Mastering Algorithms

*A systematic approach to data structures
and problem-solving techniques*

Prof. (Dr.) Rahul Bhandari

Prof. Om Prakash Suthar

bpb

www.bpbonline.com

First Edition 2025

Copyright © BPB Publications, India

ISBN: 978-93-65899-603

To View Complete
BPB Publications Catalogue
Scan the QR Code:

Dedicated to

My wife, Dr. Sunita, my lovely daughter Rudrakshi,
my parents, Veena and Ramesh Chand Bhandari,
my younger brother's family and my maternal, Karnawat family
- Prof. (Dr.) Rahul Bhandari

My parents, Mr. and Mrs. G.R. Suthar, my wife Renu,
my son Rudra, my brother Lokesh and his family, and my sisters
- Prof. Om Prakash Suthar

About the Authors

- **Prof. (Dr.) Rahul Bhandari** is a senior IEEE member. He is an accomplished academic and researcher in computer science and engineering with over a decade of experience. Currently a professor at Chandigarh University, Punjab, he holds a PhD, M.Tech, and B.E. in the field and has previously served at Chitkara University and JIET Group of Institutions. He also worked as research associate in the project, sponsored by ICMR and entitled *Validation of the Jodhpur Instrumented Kursi (JiK) against DXA to diagnose Sarcopenia* under the guidance of Dr. Vivek Vijay. His expertise spans data science, artificial intelligence, video compression, and machine learning, with numerous SCI/scopus-indexed publications and several patents, including innovations in wireless networks and healthcare technologies. A dedicated mentor, he has guided PhD and M.E. students in advanced areas like NLP and AI-driven disease detection, while excelling in teaching subjects such as algorithms and machine learning. He is also the organizing member of international conferences: Joint International Scientific Conference Information Technologies for Intelligent Decision Support 2024, SCMAI 2025.

- **Prof. Om Prakash Suthar** is an IBM Bluemix certified trainer for cloud and IoT environment. Since 2022, he has been pursuing his PhD computer vision, ML-DL domain in computer engineering at Marwadi University in Rajkot, India. He completed his M.Tech CSE from JNU Jodhpur in 2015 and his B.Tech in CSE from JIET Jodhpur in 2011. He has held academic positions at several reputed Indian institutions, including LPU. Currently, he is employed as an assistant professor (sr. scale) at the department of computer engineering at Marwadi University in Rajkot, Gujarat, India. AI, machine learning, deep learning, computer vision, and IoT comprise his research interests. With over 13 years of experience, he has authored over 14 research articles in reputed international conferences, journals and professional book chapters, and 8 patents that have been published. Various papers are in pipeline for publishing. He has reviewed various conferences and reputed journal papers.

About the Reviewer

Prof. (Dr.) Suresh, IEEE-senior member, ISTE advisor, professor and HoD-CSE, Chandigarh University, India. He is PhD, M.Tech, B.Tech in computer science and engineering, having more than 20 years of experience in technology teaching, administration, education management and accreditation evaluation process, NAAC, NBA, NIRF, coordinator-IQAC, convener and organizer of national and international conferences: ITIDS2024, SCMAI2025, FDPs, curriculum development with industry association, innovate and implement job readiness program, industry-institution partnership delivery, industry-academia collaborated research, consultation and training. He is the organizer of five international conferences with Russia, Springer, CSI, T&F, etc. He has delivered many invited and keynote talks at international and national conferences, workshops, and seminars. He has published more than 45 papers in SCI, Scopus, WOS, peer-reviewed international and national journals, and conferences. He has also published a number of books and book chapters in reputed publications like Springer, Bentham, and IGI.

Professional engagements and memberships:

- Senior member IEEE
- AI scholar expert reviewer, AEIC publishers
- ACM member
- Fellowship member, London Press Journal
- Life member of ISROSET (IJCSE- UGC Approved)
- Life member of I.S.T.E
- Member of Computer Society of India (C.S.I.)
- International Association of Computer Sc. and IT (IACSIT)
- International Association of Engineers (IAENG)
- All India Council for Technical Skill Development

Acknowledgements

Our sincere appreciation goes out to each and every person who has made a contribution to the publication of this book.

We would like to express our gratitude to our families and friends who have been there for us during the process of authoring this book. Without their words of encouragement and love, we would not have been able to overcome this obstacle.

In addition, we would like to express our deepest gratitude to our colleagues at Marwadi University and Chandigarh University, who are constantly contributing to the development of our technical capabilities. We are grateful to you for all of the efforts that you put in each day to push the limits of algorithmic thinking even farther.

We would like to express our sincere appreciation to BPB Publications for entrusting us with this book. Thank you for providing us with direction and assistance during the entire process of authoring this book.

Additionally, we would like to express our gratitude to the reviewers, technical specialists, and editors who contributed to the production of the book in its final form. There is no doubt that the quality of this book has been improved as a result of your ideas and skills.

Preface

In an era where technology drives innovation, mastering algorithms is essential for solving complex problems efficiently. *Mastering Algorithms*, an extended exploration of algorithmic foundations, equips developers and students with the tools to design, analyze, and implement high-performance solutions. From optimizing code to tackling real-world challenges, algorithms form the backbone of modern computing.

This book comprises 12 comprehensive units, guiding readers through the core of algorithmic thinking. We begin with *Algorithm and Program Performance*, laying the groundwork for evaluating efficiency. *Review of Data Structures* ensures a solid foundation, followed by in-depth explorations of *Sorting Algorithms* and *Searching Algorithms* for data manipulation. *Divide and Conquer* algorithms introduce elegant problem-solving strategies, while *Greedy Algorithms* and *Dynamic Programming* offer optimization techniques. *Backtracking* and *Branch and Bound* provide systematic approaches to complex problems, and *Graph Algorithms* address networked systems. *Computational Complexity* demystifies performance analysis, and *Other Advanced Algorithms* push the boundaries of innovation. Finally, *Most Frequently Asked Questions* prepares readers for real-world applications and interviews.

Designed for technically inclined students and professionals, this book caters to all programming levels. No prior algorithmic expertise is required, though those with experience will find advanced insights to elevate their skills. Our hands-on approach ensures you can apply concepts practically, from coding efficient solutions to mastering interview challenges.

This book is your guide to unlocking the power of algorithms, transforming ideas into impactful solutions.

Chapter 1: Algorithm and Program Performance - Algorithm and program performance refer to the efficiency and effectiveness of algorithms and the software programs that implement them. Efficient algorithms and well-optimized programs are crucial for achieving fast execution times, minimizing resource usage, and providing a responsive user experience. Topics to be covered: designing and analyzing algorithms, time and space complexity, average and worst-case analysis, asymptotic notations, and recurrence equations and their solution.

Chapter 2: Review of Data Structures - This chapter involves revisiting fundamental concepts in computer science that deal with organizing and storing data in efficient and accessible ways. Data structures provide a framework for managing data effectively, allowing for optimized operations such as insertion, deletion, retrieval, and manipulation. Topics to be covered: arrays, stacks, queues, pointers, linked lists (one-way, two-way and circular two-way), hashing, trees (BST, B-tree, balanced trees (AVL, red-black trees)), and heaps: Binomial and Fibonacci heap, etc.

Chapter 3: Sorting Algorithms - Sorting algorithms are essential techniques in computer science used to arrange elements in a specific order, typically ascending or descending. Sorting plays a fundamental role in data manipulation, enabling efficient searching, grouping, and analyzing of information.

Chapter 4: Searching Algorithms - Searching algorithms are essential techniques in computer science used to arrange elements in a specific order, typically ascending or descending. Sorting plays a fundamental role in data manipulation, enabling efficient searching, grouping, and analyzing of information.

Chapter 5: Divide and Conquer - Divide and conquer is an algorithmic strategy that breaks down a complex problem into smaller, more manageable subproblems. It solves each subproblem independently and then combines their solutions to obtain the solution to the original problem. This technique is particularly effective for problems with overlapping subproblems and optimal substructure.

Chapter 6: Greedy Algorithms - Greedy algorithms make locally optimal choices at each step to construct a globally optimal solution. While they do not guarantee the absolute best solution, they are often used when finding an optimal solution is either computationally expensive or unnecessary.

Chapter 7: Dynamic Programming - **Dynamic programming (DP)** is a powerful algorithmic technique used to solve optimization problems by breaking them down into smaller subproblems and solving each subproblem only once, storing their solutions to avoid redundant computations. DP is particularly effective when a problem has overlapping subproblems and optimal substructure, meaning the solution to a larger problem can be constructed from solutions to smaller subproblems.

Chapter 8: Backtracking - Backtracking is a systematic algorithmic technique used to solve problems by exploring all possible solutions through a trial-and-error approach. It is particularly effective for problems where you need to find one or more solutions among a large set of possibilities. Backtracking is commonly used for solving puzzles, combinatorial optimization problems, and constraint satisfaction problems.

Chapter 9: Branch and Bound - Branch and bound is an algorithmic technique used to solve optimization problems by systematically exploring the solution space and pruning branches that cannot lead to an optimal solution. It divides the problem into smaller subproblems and maintains bounds on the possible solutions within each subproblem.

Chapter 10: Graph Algorithms - Graph algorithms are a fundamental subset of algorithms in computer science that focus on solving problems related to graphs. Graphs provide a versatile way to model relationships and connections between entities, making graph algorithms essential for tasks across diverse fields.

Chapter 11: Computational Complexity - Computational complexity theory is a branch of computer science that studies the resources (such as time and space) required to solve computational problems. It categorizes problems based on their inherent difficulty and helps us understand the efficiency of algorithms.

Chapter 12: Other Advanced Algorithms - This chapter provides advanced algorithms, which are categorized into various algorithms used in cryptosystem, computational geometry, and complexity classes for randomized algorithm, NP-completeness problems, and algorithms for parallel computers.

Appendix: Most Frequently Asked Questions - This chapter provides objective-type questions asked in various examinations such as GATE, NET, etc. with solutions.

Code Bundle and Coloured Images

Please follow the link to download the
Code Bundle and the *Coloured Images* of the book:

https://rebrand.ly/96ae80

The code bundle for the book is also hosted on GitHub at
https://github.com/bpbpublications/Mastering-Algorithms.
In case there's an update to the code, it will be updated on the existing GitHub repository.

We have code bundles from our rich catalogue of books and videos available at
https://github.com/bpbpublications. Check them out!

Errata

We take immense pride in our work at BPB Publications and follow best practices to ensure the accuracy of our content to provide with an indulging reading experience to our subscribers. Our readers are our mirrors, and we use their inputs to reflect and improve upon human errors, if any, that may have occurred during the publishing processes involved. To let us maintain the quality and help us reach out to any readers who might be having difficulties due to any unforeseen errors, please write to us at :

errata@bpbonline.com

Your support, suggestions and feedbacks are highly appreciated by the BPB Publications' Family.

Did you know that BPB offers eBook versions of every book published, with PDF and ePub files available? You can upgrade to the eBook version at www.bpbonline.com and as a print book customer, you are entitled to a discount on the eBook copy. Get in touch with us at :

business@bpbonline.com for more details.

At www.bpbonline.com, you can also read a collection of free technical articles, sign up for a range of free newsletters, and receive exclusive discounts and offers on BPB books and eBooks.

Piracy

If you come across any illegal copies of our works in any form on the internet, we would be grateful if you would provide us with the location address or website name. Please contact us at business@bpbonline.com with a link to the material.

If you are interested in becoming an author

If there is a topic that you have expertise in, and you are interested in either writing or contributing to a book, please visit www.bpbonline.com. We have worked with thousands of developers and tech professionals, just like you, to help them share their insights with the global tech community. You can make a general application, apply for a specific hot topic that we are recruiting an author for, or submit your own idea.

Reviews

Please leave a review. Once you have read and used this book, why not leave a review on the site that you purchased it from? Potential readers can then see and use your unbiased opinion to make purchase decisions. We at BPB can understand what you think about our products, and our authors can see your feedback on their book. Thank you!

For more information about BPB, please visit www.bpbonline.com.

Join our Discord space

Join our Discord workspace for latest updates, offers, tech happenings around the world, new releases, and sessions with the authors:

https://discord.bpbonline.com

Table of Contents

CHAPTER 1
Algorithm and Program Performance

Introduction

In this chapter of the book, we will present an introduction to algorithms and their role in contemporary computing systems. Furthermore, this chapter introduces the concept of asymptotic notation, which we will use to analyze the growth of functions, particularly those describing algorithm runtime. We commence by briefly explaining the commonly used asymptotic notations and present an illustrative example of their application. We subsequently establish formal definitions for various asymptotic notations and outline conventions for their proper utilization.

Structure

The chapter covers the following topics:

- Introduction to algorithms
- Algorithm complexity
- Asymptotic notations
- General rules for the analysis of programs
- Recurrence relation

Objectives

The objectives of algorithm and program performance encompass a range of essential goals aimed at enhancing the efficiency and effectiveness of computational processes. One key objective is to optimize computational effectiveness, leading to quicker processing speeds. This involves the development of algorithms and programs that can execute tasks with greater speed and efficiency. Additionally, streamlining memory and hardware utilization to minimize resource usage is a crucial aim, ensuring that computational resources are utilized judiciously. Accelerating program tasks is another priority, enabling swift and flexible execution of operations, which in turn improves overall system responsiveness. Moreover, there is a focus on ensuring the ability to manage larger datasets and increased computational requirements, accommodating the growing demands of modern applications and systems. Ultimately, these objectives collectively contribute to elevating user satisfaction by providing a more responsive and efficient computing experience.

Introduction to algorithms

An algorithm is a structured sequence of steps or methods to solve problems or accomplish tasks. It consists of a precise set of rules or instructions establishing a series of actions, enabling a computer to perform specific tasks or calculations. Algorithms are foundational in computer science and have widespread applications in various domains, including data processing, software development, artificial intelligence, and solving computational problems.

Essentially, an algorithm serves as a roadmap for task execution, offering an unambiguous set of guidelines that can be followed to achieve a particular objective. The development and assessment of algorithms are pivotal in comprehending computational procedures and complexity theory, while also guaranteeing the effective utilization of computational resources. Competent algorithm design can significantly influence the performance, efficiency, and reliability of software systems and computational tasks.

Algorithm

An **algorithm** is defined as a sequence of unambiguous instructions for solving a problem, that is, for obtaining a required output for any legitimate input in a finite amount of time.

This definition can be demonstrated through *Figure 1.1*:

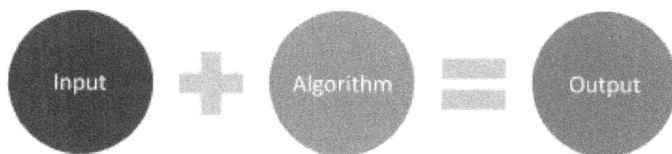

Figure 1.1: Pictorial definition of an algorithm

Algorithms play a crucial role in various fields and find extensive application in different contexts, listed as follows:

- In **computer science**, they serve as the fundamental building blocks for tasks ranging from simple sorting and searching to complex functions such as **artificial intelligence (AI)** and **machine learning (ML)**.

- In **mathematics**, they are crucial for solving problems, such as determining optimal solutions for systems of linear equations or finding the shortest path in a graph.

- In **operations research**, algorithms contribute to streamlining and making decisions for transportation, logistics, and resource allocation.

- In **AI**, they form the backbone of AI and ML, enabling the creation of intelligent systems capable of tasks such as image recognition, natural language processing, and decision-making.

- In **data science**, algorithms are indispensable for analyzing, processing, and extracting insights from extensive datasets in fields such as marketing, finance, and healthcare.

- In **cryptocurrency and blockchain**, algorithms play a vital role in ensuring secure transactions and maintaining the integrity of blockchain networks.

- In **network routing**, algorithms are pivotal in determining the most efficient routes for data packets through networks, ensuring fast and reliable data transmission.

- In **security systems**, algorithms are essential for encrypting sensitive data, securing communication, and protecting systems from cyber threats and unauthorized access.

- In **recommendation systems**, algorithms are utilized to analyze user preferences, providing personalized recommendations for products, services, and content.

These examples underscore the diverse applications of algorithms. As technology and fields continue to evolve, the role of algorithms remains indispensable, highlighting their significance in contemporary society.

Let us take the example of preparing a meal. This simple algorithm offers a basic structure for cooking a range of dishes. Additional steps may be required, depending on the intricacy of the recipe and specific cooking methods.

Algorithm 1.1: Algorithm for cooking food

The steps are as follows:

1. Collect all the necessary ingredients and cooking utensils.
2. Clean and arrange the cooking area.
3. Measure and prepare the required ingredients as per the recipe.
4. Ensure that the ingredients are properly washed, peeled, and chopped if needed.

5. Heat the cooking surface (for example, stovetop, oven) to a suitable temperature.

6. Combine the ingredients in the correct sequence, following the recipe instructions.

7. Regularly monitor the food while cooking to prevent overcooking or burning.

8. Adjust the heat levels if necessary to maintain the desired cooking temperature.

9. Incorporate seasonings and spices to enrich the flavor of the dish.

10. Fine-tune the flavors as required by tasting.

11. Transfer the cooked food to a serving dish or plate.

12. Present the food neatly for an appealing appearance.

13. Serve the dish while it is still hot and fresh.

14. Enjoy the meal with friends, family, or alone.

Likewise, algorithms aid in executing tasks in programming to achieve the desired output. The algorithm created is not reliant on a specific programming language; rather, it comprises straightforward instructions that can be applied in any language, ensuring the anticipated outcome remains consistent.

Need for algorithms

Let us consider two children, *Richard* and *Henry*, attempting to solve the Rubik's cube. Richard has a method to solve it in a specific number of steps. In contrast, Henry is confident he can solve it but does not know the procedure. Richard successfully solves the cube in just 2 minutes, while Henry struggles throughout the day, finally managing to solve it (although he might have used an unauthorized method). This illustrates that having a procedure or algorithm significantly speeds up the solving process, making it more efficient than attempting to solve it without one. Therefore, the importance of having an algorithm is evident.

Characteristics of an algorithm

Just as one might not follow written instructions for cooking a recipe but instead rely on the standard procedure, not all written instructions in programming qualify as algorithms. To be considered an algorithm, instructions must exhibit the following characteristics:

- **Clarity and precision**: An algorithm must be entirely unambiguous. Each of its steps should be precise and lead to a singular interpretation.

- **Well-defined inputs**: When an algorithm requires inputs, those inputs must be well-defined. The algorithm may accept zero or more inputs.

- **Well-defined outputs**: The algorithm should distinctly specify the output it will produce. This output should also be well-defined and must include at least one result.

- **Finiteness**: An algorithm must have a finite nature, meaning it will eventually terminate after a finite number of steps.

- **Feasibility**: An algorithm must be practical, generic, and straightforward, making it executable with existing resources. It should not rely on futuristic technologies or other elements.

- **Language independence**: The designed algorithm must be independent of any specific programming language. It should consist of straightforward instructions that can be implemented in any language, resulting in the expected output.

- **Input handling**: An algorithm can have zero or more inputs. Each instruction containing a fundamental operator may accept zero or more inputs.

- **Output production**: An algorithm should generate at least one output. Every instruction featuring a fundamental operator can accept zero or more inputs.

- **Definiteness**: All instructions within an algorithm must be unambiguous, precise, and easily understandable. Consulting any instruction in the algorithm should provide a clear understanding of what needs to be done.

- **Finiteness**: An algorithm must terminate within a finite number of steps in all test cases. Every instruction featuring a fundamental operator should conclude within a finite timeframe. Infinite loops or recursive functions lacking base conditions do not meet the criterion of finiteness.

- **Effectiveness**: An algorithm should be built using basic, simple, and practical operations, allowing it to be traced using only paper and pencil.

Designing an algorithm

As the algorithm is not tied to a specific programming language, it serves as a means to outline the logical steps for solving a problem. However, before drafting an algorithm, it is important to consider the following:

- **Clarity and precision**: The algorithm must offer unambiguous instructions.

- **Input flexibility**: An algorithm may accept zero or more well-defined inputs.

- **Output consistency**: It must yield one or more well-defined outputs that align with the desired result.

- **Termination**: Algorithms are required to conclude after a specific number of steps.

- **Finiteness:** They must reach an endpoint within a finite number of steps.

- **Language neutrality**: Step-by-step instructions in an algorithm should be independent of any specific computer code.

Let us consider some examples of algorithms which are given as follows.

Algorithm 1.2: Write an algorithm to multiply two numbers and display the result obtained from the multiplication.

1. Start

2. Get the knowledge of input. Here, we need 3 variables: a and b will be the user input, and c will hold the result.

3. Define variables a, b, and c. Variables a and b will receive input from the user, while c will store the result.

4. Acquire input values for variables a and b from the user.

5. Determine the solution using operators, data structures, and logic: $c = a * b$.

6. Ultimately, display the result c.

7. End

Algorithm 1.3: Write an algorithm to identify the maximum value among all the elements contained within the array.

1. Start

2. Define a variable called *max* and assign it the value of the first element in the array.

3. Check the variable *max* against the remaining elements of the array using a loop.

4. If *max* < *array* element, then the value in *max* will change and store array element.

5. If no element is left, return *max* otherwise go to *Step 3*.

6. End

Algorithm 1.4: Write an algorithm to find the average of 3 subjects.

1. Start

2. Read the marks of three subjects, for example, *S1, S2, S3*.

3. Compute the total of the marks for all three subjects and save the outcome in a variable called *Sum* (*Sum = S1+S2+S3*).

4. Divide the *Sum* by 3 and assign it to another variable *Average* (*Average = Sum/3*).

5. Print the value of the *Average* of three subjects.

6. End

Algorithm complexity

Algorithm complexity refers to the volume of resources, including time and memory, needed to solve a problem or execute a task. Time complexity, a widely used metric, signifies the duration an algorithm takes to generate a result relative to the input's size. Memory complexity, on the other hand, indicates the memory consumption of an algorithm. Designers aim to create algorithms with minimal time and memory complexities to enhance efficiency and scalability.

Complexity of an algorithm

The complexity of an algorithm is defining a function that describes the algorithm's efficiency based on the quantity of data it processes.

Analyzing an algorithm involves evaluating its time complexity and space complexity. Crafting an efficient algorithm ensures minimal time consumption for processing the logic.

Time complexity

Determining the time required for an algorithm to solve a problem involves evaluating loop iterations, comparisons, and related factors. Time complexity represents the duration an algorithm requires relative to its input size. The term *time* can denote the count of memory accesses performed the number of integer comparisons, the frequency of inner loop operations, or any other pertinent unit linked to the actual time taken by the algorithm.

Space complexity

Space complexity pertains to the amount of memory an algorithm uses during problem-solving. This incorporates the memory taken up by essential input variables, in addition to any extra space (excluding the input space) that the algorithm uses. For instance, if a data structure like a hash table is employed, an array is necessary to store values, thus contributing to the algorithm's space complexity as an auxiliary space. This extra space is known as **auxiliary space**. Space complexity is a metric that determines the quantity of memory (space) an algorithm requires in relation to its input size. While sometimes overlooked due to minimal or evident space usage, space complexity can become a concern akin to time complexity. The memory requirement of a program includes the following elements:

- **Instruction space**: This denotes the space required to store the compiled version of the program's instructions.

- **Data space**: Data space encompasses the memory needed for storing both constant and variable values. Data space is comprised of two components:

  o   Space utilized by constants and simple variables within the program.

  o   Space occupied by dynamically allocated objects like arrays and class instances.

- **Environment stack space**: The environment stack serves the purpose of preserving information essential for resuming the execution of partially completed functions.

The extent of instruction space necessary is contingent on various factors, including:

- The compiler employed for converting the program into machine code
- The compiler options that are in effect during the compilation process
- The specifications of the target computer

The primary goals in the design of algorithms include maximizing efficiency in time, preserving space, and upholding dependability. The excellence of a program is often indicated by its superior speed, highlighting the importance of prioritizing time-saving as a fundamental objective. Likewise, giving precedence to space efficiency over competing programs is greatly valued. Additionally, securing the program's stability and averting potential problems, such as system freezes or data distortion, is a critical aspect of maintaining a positive reputation.

The running time of an algorithm, represented by the function $f(n)$, relies not solely on the size n of the input data but also on the specific data itself. The complexity function $f(n)$ takes various forms in particular scenarios:

- **Best case**: The best-case scenario corresponds to the lowest achievable value of $f(n)$.
- **Average case**: The average case situation pertains to the expected value of $f(n)$.
- **Worst case**: The worst-case scenario refers to the highest possible value of $f(n)$ for any conceivable input.

Analysis of algorithms

The field of computer science, which studies efficiency of algorithms, is known as analysis of algorithms.

Algorithms can be evaluated using different benchmarks. Typically, this chapter concentrates on comprehending how the time or space required for solving larger instances of a problem escalates. We assign an integer, referred to as the problem's size, which functions as a measure for the volume of input data.

Asymptotic notations

The subsequent notations are frequently utilized in performance analysis to define the complexity of an algorithm:

- Big–OH (O)
- Big–OMEGA (Ω)
- THETA (θ)

Big–OH (O) notation

This notation provides the precise upper limit of the given function. Typically, it can be expressed as $f(n) = O(g(n))$. In other words, when dealing with larger values of n, the upper boundary of $f(n)$ is $g(n)$. For instance, if the algorithm is defined as $f(n) = n^3 + 10n^2 + 5n + 10$, then n^3 serves as $g(n)$. This signifies that $g(n)$ represents the highest rate of growth for $f(n)$ as n becomes larger.

It is defined as $O(g(n)) = \{f(n)$: there exist positive constants c and no such that $0 <= f(n) <= cg(n)$ for all $n >= no\}$.

Where $g(n)$ is an asymptotic tight upper bound for $f(n)$.

In *Figure 1.2*, n_0 represents the point from which we evaluate the rates of growth for an algorithm. Below this point, the rates of growth may vary:

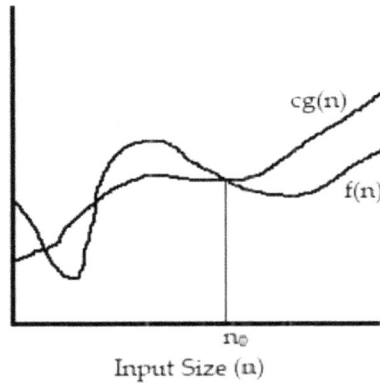

Figure 1.2: Rate growth of Big–OH (O) notation

Big–OMEGA (Ω) notation

This notation provides a more stringent lower limit for the given algorithm, denoted as $f(n) = \Omega(g(n))$. This implies that for larger values of n, the tighter lower bound of $f(n)$ is $g(n)$, as illustrated in *Figure 1.3*. For instance, if $f(n)$ is a function defined as $10n^2 + 8n + 5$, then $g(n)$ is $\Omega(n^2)$.

It is defined as $\Omega(g(n)) = \{f(n)$: there exist positive constants c and no such that $0 <= cg(n) <= f(n)$ for all $n >= no\}$.

Where $g(n)$ is an asymptotic tight lower bound for $f(n)$.

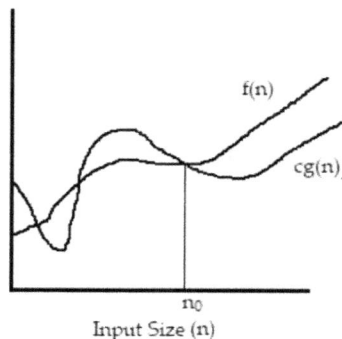

Figure 1.3: Rate growth of Big–OMEGA (Ω) notation

THETA (θ) notation

This notation determines whether the upper and lower bounds of a given function are identical. The average running time of an algorithm consistently falls between the lower and upper bounds. When the upper bound *(O)* and lower bound *(Ω)* produce equivalent outcomes, the θ notation will likewise exhibit the same rate of growth. For instance, considering the expression $f(n) = 5n + 4n$, its tight upper bound, $g(n)$, is $O(n)$. In this scenario, the rate of growth in the best-case is $g(n) = O(n)$, which aligns with the rate of growth in the worst case. Consequently, the average case will also yield the same rate. The θ notation is depicted in *Figure 1.4*.

It is defined as $θ\ (g(n)) = \{f(n)$: there exist positive constants $C1, C2$ and no such that $5\ C1g(n) <= f(n) <= C2g(n)$ for all $n >= no\}$.

$g(n)$ is an asymptotic tight bound for $f(n)$.

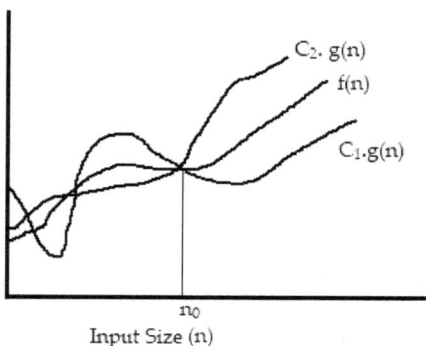

Figure 1.4: Rate growth of THETA (θ) notation

The time efficiencies of numerous algorithms can be categorized into a limited number of classes. *Table 1.1* presents these classes in ascending order of their growth orders, accompanied by their respective names and descriptions:

Class	Name	Description
1	constant	In the majority of programs, the instructions that follow are executed either once or, at the most, a few times. When all the program's instructions exhibit this trait, we define its running time as constant.
log n	logarithmic	If a program's running time is logarithmic, the program's speed diminishes slightly as n increases. This type of running time is typical in programs that tackle a substantial issue by dividing it into a more manageable problem, reducing the size by a fixed fraction. For instance, when n equals a million, log n doubles. With each doubling of n, log n increases by a constant amount, but log n does not double until n reaches n^2.
N	linear	If a program's running time is linear, typically, a minor computation is performed on each input element. This scenario is considered optimal for an algorithm that needs to handle n inputs.
n log n	linearithmic	This type of running time is observed in algorithms that resolve a problem by subdividing it into smaller sub-problems, solving them independently, and subsequently amalgamating the solutions. As 'n' doubles, the running time increases more than twofold.
n^2	quadratic	If the running time of an algorithm is quadratic, it is generally suitable for handling relatively small problems. Quadratic running times commonly emerge in algorithms that handle all pairs of data items (perhaps within a nested loop). As n doubles, the running time increases fourfold.
n^3	cubic	Likewise, an algorithm that handles triples of data items (possibly within a triple-nested loop) exhibits cubic running time and is feasible for managing only small problems. When n doubles, the running time increases eightfold.
2^n	exponential	Only a limited number of algorithms with exponential running time are viable for practical applications; these algorithms commonly emerge as brute-force solutions to problems. As n doubles, the running time quadruples.
n!	factorial	Commonly observed in algorithms that produce all permutations of a set with n elements.

Table 1.1: *Basic asymptotic efficiency classes*

Example 1.1: Let us consider a short piece of source code:

```
x = 3*y + 2; z = z + 1;
```

For scalars **y** and **z**, this code snippet consumes a fixed duration of time, denoted as *O(1)*. In terms of concrete computer instructions or clock cycles, pinpointing the exact time it takes is challenging. However, whatever the duration, it remains consistent each time this code segment is executed. *O(1)* implies a certain constant, which could be 5, 1, or 1000, for instance.

Example 1.2: If a program 1 takes $100n^2$ milliseconds and program 2 takes $5n^3$ milliseconds, then might not $5n^3$ program be better than program 1?

Since programs can be assessed by comparing functions with respect to their running time, disregarding proportional constants, a program like $5n^3$ would be superior to a program like $100n^2$.

```
5 n³/100 n² = n/20
```

Given inputs where $n < 20$, a running time of the program is $5n^3$ will outperform the one with a running time of $100n^2$. Consequently, if the program is primarily intended for small-sized inputs, opting for the program with a running time of $O(n^3)$ would be preferable.

Nonetheless, as n increases, the ratio of the running times, denoted as $n/20$, becomes progressively larger. Consequently, with an increase in the input size, the $O(n^3)$ program will require substantially more time compared to the $O(n^2)$ program. Therefore, it is consistently advisable to select a program with a lower growth rate in its running time. Functions with lower growth rates, such as $O(n)$ or $O(n \log n)$, always offer superior performance.

Example 1.3: Let us consider the analysis of a simple for loop:

```
for (i = 1; i<=n; i++)
v[i] = v[i] + 1;
```

This loop iterates precisely n times, and since constant time is taken by inner loop, the overall running time is directly related to n. This is denoted as $O(n)$. The specific number of instructions might be $50n$, with the running time measured at $17n$ microseconds. It could even be $17n + 3$ microseconds, accounting for the startup time of the loop. The big-O notation includes provisions for both a multiplication factor (such as 17) and an additive factor (such as 3). As long as it forms a linear function directly proportional to n, the appropriate notation remains $O(n)$, and the code is classified as having linear running time.

Example 1.4: Let us look at a more complicated example where we will analyze a nested for loop:

```
for (i = 1; i<=n; i++)
for (j = 1; j<=n; j++)
a[i,j] = b[i,j] * x;
```

The outer for loop runs n times, and within each iteration of the outer loop, the inner loop executes n times. Thus, the inner loop runs $n * n = n^2$ times. Since the assignment statement within the inner loop takes constant time, the overall running time of the code amounts to $O(n^2)$ steps. This code is classified as having quadratic running time.

Example 1.5: Let us consider an example of the analysis of matrix multiply.

The multiplication of two $n \times n$ matrices is denoted as A and B. The following code computes the matrix product $C = A * B$:

```
for (i = 1; i<=n; i++)
for (j = 1; j<=n; j++)
C[i, j] = 0;
for (k = 1; k<=n; k++)
C[i, j] = C[i, j] + A[i, k] * B[k, j];
```

With 3 nested for loops, each of them iterating n times, the innermost loop consequently runs $n * n * n = n^3$ times. The innermost statement, involving a scalar sum and product, requires constant $O(1)$ time. Consequently, the algorithm, on the whole, operates in $O(n^3)$ time.

General rules for the analysis of programs

In general, the runtime of a statement or group of statements can be described by the input size and/or one or more variables. The sole permissible parameter for the overall program's runtime is n, representing size of the input.

The runtime of each assignment read and write statement can typically be considered $O(1)$:

- The runtime of a sequence of statements is determined by the sum rule, meaning the runtime of the sequence is, within a constant factor, the largest runtime among any statement within the sequence.

- The runtime of an if-statement comprises the cost of conditionally executed statements, along with the time for evaluating the condition. The time to evaluate the condition is usually $O(1)$. For an if-then-else construct, the runtime is the time to evaluate the condition plus the greater of the time needed for the statements executed when the condition is true and the time for the statements executed when the condition is false.

- The time to execute a loop is the sum over all iterations of the loop, involving the time to execute the body and the time to evaluate the termination condition (usually the latter is $O(1)$). Frequently, this time, neglecting constant factors, is the product of the number of loop iterations and the maximum possible time for a single execution of the body. However, it is necessary to consider each loop separately to ensure accuracy.

Recurrence relation

A recurrence relation for a sequence of numbers S is an equation that links all terms of S, excluding a finite number of them, to preceding terms of the sequence, specifically $\{a_0, a_1, a_2, \ldots\ldots, a_{n-1}\}$, for all integers n with $n \geq n_0$, where n_0 is a non-negative integer. Recurrence relations are also known as difference equations.

Recurrence

A recurrence is a mathematical statement or inequality that characterizes a function by its values on smaller inputs.

Sequences are frequently defined in the most straightforward manner using a recurrence relation; nonetheless, directly applying a recurrence relation to compute terms can be a time-intensive task. The method of deriving a mathematical expression for the elements of a sequence from its recurring connection is recognized as solving the relation. Several trial-and-error methods for solving recurrence relations are as follows:

- Formulate simplifying assumptions regarding the inputs.
- Create a table of the initial values of the recurrence.
- Identify patterns and propose a solution.
- Generalize the outcome to eliminate the assumptions.

For example, factorial, Fibonacci, quick sort, binary search, etc.

A recurrence relation is an equation that is defined in reference to itself. No single technique or algorithm can be universally applied to solve all recurrence relations. In reality, some recurrence relations are unsolvable. The majority of the recurrence relations encountered are typically linear recurrence relations with constant coefficients. Various techniques, such as substitution, induction, characteristic roots, and generating function, are accessible for solving recurrence relations.

There are four approaches exist for resolving recurrence relations:
- Substitution method
- Iteration method
- Recursion tree method
- Master method

Substitution method

The substitution method involves two steps:

1. Predict the structure of the solution using symbolic constants.
2. Employ mathematical induction to verify the validity of the solution and determine the constants.

To utilize the inductive hypothesis, you substitute the anticipated solution for the function on smaller values, which is why the method is called the **substitution method**. While this approach is robust, it necessitates guessing the form of the solution. Despite the apparent challenge in generating a suitable guess, honing this skill through practice can swiftly enhance your intuition.

Example 1.6: Consider the recurrence $T(n) = T\left(\frac{n}{2}\right) + 1$.

We have to show that it is asymptotically bound by O *(log n)*.

Solution: For $T(n) = O$ *(log n)*

We have to show that for some constant c,

$$T(n) \le c \log \log n$$

Put this in the given recurrence equation:

$$T(n) \le c \log \log \left(\frac{n}{2}\right) + 1$$

$$= c \log \log (n) - c2 + 1$$

$$T(n) \le c \log \log (n) \, for \, c \ge 1$$

Thus, $T(n)=O(log\ n)$

Example 1.7: Consider the recurrence $T(n) = 2T\left(\frac{n}{2} + 16\right) + n$

We have to show that it is asymptotically bound by $O(log\ n)$.

Solution: For $T(n) = O$ *(n log n)*

We have to show that for some constant c,

$$T(n) \le cn \log \log n$$

Put this in the given recurrence equation,

$$T(n) \le 2\left(c\left(\frac{n}{2} + 16\right) \log \log \left(\frac{n}{2} + 16\right)\right) + n$$

$$= cn \log \log \left(\frac{n}{2}\right) + 32 + n$$

$$= cn \log \log (n) - cn2 + 32 + n$$

$$= cn \log \log (n) - cn + 32 + n$$

$$= cn \log \log (n) - (c - 1)n + 32$$

$$T(n) \le cn \log \log (n) \, for \, c \ge 1$$

Thus, $T(n)=O(n\ log\ n)$

Example 1.8: Solve the recurrence: $T(n) = 2T(\sqrt{n}) + 1$ by making a change of variable.

Solution:

$$T(n) = 2T(\sqrt{n}) + 1$$

Suppose $m = log\ log\ n \Rightarrow n = 2^m \Rightarrow \sqrt{n} = (2)^{\frac{m}{2}}$

Thus, $T(2^m) = 2T\left(\left(2^{\frac{m}{2}}\right)\right) + 1$

$$S(m) = T(2^m)$$

We have, $S(m) = 2S\left(\frac{m}{2}\right) + 1$

We know the solution to above recurrence:

$$S(m) = O(m)$$

Substituting for m we get:

$$T(n) = S(m) = O(m) = O(\log n)$$

Iteration method

The iterative method involves the fundamental concept of expanding the recurrence and representing it as a sum of terms that are solely dependent on n and initial conditions.

Example 1.9: Solve the recurrence: $T(n) = T(n-1)+1$ and $T(1) = \theta(1)$

Solution:

$$T(n) = T(n-1)+1$$
$$= (T(n-2)+1)+1$$
$$= (T(n-3)+1)+1+1$$
$$= T(n-4)+4$$
$$= T(n-5)+5$$
$$= T(n-k)+k$$

Where $k = n-1$

That is $T(n-k) = T(1) = \theta(1)$

That is $T(n) = \theta(1) + (n-1) = 1+n-1 = n = \theta(n)$

Example 1.10: Using the recurrence for the binary search given below, find the time complexity of binary search: $T(n) = T\left(\frac{n}{2}\right) + 1, T(1) = 1$

Solution:

$$T(n) = T\left(\frac{n}{2}\right) + 1$$
$$= \left(T\left(\frac{n}{4}\right) + 1\right) + 1$$
$$= T\left(\frac{n}{4}\right) + 2$$

Thus, $T(n) = T\left(\frac{n}{2^k}\right) + k$

Now we choose k such that $\frac{n}{2^k} = 1$

Thus, $n=2^k \Rightarrow k=n$

$$T(n)=T(1)+n$$

Since, $T(1)=1$ we get $T(n)=n+1$

Thus the time complexity of the binary search algorithm is n.

Recursion tree method

The method of recursion tree analysis is employed to solve repetitive relationships. It entails converting a repetitive relationship into a series of recursive trees, where every node represents the costs accumulated at different stages of recursion. By adding up the expenses at each stage, the total cost can be ascertained. The steps involved in addressing a repetitive relationship using the recursion tree technique are as follows:

1. Draw a recursive tree that corresponds to the provided repetitive relationship.
2. Calculate the expense at each stage and determine the total number of stages in the recursion tree.
3. Count the total number of nodes at the final stage and evaluate the expenses associated with the last stage.
4. Combine the costs across all stages in the recursive tree.

Example 1.11: Solve the recurrence relation: $T(n)=2T\left(\frac{n}{2}\right)+c$ using recursion tree method.

Solution:

1. Generate a tree through recursion as shown in *Figure 1.5*:

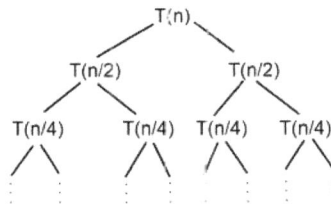

Figure 1.5:*Recursion tree*

2. Determine the work accomplished or cost at each level of a tree and count the total levels in the recursion tree as shown in *Figure 1.6*:

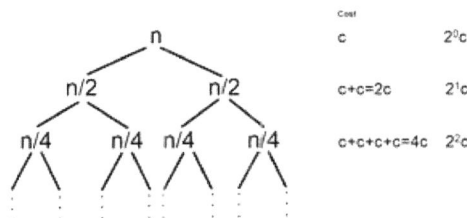

Figure 1.6: *Recursion tree*

Calculate the entire number of levels.

Select the most extended path from the starting node to the endpoint node:

$$\frac{n}{2^0} \rightarrow \frac{n}{2^1} \rightarrow \frac{n}{2^2} \rightarrow \cdots \cdots \rightarrow \frac{n}{2^k}$$

Size of problem at last level $=\frac{n}{2^k}$. At the last level, size of the problem becomes 1:

$$\frac{n}{2^k} = 1$$

$$2k = n$$

$$k = n$$

Total number of levels in recursive tree $=k+1=n+1$

3. Count the total number of nodes in the last level and calculate the cost of the last level.

No. of nodes at level $0 = 2^0 = 1$

No. of nodes at level $1 = 2^1 = 2$

 No. of nodes at level $n =2n=nn =n$

Cost of sub-problems at level n *(last level)* $= n*T(1) = n*1 = n$

4. Sum up the cost of all the levels in the recursive tree.

$$T(n) = c + 2c + 4c + \text{---} + \textit{(no. of levels-1) times} + \textit{last level cost}$$

$$= c + 2c + 4c + \text{---} +n \ \textit{times} + \theta\ (n)$$

$$= c\ (1 + 2 + 4 + \text{---} +n\ \textit{times}) + \theta\ (n)$$

$$1 + 2 + 4 +\ldots +n\ \textit{times} \rightarrow 2^0 + 2^1 + 2^2 +\ldots +n\ \textit{times}$$

The aforementioned series is a **geometric progression (GP)**, so:

$$= c\ (n) + \theta\ (n)$$

Thus, $T\ (n) = \theta\ (n)$

Master's method

The master method functions as a methodical strategy for identifying the asymptotic patterns of a broad spectrum of recurring equations. Its application is tailored for the resolution of recurring equations structured as:

$$T(n) = \{c\ ; if\ n < d\ aT\left(\frac{n}{b}\right) + f(n)\ ; if\ n \geq d$$

For an integer constant $d > 1$, positive constants $a > 0$, $c > 0$, and $b > 1$, and a positive function $f(n)$ for $n \geq d$, the master method's approach to solving these recurring equations relies on directly presenting the solution based on the application of one of three distinct scenarios. These cases are determined by contrasting $f(n)$ with a particular function, n^a.

Theorem 1.1: Let $f(n)$ and $T(n)$ be defined as previously mentioned.

We have three cases:

- **Case 1:** If there is a small constant $\epsilon > 0$, such that $f(n)$ is $\Theta(n^{a-\epsilon})$, then $T(n)$ is $\Theta(n^a)$.

- **Case 2:** If there is a constant $K \geq 0$, such that $f(n)$ is $\Theta(n^a \log^k n)$, then $T(n)$ is $\Theta(n^a \log^{k+1} n)$.

- **Case 3:** If there are small constant $\epsilon > 0$ and $\delta < 1$, such that $f(n)$ is $\Omega(n^{a+\epsilon})$ and a $f(n/b) < \delta f(n)$, for $n \geq d$, then $T(n)$ is $\Theta(f(n))$.

Case 1 identifies situations where $f(n)$ diminishes polynomially compared to the special function, n^a.

Case 2 distinguishes situations in which $f(n)$ approaches the special function asymptotically.

Case 3 outlines scenarios in which $f(n)$ grows polynomially as compared to the special function.

The application of the master method is demonstrated through a few examples (with each taking the assumption that $T(n) = c$ for $n < d$, for constants $c > 1$ and $d > 1$).

Example 1.12: Solve the recurrence relation: $T(n) = 9T\left(\frac{n}{3}\right) + n$

Solution: Here $a = 9$, $b = 3$, $f(n) = n$, and $n^a = n^9 = \Theta(n^2)$.

Since $f(n) = O(n^{9-\epsilon})$ for $\epsilon = 1$, case 1 of the master theorem applies.

The solution is $T(n) = \Theta(n^2)$.

Example 1.13: Solve the recurrence relation: $T(n) = T\left(\frac{2n}{3}\right) + 1$

Solution: Here $a = 1$, $b = 3/2$, $f(n) = 1$, and $n^a = n^0 = 1$.

Since, $f(n) = \Theta(n^a)$, Case 2 of the master theorem applies.

So, the solution is $T(n) = \Theta(\log n)$.

Conclusion

This chapter highlights the critical importance of optimizing computational efficiency, minimizing resource usage, and enhancing overall system responsiveness. By giving priority to these factors, it becomes feasible to attain accelerated processing speeds, decrease execution time, and ensure the seamless management of extensive data and increased computational requirements. These endeavors contribute to a more efficient and effective utilization of computational resources, ultimately resulting in enhanced program performance and user satisfaction.

The next chapter will provide an overview of essential data structures, frequently employed in the field of computer science and programming.

Exercise

1. Obtain the running time for the following sample snippets:

   a) for(i←2 to k-1)
   ```
   {
   for(j←3 to k-2)
   {
   A←A+2;
   }
   }
   ```

   b) max←A[0]
   ```
   for(i←1 to n-1)
       do if max<A[i]
              then max←A[i]
   return max
   ```

2. Arrange the following growth rates in the increasing order:

   $O(n^4)$, $O(1)$, $O(n^3)$, $O(n^2 \log n)$, $\Omega(n^{1.5})$, $\Theta(n^{1.5})$, $\Theta(n \log n)$

3. Can the master method be applied to the recurrence relation, $(n)=4T\left(\frac{n}{3}\right)+n$? Give the reason of your answer. Also give an asymptotic upper bound for this recurrence.

4. Solve the following recurrence relations:

   (a) $T(n) = 2T\left(\frac{n}{2}\right) + n^3$

   (b) $T(n) = 5T\left(\frac{n}{4}\right) + n^2$

   (c) $T(n) = 14T\left(\frac{n}{2}\right) + n^2$

   (d) $T(n) = T\left(\frac{9n}{10}\right) + n$

5. Use a recursion tree to give an asymptotic tight solution to the recurrence:

   T(n)=T(n-a)+T(a)+cn Where a ≥ 1 and c > 0 are constants.

6. Solve the following recurrence relation.

   $$T(1) = 1$$

   $$T(n) = 3T\left(\frac{n}{2}\right) + 2n^{1.5}$$

CHAPTER 2
Review of Data Structures

Introduction

In this chapter, we will present a review of data structures that involves revisiting fundamental concepts in computer science that deal with organizing and storing data in efficient and accessible ways. Data structures provide a framework for managing data effectively, allowing for optimized operations such as insertion, deletion, retrieval, and manipulation. The chapter examines the primary classifications of data structures, including arrays, linked list, queues, stacks, and trees, with an emphasis on their respective advantages and limitations. The discourse encompasses the significance of carefully choosing an appropriate data format for particular jobs in order to enhance efficiency and optimize performance. In this chapter, we have used different linear and non-linear data structures with their algorithms and solved examples. It subsequently indicates the complexity of all the algorithms.

Structure

The chapter covers the following topics:

- Introduction to data structures
- Array
- Stack
- Queue

- Pointers
- Linked lists
- Hashing
- Trees
- Heap

Objectives

The focus of this chapter is to provide a comprehensive overview of essential data structures, frequently employed in the field of computer science and programming, with their strengths, weaknesses, and applications of various data structures. The chapter also aims to facilitate a deeper understanding of how the choice of data structure impacts algorithm design and computational efficiency.

Introduction to data structures

Data structures are a fundamental concept in computer science that involves the organization, storage, and manipulation of data in a way that enables efficient access and modification. They are essential for handling various computational issues and form the building blocks of software and algorithms. It is a form of storage utilized to store and arrange data. Data organization on a computer is a systematic method employed to facilitate quick access and updating of information.

Purpose of data structures

Data structures are designed to achieve specific objectives, such as:

- **Enhancing efficiency**: The main purpose of data structures is to make it easier to view and change data. This efficiency is very important for making algorithms and software systems work better. Developers can greatly cut down on the time and resources needed to process and handle data by picking the right data structure for each job.

- **Abstraction**: Data structures provide a level of abstraction that makes it easier to work with and handle large amounts of complex data in software development. They protect coders from the details of managing memory and storing data by letting them work with data in a more abstract and high-level way. This level of abstraction makes it easier to see how data can be used in a problem or application.

- **Organization**: When it comes to solving a problem or accomplishing a task, data structures are crucial for arranging information in a way that makes sense. They allow for information to be arranged in a way that is both readable and easily accessible.

The following figure represents the classification of data structure into two categories, i.e., linear and non-linear data structure:

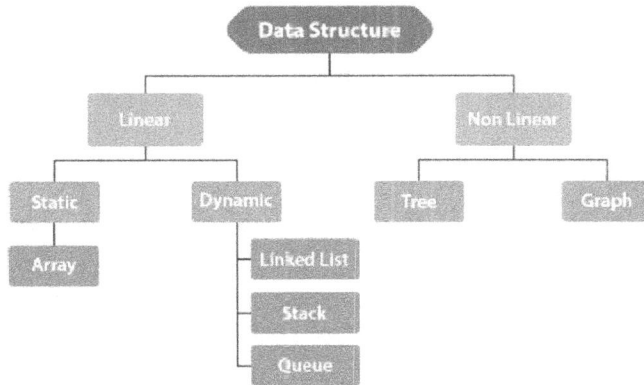

Figure 2.1: *Classification of data structures*

When selecting data structures, you must perform the following steps:

1. Analysis of the problem to determine basic operations like insert, delete, and search data in data structures.

2. Determine the exact number of resources that can be used for each task.

3. Figure out which data structure is ideal for these needs:

    a. Data and operations that are to be performed on them.

    b. Representation of data.

    c. Implementation of that representation.

Array

An array is a fixed-size, sequence grouping of items with the same kind of data. So, it is a linear data structure, i.e., the collection of homogeneous data elements at contiguous memory locations.

Refer to the following example, **int Age[10]**, showing 10 data items indexed from 0 to 9:

Age 0	Age 1	Age 2	Age 3	Age 4	Age 5	Age 6	Age 7	Age 8	Age 9
40	45	32	26	29	23	34	30	12	11

Table 2.1: *Example of an array*

Declaring and storing an array

An array declaration can be explained in three different ways:

1. `int Ar[3] = {11, 12, 25}`   `[Compile Time]`
2. `int i, Ar[3];`   `[Run time]`
      `for (i=0 ; i< 3; i++)`
          `Ar[i] = i;`
3. `int i, Ar[3];`   `[Run time]`
      `for (i=0 ; i< 3 ; i++)`
          `scanf("%d", &Ar[i]);`

Some applications of array data structures are mentioned as follows:

- Contacts on a cell phone indicate the array structure and maintain dictionary order.
- Book titles in a library management system represent an array formation.
- Speech processing involves representing each speech signal as an array.
- The display screen is also a multidimensional array of pixels.

Address calculation of array elements

In this section, we will be able to pinpoint memory precisely, where a single array element is stored. The initial byte of the array is represented by the address of the array's name. By referring to the array by its name, we are referring to the array's initial byte. The index or subscript specifies the position in the array relative to the array's initial position. Since an array's data elements are kept in successive memory locations, it is sufficient to keep track of only the base address, or the location of the first member in the array. Using the starting point's address, we can easily determine the location of any further data components. The calculating formula is as follows:

Address of array data element, `Arr[k] = Base_Address[Arr] + w(k - lower_bound)`.

Example 2.1: An array `int S_marks[ ] = {98,65,77,54,89,91,32,84}` is shown. Determine the address of `S_marks[4]` if the base address is 1000:

98	65	77	54	89	91	32	84
S_marks[0]	S_marks[1]	S_marks[2]	S_marks[3]	S_marks[4]	S_marks[5]	S_marks[6]	S_marks[7]
1000	1002	1004	1006	1008	1010	1012	1014

Figure 2.2: Array S_marks structure

Solution: Since we know that two bytes are needed to store an integer value. Therefore, its size is two bytes, shown as follows:

S_marks[4] = 1000 + 2(4 − 0)

= 1000 + 2(4) = 1008

Declaration of 2D array

The most basic type of multi-dimensional array in C is the 2D array, or two-dimensional array, which can be thought of as a table with X rows and Y columns. The row numbers fall within the range of 0 to (X-1), and the column numbers fall within the range of 0 to (Y-1).

```
data_type array_name[rowsize] [colsize];
```

This statement shows the declaration syntax of 2D array.

`int marks[3][3];` represents 2D array name marks having 3 rows and 3 columns. The memory representation is as follows:

00	01	02
10	11	12
20	21	22

marks

Table 2.2: 2D array structure of 3X3

These elements are stored sequentially in two ways, **row major order (RMO)** and **column major order (CMO)**, described as follows:

- **RMO:**

(0,0)	(0,1)	(0,2)	(1,0)	(1,1)	(1,2)	(2,0)	(2,1)	(2,2)

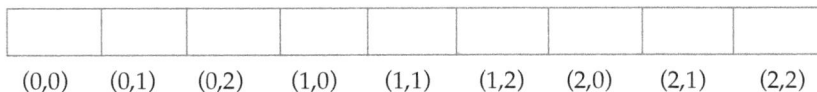

Table 2.3: 2D array structure using RMO

The preceding structure shows the sequential RMO structure that reads 2D array row-wise.

`A[M][N];`

The formula to calculate address of any data element in 2D array using RMO is as follows:

Address A[i, j] = Base_Address+ w*{ N(i-1) + (j-1)}

The equation demonstrates the following:

- *w* is the number of words stored per memory location.
- *N* is the number of elements in one row (number of columns).
- *i* and *j* are the subscripts of the array element.

Example 2.2: An array **int A[20][5]** is shown with *Base_Address=1000*, and number of words per memory location=2. Compute the address of element A[18,4]. Assume the elements are stored in RMO.

Solution: *Address of A[i, j] = Base_Address+ w * [N*(i-1) + (j-1)]*

*Address of A[18,4] = 1000 + 2 * [5 * (18-1) + (4-1)]*

*= 1000 + 2 * [85 + 3]*

= 1176

- **CMO**:

2	1	3	4	3	6	6	5	9
(0,0)	(1,0)	(2,0)	(0,1)	(1,1)	(2,1)	(0,2)	(1,2)	(2,2)

Table 2.4: 2D array structure using CMO

The preceding structure shows the sequential CMO structure that reads the 2D array column-wise:

2　4　6

1　3　5

3　6　9

A[M][N];

The formula to calculate the address of any data element in 2D array using CMO is as follows:

Address A[i, j] = Base_Address+ w*{ M(j-1) + (i-1)}

The equation demonstrates the following:

- w is the number of words stored per memory location.
- ī is the number of elements in one column (number of rows).
- *i* and *j* are the subscripts of the array element.

Example 2.3: The array **int A[10][10]**, *Base_Address=1000*, and number of words per memory location=2. Compute the address of element A[8,5]. Assume the elements are stored in CMO.

Solution: *Address of A[i, j] = Base_Address+ w * [M*(j-1) + (i-1)]*

*Address of A[8,5] = 1000 + 2 * [10 * (5-1) + (8-1)]*

*= 1000 + 2 * [40 + 7]*

= 1094

Array operations

Several operations can be executed on arrays, encompassing the following tasks:

- Traversing an array
- Inserting an item into an array
- Searching for an item in an array
- Deleting an item from an array
- Merging two arrays
- Sorting an array in an ascending or descending order

Let us discuss the topics in detail:

- **Traversal:** In order to perform a traversal operation in an array, or just traverse an array, you must access or print every array element precisely once so, that you can verify or use the data items (values) of the array in some other operation or process (sometimes referred to as visiting the array). The following shows the initialization of an array for traversal:

  A[ ] is the array.

  The lower bound is the starting index.

  The upper bound is the last index.

  Algorithm 2.1: Array traversal

  1. `Set i = lower_bound`
  2. `Repeat Steps 2 to 4 while i < = upper_bound`
  3. `Print (A[i])`
  4. `Set i = i + 1`
  5. `Exit`

  First, we set the index to the array's minimum value. The second step is a while loop. The third step involves handling each array element according to its index value and name. The index is increased in *Step 4* so that the next element in the array may be accessed and worked with. *Step 2's* while loop runs until the array's elements have been processed, or until i is greater than the upper bound of the array.

  Program 2.1: Using an array to read and show N numbers

```
#include <stdio.h>
#include <conio.h>
int main()
{
    int i, n, arr[20];
```

```
clrscr();
printf("\n Enter the number of elements in the array : ");
scanf("%d", &n);
for(i=0;i<n;i++)
{
        printf("\n arr[%d] = ", i);
        scanf("%d",&arr[i]);
}
printf("\n The array elements are ");
for(i=0;i<n;i++)
        printf("\t %d", arr[i]);
return 0;
}
```

Output:

Enter the number of elements in the array: 5
arr[0] = 10
arr[1] = 20
arr[2] = 30
arr[3] = 40
arr[4] = 50
The array elements are 10 20 30 40 50

Adding an item to the end of an existing array is a straightforward operation. We can easily set the value by adding one to the current upper_bound. Here, the array's allotted memory area is still accessible. For example, if an array is stated to have ten components, but now it has only eight elements, then there is space to accommodate two additional elements. We cannot add anything else if there are already ten elements in there.

Algorithm 2.2: Array insertion at the end

The algorithm is as follows:

1. **Set upper_bound = upper_bound + 1**
2. **Set A[upper_bound] = VALUE**
3. **EXIT**

The process of adding an item to the end of an array is done by using an algorithm. We increase the upper_bound by one in the first step. In *Step 2*, the upper_bound is used to determine where to put the updated value:

- **Insert an element in the middle of an array**: The algorithm **INSERT** is declared as **INSERT (Arr, Num, POS, VAL)**.

The arguments for the insertion of an element into an array are as follows:

○ **Arr**, represents the array in which the element is to be inserted.

○ **Num**, indicating the total number of elements currently present in the array.

○ **POS**, denoting the desired spot, where the component will be placed.

○ **VAL** represents the specific value that is to be inserted into the array.

Algorithm 2.3: Demonstrating the algorithm for insertion in the array in the middle

The algorithm is as follows:

1. **Set i = Num.**
2. **Repeat Steps 3 and 4 while i > = POS .**
3. **Set Arr[i + 1] = A[i].**
4. **Set i = i - 1.**
5. **[End of the Loop]**
6. **Set Num = Num + 1.**
7. **Set Arr[POS] = VAL.**
8. **EXIT**

In the first step, the variable i is initialized with the entire number of elements in the array. During *Step 2*, a while loop is conducted in order to shift all elements with an index larger than POS, one place to the right, creating room for the insertion of a new element. In *Step 5*, the total number of elements in the array is incremented by 1. At the end, in *Step 6*, the new value is placed at the desired position. *Figure 2.3* demonstrates the insertion of a data element at the middle in a 1D array:

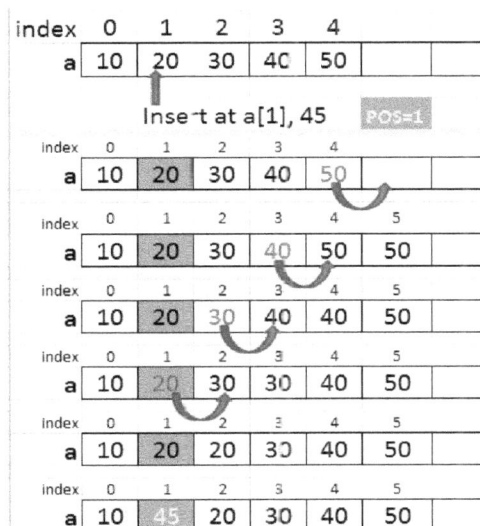

Figure 2.3: Insertion at middle

Program 2.2: Put a value into an array at a specific spot

```c
#include <stdio.h>
#include <conio.h>
int main()
{
        int i, n, num, pos, arr[10];
        clrscr();
        printf("\n Enter the number of elements in the array : ");
        scanf("%d", &n);
        for(i=0;i<n;i++)
        {
                printf("\n arr[%d] = ", i);
                scanf("%d", &arr[i]);
        }
        printf("\n Enter the number to be inserted : ");
        scanf("%d", &num);
        printf("\n Enter the position at which the number has to be added : ");
        scanf("%d", &pos);
        for(i=n-1;i>=pos;i--)
                arr[i+1] = arr[i];
        arr[pos] = num;
        n = n+1;
        printf("\n The array after insertion of %d is : ", num);
        for(i=0;i<n;i++)
                printf("\n arr[%d] = %d", i, arr[i]);
        getch();
        return 0;
}
```

Output:

```
Enter the number of elements in the array: 5
arr[0] = 1
arr[1] = 2
arr[2] = 3
arr[3] = 4
arr[4] = 5
Enter the number to be inserted: 0
Enter the position at which the number has to be added: 3
```

```
The array after the insertion of 0 is:
arr[0] = 1
arr[1] = 2
arr[2] = 3
arr[3] = 0
arr[4] = 4
arr[5] = 5
```

- **Deletion**: The act of deleting an element from an array involves the removal of a specific data element from an array that already exists. If the removal of an element is required from the end of the given array, then the process of deletion can be considered straightforward. It is necessary to do a subtraction operation by decrementing the value of the upper bound by one.

Algorithm 2.4: Array deletion at the end

The algorithm is as follows:

1. **Set upper_bound = upper_bound - 1**
2. **EXIT**

The process of removing an item at the end of an array is done by using an algorithm. We decrease the upper_bound by one in the first step, then return. Delete an element from the middle of an array. The algorithm deletion is stated as **DELETE (Arr, Num, POS)**.

The arguments for the deletion of an element from an array are as follows:

- **Arr**, represents the array in which the element is to be inserted.

- **Num**, indicating the total number of elements currently present in the array.

- **POS**, denoting the desired position at which the element is to be deleted.

Algorithm 2.5: Insertion in the array at the middle:

1. **Set i = POS**
2. **Repeat step 3 & 4 while i < = Num - 1**
3. **Set Arr[i] = Arr[i + 1]**
4. **Set i = i + 1**
5. **[End of the Loop]**
6. **Set Num = Num - 1**
7. **EXIT**

The algorithm commences by initializing the variable I, with the position from which the element is to be eliminated. During *Step* 2, a while loop is implemented to shift any elements with an index larger than POS one position to the left, in order to fill the gap left by the removed element. When referring to the act of deleting an element, it is more accurate to state that the element is overwritten with the value of its subsequent element. In the fifth step, the total number of elements in the array is reduced by one through the process of decrementing. The complete process of deletion of a data element at a given location in 1D array is explained in *Figure 2.4*:

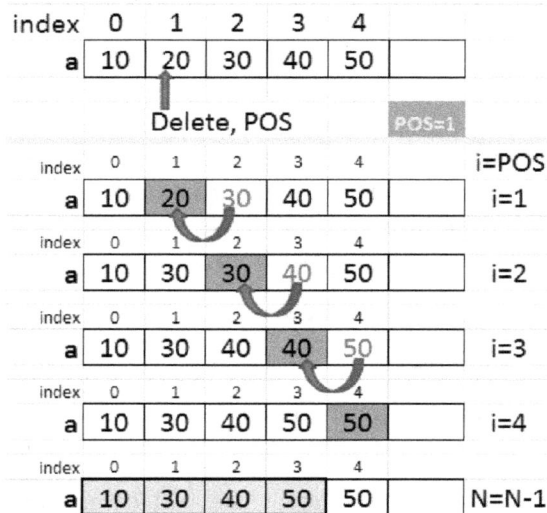

Figure 2.4: Deletion of an element at given position

Program 2.3: Delete a number from a given location in an array

```c
#include <stdio.h>
#include <conio.h>
int main()
{
    int i, n, pos, arr[10];
    clrscr();
    printf("\n Enter the number of elements in the array : ");
    scanf("%d", &n);
    for(i=0;i<n;i++)
    {
        printf("\n arr[%d] = ", i);
        scanf("%d", &arr[i]);
    }
    printf("\nEnter the position from which the number has to be deleted : ");
    scanf("%d", &pos);
    for(i=pos; i<n-1;i++)
        arr[i] = arr[i+1];
    n--;
    printf("\n The array after deletion is : ");
```

```
        for(i=0;i<n;i++)
                printf("\n arr[%d] = %d", i, arr[i]);
        getch();
        return 0;
}
```

Output:

```
Enter the number of elements in the array : 5
arr[0] = 1
arr[1] = 2
arr[2] = 3
arr[3] = 4
arr[4] = 5
Enter the position from which the number has to be deleted : 3
The array after deletion is :
arr[0] = 1
arr[1] = 2
arr[2] = 3
arr[3] = 5
```

* **Merging two arrays**: The process of merging two arrays into a third array involves initially duplicating the first array's elements into the third array, followed by duplicating the second array's elements into the third array. Consequently, the merged array comprises the first array's elements followed by the second array's elements. In the case of unsorted arrays, the process of merging them is straightforward, as it involves merely duplicating one array's elements into another. However, the process of merging becomes more complex when dealing with sorted arrays, as the resulting merged array must likewise maintain a sorted order. Firstly, let us initiate a discussion regarding the merge operation applied to arrays that have not been sorted. The following structure shows the merging of two arrays:

55	45	57	41

Table 2.5: Array 1

22	43	84	92	73

Table 2.6: Array 2

The merged array is named array 3 as follows:

55	45	57	41	22	43	84	92	73

Table 2.7: Array 3

Program 2.4: Merge two unsorted arrays

```c
#include <stdio.h>
#include <conio.h>
int main()
{
        int arr1[10], arr2[10], arr3[20];
        int i, n1, n2, m, index=0;
        clrscr();
        printf("\n Enter the number of elements in array1 : ");
        scanf("%d", &n1);
        printf("\n\n Enter the elements of the first array");
        for(i=0;i<n1;i++)
        {
                printf("\n arr1[%d] = ", i);
                scanf("%d", &arr1[i]);
        }
        printf("\n Enter the number of elements in array2 : ");
        scanf("%d", &n2);
        printf("\n\n Enter the elements of the second array");
        for(i=0;i<n2;i++)
        {
                printf("\n arr2[%d] = ", i);
                scanf("%d", &arr2[i]);
        }
        m = n1+n2;
        for(i=0;i<n1;i++)
        {
                arr3[index] = arr1[i];
                index++;
        }
        for(i=0;i<n2;i++)
        {
                arr3[index] = arr2[i];
                index++;
        }
        printf("\n\n The merged array is");
        for(i=0;i<m;i++)
                printf("\n arr[%d] = %d", i, arr3[i]);
        getch();
        return 0;
}
```

Output:

```
Enter the number of elements in array1 : 3
```

```
Enter the elements of the first array
arr1[0] = 1
arr1[1] = 2
arr1[2] = 3
Enter the number of elements in array2 : 3
Enter the elements of the second array
arr2[0] = 4
arr2[1] = 5
arr2[2] = 6
The merged array is
arr[0] = 1
arr[1] = 2
arr[2] = 3
arr[3] = 4
arr[4] = 5
arr[5] = 6
```

Merging two sorted arrays

When confronted with the requirement of merging two sorted arrays into a resultant array that must likewise be sorted, the process of merging becomes more challenging. The process of merging can be elucidated through the utilization of the following tables:

41	45	55	57

Table 2.8: Array 1

22	43	73	84	92

Table 2.9: Array 2

The merged table is as follows:

22	41	43	45	55	57	73	84	92

Table 2.10: Array 3

The example demonstrates the process of creating a merged array by combining two arrays that are already sorted. Here, we first compare the first element of array1 with the first element of array 2 and then put the smaller element in the merged array. Since 41 > 22, we put 22 as the first element in the merged array. We then compare the second element of the second array with the first element of the first array. Since 41 < 43, now 41 is stored as the second element of the merged array. Next, the second element of the first array is compared with the second element of the second array. Since 45 > 43, we store 43 as the third element of the merged array. Now, we will compare the second element of the first array with the third element of the second array. Because 45 < 73, we store 45 as the fourth element of the merged array. This procedure will be repeated until elements of both arrays are placed in the right location in the merged array.

Program 2.5: Merge two sorted arrays

```c
#include <stdio.h>
#include <conio.h>
int main()
{
        int arr1[10], arr2[10], arr3[20];
        int i, n1, n2, m, index=0;
        int index_first = 0, index_second = 0;
        clrscr();
        printf("\n Enter the number of elements in array1 : ");
        scanf("%d", &n1);
        printf("\n\n Enter the elements of the first array");
        for(i=0;i<n1;i++)
        {
                printf("\n arr1[%d] = ", i);
                scanf("%d", &arr1[i]);
        }
        printf("\n Enter the number of elements in array2 : ");
        scanf("%d", &n2);
        printf("\n\n Enter the elements of the second array");
        for(i=0;i<n2;i++)
        {
                printf("\n arr2[%d] = ", i);
                scanf("%d", &arr2[i]);
        }
        m = n1+n2;
        while(index_first < n1 && index_second < n2)
        {
                if(arr1[index_first]<arr2[index_second])
                {
                        arr3[index] = arr1[index_first];
                        index_first++;
                }
                else
                {
                        arr3[index] = arr2[index_second];
                        index_second++;
                }
                index++;
        }
```

```
      // if elements of the first array are over and the second array has
      some elements
      if(index_first == n1)
      {
            while(index_second<n2)
            {
                  arr3[index] = arr2[index_second];
                  index_second++;
                  index++;
            }
      }
      // if elements of the second array are over and the first array has
      some elements
      else if(index_second == n2)
      {
            while(index_first<n1)
            {
                  arr3[index] = arr1[index_first];
                  index_first++;
                  index++;
            }
      }
      printf("\n\n The merged array is");
      for(i=0;i<m;i++)
            printf("\n arr[%d] = %d", i, arr3[i]);
      getch();
      return 0;
}
```

Output:
```
Enter the number of elements in array1 : 3
Enter the elements of the first array
arr1[0] = 1
arr1[1] = 3
arr1[2] = 5
Enter the number of elements in array2 : 3
Enter the elements of the second array
arr2[0] = 2
arr2[1] = 4
arr2[2] = 6
The merged array is
arr[0] = 1
arr[1] = 2
```

```
arr[2] = 3
arr[3] = 4
arr[4] = 5
arr[5] = 6
```

Stack

A stack is a type of linear data structure that adheres to the notion of adding and removing elements exclusively from one end, known as the top. Therefore, a stack is sometimes referred to as a **last-in-first-out** (**LIFO**) data structure, as the piece that was most recently put, is the first one to be removed.

The basic operations that can be performed on the stacks are push, pop, and peek. Stacks are widely used in computer science for a variety of applications with the inclusion of function calls, evaluation of expression, and memory management.

Figure 2.5 illustrates a stack of plates arranged one over the other. This visual metaphor is commonly used to explain the LIFO principle in data structures.

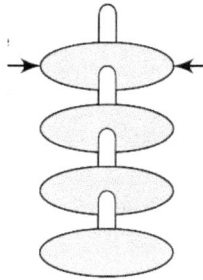

Figure 2.5: Stack of plates

The other plate will be placed over the TOP plate, and this new inserted plate will be removed first.

The concept of stacks can be elucidated through the use of an analogy. Consider a stack of plates, as depicted in the figure, where each plate is positioned atop another. When desiring to remove a plate, the topmost plate is the first to be taken away. Consequently, the addition and removal of an element, represented by a plate, can solely occur at the highest position within the stack.

Some applications of stack data structures are mentioned as follows:

- Reversing a list
- Parentheses checker
- Conversion of an infix expression into a postfix expression
- Evaluation of a postfix expression

- Conversion of an infix expression into a prefix expression
- Evaluation of a prefix expression
- Tower of Hanoi using recursion
- Undo-redo operation, etc.

Stacks can be implemented using either arrays or linked lists. In the following sections, we will discuss the array implementation of stacks.

Stack operations

The stack data structure facilitates three fundamental operations, namely push, pop, and peek. The push action is responsible for appending an element to the TOP of the stack, while the pop operation is responsible for removing the element from the TOP of the stack. The peek operation retrieves the value of the element located at the TOP of the stack.

Push operation

The push action is employed to insert an element onto the stack. The addition of the new element occurs at the highest place inside the stack. Prior to inserting the value, it is imperative to verify whether TOP is equal to MAX-1. This is necessary since it indicates that the stack has reached its maximum capacity, rendering any further insertions impossible. If an endeavor is made to insert a value into a stack that has already reached its maximum capacity, a notification indicating an overflow condition is displayed:

6				6				6		
5				5				5		
4				4		TOP		4	50	TOP
3	23	TOP		3	23			3	23	
2	17			2	17			2	17	
1	25			1	25			1	25	
0	15			0	15			0	15	
Index	Stack, S			Index	Stack, S			Index	Stack, S	
	MAX=7								MAX=7	

Table 2.11: Stack push operation

The diagram illustrates the algorithm for inserting an element into a stack. In the initial step, the first task is to examine the presence of the OVERFLOW condition. During *Step 2*, the value of TOP is incremented in order to indicate the subsequent location inside the array. During the third step, the value is put into the stack at the specific location indicated by the TOP pointer.

Algorithm 2.6: Insert an element in the stack

1. `If TOP = MAX - 1, print OVERFLOW. Go to Step 4. [End of IF].`
2. `Set TOP = TOP + 1.`
3. `Set Stack[TOP] = Value.`
4. `END`

Pop operation

The pop action is utilized to remove the uppermost element from the stack. Prior to deleting the value, it is imperative to verify if TOP=NULL, as this condition indicates that the stack is devoid of elements and further deletions are not feasible. If an endeavor is made to remove a value from a stack that is now devoid of elements, an underflow notification is generated. The following table illustrates the algorithm for inserting an element into a stack:

6			6			6			
5			5			5			
4			4			4			
3	23	TOP	3	23		3	23		
2	17		2	17	TOP	2	17	TOP	
1	25		1	25		1	25		
0	15		0	15		0	15		
Index	Stack, S					Index	Stack, S		
	MAX=7						MAX=7		

Table 2.12: Stack pop operation

In the initial step, the first task is to examine the presence of the OVERFLOW condition. During *Step 2*, the value of TOP is incremented in order to indicate the subsequent location inside the array. During the third step, the value is put into the stack at the specific location indicated by the TOP pointer.

Algorithm 2.7: Delete an element from a stack

1. `If TOP = NULL, print UNDERFLOW. Go to Step 4. [End of IF]`
2. `Set Value = Stack[TOP].`
3. `Set TOP = TOP - 1.`
4. `END`

In order to remove the element at the top of the stack, it is necessary to first verify if the value of the TOP pointer is equal to NULL. If the condition is determined to be false, the value referenced by the variable TOP is subsequently decreased.

Peek operation

The peek operation is a function that retrieves the value of the topmost element in a stack, without removing it from the stack. The peek action involves an initial check to determine if the stack is empty. This check is performed by verifying if the TOP pointer is NULL. If the stack is indeed empty, an appropriate message is written. However, if the stack is not empty, the value is returned:

Index	Stack S	
6		
5		
4		
3	23	TOP
2	17	
1	25	
0	15	
Index	Stack S	
	MAX=7	

Table 2.13: Stack peek operation

The peek action will yield the number 23, as it corresponds to the element situated at the top of the stack.

Algorithm 2.8: Peek operation in the stack

1. **If TOP = NULL, Print STACK IS EMPTY, then go to Step 3.**
2. **Return Stack[TOP]**
3. **END**

Program 2.6: Push, pop, and peek operations on a stack

```
#include <stdio.h>
#include <stdlib.h>
#include <conio.h>
#define MAX 3 // Altering this value changes size of stack created
int st[MAX], top=-1;
int main(int argc, char *argv[]) {
    int val, option;
    do
    {
        printf ("\n *****MAIN MENU*****\n 1. PUSH \n 2. POP \n 3. PEEK
        \n 4. DISPLAY\n 5. EXIT ");
        printf("\n Enter your option: ");
        scanf("%d", &option);
```

```
            switch(option)
            {
            case 1: printf("\n Enter the number to be pushed on stack: ");
                    scanf("%d", &val);
                    push(st, val);
                    break;
            case 2: val = pop(st);
                    if(val != -1)
                            printf("\n The value deleted from stack is: %d",
                    val);
                    break;
            case 3: val = peek(st);
                    if(val != -1)
                            printf("\n Value stored at top of stack is: %d",
                    val);
                    break;
            case 4: display(st);
                    break;
        } while(option != 5);
        return 0;
}
void push(int st[], int val){
        if(top == MAX-1)
                printf("\n STACK OVERFLOW");
        else{
                top++;
                st[top] = val;
        }
}
int pop(int st[]){
        int val;
        if(top == -1){
                printf("\n STACK UNDERFLOW");
                return -1;
        }
        else{
                val = st[top];
                top--;
                return val;
        }
}
void display(int st[]){
        int i;
        if(top == -1)
                printf("\n STACK IS EMPTY");
```

```
        else
        {
                for(i=top;i>=0;i--)
                        printf("\n %d",st[i]);
                printf("\n"); // Added for formatting purposes
        }
}
int peek(int st[])
{
        if(top == -1)
        {
                printf("\n STACK IS EMPTY");
                return -1;
        }
        else
                return (st[top]);
}
```

Output:

```
*****MAIN MENU*****
1. PUSH
2. POP
3. PEEK
4. DISPLAY
5. EXIT
Enter your option : 1
Enter the number to be pushed on stack : 555
```

Linked list representation of stack

The process of creating a stack by using an array has been observed. The process of constructing a stack by using this method is quite straightforward; nevertheless, it is important to note that a limitation of this approach is the requirement to declare the array with a pre-determined size. If the stack is either relatively tiny or its maximum size is pre-determined, the array implementation is typically chosen over the linked representation.

The linked representation of a stack with n members has a storage need of $O(n)$, and the operations typically have a time requirement of $O(1)$.

Queue

When an element is added to a queue, it will be withdrawn in the same order that it was added. This data structure is known as a **first-in, first-out** (**FIFO**) queue. Elements are added to a queue at one end, called the **REAR** and taken out at the other end, called the **FRONT**.

Both arrays and linked lists are viable implementations of queues. This section will demonstrate the implementation of queues by using each of these data types.

Queue can handle multiple data items. We can access the data elements in the queue from both ends and they are flexible and fast to access. *Figure 2.6* shows the basic structure of queue with two pointer FRONT and REAR:

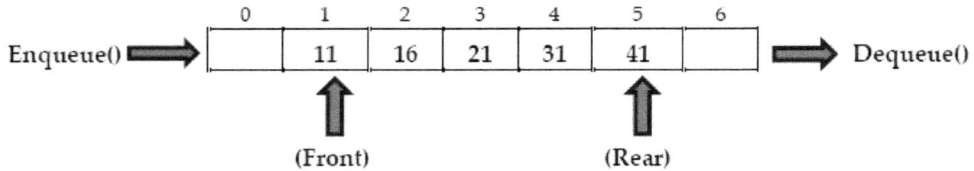

Figure 2.6: Structure of queue

The applications of queue data structures are mentioned as follows:

- Printers and single shared resources utilize the queue structure.
- Both slow and fast devices synchronize with the queue.
- In networking, queue is used in switch or router and mail queue.
- Within a single source program, there may be multiple queue requests.

Queue operations

Linear arrays provide a simple and efficient way to represent queues. As previously mentioned, each queue is equipped with FRONT and REAR variables that indicate the positions where deletions and insertions can be performed, respectively. The following table displays the array representation of the queue:

0	1	2	3	4	5
11	16	21	31	41	
Initial queue					
0	1	2	3	4	5
11	16	21	31	41	46
Queue after insertion of new element 46					
0	1	2	3	4	5
	16	21	31	41	46
Queue after deletion of an element 11					

Table 2.14: Queue insertion and deletion operation

Let us discuss insertion and deletion in the queue.

In the example, we will consider FRONT = 0 and REAR = 4. We would save the value in the position pointed by REAR and increment REAR by 1 if we wanted to add another element with a value of 46. Following addition, the queue would look like this: FRONT = 0 and REAR = 5. We always use the same method when adding new elements. To remove an item from a queue, we increment the FRONT value. After the deletion, FRONT becomes 1 and REAR becomes 5.

Prior to entering an element into a queue, it is necessary to verify if there are any overflow circumstances. An overflow will arise if we attempt to enter an element into a queue that is already at its maximum capacity. An overflow condition occurs when the value of REAR is equal to MAX - 1, where MAX represents the size of the queue. Please note that we have used MAX - 1 in our expression to account for the fact that the index begins at 0.

Prior to removing an element from a queue, it is necessary to verify if there are any underflow circumstances. An underflow problem arises while attempting to remove an element from a queue that is already devoid of any elements. If the value of FRONT is -1 and the value of REAR is -1, it indicates that the queue is empty and there are no elements present.

Algorithm 2.9: Insert an element in a queue

1. `IF variable REAR = MAX - 1, print OVERFLOW message. Go to Step 4. [END of IF]`
2. `IF FRONT =-1 and REAR = -1, SET FRONT = 0, REAR = 0. Else, SET REAR++. [END of IF].`
3. `Set Queue [REAR] = Value`
4. `END`

Algorithm 2.10: Remove an item from a given queue

1. `If FRONT == -1 or FRONT > REAR, print OVERFLOW. Else, set value = Queue[FRONT], and set FRONT = FRONT + 1. [End of IF]`
2. `END`

Program 2.7: Insert, delete, and peek operations in a queue

```
#include <stdio.h>
#include <stdlib.h>
#include <conio.h>
#define MAX 10
int queue[MAX], int front = -1, rear = -1;
int main(){
        int option, val;
        do{
                printf("\n\n ***** MAIN MENU *****\n1. Insert \n2. Delete \n3.
                Peek \n3. Display \n5. Exit");
                printf("\n Enter your option : ");
```

```
            scanf("%d", &option);
            switch(option)
            {       case 1:    insert();
                            break;
                    case 2:    val = delete_element();
                            if (val != -1)
                                    printf("\n The number deleted is : %d",
                            val);
                            break;
                    case 3:    val = peek();
                            if (val != -1)
                                    printf("\n The first value in queue is :
                            %d", val);
                            break;
                    case 4:    display();
                            break;
            }
    }while(option != 5);
    return 0;
}
void insert(){
    int num;
    printf("\n Enter the number to be inserted in the queue: ");
    scanf("%d", &num);
    if(rear == MAX-1)
            printf("\n OVERFLOW");
    else if(front == -1 && rear == -1)
            front = rear = 0;
    else
            rear++;
    queue[rear] = num;
}
int delete_element(){
    int val;
    if(front == -1 || front>rear){
            printf("\n UNDERFLOW");
            return -1;
    }
    else{
            val = queue[front];
            front++;
            if(front > rear)
                    front = rear = -1;
```

```
                    return val;
            }
}
int peek(){
        if(front==-1 || front>rear){
                printf("\n QUEUE IS EMPTY");
                return -1;
        }
        else
                return queue[front];
}
void display(){
        int i;
        printf("\n");
        if(front == -1 || front > rear)
                printf("\n QUEUE IS EMPTY");
        else{
                for(i = front;i <= rear;i++)
                        printf("\t %d", queue[i]);
        }
}
```

Output:

```
***** MAIN MENU *****"
1. Insert
2. Delete
3. Peek
4. Display
5. EXIT
Enter your option : 1
Enter the number to be inserted in the queue : 50
```

If the queue is either relatively tiny or its maximum size is predetermined, then implementing the queue by using an array is an efficient approach. However, if the size of the array cannot be pre-determined, the alternative option, namely the linked form, is employed.

The storage complexity of a queue implemented by using a linked representation with n members is $O(n)$, but the time complexity for operations is typically $O(1)$.

The different types of queues are mentioned as follows:

- **Circular queue**: Assuming we wish to add a new element to the queue, despite having adequate space, the overflow situation persists if the condition REAR = MAX -1 remains true. A significant limitation of a linear queue is evident. In order to address this issue, we have two potential resolutions. Initially, perform a leftward shift of the elements to create a vacant space that can be effectively occupied and exploited. However, this process can be exceedingly time-consuming, particularly when the backlog is of considerable size.

An alternative is to employ a circular queue. In a circular queue, the first index immediately follows the last index. It is filled only when the FRONT pointer is at position zero and the REAR pointer is at position MAX - 1. A circular queue is implemented by using the same approach as a linear queue. The sole distinction will be in the code that executes insertion and deletion operations. When it comes to insertion, it is now necessary to verify the following three conditions:

- o   If the value of FRONT is 0, and the value of REAR is MAX -1, at that time the circular queue is considered to be full.

- o   If the value of REAR! is MAX - 1, then the REAR will be increased and the value will be entered.

- o   If the value of the FRONT is not equal to 0 and the value of the REAR is equal to MAX - 1, then it can be concluded that the queue is not full. To insert the new element, assign the value of the REAR as zero.

- **Deque**: The data structure that permits the addition or removal of components at both ends is called a **deque**, which is also called a **double-ended queue**. The data structure is sometimes referred to as a head-tail linked list due to its ability to assemble or disassemble by removing members from the head or tail end.

  Nevertheless, it is not possible to insert or remove elements from the middle. Two types of circular memory structures are circular arrays and circular doubly linked lists. They are used to implement a deque. A deque is a data structure that utilizes two pointers, LEFT and RIGHT, to indicate the positions at each end of the deque. The items in a deque span from the leftmost end to the rightmost end, and due to their circular nature, dequeue[N–1] is immediately followed by dequeue [0].

  There exist two variations of a double-ended queue. The items encompass the following:

  - o   **Restricted input deque**: In this deque, insertions are limited to one end, while deletions can occur from either end.

  - o   **Output-restricted deque**: In this deque, deletions are limited to one of the ends, while insertions can be performed on both ends.

- **Priority queue**: In a priority queue, each element has a specific position in the hierarchy. The element's priority will define the sequence in which the elements will be processed. The fundamental principles governing the processing of components in a priority queue are as follows:

o Components having a higher priority are processed prior to those with a lower priority.

o Elements of equal priority are handled in the order they were received, following a first-come-first-served approach.

A priority queue can be conceptualized as an altered queue where the element with the highest priority is retrieved first when an element needs to be removed from the queue. The element's priority can be determined by considering multiple aspects. Priority queues are extensively utilized in operating systems to prioritize the execution of the most important processes. The process's priority can be determined by the amount of CPU time it needs to complete execution. In this scenario, with three processes, the second process, which requires 4 nanoseconds to complete, will be assigned the greatest priority and will therefore be run first. Nevertheless, CPU time is merely one of several factors that determine the priority. Another factor to consider is the prioritization of one process over another. If we need to simultaneously execute two processes, where one process involves online order booking and the other involves printing stock details, it is evident that the online booking process takes precedence and should be completed first.

- **Multiple queue**: When utilizing an array to create a queue, it is necessary to have prior knowledge of the array's size. If the authorized space for the queue is reduced, it will result in frequent occurrences of overflow circumstances. In order to address this issue, it will be necessary to make modifications to the code in order to allocate additional space for the array.

If we give a substantial amount of space for the queue, it will lead to excessive memory wastage. Hence, there exists a compromise between the occurrence rate of overflows and the allocated space.

An optimal approach to address this issue is to implement multiple queues or incorporate various queues into a single array of ample capacity. A collection of elements of the data structure Queue[n] is utilized to denote two separate queues, namely Queue A and Queue B. The choice of n ensures that the total size of both queues will never surpass n. When working with these queues, it is crucial to observe that queue A will expand from left to right, whereas queue B will expand from right to left simultaneously.

Pointers

A pointer, in the context of computer science and data structures, is a variable that saves the location in memory of another variable. Pointers are extensively utilized in programming languages such as C and C++, serving as a potent tool for manipulating memory and data structures. Comprehending pointers is essential for optimizing memory allocation and handling of intricate data structures.

Some key concepts related to pointers in data structures are mentioned as follows:

- **Memory address**: A pointer stores the memory location of a variable or an object. The memory address corresponds to the specific region in the computer's memory where the data is stored.

- **Declaration and initialization**: In order to declare a pointer, one must first identify the data type they are pointing to, followed by an asterisk (*). For instance, the declaration **int *ptr;** signifies the creation of a pointer that points to an integer. Prior to utilization, it is imperative to initialize pointers in order to prevent them from referencing an indeterminate memory location.

- **Pointer arithmetic**: Pointers are capable of being incremented or decremented, and arithmetic operations can be executed on them. This is especially advantageous when dealing with arrays and traversing memory.

- **Dereferencing**: Dereferencing a pointer involves retrieving the value stored at the specific memory address to which it is pointing. This is accomplished by using the dereference operator (*). For instance, the expression **int x = *ptr;** retrieves the value stored at the memory address indicated by **ptr** and assigns it to the variable x.

- **Dynamic memory allocation**: Pointers are frequently employed for dynamic memory allocation, a process in which memory is allocated or deallocated while the program is running. The C programming language utilizes functions such as **malloc()** and **free()** to manage dynamic memory.

- **Pointers and data structures**: Pointers are essential for constructing diverse data structures, such as linked list, trees, and graphs. They facilitate efficient manipulation and traversal of these structures.

- **Pointer to pointer (double pointer)**: Pointers can reference other pointers as well. This is particularly advantageous in situations where there is a need to alter the value of a pointer itself, such as via function parameters or when allocating dynamic memory.

- **Null pointers**: Pointers can have a special value called **NULL** (or **nullptr** in C++), which indicates that they do not indicate a legitimate location in memory.

Pointers offer a degree of indirection, enabling greater flexibility and efficiency in memory and data structure management. However, they also require careful handling to stay away from typical problems like memory leaks, dangling pointers, and segmentation faults.

Program 2.8: Dynamic memory allocation using single pointer

```
#include <stdio.h>
#include <stdlib.h>
int main() {
```

```
    // Declare a single pointer to an integer
    int *ptr;
    // Allocate memory for a single integer dynamically
    ptr = (int *)malloc(sizeof(int));
    // Check if memory allocation was successful
    if (ptr == NULL) {
        printf("Memory allocation failed. Exiting program.\n");
        return 1; // Exit with an error code
    }
    // Input a value into the allocated memory
    printf("Enter an integer: ");
    scanf("%d", ptr);
    // Display the value using the pointer
    printf("Value entered: %d\n", *ptr);
    // Deallocate the allocated memory
    free(ptr);
    return 0; // Exit program successfully
}
```

This program does the following:

- It declares a single pointer to an integer (**int *ptr**).

- It allocates memory for an integer using **malloc**.

- It inputs an integer from the user and stores it in the allocated memory.

- It displays the entered value by using the pointer.

- It deallocates the allocated memory using free.

Remember that using malloc and free requires careful handling to avoid memory leaks. Additionally, always check if memory allocation was successful before using the allocated memory, as demonstrated in the program.

Program 2.9: Double pointer to dynamically allocate a 2D array

```
#include <stdio.h>
#include <stdlib.h>
int main() {
    int rows, cols;
    printf("Enter the number of rows: ");
    scanf("%d", &rows);
    printf("Enter the number of columns: ");
    scanf("%d", &cols);
    int **matrix;
    matrix = (int **)malloc(rows * sizeof(int *));
    if (matrix == NULL) {
```

```
        printf("Memory allocation failed. Exiting program.\n");
        return 1; // Exit with an error code
    }
    for (int i = 0; i < rows; i++) {
        matrix[i] = (int *)malloc(cols * sizeof(int));
        if (matrix[i] == NULL) {
            printf("Memory allocation failed. Exiting program.\n");
            for (int j = 0; j < i; j++) {
                free(matrix[j]);
            }
            free(matrix);
            return 1; // Exit with an error code
        }
    }
    printf("Enter elements of the matrix:\n");
    for (int i = 0; i < rows; i++) {
        for (int j = 0; j < cols; j++) {
            printf("Element at [%d][%d]: ", i, j);
            scanf("%d", &matrix[i][j]);
        }
    }
    printf("\nMatrix entered:\n");
    for (int i = 0; i < rows; i++) {
        for (int j = 0; j < cols; j++) {
            printf("%d\t", matrix[i][j]);
        }
        printf("\n");
    }
    for (int i = 0; i < rows; i++) {
        free(matrix[i]);
    }
    free(matrix);
    return 0; // Exit program successfully
}
```

This program does the following:

- Takes user input for the number of rows and columns of a 2D array.
- Allocates memory for the 2D array using a double pointer.
- Inputs values into the 2D array.
- Displays the entered 2D array.
- Deallocates the allocated memory.

Make sure to handle memory deallocation properly, especially when working with double pointers, to avoid memory leaks. The program includes error handling for failed memory allocation to ensure proper cleanup before exiting.

Linked lists

A linked list is a data structure consisting of nodes, where each node is connected to the next node through links, creating a linear representation. So, a linked list is a linear data structure that consists of a collection of data pieces. These bits of data are referred to as nodes. It is a data structure that can be utilized to construct additional data structures. Therefore, it serves as a fundamental component for implementing data structures such as stacks, queues, and their variations. It can be conceptualized as a series of nodes, resembling a train, where each node holds one or more data fields and a reference to the next node. The following figure represents the linked list structure:

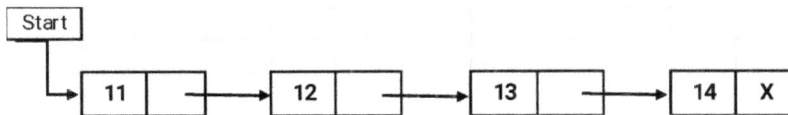

Figure 2.7: Linked list representation

A linked list consists of nodes, each containing an integer and a pointer to the next node. The left part of the node holds the data, which can be a simple data type, an array, or a structure. The right part of the node holds a pointer to the next node in the sequence. The last node does not have a connected next node and is indicated by a special value called **NULL**, represented as X. In programming, NULL is typically defined as -1. Therefore, a NULL pointer signifies the end of the list. Since each node in a linked list contains a pointer to another node of the same type, it is also referred to as a self-referential data type.

We can implement a linked list by using the following code:

```
struct node
{
int data;
struct node *next;
};
```

Singly linked list

A **singly linked list** (**SLL**) is a basic form of a linked list where each node holds data and a pointer to the next node of the same data type. The pointer in each node stores the address of the next node in the sequence, enabling the traversal of data in only one direction.

Traversing a linked list

Let us look at the algorithm.

Algorithm 2.11: Traverse singly linked list

1. `[Initialize], Set ptr = Start.`
2. `Repeat steps 3 and 4 while ptr != NULL.`
3. `Apply process to ptr | Data.`
4. `Update ptr = ptr | next. [End of Loop]`
5. `End`

For a single linked list, the time complexity of traversal is $O(n)$, where n is the number of nodes.

As you move through a uniquely linked list, you typically start from the head (the first node) and move through the list one node at a time until you reach the end (where the final node's next pointer is empty). Since you visit each node once, the time complexity is directly proportional to the number of nodes in the linked list.

In Big O Notation, $O(n)$ represents linear time complexity, meaning the time required for the operation grows linearly with the size of the input (in this case, the number of nodes in the linked list).

Searching an element in a linked list

This operation searches for an element in the given linked list and checks whether the input element exists in the list or not.

Algorithm 2.12: Search an element in a singly linked list

1. `[Initialization]. Assign the value of Start to ptr.`
2. `Repeat` *Step 3* `as long as ptr is not equal to NULL.`
3. `If VAL is equal to ptr | data. Assign the value of ptr to pos and jump to` *Step 5.* `Else, move ptr to ptr | Next. [End of If] and [End of the Loop].`
4. `Assign NULL to pos.`
5. `Exit`

In a singly linked list, searching for an element involves traversing the list from the beginning until you find the desired element or reach the end. If the list contains n elements, then this operation will take $O(n)$ time to complete. This is because, in the worst case, you may need to visit each node in the list once to find the target element.

Insertion in singly linked list

Here, we will examine the process of adding a new node to an existing linked list. We will analyze four examples to determine the insertion process:

- **First scenario**: The new node is added at the very beginning.
- **Second scenario**: The new node is appended to the end in this case.
- **Third scenario**: A specific node is placed before the new one.
- **Fourth scenario**: The new node is appended to an existing one.

The first scenario shows the insertion at the beginning of the list.

Algorithm 2.13: Insert at the beginning of SLL

1. `If Avail is NULL. Write OVERF_OW message. Go to Step 7 and [End of If].`
2. `Set NEW_NODE = Avail`
3. `Set Avail to Avail | NEXT`
4. `Set DATA to VAL`
5. `Set NEW_NODE | NEXT to START`
6. `Set START to NEW_NODE`
7. `Exit`

During *Step 1*, our initial task is to verify the availability of memory for the new node. If the available memory has been completely used, an **OVERFLOW** notice is displayed. Alternatively, if there is an unoccupied memory cell, we reserve space for the new node. Assign the value **VAL** to the **DATA** portion of the node and assign the next part to the address location of the first node in the list, which is held in the variable **START**. Since the new node is added to the list's starting point, it will be designated as the **START** node. A new variable called **START** will now hold the address of the **NEW_NODE**. Remember these two procedures:

- Assign the value of **Avail** to the variable **NEW_NODE**.
- Assign the value of **Avail** to the next node in the linked list.

These steps reserve memory for the newly created node. In the C programming language, there exist functions such as **malloc()**, **alloc,** and **calloc()** that handle the task of memory allocation on behalf of the user.

The second scenario shows the insertion at the end.

Algorithm 2.14: Insert at the end in SLL

1. `If AVAIL is NULL. Write OVERFLOW message. Go to Step 7 and [END of If statement].`
2. `Set NEW_NODE to AVAIL`
3. `Set AVAIL to AVAIL | NEXT`
4. `Set NEW_NODE | DATA to VAL`
5. `Set NEW_NODE | NEXT to NULL`
6. `Set PTR to START`

7. Repeat the Step 8 While variable PTR | NEXT is != NULL.
8. Set PTR to PTR | NEXT and [END of while Loop].
9. Set PTR | NEXT to NEW_NODE
10. EXIT

The third scenario shows the insertion after a given node.

Algorithm 2.15: Insert after a given node in SLL

1. If AVAIL is NULL. Write OVERFLOW message and jump to the Step 12.
2. Set NEW_NODE to AVAIL
3. Set AVAIL to AVAIL | NEXT
4. Set NEW_NODE | DATA to VAL
5. Set PTR to START
6. Set PREPTR to PTR
7. Repeat Step 8 and 9 While PREPTR | DATA is != NUM
8. Set PREPTR to PTR
9. Set PTR to PTR | NEXT. [END of the while Loop] and [END of the If statement].
10. Update PREPTR | NEXT to NEW_NODE
11. Set NEW_NODE | NEXT to PTR
12. Exit

The fourth scenario shows the insertion before a given node.

Algorithm 2.16: Insert a node before a given node in SLL

1. If AVAIL is NULL. Write OVERFLOW message and jump to Step 12. Then, [END of If statement]
2. Set NEW_NODE to AVAIL
3. Set AVAIL to AVAIL | NEXT
4. Set NEW_NODE | DATA to VAL
5. Set PTR to START
6. Set PREPTR to PTR
7. Repeat Steps 8 and 9, while PTR | DATA is != NUM.
8. Set PREPTR to PTR
9. Set PTR to PTR | NEXT. [END of the while Loop]
10. Update PREPTR | NEXT to NEW_NODE
11. Set NEW_NODE | NEXT to PTR
12. Exit

So, the time complexity for insertion in a singly linked list is generally *O(1)* for insertion at the beginning and *O(n)* for insertion at the end or a specific position in the middle.

Deletion in singly linked list

Here, we will examine the process of removing a node from an existing linked list. We will analyze three examples to determine the deletion process:

- **Situation 1**: Remove an initial node.
- **Situation 2**: Remove the last node.
- **Situation 3**: Remove a node after a specified node.

The first case shows the deletion at the beginning of the list.

Algorithm 2.17: Delete the first node in SLL

```
1.  If START is NULL
                    Write "UNDERFLOW" message
                    Goto Step 5
            [END of the If statement]
2.  Set PTR to START
3.  Set START to START | NEXT
4.  FREE the PTR pointer
5.  Exit
```

Initially, we verify the presence or absence of the connected list. If the value of **START** is **NULL**, it indicates that there are no nodes in the list and control is passed to the final step of the algorithm. Nevertheless, if the linked list contains nodes, we employ a pointer variable PTR that is assigned to reference the initial node in the list.

In order to accomplish this, we begin by initializing **PTR** with **START**, which holds the memory address of the first node in the list. During *Step 3*, the **START** pointer is updated to refer to the next node in the sequence. Then, the memory location engaged by the node pointed to by the **PTR** pointer (which is initially the first node of the list) is deallocated and returned to the free pool.

The second case shows the deletion at the end of the list.

Algorithm 2.18: Delete the last node in SLL

```
1.  If START is NULL then
                    Write "UNDERFLOW" message
                    Goto Step 8
        [END of If statement]
2.  Set PTR to START
3.  Repeat Step 4 and 5 While PTR| NEXT is not equal to NULL
4.  Set PREPTR to PTR
5.  Set PTR to PTR | NEXT
            [END of the while Loop]
```

6. `Set PREPTR | NEXT to NULL`
7. `FREE PTR pointer`
8. `Exit`

The third case shows deletion after a given node in the list.

Algorithm 2.19: Delete a node after a node in SLL

1. `If START is equals to NULL`
   `Write "UNDERFLOW" message`
   `Goto the Step 10`
   `[END of If statement]`
2. `Set PTR to START`
3. `Set PREPTR to PTR`
4. `Repeat Step 5 and 6 While PREPTR | DATA is not equal to NUM`
5. `Set PREPTR to PTR`
6. `Set PTR to PTR | NEXT`
   `[END of the while Loop]`
7. `Set TEMP to PTR`
8. `Set PREPTR | NEXT to PTR | NEXT`
9. `FREE PTR pointer`
10. `Exit`

So, the deletion at the beginning of a singly linked list involves updating the head to the next node. This operation holds constant time $O(1)$, irrespective of the size of the list.

In a single linked list, removing the last node requires traversing the entire list to reach the second-to-last node. This makes the time complexity linear and proportional to the number of elements in the list. The time complexity will be $O(n)$. Deleting a node from a specific position in the middle of a singly linked list requires traversing the list to find the node to be deleted and updating the pointers of the adjacent nodes. The time complexity is again linear, dependent on the size of the list, i.e., $O(n)$.

Two way or doubly linked list

A **doubly linked list** (**DLL**), also termed a 2-way linked list, is a more intricate variant of a linked list that contains a pointer to both the next and prior nodes in the sequence. Thus, it comprises three components: data, a pointer variable to the next node, and another pointer variable to the prior node.

By using the C language structure, a doubly linked list can be written as:

```
struct node1
{
struct node1 *previous;
```

```
int Data;
struct node1 *Next;
};
```

The initial node's PREV field and the final node's NEXT field will both be assigned the value NULL. The PREV field stores the address of the previous node, allowing for backward traversal of the list.

Therefore, it is evident that a doubly linked list requires a greater amount of memory per node and more costly fundamental operations. On the other hand, a doubly linked list offers the convenience of manipulating list elements by keeping references to nodes in both the forward and backward directions. *Figure 2.8* shows the representation of the two-way linked list:

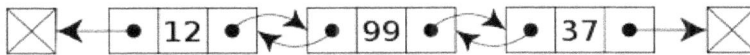

Figure 2.8: Two-way linked list representation

The primary benefit of utilizing a doubly linked list is that it enhances search efficiency by a factor of two. The doubly linked list can be used to denote other data structures like trees and graphs.

Insertion in two-way linked list

Adding a new node to an existing doubly linked list is demonstrated in this section. The process of inserting is going to be examined in four separate cases:

- **Instance 1**: The initial position of the new node is placed.
- **Instance 2**: The new node is appended to the end in this case.
- **Instance 3**: A specific node is placed before the new one.
- **Instance 4**: A specific node is preceded by the new node.

Algorithm 2.20: Insertion at the beginning of the DLL

```
1.  If AVAIL is equal to NULL
                Write "OVERFLOW" message
                Goto the Step 9
    [END of the If statement]
2.  Set variable NEW_NODE to AVAIL
3.  Set AVAIL to AVAIL | NEXT
4.  Set NEW_NODE | DATA to Value
5.  Set NEW_NODE | PREV to NULL
6.  Set NEW_NODE | NEXT to START
```

7. `Set START | PREV to NEW_NODE`
8. `Set START to NEW_NODE`
9. `Exit`

Algorithm 2.20: Add a new node at the start of a doubly linked list

During *Step 1*, our initial task is to verify the availability of memory for the new node. If the available memory has been completely used, then an OVERFLOW notification is displayed.

Alternatively, if there is an unoccupied memory cell, we assign space for the new node. Assign the **DATA** part of the node with the provided **VALUE**, then initialize the **NEXT** part with the memory location of the first node in the list, which is saved in the **START** variable. Now, as the new node is inserted at the beginning of the list, it will be designated as the **START** node. Consequently, the address of the **NEW_NODE** will now be stored in the **START** pointer variable.

Instance two demonstrates *Algorithm 2.21,* it shows the insertion at the end in DLL:

1. `If AVAIL is equal to NULL`
   `Write "OVERFLOW" message`
   `Goto the Step 11`
   `[END of the If statement]`
2. `Set NEW_NODE to AVAIL`
3. `Set AVAIL to AVAIL | NEXT`
4. `Set NEW_NODE | DATA to VALUE`
5. `Set NEW_NODE | NEXT to NULL`
6. `Set PTR to START`
7. `Repeat Step 8 while PTR | NEXT is not equal to NULL`
8. `Set PTR to PTR | NEXT`
9. `[END of the while Loop]`
10. `Set PTR | NEXT to NEW_NODE`
11. `Set NEW_NODE | PREV to PTR`
12. `Exit`

Algorithm 2.22: Insert after a given node in DLL

1. `If AVAIL is NULL`
   `Write "OVERFLOW" message`
   `Goto Step 12`
2. `Set NEW_NODE to AVAIL`
3. `Set AVAIL to AVAIL | NEXT`
4. `Set NEW_NODE | DATA to VALUE`
5. `Set PTR to START`

6. `Repeat Step 7 While PTR | DATA is not equal to NUM`
7. `Set PTR to PTR | NEXT`
8. `[END of the while Loop]`
9. `[END of the If statement]`
10. `Update NEW_NODE | NEXT to PTR | NEXT`
11. `Update NEW_NODE | PREV to PTR`
12. `Update PTR | NEXT to NEW_NODE`
13. `Update PTR | NEXT | PREV to NEW_NODE`
14. `Exit`

Insertion at the beginning or end of a doubly linked list has a *O(1)* constant time complexity.

In the worst-case scenario, inserting data into a given location in the list takes *O(n)* time, where n is the total number of nodes in the list.

Deletion in doubly linked list

In this scenario, we will check how a node is removed from an already existing two-way linked list. We will take three situations and then find the deletion process in each case:

- **Case 1**: Delete a node at the beginning.
- **Case 2**: Delete a node at the end.
- **Case 3**: Delete a node after a given node.

Algorithm 2.23: Deletion of the first node in DLL

1. `If START is equal to NULL`
       `Write "UNDERFLOW" message`
       `Goto Step 6`
   `[END of If statement]`
2. `Set PTR pointer to START`
3. `Set START to START | NEXT`
4. `Set START | PREV to NULL`
5. `FREE PTR pointer`
6. `Exit`

Algorithm 2.24: Deletion at the end of the list

1. `If START is equal to NULL`
       `Write "UNDERFLOW" message`
       `Goto Step 7`
   `[END of If statement]`
2. `Set PTR to START`

```
3.  Repeat Step 4 While PTR | NEXT is not equal to NULL
4.  Set PTR to PTR - > NEXT
          [END of the while Loop]
5.  Set PTR | PREV | NEXT to NULL
6.  FREE PTR pointer
7.  Exit
```

Algorithm 2.25: Delete a node after a node in DLL

```
1.  If START is equal to NULL
              Write "UNDERFLOW" message
              Goto Step 9
    [END of If statement]
2.  Initialize PTR to START
    Repeat Step 4 While PTR | DATA is not equal to NUM
    Set PTR to PTR | NEXT
              [END of the while Loop]
3.  Set TEMP to PTR - > NEXT
4.  Set PTR | NEXT to TEMP | NEXT
5.  Set TEMP | NEXT | PREV to PTR
6.  Free TEMP
7.  Exit
```

Deletion at the beginning or end of a doubly linked list has a constant time complexity of $O(1)$.

When deleting a node at a specific position in a doubly linked list, the time complexity is $O(n/2)$ on average, where n is the number of nodes in the list. In the worst case, it is still $O(n)$. This is because, on average, you need to traverse half of the list to find the node to delete. In the worst case, you may need to traverse the entire list.

Circular doubly linked list

A circular doubly linked list is a discrepancy of a doubly linked list in which the end node of the list is linked to the first node, forming a circle or loop. In a standard doubly linked list, the end node points to null to signify the end of the list. A circular doubly linked list, on the other hand, is always in a loop since the last node's pointer always points back to the first. *Figure 2.9* shows the representation of a circular doubly linked list:

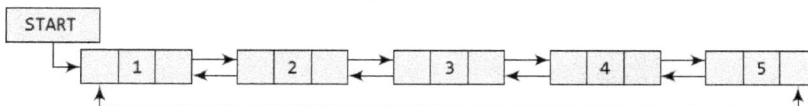

Figure 2.9: Circular doubly linked list representation

Due to its structure consisting of three parts, a circular DLL requires additional space per node and incurs higher costs for fundamental operations. On the other hand, a circular doubly linked list offers the convenience of manipulating list elements by keeping references to nodes in both the forward and backward directions. A significant advantage of utilizing a circular DLL is that it enhances the efficiency of search operations by a factor of two.

Insertion in circular doubly linked list

Adding a new node to an existing circular DLL is demonstrated in this section. We shall split the instances into two parts:

- **Instance 1**: The initial position of the new node is placed.
- **Instance 2**: The new node is appended to the end in this case.

Algorithm 2.26: Insertion at the beginning of the circular DLL

```
1. If AVAIL is equal to NULL
                Write "OVERFLOW" message
                Goto Step 13
   [END of the If statement]
2. Set NEW_NODE to AVAIL
3. Set AVAIL to AVAIL - > NEXT
4. Set NEW_NODE | DATA to VALUE
5. Set PTR pointer to START
6. Repeat the Step 7 while PTR | NEXT is not equals to START
7. Set PTR to PTR | NEXT
8. [END of the while loop]
9. Set PTR | NEXT to NEW_NODE
10. Set NEW_NODE | PREV to PTR
11. Set NEW_NODE | NEXT to START
12. Set START | PREV to NEW_NODE
13. Set START to NEW_NODE
14. then Exit
```

Case 2 insertion at the end.

Algorithm 2.27: Insert at the end in CDLL

```
Step 1:        If AVAIL is equals to NULL
                    Write "OVERFLOW" message
                    Jump to Step 12
               [END of If statement]
```

```
Step 2:        Set NEW_NODE to AVAIL
Step 3:        Set AVAIL to AVAIL | NEXT
Step 4:        Set NEW_NODE | DATA to VALUE
Step 5:        Set NEW_NODE | NEXT to START
Step 6:        Set PTR to START
Step 7:        Repeat the Step 8 While PTR | NEXT is not equals to START
Step 8:                Set PTR to PTR | NEXT
                   [END of the while loop]
Step 9:        Set PTR | NEXT to NEW_NODE
Step 10.       Set NEW_NODE | PREV to PTR
Step 11.       Set START | PREV to NEW_NODE
Step 12:       Exit
```

The constant-time complexity of inserting at the start or end of a circular doubly linked list is $O(1)$. At worst, inserting data at a given point in the list takes $O(n/2)$ time, where n is the total number of nodes.

Deletion in circular doubly linked list

Here, we will examine the process of removing a node from an existing circular doubly linked list. We shall examine two instances.

In Case 1, the new node is deleted at the beginning of the list, while in case 2, the new node is deleted at the end.

Let us look at Case 1, which involves the deletion at the beginning of the list.

Algorithm 2.28: Delete first node in CDLL

```
Step 1:        If START is equals to NULL
                       Write "UNDERFLOW" message
                       Then Goto Step 8
                   [END of the If statement]
Step 2:        Initialize PTR to START
Step 3:        Repeat the Step 4 while PTR | NEXT is != START
Step 4:                Move PTR to PTR | NEXT
                   [END of the while Loop]
Step 5:        Set PTR | NEXT to START | NEXT
Step 6:        Update START | NEXT | PREV to PTR
Step 7:        Free the START pointer
Step 8:        Finally set START to PTR | NEXT
```

Case 2 involves the deletion at the end of the list

Algorithm 2.29: Delete the last node in CDLL

```
Step 1:        If START is equals to NULL
                        Write "UNDERFLOW" message
                        Then Goto Step 8
                   [END of the If statement]
Step 2:        Initialize PTR pointer to START
Step 3:        Repeat the Step 4 While PTR | NEXT is != START
Step 4:            Set PTR to PTR - > NEXT
                   [END of the while Loop]
Step 5:        Update PTR | PREV | NEXT to START
Step 6:        Set START | PREV to PTR | PREV
Step 7:        Free PTR pointer
Step 8:        Then Exit
```

The operation deletion in a circular DLL is generally *O(1)* if you have a reference to the node and *O(n)* if you need to search for the node.

Hashing

Hashing is a method employed in the examination of algorithms and data structures, specifically in the field of searching and retrieving information from extensive datasets. The main objective of hashing is to efficiently map data of any size to fixed-size values, usually integers, while preventing collisions, which occur when two distinct bits of data are mapped to the same spot.

The following is a fundamental explanation of how hashing operates within the framework of algorithm analysis:

- **Hash function**: A hash function is a mathematical function that takes an input, sometimes known as a key, and generates a fixed-size output, typically referred to as a hash code. The hash code functions as the index or location inside the data structure where the appropriate data should be stored or retrieved.

    o The general idea of using the key to determine the address of records is an excellent idea. But it must be modified to prevent the wastage of space.

    o The modification takes the form of a function H from the set K of keys into the set L of memory addresses.

    H: K → L

    o Two principal criteria used in selecting a hash function H are:

    ▪ H should be very easy and quick to compute.

    ▪ H should be uniformly distributing the hash address throughout the set L so that the number of collisions is minimized.

- **Hash table**: It is a data structure that uses a hash function to map keys to specific places in an array. We utilize a hash function that retrieves the final two digits of the key. Consequently, we assign the keys to specific positions in an array, known as array locations or array indices. By utilising a hash function, which creates an address from the key and determines the index of the array where the value is kept, a value stored in a hash table can be found in constant time, denoted as *O(1)*.

Different hash functions:

  - **The division method**: This is the most basic approach to hashing an integer x. This approach involves dividing the value of x by M and subsequently utilising the resulting remainder. The hash function in this scenario can be expressed as follows:

    H(x) = x mod M

    The division method is highly efficient for any value of M, as it only takes a single division operation, resulting in quick performance. Nevertheless, it is imperative to use caution while choosing an appropriate value for M.

    For instance, let us assume that M is an even number. In this case, H(x) will also be even if x is even, whereas H(x) will be odd if x is odd. If all potential keys have an equal probability of occurring, then this situation does not pose an issue. However, if the probability of even keys is higher than that of odd keys, the division algorithm will not distribute the hashed values evenly.

    It is often advisable to select M as a prime integer because doing so enhances the probability of achieving a uniform mapping of keys to a range of output values. M should also be sufficiently distant from the precise powers of two. Given *H(x)=x mod 2^k* function, the binary form of x will only have its lowest k bits extracted.

Example 2.4: Find the matching hash values for keys 5462 and 1234.

Solution: Consider the value of *M = 97*, hash values can be evaluated as:

H(5642) = 5642 % 97 = 16

H(1234) = 1234 % 97 = 70

- **Multiplication method**: The procedure for the multiplication method consists of the following steps:

  1. Select a constant A within the range of 0 to 1,
  2. Compute the product of the key k and A.
  3. Obtain the decimal portion of the product of k and A.
  4. Compute the product of the outcome from Step 3 and the magnitude of the hash table (m).

Therefore, the hash function can be expressed like: *H(k) = [M (KA mod 1)]*

Where (*KA mod 1*) represents the fractional part of KA, and the total number of indices in the given hash table is denoted by M.

Example 2.5: Find the correct location in a 1000-by-key hash table for the key 12345.

Solution: We will consider $A = 0.619034$, $M = 1000$, and $K = 12345$

$H(12345) = [1000 (12345 \times 0.619034 \bmod 1)]$

$H(12345) = [1000 (7641.97473 \bmod 1)]$

$H(12345) = [1000 (0.97473)]$

$H(12345) = [974.73]$

$H(12345) = 974$

- **Mid-square method**: This method is an effective hashing function that operates in two distinct steps:
    1. Calculate the square of the key value. That is, determine the value of k2.
    2. Retrieve the middle r digits from the outcome received in *Step 1*.

The algorithm is effective because the majority or all of the digits in the key value have an impact on the outcome. This occurs because each individual digit in the original key value collectively contributes to generating the middle digits of the squared value. Consequently, the outcome is not influenced by the prevalence of either the lowest or highest digit in the initial key value.

In the mid-square approach, the selection of r digits must be consistent across all keys. Thus, the hash function can be expressed as follows: $h(k) = s$, where s is derived by picking *r* digits from the square of k.

Example 2.6: Use the mid-square method to determine the hash value of keys 5642 and 1234. The hash table occupies one hundred memory spaces.

Solution: Be aware that the hash table uses 100 memory regions with indices ranging from zero to 99. This implies that r= 2 is the minimum number of digits required to map the key to a place in the hash table.

When $K = 5642$, $K^2 = 31832164$, $H (5642) = 21$

When $K = 1234$, $K^2 = 1522756$, $H (1234) = 27$

Keeping with the right-hand side of the equation, the third and fourth digits are selected.

- **Folding method**: The folding technique operates through the sequential execution of two distinct steps:
    1. Partition the key value into multiple segments. That is, partition k into k_1, k_2, ..., k_n, where the exception of the final partition, every partition has an identical number of digits, which may have fewer digits than the others.

2. Incorporate the different components. i.e., acquire the total of K_1, K_2, ..., K_n. The hash-value is generated by disregarding the final carry, if one exists.

It should be noted that the number of digits in each section of the key will differ based on the size of the hash table. For instance, if the hash table has a size of 1000, it means that there are 1000 slots or positions available in the hash table. To address these 1000 places, we require at least three digits; consequently, every section of the key, with the exception of the last part, needs to have three digits.

Example 2.7: Utilizing the folding approach, determine the hash value for keys 5678, 322, and 34567 in a hash table with 100 places.

Solution: Since there are 100 memory locations to address, we will break the key into parts where each part (except the last) will contain two digits.

Key 5679   Parts are 56 and 79   Sum 135   Hash value 35 (ignore the last carry)

Key 322   Parts are 32 and 2   Sum 34   Hash value 34

Key 35568   Parts are 35, 56 and 8   Sum 99   Hash value 99

- **Chaining**: In the hash table, each bucket holds a linked list (or another data structure) to store numerous items that have the same hash code. Thus, different keys that generate the identical hash value can reside together within a single bucket.

- **Open addressing**: In the event of a collision, this technique entails locating another position inside the hash table to accommodate the conflicting item. This may entail looking for the subsequent accessible position using techniques like linear probing or quadratic probing.

Hashing is frequently employed in algorithms that necessitate efficient data retrievals, such as hash-based search structures, caches, and diverse database indexing strategies. When evaluating methods that utilize hashing, it is crucial to take into account the effectiveness of the hash function, the dispersion of hash codes, and the approach to resolving collisions. A well-constructed hash function can result in a more evenly distributed allocation of data, hence decreasing the probability of collisions and enhancing overall efficiency.

Trees

Trees are hierarchical non-linear data structures that are made out of nodes linked together by edges. Every tree starts at the root node and branches outward from there with one or more child nodes at each level, except for the root node, which has zero or more children.

There are various types of trees used in algorithm design and analysis, and they serve different purposes. Some common types of trees include:

- **Binary tree**: In a binary tree, the number of children per node is strictly limited to two: the left child and the right child.

- **Binary search tree (BST)**: The BST is a kind of binary tree where the left subtree of a node consists exclusively of nodes with keys that are less than the key of the node, and the right subtree consists exclusively of nodes with keys that are higher than the key of the node. The ordering aspect of this data structure enhances its efficiency for searching, insertion, and deletion operations.

- **AVL tree**: One kind of binary search tree is the AVL tree that automatically maintains balance. The balance of the tree is maintained by ensuring that the difference in heights between the two child subtrees of each node is no more than one.

- **Heap**: A heap is a data structure that is built on a tree and fulfils the heap attribute. In a maximum heap, the value of each node is always larger than or equal to the values of its child nodes. A min-heap is a data structure where the value of each node is smaller or equal to the values of its child nodes.

Trees are utilised in algorithms for several objectives, including optimizing data organization, facilitating element search, and illustrating hierarchical connections. Algorithmic design and analysis frequently entail the utilisation or construction of tree structures to enhance specific operations or represent connections between elements in a problem.

The application of trees is mentioned as follows:

- Trees serve as a means of storing both basic and intricate information. In this context, simple refers to an integer or character value, while complex refers to a structure or record.

- Trees are commonly employed for the implementation of various data structures such as hash tables, sets, and maps.

- Red-black tree, one kind of self-balancing tree, is utilized in kernel scheduling for preempting massively multiprocessor computer operating systems.

- B-trees are commonly employed for storing tree structures on disc, serving as an alternative form of trees. They are utilised for the purpose of cataloguing a substantial quantity of records.

- B-trees are utilised as supplementary indexes in databases, enabling efficient select operations to satisfy certain range conditions.

- There is another usage for trees in file system directories, database design etc.

Binary search tree

The BST, sometimes termed as an, is an ordered binary tree type of binary tree where nodes are organized in a specific order. Within a binary search tree, every node in the left subtree has a value lower than the root node. Similarly, all the nodes in the right subtree possess a value that is either equivalent to or larger than the value of the root node. Each subtree in the tree is subject to the same rule.

The search operation typically takes $O(log_2 n)$ time to complete because we remove half of the subtree at each stage.

We do not need to traverse the entire tree for searching an element due to its efficiency in searching, widely used in dictionary problems. We can get all values in sorted order by just doing the inorder traversal of BST.

Example 2.8: Make a binary search tree with these pieces of information:

45, 39, 56, 12, 34, 78, 32, 10, 89, 54, 67, 81

Solution: The solution is given in the following figure:

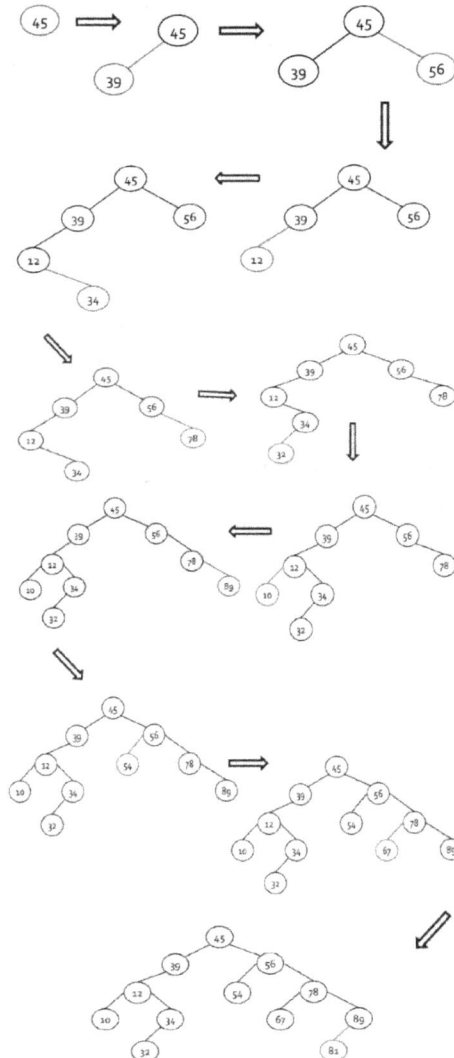

Figure 2.10: Finding the final BST

So, in the preceding over tree structure, we first pick up value 45 and make it the root node. Now, the next value, 39 is compared with the root value, 39 < 45, so place 39 as the left child of the root. The next value is 56, 56 > 45, place 56 as the right child of the root. The next value is 12, which is compared with the root node first and then compared with the left child 39. Since 12 < 39, put this to the left of 39. Now another value is 34, which will be compared in the left subtree, placed as the right child of the 12. The next value is 78, 78 > 45, so we will process it in the right subtree. It is also greater than 56, so it is a right child to 56. Next is 32, compare it in the left subtree, and next place it as the left child of 34. Now another value is 10, which is compared with 45, then compared with 39, then compared with 12. So, 10 < 12, thus, make it the left child of 12. The next value is 89, which will be compared in the right subtree and placed as the right child of 78. The next three values are 54, 67, and 81, all these values are greater than the root node, so we will place these values in the right subtree one by one at their correct positions.

B-tree

B-tree is a data structure that automatically adjusts its balance and keeps data sorted. It enables efficient operations such as searching, accessing data in order, inserting new data, and deleting data, all of which can be done in logarithmic time. It is an abstract representation of the binary search tree. B-trees are highly suitable for storage systems with slow, cumbersome data access, like hard drives, flash memory, and CD-ROMs. The value of 't' is contingent upon the size of the disc block.

A B-tree node can accommodate many keys, enabling the tree to have a higher branching factor and hence a shorter height. The limited height of this structure reduces the amount of disc input/output, hence enhancing the speed of search and insertion operations. A B-trees achieves balance by enforcing a minimum number of keys in each node, hence assuring constant balance throughout the tree. The equilibrium ensures that the Time Complexity for operations like searching, insertion, and deletion is consistently *O(log n)*, irrespective of the starting structure of the tree.

Features of B-tree are mentioned as follows:

- All the leaves are situated at the same level.

- A B-tree is characterised by the parameter 't', which represents the minimal degree. The value of 't' depends upon the size of the disc block.

- Each node, excluding the root, can have a maximum of t-1 keys. A minimum of one key is required for the root.

- Each node, including the root, can have a maximum of the $(2t - 1)$ keys.

- A node's total number of children is equivalent to the number of keys it contains, plus one.

- The keys of a node are arranged in ascending order. The child located b/w 2 keys, K1 and K2, encompasses all keys inside the range defined by K1 and K2.

- The B-tree expands and contracts starting from the root, which is in contrast to the BST. BST trees expand downwards and contracts above.

- Each operation on a balanced BST takes *O(log n)* time, just like any other balanced BST.

- Node insertion in a B-tree occurs exclusively at leaf nodes.

Example 2.9: Use the numbers 11–18 to construct a three-order B-tree.

Solution: The first element is 11, inserted into a new node, i.e., root node:

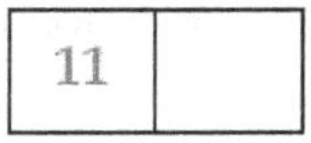

Figure 2.11: Add first element to root node

The second element is 12, added to the same leaf node, value 12 can be inserted at an empty position:

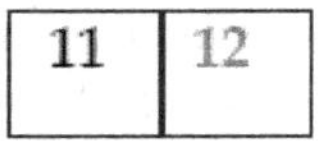

Figure 2.12: Add second element to leaf node

The third element, 13, is added to the same leaf, but we do not have free space in the leaf. So, we split the node by transferring the middle value 12 to its parent node. But there is no parent, so we make the middle-value node the parent node:

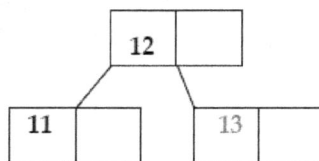

Figure 2.13: Splitting the node

The fourth value is 14, 14 > 12, so we move to the right of 12. We reach the leaf node having value 13, it has empty space, and we place value 14 there:

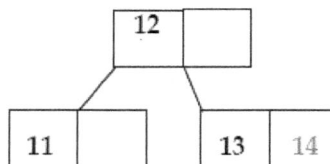

Figure 2.14: Adding the fourth element

The fifth value is 15, 15 > 12(root node), it is not a leaf node, we proceed to the leaf node, which is already full. We divide that node by transferring the middle value 14 to its parent node 12. So, there is an empty space in its parent, so 14 is added to the parent and 15 is added to a new leaf node:

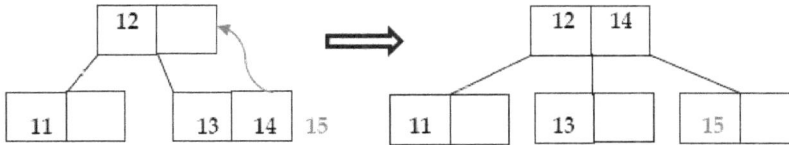

Figure 2.15: Add fifth element to new leaf node

The sixth number is 16, i.e., greater than root values 12 and 14, and it is not a leaf node, so we move to the right of 14 and reach to the leaf node (15). It has vacant space, add 16 here:

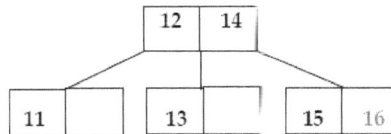

Figure 2.16: Adding element to leaf node

The seventh number is 17, larger than 12 and 14, and not a leaf node. So, we move right of 14, we reach at the leaf node which is already full. We split the node by transferring the middle value 16 to its ancestor (12 and 14), but the parent is also full. So, again, split by sending the middle value 14 to its parent, but the parent does not exist. So, 14 becomes the new root node:

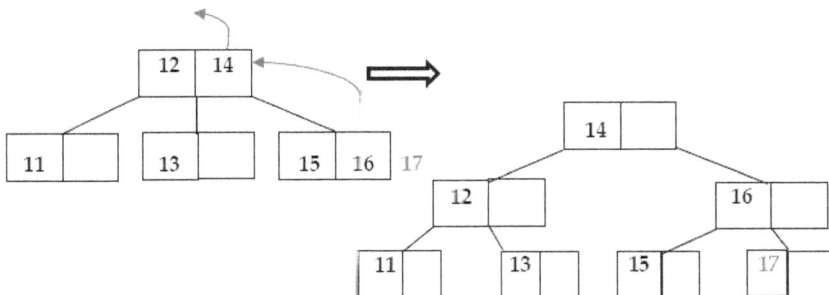

Figure 2.17: 14 becomes new root node

The eighth value is 18, larger than the root node 14, and it is not a leaf node. So, we proceed to the right subtree, reach at 16 again. As 18 > 16 is also not a leaf node, we move to a leaf node 17. There is empty space, place 18 with 17 at a leaf node position:

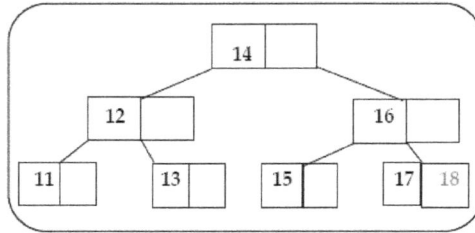

Figure 2.18: Final tree

AVL tree

The AVL tree, developed by *Adelson, Velsky,* and *Landis,* is a binary search tree that can balance itself. There can be no more than a one-degree difference between a node's two child trees in an AVL tree. The AVL tree is referred to as a height balanced tree because of this characteristic.

The advantage of the AVL tree is that it takes $O(log_2n)$ time to execute search, insertion, and deletion operations in both the worst and average-case scenarios.

It keeps the balance factor variable, which is an extra one in an AVL tree structure.

It is possible to determine a node's balance factor by deducting the heights of its right and left subtrees.

$$bf = Height\ of\ Left\ subtree - Height\ of\ Right\ subtree$$

$$bf = hL - hR$$

The term height balanced describes a binary search tree where each node's balancing factor is either 1, 0, or -1.

It may be necessary to rebalance the tree if AVL tree insertions or deletions upset the balance factor of nodes. By rotating the tree at the essential node, the equilibrium is restored.

Four kinds of rotations are applied, which are **left-left (LL)**, **right-right (RR)**, **left-right (LR)**, and **right-left (RL)**.

Insertion operation of AVL tree consists of the following steps:

1. Insertion of the new node occurs at the leaf node.

2. Nodes that are on a path between the tree's root and the newly inserted leaf are the only ones whose balance factor can be altered by this technique of insertion.

3. Every node along this route has the potential to undergo the following transformations:

    a. After insertion, the node becomes balanced, even though it was previously heavy on one side or the other.

b. After insertion, the node becomes unbalanced and favors one side over the other.

c. The new node has been added to the heavy subtree, making it an unbalanced subtree because the node was either left or right-heavy before A crucial node is one such node.

Figure 2.19 illustrates the balanced AVL tree structure after insertion:

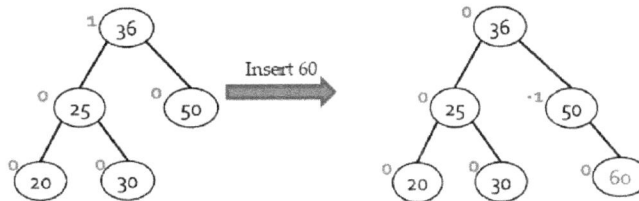

Figure 2.19: Balanced tree

The tree is rebalanced by performing rotations at the critical node.

The four types of rotations are mentioned as follows:

*   The new node is inserted into the critical node's left subtree as part of the **LL rotation**.

*   When performing **RR rotation**, a new node is added to the critical node's right subtree.

*   The new node is inserted into the right subtree of the critical node's left subtree during the **LR rotation**.

*   The new node is inserted into the critical node's left subtree of the right subtree via **RL rotation**.

So, in the AVL tree:

*   **Search operation**: The time complexity is $O(log_2 n)$.

    The search operation in AVL trees is the same as binary search tree operations. The tree is balanced, so the height is guaranteed to be logarithmic with respect to the number of nodes.

*   **Insertion operation**: The time complexity is $O(log_2 n)$.

    During insertion, the AVL tree may need to perform rotations to maintain balance. However, since the height of the tree is logarithmic, the overall complexity remains $O(log_2 n)$.

*   **Deletion operation**: The time complexity is $O(log_2 n)$.

    Similar to insertion, deletion in AVL trees may require rotations to restore balance. The height of the tree remains logarithmic, resulting in $O(log_2 n)$ time complexity.

- **Rotations**: Time complexity is *O(1)* per rotation.

  Rotations (single or double) are constant time operations, as they involve rearranging pointers without traversing the entire tree.

Red-black tree

A **red-black (RB)** tree is a type of BST that automatically maintains balance by assigning each node an additional attribute indicating its color, which may be either red or black.

During the process of adding a new node, the new node is consistently added as a red node. When we insert a new node, if the tree is in violation of the properties of a red-black tree, we do the following activities:

- **Change the color**: This step involves color changing of the node from red to black or vice versa.
- **Rotate**: Denote the tree rotation in a particular direction.

Recolouring refers to the alteration of the colour of a node, such that if it is initially red, it is changed to black, and vice versa. It is important to mention that the color of the NULL node is consistently black. In addition, our initial approach is to attempt recolouring. If recolouring proves unsuccessful, we then proceed with rotation. The algorithms primarily consist of two scenarios, which are determined by the color of the uncle node. If the uncle is red in color, we proceed with the process of altering the color. If the uncle node has a black color, we perform rotations and recoloring.

Example 2.10: Construct a red black tree having elements 3, 22, 33, 18 in a blank tree structure.

Solution: The first element is 3, inserted into the tree, i.e., the root node:

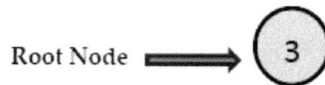

Figure 2.20: RB tree step 1

The second element is 22, inserted right to the root node:

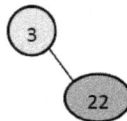

Figure 2.21: RB tree step 2

The third element is 33, which is greater than 3 and 21. So, we will add it in the right sub tree. Here, two nodes have the color red. So, we rotate RR and recolour the balanced tree as follows:

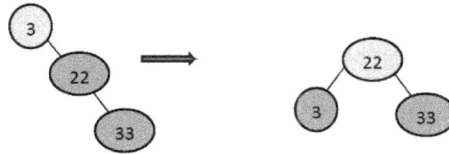

Figure 2.22: RB tree step 3

The fourth element is 18. Since 18 < 22, we move towards the left subtree, but 18 > 3, so we put it as the right child of 3. After adding the new node, we rearrange the colour of the tree:

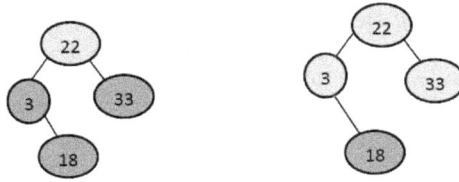

Figure 2.23: RB tree step 4

The time complexity of various operations in a red-black tree is generally expressed in terms of big O notation. Here are the typical time complexities for red-black tree operations:

- **Search**: $O(log\ n)$, the height of an RB tree is guaranteed to be logarithmic, which guarantees efficient search operations.

- **Insertion**: $O(log\ n)$, the insertion procedure may need several recoloring and rotations operations, but the overall time complexity remains $O(log\ n)$ because of the balanced structure of red-black trees.

- **Deletion**: $O(log\ n)$, deletion, like insertion, may necessitate rotations and recoloring, but the time complexity remains $O(log\ n)$ because of the balanced features of the tree.

Heap

A heap is a tree-based data structure in computer science that adheres to the heap property. Heaps are frequently employed for the implementation of priority queues, which are data structures that store elements along with their corresponding priorities and enable efficient retrieval of the element with the highest (or lowest) priority.

There are two main types of heaps, described as follows:

- **Max heap**: A max heap is a data structure where the value of each node is larger than or equal to the values of its descendants. Consequently, the element with the greatest value is consistently located at the root. In a max heap, each node i, except for the root, has a value that is less than or equal to its parent's value. This is the main characteristic of a max heap.

- **Min heap**: In a minimum heap, the value of each node is smaller than or equal to the values of its offspring. Consequently, the element with the minimum value is consistently located at the root. A fundamental characteristic of a min heap is that, for each node i that is not the root, the value of i is larger than or equal to the value of its parent.

Heap operations typically include the following:

- **Insertion operation**: To add a new element to the heap. the time complexity of insertion in a heap is *O(log n)*.

- **Deletion**: Removing the element with the highest (for max heap) or lowest (for min heap) priority deletion in the worst-case scenario, the time complexity is *O(log n)*.

- **Heapify**: Ensuring that the heap property is maintained after an insertion or deletion operation. Building a heap from an array of n elements can be done in *O(n)* time using a bottom-up approach called heapify.

Binomial heap

A group of binomial trees is called a binomial heap. A binomial tree B_k is a tree that is defined recursively in a specific order. A binomial tree B_0 consists of a solitary node.

A binomial tree B_k is composed of two binomial trees B_k-1 that are interconnected. The root of one is the leftmost offspring of the root of the other.

Properties of a binomial tree are as follows:

- The height of the tree is k.
- Binomial tree with B_k has 2_k nodes.
- There are exactly *(k j)* nodes at depth i for all the i having range 0 - k.

A binomial heap, H denotes the collection of binomial trees. Several qualities exist, shown as follows:

- Every binomial tree in H is arranged in a heap order. The key value of a node is always greater than or equal to the key value of its parent node.

- There exists a maximum of 1 binomial tree in H, in which the root of the tree has a certain degree.

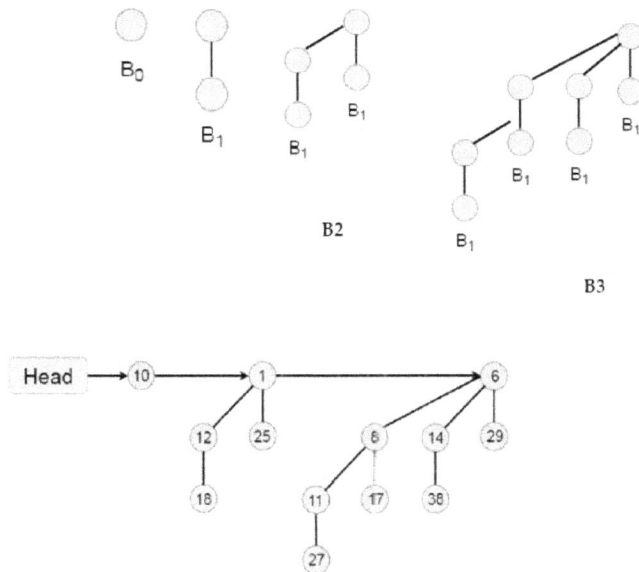

Figure 2.24: Binomial heap

The binomial heap H comprises binomial trees B_0, B_2, and B_3, which contain nodes 1, 4, and 8, respectively. The total number of nodes, n, is 13. The roots of the binomial trees are connected by a linked list, arranged in ascending order of degree.

Fibonacci heap

A data structure known as a Fibonacci heap offers efficient time complexity for multiple operations, including insert, merge, decrease key, and extract minimum. It outperforms other heap data structures, such as binary heaps or binomial heaps, in terms of amortised time complexity. *Michael L. Fredman* and *Robert E. Tarjan* introduced it in 1984.

The effectiveness of the Fibonacci heap is attributed to several inherent properties:

- **Amortized time**: The amortized time complexity of key operations such as insert, reduce key, and delete is superior to that of other heap structures, rendering it appropriate for specific algorithms and applications.

- **Merging mechanism**: Fibonacci heap distinguishes itself from other heap structures by employing a slow merging mechanism. Consequently, the two heaps are not instantaneously merged during the merge procedure. Alternatively, a circular doubly linked list is generated to connect the root nodes of the two heaps. This methodical methodology enables the attainment of amortized constant time for merging procedures.

- **Potential approach**: The evaluation of Fibonacci heap operations is commonly conducted with the potential approach. This approach takes into account not just the current work performed by an operation, but also the possibility of saving future work. This results in more advantageous amortized time complexities.

The reduce key action in a Fibonacci heap can be executed in constant time without the need to consolidate the heap. This is an additional component that contributes to the effectiveness of the data structure.

Fibonacci heaps consist of a collection of trees. They have a loose foundation derived from binomial heaps. In contrast to trees in binomial heaps, in Fibonacci heaps, trees are rooted but not arranged in a specific way. Every node x in Fibonacci heaps possesses a pointer p[x] that points to its parent, as well as a pointer child[x] that denotes to its children. The children of x are interconnected in a circular, doubly linked list referred to as the child list of x. Each kid y in a child list possesses pointers left[y] and right[y] that shows the left and right siblings of y, respectively. If the node y is the lone child, then the values of left[y] and right[y] are both set to y. The placement of siblings in a child list is random. Fibonacci heap is shown in the following figure:

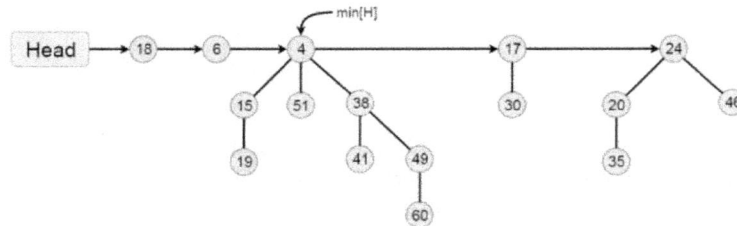

Figure 2.25: Fibonacci heap

In the Fibonacci heap, insertion, decrease key, and merge operation time complexity is amortized *O(1)*, and in the deletion operation, the time complexity is amortized *O(log n)*, where '*n*' represents the number of items in the heap.

Conclusion

This chapter provided a comprehensive overview of fundamental data structures, emphasizing their roles in efficiently organizing and managing data. By exploring both linear structures like arrays, stacks, queues, and linked lists, as well as non-linear ones such as trees and heaps, we gained insight into their unique use cases, advantages, and trade-offs. Additionally, concepts like hashing and pointers were discussed to highlight their importance in memory management and fast data access. Through algorithms and examples, we analyzed how the right choice of data structure can significantly impact an application's performance. Understanding these core structures lays the groundwork for mastering more advanced computational techniques.

In the next chapter, *Sorting Algorithms*, we will study a variety of sorting methods ranging from basic techniques like bubble and insertion sort to more advanced ones such as radix and bucket sort, focusing on their logic, implementation, and efficiency.

Exercise

1. Let us pretend we have a 2-dimensional array Arr1[10][10] with a base address of 2000 and 2 bytes each entry. Presuming the items are stored in column major order, we can now calculate the address of the element Arr1[7][4].

2. Write a program using pointers to interchange the second largest and the second smallest number in the given array.

3. Write a program to implement Tower of Hanoi using recursion and find the complexity of the recursive algorithm and also justify your answer.

4. Design code that creates an array-based queue that accepts insertions at both ends.

5. Write a program to perform followings:

   a. Remove the first occurrence of a specific character in a linked list.

   b. Remove the last occurrence of a specific character.

   c. Remove all instances of a certain character.

6. Write a program to form a linked list of floating-point numbers. Display the sum and mean of these numbers.

7. 10, 3, 15, 22, 6, 45, 65, 23, 78, 34. 5. Create BST and find its inorder, preorder and postorder traversal.

8. Construct the AVL tree (height balanced tree) for the following data: 42, 06, 54, 62, 88, 50, 22, 32, 12, 33. After creating AVL tree structure delete node 50 and 80 from the AVL tree.

9. Create a B-tree for following data:

   a. Insert 1, 6, 8, 12, 14, 16, 19, and 21 in the tree.

   b. Delete 19 and 21 from the tree.

10. Compare the binomial heap and Fiboracci heap.

Join our Discord space

Join our Discord workspace for latest updates, offers, tech happenings around the world, new releases, and sessions with the authors:

https://discord.bpbonline.com

CHAPTER 3
Sorting Algorithms

Introduction

In this chapter of the book, we will present sorting algorithms and their concept in the field of computer science. Sorting algorithms serve as essential tools in computer science, facilitating the arrangement of data in particular orders, usually in ascending or descending sequences. Their significance extends to various applications, such as data analysis, database management, and information retrieval systems. Through effective data organization, sorting algorithms expedite search and retrieval operations, streamline data analysis, and bolster the overall performance of computing systems. Comprehending these algorithms is crucial for maximizing the efficiency and efficacy of data handling across various fields of research and practical implementation.

Structure

The chapter covers the following topics:

- Sorting
- Bubble sort
- Selection sort
- Insertion sort
- Shell sort

- Counting sort
- Radix sort
- Bucket sort

Objectives

This chapter aims to arrange a set of data in a specific order, either ascending or descending. The goal is to efficiently restructure elements, reducing the need for extensive comparisons and exchanges, all in an effort to improve the effectiveness of search and retrieval operations, simplify data analysis, and boost the overall performance of systems. These algorithms hold significant importance across diverse disciplines, such as computer science, data analysis, and information management, facilitating the efficient management and manipulation of large data.

Sorting

Sorting is a fundamental operation in computer science and is used to arrange elements in a specific order. The order could be numerical (ascending or descending) or lexicographical (dictionary order). Sorting algorithms play a crucial role in optimizing data retrieval and making information more accessible. There are various sorting algorithms, each with its own set of characteristics and best-use scenarios.

Sorting is essential for organizing and retrieving information efficiently. In many applications, data is unsorted and needs to be arranged in a meaningful way for analysis or presentation. Here are some common scenarios where sorting is crucial:

- **Searching**: Sorted data allows for more efficient search operations, such as binary search, which relies on the order of elements.

- **Data presentation**: For better readability and user experience, it is often desirable to present data in a sorted form.

- **Algorithmic operations**: Many algorithms and data structures, such as binary search trees, rely on sorted data to perform efficiently.

Key concepts

Let us discuss comparison-based vs. non-comparison-based sorting:

- **Comparison-based sorting**: These algorithms sort elements by comparing them using a comparison operator ($<, >, =$). Examples include bubble sort, selection sort, merge sort, and quick sort.

- **Non-comparison-based sorting**: These algorithms exploit specific properties of the data and do not rely solely on element comparisons. Examples include counting sort and radix sort.

Let us discuss stable vs. unstable sorting:

- If a sorting algorithm, after sorting the contents, does not change the sequence of similar content in which they appear, it is called **stable sorting**. This is shown in the following figure:

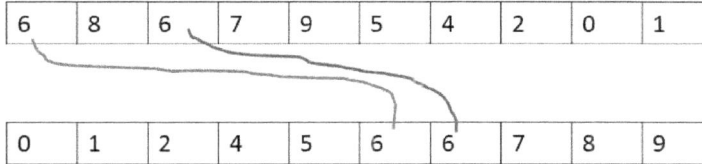

6	8	6	7	9	5	4	2	0	1

0	1	2	4	5	6	6	7	8	9

Figure 3.1: Stable sorting algorithms

- If a sorting algorithm, after sorting the contents, changes the sequence of similar content in which they appear, it is called **unstable sorting**. This is shown in the following figure:

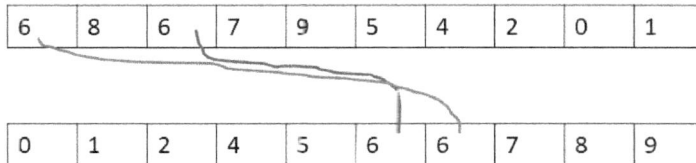

6	8	6	7	9	5	4	2	0	1

0	1	2	4	5	6	6	7	8	9

Figure 3.2: Unstable sorting algorithms

Refer to the following list for an overview of the general types of sorting:

- **In-place sorting**: Sorting algorithms may require some extra space for comparison and temporary storage of a few data elements. These algorithms do not require any extra space, and sorting is said to happen in-place or, for example, within the array itself. This is called in-place sorting. Bubble sort is an example of in-place sorting.

- **Adaptive sorting**: A sorting algorithm is said to be adaptive if it takes advantage of already sorted elements in the list that is to be sorted. That is, while sorting if the source list has some element already sorted, adaptive algorithms will take this into account and will try not to re-order them.

- **Time and space complexity**: Sorting algorithms are analyzed based on their time and space complexity. Time complexity describes the computational time required, while space complexity refers to the additional memory needed. Some of the popular sorting algorithms are as follows:

  o Bubble sort

  o Selection sort

  o Insertion sort

    o Shell sort

    o Counting sort

    o Radix sort

    o Bucket sort

Understanding these concepts and algorithms provides a foundation for choosing the most appropriate sorting algorithm based on the specific requirements of a given task.

Bubble sort

The fundamental principle of the bubble sort algorithm involves iteratively traversing a list, checking adjacent elements, and swapping them if they are not in the correct sequence. This procedure continues until the entire list is arranged in the correct order.

Algorithm 3.1: Algorithm of bubble sort

```
bubbleSort(arr: list)
    n = length(arr)
    for i = 0 to n-1 do:
        swapped = False
        for j = 0 to n-i-1 do:
            if arr[j] > arr[j+1] then:
                swap(arr[j], arr[j+1])
                swapped = True
        if swapped = False then:
            break
```

Following is a concise overview highlighting the main principles of the bubble sort algorithm:

- **Comparison of adjacent elements**:

    o Initially, the algorithm compares the initial two elements within the list.

    o When the first element surpasses the second, a swap occurs; otherwise, they retain their positions.

    o This comparison and potential swap routine continues for each adjacent pair of elements in the list.

- **Passes through the list**:

    o With each iteration through the list, the largest unsorted element gradually moves to its proper place at the list's end, resembling a bubble-up motion.

    o Following the initial pass, the largest element invariably settles at the list's conclusion.

- Subsequent passes ensure the placement of the second-largest element, and this pattern continues until all elements find their correct positions.

- **Repeated passes**: The iteration continues for the remaining unsorted elements until no further swaps are necessary, signaling that the entire list has been sorted.

- **Optimization and early exit**:

    o An optimization for bubble sort involves using a flag to track if any swaps occurred during a pass.

    o If no swaps happen during a pass, it means the list is already sorted, allowing the algorithm to terminate early.

In comparison to more advanced sorting techniques like quick sort or merge sort, bubble sort is deemed inefficient for handling large datasets. Nonetheless, its straightforward nature and ease of comprehension make it a popular choice for educational purposes.

Program 3.1: Implementation of bubble sort

```cpp
#include <iostream>
using namespace std;

// Function to perform bubble sort
void bubbleSort(int arr[], int n) {
    for (int i = 0; i < n - 1; ++i) {
        // Last i elements are already in place, so no need to check them
        for (int j = 0; j < n - i - 1; ++j) {
            // Swap if the element found is greater than the next element
            if (arr[j] > arr[j + 1]) {
                // Swap arr[j] and arr[j+1]
                int temp = arr[j];
                arr[j] = arr[j + 1];
                arr[j + 1] = temp;
            }
        }
    }
}

// Function to print an array
void printArray(int arr[], int size) {
    for (int i = 0; i < size; ++i) {
        cout << arr[i] << " ";
    }
    cout << endl;
}
```

```
// Example usage
int main() {
    int arr[] = {64, 34, 25, 12, 22, 11, 90};
    int n = sizeof(arr) / sizeof(arr[0]);

    cout << "Original array: ";
    printArray(arr, n);

    // Sorting the array using bubble sort
    bubbleSort(arr, n);

    cout << "Sorted array: ";
    printArray(arr, n);

    return 0;
}
```

Following is the explanation of code:

- The **bubbleSort** function executes the bubble sort algorithm on an array of integers.

- It involves two nested loops: the outer loop (**i**) manages passes through the array, while the inner loop (**j**) navigates the unsorted segment of the array.

- Within the inner loop, elements are compared in pairs, and if they are in the incorrect order, they are swapped.

- **printArray** serves as a utility function to display the elements within an array.

- Inside the **main()** function, an array example is created, sorted using **bubbleSort**, and subsequently printed to exhibit the sorting process.

Complexity analysis

An algorithm's time complexity quantifies the time it requires to execute relative to the input size. In the case of bubble sort, its time complexity is commonly denoted in big O notation, indicating the maximum rate of growth for the algorithm.

In the case of bubble sort:

- **Worst case time complexity ($O(n^2)$)**: Bubble sort exhibits its worst-case scenario when the input list is arranged in reverse order. Here, the algorithm necessitates the highest count of comparisons and swaps to position the largest element correctly in each pass through the list. The quantity of comparisons and swaps escalates quadratically concerning the input list's size, leading to a time complexity of $O(n^2)$.

- **Best case time complexity ($O(n)$)**: Bubble sort demonstrates its best-case scenario when the input list is already in sorted order. Despite needing passes through the list to verify that no swaps are required, the algorithm terminates early in each pass as no swaps are necessary. The count of comparisons remains proportional to n, while the number of swaps remains minimal, leading to a best-case time complexity of $O(n)$.

- **Average case time complexity ($O(n^2)$)**: The average-case time complexity of bubble sort is $O(n^2)$. This estimation arises from the fact that, on average, it performs roughly $n^2/4$ comparisons and $n^2/4$ swaps when sorting a random arrangement of elements.

Selection sort

The selection sort algorithm divides an input list into two segments: the sorted and the unsorted. Initially, the sorted segment is empty, and the unsorted segment contains the complete list.

Throughout each iteration, the algorithm examines the unsorted segment, identifies the smallest element, and exchanges it with the leftmost unsorted element. This process progressively expands the sorted segment by integrating one element and reduces the unsorted segment by one element.

Algorithm 3.2: Algorithm of selection sort

```
selection_sort (arr)
    n = length of arr
    for i from 0 to n - 2 do
        min_index = i
        // Find the index of the minimum element in the unsorted part
        for j from i + 1 to n - 1 do
            if arr[j] < arr[min_index] then
                min_index = j
        // Swap the found minimum element with the first unsorted element
        swap arr[i] with arr[min_index]
    end for
end SelectionSort
```

Program 3.2: Implementation of selection sort

```cpp
#include <iostream>
#include <vector>

// Function to perform Selection Sort
void selectionSort(std::vector<int> &arr) {
    int n = arr.size();

    // Iterate through the array
```

```cpp
    for (int i = 0; i < n - 1; ++i) {
        // Assume the current index has the minimum value
        int min_index = i;

        // Find the index of the minimum element in the unsorted segment
        for (int j = i + 1; j < n; ++j) {
            // Compare current element with the assumed minimum
            if (arr[j] < arr[min_index]) {
                // If a smaller element is found, update the minimum index
                min_index = j;
            }
        }

        // Swap the found minimum element with the first unsorted element
        std::swap(arr[min_index], arr[i]);
    }
}

int main() {
    // Example vector of integers
    std::vector<int> elements = {64, 25, 12, 22, 11};

    // Display the original array
    std::cout << "Original Array: ";
    for (int elem : elements) {
        std::cout << elem << " ";
    }
    std::cout << std::endl;

    // Sort the array using Selection Sort
    selectionSort(elements);

    // Display the sorted array
    std::cout << "Sorted Array: ";
    for (int elem : elements) {
        std::cout << elem << " ";
    }
    std::cout << std::endl;

    return 0;
}
```

Following is the explanation of code:

- The **selectionSort** function arranges the given vector **arr** utilizing the selection sort algorithm.

- The outer loop (**for (int i = 0; i < n - 1; ++i)**) cycles through the array.
- Within this loop, **min_index** is initially designated as **i**, presuming that the current index contains the minimum value.
- The inner loop (**for (int j = i + 1; j < n; ++j)**) identifies the index of the minimum element in the unsorted segment by comparing each element with the assumed minimum.
- If a smaller element is discovered, **min_index** is updated.
- Ultimately, the smallest element found in the unsorted segment gets swapped with the leftmost unsorted element.

In the **main** function:

- Elements initialized with vector.
- The original array is displayed.
- The **selectionSort** function is executed to sort the array.
- The sorted array is displayed after the sorting process.

Complexity analysis

The complexity analysis of selection sort involves evaluating its time and space complexities:

- **Time complexity**: In both the worst-case and average-case scenarios, selection sort requires roughly $n^2/2$ comparisons and n swaps, where n represents the number of elements in the array. Consequently, the time complexity of selection sort remains $O(n^2)$ across all cases.

  Best-case: The best-case scenario arises when the input array is already sorted. However, even in the best-case, selection sort performs roughly $n^2/2$ comparisons as it still iterates through the array to locate the minimum element in each iteration.

  Consequently, the best-case time complexity of selection sort remains $O(n^2)$.

- **Space complexity**: Selection sort operates in-place, meaning it does not require additional memory proportional to the input size. It only uses a constant amount of extra space for variables like indices and temporary variables.

  Therefore, the space complexity of selection sort is $O(1)$ or constant space.

Insertion sort

Insertion sort is a straightforward sorting algorithm that constructs the final sorted array by gradually incorporating one element at a time. It traverses the input array, extracting each element and positioning it in its appropriate sorted position within the array.

Refer to the following list for a description of the **insertion sort** algorithm:

1. Commence from the second element (index 1) in the array.

2. Compare this element with the elements to its left (within the sorted section).

3. Shift elements larger than the current element one position forward to generate space for the current element.

4. Position the current element into its suitable sorted position among the elements to its left.

5. Carry out this procedure for each remaining element in the array until the entire array is sorted.

Algorithm 3.3: Algorithm of insertion sort

```
insertionSort(arr):
    n = length of arr
    for i = 1 to n - 1 do
        key = arr[i]
        j = i - 1
        // Move elements greater than key to one position ahead
        while j >= 0 and arr[j] > key do
            arr[j + 1] = arr[j]
            j = j - 1
        arr[j + 1] = key
```

Program 3.3: Insertion sort

```cpp
#include <iostream>
#include <vector>
// Function to perform Insertion Sort
void insertionSort(std::vector<int> &arr) {
    int n = arr.size();
    for (int i = 1; i < n; ++i) {
        int key = arr[i];
        int j = i - 1;
        // Move elements greater than key to one position ahead
        while (j >= 0 && arr[j] > key) {
            arr[j + 1] = arr[j];
            j = j - 1;
        }
        arr[j + 1] = key;
    }
}
```

```
irt main() {
    std::vector<int> elements = {64, 25, 12, 22, 11};

    std::cout << "Original Array: ";
    for (int elem : elements) {
        std::cout << elem << " ";
    }
    std::cout << std::endl;
    insertionSort(elements);
    std::cout << "Sorted Array: ";
    for (int elem : elements) {
        std::cout << elem << " ";
    }
    std::cout << std::endl;
    return 0;
}
```

The following is the explanation of the preceding code:

- The **insertionSort** function organizes the given vector **arr** using the insertion sort algorithm.

- The outer loop (**for (int i = 1; i < n; ++i)**) navigates through the array, commencing from the second element.

- For each element at index **i**, it undergoes comparison with the elements to its left and is inserted into the appropriate position among the sorted elements.

- The inner loop (**while (j >= 0 && arr[j] > key)**) shifts elements greater than the **key** (the current element being sorted) one position ahead to make room for the **key**.

- Subsequently, the **key** element is placed in its correct sorted location.

- The **main** function initializes an example vector with elements, displays the original array, performs sorting using **insertionSort**, and showcases the resulting sorted array.

Complexity analysis

The complexity of insertion sort can be understood as follows:

- **Time complexity**: The time complexity of the insertion sort algorithm is as follows:

    o   In the worst-case scenario, where the array is in reverse order, insertion sort takes the maximum time to sort the elements.

o The outer loop executes *n-1* times (where n represents the number of elements in the array).

o In the worst-case, each iteration of the inner loop might compare and shift nearly all elements to the right, resulting in approximately *n/2* comparisons on average.

o As a result, in the worst-case, insertion sort performs approximately $O(n^2)$ comparisons and shifts to sort an array comprising *n* elements.

o In the best-case scenario, where the array is already sorted, insertion sort performs $O(n)$ comparisons since each element is already in its correct position. However, it still executes $O(n)$ shifts.

• **Space complexity**: Insertion sort maintains a space complexity of $O(1)$ as it conducts an in-place sorting of the array, utilizing a constant amount of extra space for temporary variables, regardless of the input size.

While insertion sort exhibits efficiency for small datasets or partially sorted arrays due to its simplicity and linear-time performance in the best-case, it becomes less efficient for larger datasets because of its quadratic time complexity in the worst-case.

Shell sort

Shell sort, also known as Shell's method, is an efficient variation of insertion sort. It enhances insertion sort by enabling elements to be compared and moved over longer distances, thereby reducing the number of shifting operations.

Gap sequence

Shell sort utilizes a sequence of decreasing gaps (referred to as h-sorted), starting with a substantial gap and reducing it to a size of 1. Commonly used sequences include the Knuth sequence (*3x + 1*) or other predefined sequences.

Gap-sorted insertion can be described as follows:

1. The algorithm applies insertion sort for each gap.

2. Elements separated by a distance of gap are compared and moved to their appropriate positions within the subarrays.

3. The sequence of gaps determines the number of subarrays and their individual sizes.

4. As the algorithm progresses, it reduces the gap size.

5. Eventually, the gap diminishes to 1, resulting in a final pass of the insertion sort that effectively resembles a nearly sorted array.

Algorithm 3.4: Algorithm of shell sort

```
ShellSort (arr):
    n = length of arr
    // Start with a large gap
    for gap = n/2; gap > 0; gap = gap / 2 do
        // Perform insertion sort for each gap
        for i = gap to n - 1 do
            temp = arr[i]
            j = i
            // Compare elements at a distance of gap and swap if necessary
            while j >= gap and arr[j - gap] > temp do
                arr[j] = arr[j - gap]
                j = j - gap
            arr[j] = temp
```

Program 3.4: Implementation of shell sort

```cpp
#include <iostream>
#include <vector>
// Function to perform Shell Sort
void shellSort(std::vector<int>& arr) {
    int n = arr.size();
    // Generate gap sequence (Knuth sequence)
    int gap = 1;
    while (gap <= n / 3) {
        gap = gap * 3 + 1;
    }
    while (gap > 0) {
        for (int i = gap; i < n; ++i) {
            int temp = arr[i];
            int j = i;
            // Perform Insertion Sort on subarrays
            while (j >= gap && arr[j - gap] > temp) {
                arr[j] = arr[j - gap];
                j -= gap;
            }
            arr[j] = temp;
        }
        gap /= 3; // Reduce the gap
```

```
    }
}

int main() {
    std::vector<int> elements = {64, 25, 12, 22, 11};

    std::cout << "Original Array: ";
    for (int elem : elements) {
        std::cout << elem << " ";
    }
    std::cout << std::endl;
    shellSort(elements);
    std::cout << "Sorted Array: ";
    for (int elem : elements) {
        std::cout << elem << " ";
    }
    std::cout << std::endl;
    return 0;
}
```

Complexity analysis

The complexity of the shell sort algorithm can be understood as follows:

- **Time complexity**: The time complexity of the shell sort algorithm is as follows:

  o Shell sort's time complexity relies on the gap sequence used.

  o Typically, the average time complexity ranges between $O(n \log2 n)$ and $O(n\{4/3\})$.

  o In specific scenarios with particular gap sequences, the worst-case time complexity can reach $O(n2)$, resembling insertion sort's worst-case scenario.

  o However, for many practical cases and specific gap sequences, shell sort surpasses $O(n^2)$ algorithms like insertion sort or bubble sort.

- **Space complexity**: Having a space complexity of $O(1)$, shell sort arranges the array in place, utilizing a set amount of additional space for temporary variables.

Shell sort improves upon insertion sort by allowing elements to move more than one position at a time towards their sorted positions, thereby reducing the number of comparisons and swaps. The efficiency of shell sort heavily depends on the chosen gap sequence.

Counting sort

Counting sort, an integer sorting technique, does not rely on comparisons between elements. Instead, it tallies the occurrences of unique elements within an input array. Using this tally, it arranges the elements into their rightful sorted sequence. It involves the following:

1. **Counting occurrences**: Let us talk about counting occurrences:

    a. Determine the range of elements within the input array and create a count array (commonly known as a frequency array) to store the occurrence count of each element.

    b. Iterate through the input array, incrementing the count of each element in the count array.

2. **Cumulative sum**: Let us talk about cumulative sum:

    a. Adjust the count array to hold the cumulative sum of counts.

    b. This cumulative sum indicates the index positions where elements should be placed within the sorted array.

3. **Sorting**: Sorting involves the following:

    a. Traverse the input array once more.

    b. For each element, determine its position using the count array and place it correctly in the sorted array.

    c. Decrease the count in the count array to manage duplicate elements.

Algorithm 3.5: Algorithm of counting sort

```
countingSort(arr):
    n = length of arr
    max_element = maximum element in arr
    min_element = minimum element in arr (if negative numbers are present)
    range = max_element - min_element + 1

    // Create count array and initialize with zeros
    count[range] = {0}

    // Count occurrences of each element
    for i = 0 to n - 1 do
        count[arr[i] - min_element]++

    // Modify count array to store cumulative sum
    for i = 1 to range - 1 do
        count[i] += count[i - 1]
```

```
// Create the sorted array using count array
sorted[n] = {0}
for i = n - 1 to 0 do
    sorted[count[arr[i] - min_element] - 1] = arr[i]
    count[arr[i] - min_element]--

// Copy the sorted array back to the original array
for i = 0 to n - 1 do
    arr[i] = sorted[i]
```

Program 3.5: Implementation of counting sort

```cpp
#include <iostream>
#include <vector>

void countingSort(std::vector<int>& arr) {
    int n = arr.size();

    // Find the maximum and minimum elements in the array
    int max_element = *std::max_element(arr.begin(), arr.end());
    int min_element = *std::min_element(arr.begin(), arr.end());

    int range = max_element - min_element + 1;

    // Create a count array to store the count of each element
    std::vector<int> count(range, 0);

    // Count occurrences of each element
    for (int i = 0; i < n; ++i) {
        count[arr[i] - min_element]++;
    }

    // Modify count array to store cumulative sum
    for (int i = 1; i < range; ++i) {
        count[i] += count[i - 1];
    }

    // Create the sorted array using count array
    std::vector<int> sorted(n);
    for (int i = n - 1; i >= 0; --i) {
        sorted[count[arr[i] - min_element] - 1] = arr[i];
        count[arr[i] - min_element]--;
    }

    // Copy the sorted array back to the original array
    for (int i = 0; i < n; ++i) {
        arr[i] = sorted[i];
    }
}
```

```
int main() {
    std::vector<int> elements = {64, 25, 12, 22, 11};

    std::cout << "Original Array: ";
    for (int elem : elements) {
        std::cout << elem << " ";
    }
    std::cout << std::endl;

    countingSort(elements);

    std::cout << "Sorted Array: ";
    for (int elem : elements) {
        std::cout << elem << " ";
    }
    std::cout << std::endl;

    return 0;
}
```

The following is the explanation of code:

- The **countingSort** function arranges the given vector, **arr**, using the counting sort algorithm.

- It identifies the range of elements by determining the maximum and minimum values within the array.

- A **count** array is created to monitor the occurrence count of each element.

- It tallies and stores the occurrences of each element from the input array into the **count** array.

- The **count** array is modified to represent the cumulative count of elements.

- A sorted array is created by accurately positioning elements based on information from the **count** array.

- Finally, the sorted array is copied back into the original array.

The counting sort algorithm efficiently sorts integers within a specific range by counting the occurrences of each element to determine their positions in the sorted array. This implementation works well for positive integers. However, to handle a broader range of integers, including negative values, adjustments might be necessary.

Complexity analysis

The complexity analysis of counting sort is as follows:

- **Time complexity**: The time complexity of the counting sort algorithm can be explained as follows:

o   Counting sort demonstrates a time complexity of $O(n + k)$, where n stands for the quantity of elements in the input array, and k denotes the input range.

o   The algorithm consists of two primary phases: counting occurrences and generating the sorted array based on the count data.

o   Counting the occurrences of each element in the input array takes $O(n)$ time.

o   Generating the sorted array using the count information requires $O(n + k)$ time.

- **Space complexity**: The space complexity of the counting sort algorithm is as follows:

   o   Counting sort demonstrates a space complexity of $O(n + k)$, where n represents the number of elements in the input array and k signifies the range of input values.

   o   Additional space is required for both the count array and the sorted array.

Counting sort showcases notable efficiency in sorting a range of integers. However, its effectiveness may diminish if the range of elements substantially exceeds the number of elements to be sorted, primarily due to increased space requirements.

Radix sort

Radix sort is a non-comparative integer sorting algorithm that operates by sorting elements digit by digit, either from the **least significant digit (LSD)** to the **most significant digit (MSD)** or vice versa. This algorithm functions based on the concept of categorizing elements into buckets according to their digit values. The steps involved are as follows:

1.   **LSD radix sort**: This involves the following procedure:

   a.   Sorting initiates from the rightmost (least significant) digit and progresses towards the leftmost (most significant) digit.

   b.   Each digit column undergoes stable sorting methods such as counting sort or bucket sort.

2.   **Digit extraction**: In digit extraction, the following is done:

   a.   Traverse through the elements, extracting the current digit (from LSD to MSD) to categorize elements into their respective buckets.

   b.   Elements with the same digit value are grouped into the same bucket.

3.   **Bucketing and combining**: Once the elements are sorted according to the current digit, reassemble them into a single array.

4.   **Repeat for all digits**: Continue the process for each digit position until the entire array is sorted.

    a. When sorting decimal numbers, the typical procedure involves executing radix sort on each digit (0-9) from right to left.

Algorithm 3.6: Algorithm of radix sort

```
LSD Radix sort (sorting from least significant digit):
    radixSort(arr):
        n = length of arr
        max_element = maximum element in arr

        // Perform sorting for each digit place, starting from the least
significant digit
        for exp = 1 to max_element do
            // Initialize count array for each digit (0-9)
            count[10] = {0}

            // Count occurrences of each digit in the current place
            for i = 0 to n - 1 do
                digit = (arr[i] / exp) % 10
                count[digit]++

            // Modify count array to store cumulative sum
            for i = 1 to 9 do
                count[i] += count[i - 1]

            // Create the sorted array using count array
            sorted[n] = {0}
            for i = n - 1 to 0 do
                digit = (arr[i] / exp) % 10
                sorted[count[digit] - 1] = arr[i]
                count[digit]--

            // Copy the sorted array back to the original array
            for i = 0 to n - 1 do
                arr[i] = sorted[i]
```

Program 3.6: Implementation of radix sort

```cpp
#include <iostream>
#include <vector>

void countingSort(std::vector<int>& arr, int exp) {
    int n = arr.size();
    std::vector<int> output(n);
    std::vector<int> count(10, 0);

    for (int i = 0; i < n; ++i)
        count[(arr[i] / exp) % 10]++;
```

```
    for (int i = 1; i < 10; ++i)
        count[i] += count[i - 1];

    for (int i = n - 1; i >= 0; --i) {
        output[count[(arr[i] / exp) % 10] - 1] = arr[i];
        count[(arr[i] / exp) % 10]--;
    }

    for (int i = 0; i < n; ++i)
        arr[i] = output[i];
}

void radixSort(std::vector<int>& arr) {
    int max_element = *std::max_element(arr.begin(), arr.end());

    for (int exp = 1; max_element / exp > 0; exp *= 10)
        countingSort(arr, exp);
}

int main() {
    std::vector<int> elements = {170, 45, 75, 90, 802, 24, 2, 66};

    std::cout << "Original Array: ";
    for (int elem : elements) {
        std::cout << elem << " ";
    }
    std::cout << std::endl;

    radixSort(elements);

    std::cout << "Sorted Array: ";
    for (int elem : elements) {
        std::cout << elem << " ";
    }
    std::cout << std::endl;

    return 0;
}
```

Let us look at the explanation of the code:

o The **radixSort** function arranges the given vector **arr** using LSD radix sort.

o It determines the maximum element in the array to establish the number of digits in the largest number.

o The **countingSort** function is a modified counting sort explicitly crafted to sort digits at each place value.

o   The **main** function initializes an example vector, sorts it using **radixSort**, and displays the sorted array.

Radix sort operates by sorting individual digits at each place value, effectively organizing the entire array based on these digits, either from the least significant to the most significant or vice versa. This iterative process ultimately results in a fully sorted array.

Complexity analysis

The complexity analysis of radix sort is as follows:

- **Time complexity**: The time complexity of the radix sort algorithm can be explained as follows:

  o   The time complexity of radix sort is $O(n*k)$, where n denotes the number of elements in the input array and k represents the number of digits or characters in the largest number or key.

  o   The algorithm involves iterating through each digit of every element and performing a stable sort (such as counting sort or bucket sort) for each digit.

  o   The number of iterations through the digits is determined by the quantity of digits present in the largest element.

  o   Since each iteration processes the entire array, the time complexity grows linearly with the number of digits.

- **Space complexity**: The space complexity of the radix sort algorithm can be explained in the following manner:

  o   The space complexity of radix sort is $O(n + k)$, where n represents the number of elements in the input array, while k denotes the range of input values.

  o   Additional space is required for creating count arrays and auxiliary arrays during the sorting process.

  o   If counting sort is used as a subroutine, additional space is needed for the count array, which increases in size proportionally to the range of elements.

Radix sort demonstrates efficiency in sorting integers or fixed-length strings when the number of digits is confined and predetermined. Its time complexity shows linearity in relation to both the number of elements and the number of digits in the largest element. This characteristic makes it suitable for specific scenarios that adhere to the constraints of the input data.

Bucket sort

Bucket sort is a distribution-based sorting algorithm that segments the input into several buckets, each capable of accommodating a specific range of values. After distributing the elements across these buckets, each bucket undergoes individual sorting, often utilizing another sorting algorithm or recursively employing the bucket sort algorithm itself. Ultimately, the sorted elements from all buckets are merged together to create the final sorted array.

The algorithm's description is as follows:

1. **Creating buckets**: The first step involves:

    a. Determine the number of buckets needed.

    b. Traverse through the input array and assign elements to their respective buckets using a mapping function that allocates elements to specific buckets.

2. **Sorting individual buckets**: This can be done as follows:

    a. Conduct separate sorting for each bucket, employing either another sorting algorithm or employing bucket sort recursively when required.

    b. Each bucket can undergo sorting using a suitable sorting algorithm, typically insertion sort or quick sort, acknowledged for their efficiency on smaller datasets.

3. **Concatenating buckets**: Combine all the sorted buckets to form the final sorted array.

The key points of bucket sorting are as follows:

- **Bucket distribution**: Elements are assigned to buckets using a function that evenly distributes elements across buckets, ensuring a reasonably uniform distribution.

- **Bucket sort variation**: When the range of input values is known and comfortably fits within the available memory, bucket sort can operate independently as a sorting algorithm.

- **Stability**: The stability of bucket sort relies on the stability of the sorting algorithm employed for sorting individual buckets. For instance, when a stable sorting algorithm like insertion sort is utilized, it maintains the overall stability of bucket sort.

Bucket sort operates efficiently with uniformly distributed data and proves especially valuable when the input range is well-defined and limited. However, its efficiency may decrease when dealing with non-uniform data distributions or if the number of elements in a single bucket significantly exceeds expectations.

Algorithm 3.7: Algorithm of bucket sort

```
bucketSort(arr):
    n = length of arr
    create n empty buckets
```

```
// Distribution of elements into buckets
for i = 0 to n - 1 do
    index = n * arr[i] // Determine which bucket the element should
go to
    insert arr[i] into bucket[index]

// Sorting individual buckets
for i = 0 to n - 1 do
    sort bucket[i] using a suitable sorting algorithm (e.g.,
Insertion Sort, Quick Sort)

// Concatenate sorted buckets to get the final sorted array
concatenate all elements in bucket[i] to the output array
```

Program 3.7: Implementation of bucket sort

```cpp
#include <iostream>
#include <vector>
#include <algorithm>

// Function to perform Bucket Sort
void bucketSort(std::vector<float>& arr) {
    int n = arr.size();

    // Create n empty buckets
    std::vector<std::vector<float>> buckets(n);

    // Distribution of elements into buckets
    for (int i = 0; i < n; ++i) {
        int index = n * arr[i];
        buckets[index].push_back(arr[i]);
    }

    // Sorting individual buckets (using a suitable sorting algorithm)
    for (int i = 0; i < n; ++i) {
        std::sort(buckets[i].begin(), buckets[i].end());
    }

    // Concatenate sorted buckets to get the final sorted array
    int index = 0;
    for (int i = 0; i < n; ++i) {
        for (float num : buckets[i]) {
            arr[index++] = num;
        }
    }
}
```

```
    }

    int main() {
        std::vector<float> elements = {0.42, 0.32, 0.33, 0.52, 0.37, 0.47,
0.51};

        std::cout << "Original Array: ";
        for (float elem : elements) {
            std::cout << elem << " ";
        }
        std::cout << std::endl;

        bucketSort(elements);

        std::cout << "Sorted Array: ";
        for (float elem : elements) {
            std::cout << elem << " ";
        }
        std::cout << std::endl;

        return 0;
    }
```

Let us look at the explanation of code:

- The **bucketSort** function sorts the provided vector **arr** using bucket sort.

- It creates **n** empty buckets and allocates elements into the respective buckets based on a function that determines the bucket index for each element.

- Each bucket undergoes individual sorting using **std::sort**, a sorting algorithm.

- Finally, the sorted elements from all buckets are merged to generate the final sorted array.

Complexity analysis

The complexity analysis of bucket sort is as follows:

- **Time complexity**: The time complexity of bucket sort relies on various factors:
    o **n**: The number of elements to be sorted.
    o **k**: The number of buckets created.
    o **m**: The average number of elements in each bucket.

  In the average-case, when elements are uniformly distributed across buckets:
    o Distributing elements into buckets takes $O(n)$ time.

     o   Sorting each individual bucket using an efficient algorithm (like insertion sort, quick sort, etc.) requires $O(m*log\ m)$ time per bucket on average.

The total time complexity can be approximated as $O(n + k * m * log\ m)$.

When m is close to n and elements are evenly distributed across buckets, bucket sort approaches $O(n * log\ n)$ time complexity. However, uneven distribution of elements leading to a few buckets holding a large number of elements (resulting in large **m**) can degrade the time complexity, approaching $O(n^2)$ due to the sorting of such large buckets.

- **Space complexity**: The space complexity of bucket sort is $O(n + k)$, where:

     o n represents the number of elements in the input array.

     o k denotes the number of buckets created.

Bucket sort exhibits efficiency when the elements are evenly distributed across buckets. However, its performance can vary based on the data distribution and the sorting algorithm chosen for sorting individual buckets. Adjustments in bucket creation or the selection of sorting algorithms for buckets can significantly influence its practical efficiency.

Conclusion

In summary, this chapter covered a variety of sorting algorithms, such as bubble sort, selection sort, and insertion sort. Understanding these methods equips you to select and implement the most appropriate algorithm for different scenarios, ensuring efficiency and optimal performance. In the next chapter, we will focus on searching algorithms, such as linear search, binary search, interpolation search, jump search, exponential search, Fibonacci search, and sublist search.

Exercise

1. Implement the bubble sort algorithm in your preferred programming language. Analyze its time complexity in best, average, and worst cases.

2. Given the following unsorted list: [45, 12, 89, 33, 22, 10], manually trace and show the steps of selection sort to sort the list in ascending order.

3. Compare insertion sort and selection sort. Which performs better on nearly sorted data? Justify your answer with an example.

4. Design a program that implements shell sort. Use a gap sequence of your choice and discuss its impact on performance.

5. Use counting sort to sort the array: [4, 2, 2, 8, 3, 3, 1]. Show the intermediate counting array and explain how the algorithm works step by step.

6. Explain how radix sort works and apply it to sort the list: [170, 45, 75, 90, 802, 24, 2, 66]. Use the LSD approach.

7. Design and implement bucket sort for sorting a list of floating-point numbers in the range [0,1). Use at least five buckets and show step-by-step bucket assignment and sorting.

8. Write a function that takes a list of integers and a sorting algorithm choice (bubble, insertion, or selection) and returns the sorted list. Demonstrate how modular design can be applied to sorting algorithms.

9. Suppose you have a dataset with millions of integers in a small range (e.g., 1–100). Which sorting algorithm would you choose and why? Analyze the efficiency compared to other algorithms.

Join our Discord space

Join our Discord workspace for latest updates, offers, tech happenings around the world, new releases, and sessions with the authors:

https://discord.bpbonline.com

CHAPTER 4
Searching Algorithms

Introduction

In this chapter of the book, we will discuss searching algorithms and their utility in the field of computer science engineering. The act of searching is a fundamental and essential operation in computer science, involving the precise identification of a specific element within a collection of data. This exploration spans various data structures, such as lists, arrays, trees, and others, emphasizing the critical nature of efficient searching across diverse applications and problem-solving scenarios. Playing a pivotal role in this endeavor are searching algorithms, acting as the cornerstone in determining the most optimal and effective approaches to locate the desired item. These algorithms serve as the backbone of the search process, supplying the computational process necessary for navigating and extracting pertinent information from intricate data structures.

Structure

This searching algorithm chapter covers the following topics:

- Searching
- Linear search
- Binary search
- Interpolation search

- Jump search
- Exponential search
- Fibonacci search
- Sublist search

Objectives

This chapter provides readers with the knowledge of searching algorithms by means of usage and implementation. The fundamental ideas are time and space efficiency, accuracy, and adaptation for various data structures and scalability for growing datasets. Readers will be shown the selection process of best algorithms coupled with actual implementation and maintenance techniques depending on problem needs.

Searching

In the context of data structures, searching refers to the process of locating a particular element within a collection of data. The goal is to determine whether a specific item exists in the data structure and, if so, to find its location or retrieve it. The search operation is fundamental and common in various applications, and it is crucial for efficiently accessing and manipulating data.

The importance of searching

Searching is a fundamental operation in computer science and data processing that serves several essential purposes, which are as follows:

- **Retrieval of information**: One of the primary reasons for searching is to locate specific pieces of information within a dataset. This could be anything from finding a particular record in a database, locating a file on a computer, or searching for a specific value in an array.

- **Data analysis**: In many applications, searching is a crucial step in data analysis. Researchers, analysts, and scientists often need to search through large datasets to identify patterns, trends, or specific data points relevant to their study.

- **Information retrieval systems**: Search is a key component in information retrieval systems, such as search engines. Users rely on search functionality to find relevant documents, websites, or information on the internet.

- **Database operations**: Databases store vast amounts of information, and searching is essential for retrieving specific records or subsets of data. Efficient searching algorithms are crucial for optimizing the performance of database queries.

- **Sorting and filtering**: Searching is often used in conjunction with sorting and filtering operations. For example, in a list or database, users may want to search for specific items based on certain criteria while also sorting the results in a particular order.

- **Algorithmic problem-solving**: Many algorithmic problems involve searching for a solution within a given space. Efficient search algorithms are critical for solving problems in areas such as artificial intelligence, optimization, and computational biology.

- **Navigation**: In various applications, users navigate through data structures by searching. This is common in file systems, directories, and other hierarchical structures.

- **Decision-making**: In decision-making processes, searching is often employed to find the best solution or optimal choice among a set of alternatives.

Linear search

Linear search, also called sequential search, is a very simple method used for searching an array for a particular value. It works by comparing the value to be searched with every element of the array one by one in a sequence until a match is found. Linear search is mostly used to search an unordered list of elements (an array in which data elements are not sorted). For example, consider an array, **Array1[]**, which is declared and initialized as follows:

```
int Array1[] = {11, 18, 12, 17, 13, 14, 19, 10, 16, 15};
```

In this array, the value to be searched is **VAL = 17**, then searching means to find whether the value **17** is present in the array or not. If yes, then it returns the position of its occurrence. Here, **POS = 3** (index starting from 0).

Algorithm 4.1: Algorithm of linear search

```
LINEAR_SEARCH(A, N, VAL)
Step 1: [INITIALIZE] SET POS = -1
Step 2: [INITIALIZE] SET I = 1
Step 3: Repeat Step 4 while I<=N
Step 4: IF A[I] = VAL
SET POS = I
PRINT POS
Go to Step 6
[END OF IF]
[END OF LOOP]
Step 6: EXIT
SET I = I + 1
```

```
Step 5: IF POS = -1
PRINT VALUE IS NOT PRESENT
IN THE ARRAY
[END OF IF]
```

In *Step 1* and *Step 2* of the algorithm, we initialize the value of **POS** and **I**. In *Step 3*, a while loop is executed that would be executed till **I** is less than **N** (total number of elements in the array). In *Step 4*, a check is made to see if a match is found between the current array element and **VAL**. If a match is found, then the position of the array element is printed; else, the value of **I** is incremented to match the next element with **VAL**. However, if all the array elements have been compared with **VAL** and no match is found, then it means that **VAL** is not present in the array.

Complexity of linear search algorithm

The linear search algorithm, also known as sequential search, has a time complexity of $O(n)$, where n is the number of elements in the array. The complexity analysis is as follows:

- **Time complexity**: The time complexity analysis is different based on the scenario, shown as follows:

  o **Worst-case scenario**: In the worst-case scenario, the element being searched for is at the last position in the array or is not present at all. In this case, the algorithm needs to iterate through the entire array to determine that the element is not present. The maximum number of comparisons is n. Therefore, the worst-case time complexity is $O(n)$.

  o **Best-case scenario**: The best-case scenario occurs when the element being searched is found at the beginning of the array. In this case, the algorithm makes only one comparison. The best-case time complexity is $O(1)$. However, best-case time complexity is not commonly used for representing the efficiency of an algorithm because it does not provide a meaningful average case.

  o **Average-case scenario**: In the average case, the linear search algorithm, on average, needs to inspect half of the array elements before finding the target element (if it exists). Therefore, the average-case time complexity is $O(n/2)$, which is still expressed as $O(n)$ in big O notation.

- **Space complexity**: The space complexity of the linear search algorithm is $O(1)$ because it uses a constant amount of extra space for variables (like loop counters and temporary variables) that do not depend on the input size.

Program 4.1: Implementation of linear search

```
#include <stdio.h>
#include <stdlib.h>
```

```
#include <conio.h>
#define size 20 // Added so the size of the array can be altered more easily
int main(int argc, char *argv[]) {
int arr[size], num, i, n, found = 0, pos = -1;
printf("\n Enter the number of elements in the array : ");
scanf("%d", &n);
printf("\n Enter the elements: ");
for(i=0;i<n;i++)
{
scanf("%d", &arr[i]);
}
printf("\n Enter the number that has to be searched : ");
scanf("%d", &num);
for(i=0;i<n;i++)
{
if(arr[i] == num)
{
found =1;
pos=i;
printf("\n %d is found in the array at position= %d", num,i+1);
*+1 added in line 23 so that it would display the number in
    the first place in the array as in position 1 instead of 0 */
break;
}
}
if (found == 0)
printf("\n %d does not exist in the array", num);
return 0;
}
```

Binary search

Binary search is a searching algorithm that works efficiently with a sorted list. The mechanism of binary search can be better understood by an analogy of a telephone directory. When we are searching for a particular name in a directory, we first open the directory from the middle and then decide whether to look for the name in the first part of the directory or in the second part of the directory. Again, we open some page in the middle, and the whole process is repeated until we finally find the right name.

Let us consider another analogy. To find words in a dictionary, we first open the dictionary somewhere in the middle. Then, we compare the first word on that page with the desired word whose meaning we are looking for. If the desired word comes before the word on the page, we look in the first half of the dictionary; otherwise, we look in the second half. Again, we open a page in the first half of the dictionary, compare the first word on that page with the desired word, and repeat the same procedure until we finally get the word. The same mechanism is applied in binary search.

Now, let us consider how this mechanism is applied to search for a value in a sorted array. Consider an array, **A[ ]**, that is declared and initialized as follows:

```
int A[] = {0, 1, 2, 3, 4, 5, 6, 7, 8, 9, 10};
```

Here, the value to be searched is **VAL = 9**. The algorithm will proceed in the following manner:

- **BEG = 0, END = 10, MID = (0 + 10)/2 = 5**
- **Now, VAL = 9 and A[MID] = A[5] = 5**
- **A[5] is less than VAL, therefore, we now search for the value in the second half of the array. So, we change the values of BEG and MID.**
- **Now, BEG = MID + 1 = 6, END = 10, MID = (6 + 10)/2 =16/2 = 8**
- **VAL = 9 and A[MID] = A[8] = 8**
- **[8] is less than VAL, therefore, we now search for the value in the second half of the segment.**
- **So, again, we change the values of BEG and MID.**
- **Now, BEG = MID + 1 = 9, END = 10, MID = (9 + 10)/2 = 9**
- **Now, VAL = 9 and A[MID] = 9**

In this algorithm, we see that **BEG** and **END** are the beginning and ending positions of the segment that we are looking to search for the element. **MID** is calculated as **(BEG + END)/2**. Initially, **BEG = lower_bound** and **END = upper_bound**. The algorithm will terminate when **A[MID] = VAL**. When the algorithm ends, we will set **POS = MID**. **POS** is the position at which the value is present in the array.

However, if **VAL** is not equal to **A[MID]**, then the values of **BEG**, **END**, and **MID** will be changed depending on whether **VAL** is smaller or greater than **A[MID]** in the following manner:

- If **VAL < A[MID]**, then **VAL** will be present in the left segment of the array. So, the value of **END** will be changed as **END = MID - 1**.

- If **VAL > A[MID]**, then **VAL** will be present in the right segment of the array. So, the value of **BEG** will be changed as **BEG = MID + 1**.

Finally, if **VAL** is not present in the array, then eventually, **END** will be less than **BEG**. When this happens, the algorithm will terminate, and the search will be unsuccessful.

Algorithm 4.2: Algorithm of binary search

```
BINARY_SEARCH(A, lower_bound, upper_bound, VAL)
Step 1: [INITIALIZE] SET BEG = lower_bound
```

```
END = upper_bound, POS = - 1
Step 2: Repeat Steps 3 and 4 while BEG <= END
Step 3: SET MID = (BEG + END)/2
Step 4: IF A[MID] = VAL
SET POS = MID
PRINT POS
Go to Step 6
ELSE IF A[MID] > VAL
SET END = MID - 1
ELSE
SET BEG = MID + 1
[END OF IF]
[END OF LOOP]
Step 5: IF POS = -1
PRINT "VALUE IS NOT PRESENT IN THE ARRAY."
[END OF IF]
Step 6: EXIT
```

In *Step 1*, we initialize the value of variables **BEG**, **END**, and **POS**. In *Step 2*, a while loop is executed until **BEG** is less than or equal to **END**. In *Step 3*, the value of **MID** is calculated. In *Step 4*, we check if the array value at **MID** is equal to **VAL** (the item to be searched in the array). If a match is found, then the value of **POS** is printed, and the algorithm exits. However, if a match is not found, and if the value of **A[MID]** is greater than **VAL**, the value of **END** is modified. Otherwise, if **A[MID]** is greater than **VAL**, then the value of **BEG** is altered. In *Step 5*, if the value of **POS** = **−1**, then **VAL** is not present in the array, and an appropriate message is printed on the screen before the algorithm exits.

Program 4.2: Implementation of binary search

```c
#include <stdio.h>
#include <stdlib.h>
#include <conio.h>
#define size 10 // Added to make changing size of array easier
int smallest(int arr[], int k, int n); // Added to sort array
void selection_sort(int arr[], int n); // Added to sort array
int main(int argc, char *argv[]) {
int arr[size], num, i, n, beg, end, mid, found=0;
printf("\n Enter the number of elements in the array: ");
scanf("%d", &n);
printf("\n Enter the elements: ");
for(i=0;i<n;i++)
{
```

```
scanf("%d", &arr[i]);
}
selection_sort(arr, n); // Added to sort the array
printf("\n The sorted array is: \n");
for(i=0;i<n;i++)
printf(" %d\t", arr[i]);
printf("\n\n Enter the number that has to be searched: ");
scanf("%d", &num);
beg = 0, end = n-1;
while(beg<=end)
{
mid = (beg + end)/2;
if (arr[mid] == num)
{
printf("\n %d is present in the array at position %d", num, mid+1);
found =1;
break;
}
else if (arr[mid]>num)
end = mid-1;
else
beg = mid+1;
}
if (beg > end && found == 0)
printf("\n %d does not exist in the array", num);
return 0;
}
int smallest(int arr[], int k, int n)
{
int pos = k, small=arr[k], i;
for(i=k+1;i<n;i++)
{
if(arr[i]< small)
{
small = arr[i];
pos = i;
}
}
```

```
return pos;
}
void selection_sort(int arr[],int n)
{
int k, pos, temp;
for(k=0;k<n;k++)
{
pos = smallest(arr, k, n);
temp = arr[k];
arr[k] = arr[pos];
arr[pos] = temp;
}
}
```

Complexity of binary search algorithm

The binary search algorithm is more efficient compared to linear search, especially for sorted arrays. Let us analyze the complexity of the binary search algorithm:

- **Time complexity**: The time complexity analysis is as follows:
  - **Worst-case scenario**: In the worst-case scenario, the element being searched is either not present in the array or is at the last position. The binary search algorithm divides the array in half at each step, and the search space is reduced by half in each iteration. The maximum number of comparisons needed to find the element is logarithmic with base 2 of the number of elements in the array. Therefore, the worst-case time complexity is $O(log\ n)$, where n is the number of elements in the array.
  - **Best-case scenario**: The best-case scenario occurs when the element being searched is exactly in the middle of the array. In this case, the algorithm finds the element in the first comparison. The best-case time complexity is $O(1)$. However, similar to linear search, the best-case is not commonly used for representing the efficiency of an algorithm because it does not provide a meaningful average case.
  - **Average-case scenario**: On average, binary search also requires logarithmic time. The average-case time complexity is $O(log\ n)$, which is considered very efficient.
- **Space complexity**: The space complexity of binary search is $O(1)$ because it uses a constant amount of extra space for variables (like low, high, and mid) that do not depend on the input size.

Interpolation search

Interpolation search, also known as extrapolation search, is a searching technique that finds a specified value in a sorted array. The concept of interpolation search is similar to how we search for names in a telephone book or for keys by which a book's entries are ordered. For example, when looking for a name, such as *Bharat*, in a telephone directory, we know that it will be near the extreme left, so applying a binary search technique by dividing the list in two halves each time is not a good idea. We must start scanning the extreme left in the first pass itself.

In each step of the interpolation search, the remaining search space for the value to be found is calculated. The calculation is done based on the values at the bounds of the search space and the value to be searched. The value found at this estimated position is then compared with the value being searched for. If the two values are equal, then the search is complete.

However, in case the values are not equal, then depending on the comparison, the remaining search space is reduced to the part before or after the estimated position. Thus, we see that interpolation search is similar to the binary search technique. However, the important difference between the two techniques is that binary search always selects the middle value of the remaining search space. It discards half of the values based on the comparison between the value found at the estimated position and the value to be searched. But in interpolation search, interpolation is used to find an item near the one being searched for, and then linear search is used to find the exact item.

Algorithm 4.3: Algorithm of interpolation search

```
INTERPOLATION_SEARCH (A, lower_bound, upper_bound, VAL)
Step 1: [INITIALIZE] SET LOW = lower_bound,
HIGH = upper_bound, POS = -1
Step 2: Repeat Steps 3 to 4 while LOW <= HIGH
Step 3: SET MID = LOW + (HIGH - LOW) ×((VAL - A[LOW]) / (A[HIGH] - A[LOW]))
Step 4: IF VAL = A[MID]
POS = MID
PRINT POS
Go to Step 6
ELSE IF VAL < A[MID]
SET HIGH = MID - 1
ELSE
SET LOW = MID + 1
[END OF IF]
[END OF LOOP]
Step 5: IF POS = -1
PRINT "VALUE IS NOT PRESENT IN THE ARRAY"
```

[END OF IF]
Step 6: EXIT

Example 4.1: Given a list of numbers **arr[] = {11, 13, 15, 17, 19, 21, 23, 25, 27, 29, 31}**. Search for value 19 using interpolation search technique.

Solution: The solution is as follows:

Low = 0, High = 10, VAL = 29, a[Low] = 11, a[High] = 31

$Middle = Low + (High - Low) \times ((VAL - a[Low]) / (a[High] - a[Low]))$

$\qquad = 0 + (10 - 0) \times ((29 - 11) / (31 - 11))$

$\qquad = 0 + 10 \times 0.9 = 9$

arr[middle] = arr[9] = 29 which is equal to value to be searched.

	VAL							
Low	Item to be searched							High

$Middle = (Low + High) / 2$

(Binary search approach for division of given array list in 2 halves)

	VAL							
Low	searche d item							High

$Middle = Low + (High - Low) \times ((key - Arr[Low]) / (Arr[High] - Arr[Low]))$

(Interpolation search approach for division of given array list in 2 halves)

Program 4.3: Implementation of interpolation search

```c
#include <stdio.h>
#include <conio.h>
#define MAX 20
int interpolation_search(int a[], int low, int high, int val)
{
int mid;
while(low <= high)
{
mid = low + (high - low)*((val - a[low]) / (a[high] - a[low]));
```

```
if(val == a[mid])
return mid;
if(val < a[mid])
high = mid - 1;
else
low = mid + 1;
}
return -1;
}
int main()
{
int arr[MAX], i, n, val, pos;
clrscr();
printf("\n Enter the number of elements in the array : ");
scanf("%d", &n);
printf("\n Enter the elements : ");
for(i = 0; i <n; i++)
scanf("%d", &arr[i]);
printf("\n Enter the value to be searched : ");
scanf("%d", &val);
pos = interpolation_search(arr, 0, n-1, val);
if(pos == -1)
printf("\n %d is not found in the array", val);
else
printf("\n %d is found at position %d", val, pos);
getche();
return 0;
}
```

Complexity of interpolation search algorithm

Interpolation search is an algorithm for searching for a target value within a sorted array of elements. It improves upon binary search by making a more informed guess about the position of the target element based on the distribution of values in the array. Let us analyze the complexity of the interpolation search algorithm:

- **Time complexity**: The time complexity analysis is as follows:

    o **Worst-case scenario**: The worst-case scenario for interpolation search occurs when the target element is either the smallest or largest element in the array or when the values in the array are not uniformly distributed. In such cases, the interpolation search may degrade to perform a linear search, leading to a worst-case time complexity of *O(n)*. This happens because the interpolation formula may not provide a good estimate of the target's position, causing the algorithm to traverse through a significant portion of the array.

  o **Best-case scenario**: The best-case scenario for interpolation search occurs when the target element is found at the middle of the array in the first iteration. In this case, the time complexity is *O(1)*, as the algorithm directly finds the target without any further comparisons.

  o **Average-case scenario**: The average-case time complexity of interpolation search is typically expressed as *O(log(log(n)))*. This means that, on average, the algorithm performs logarithmic time operations. However, it is important to note that this average-case complexity assumes a uniform distribution of elements in the array. The interpolation search algorithm calculates an approximate position for the target element based on the values at the ends of the array and uses this estimate to guide the search towards the target.

• **Space complexity**: The space complexity of the interpolation search algorithm is *O(1)*, meaning it requires constant space regardless of the size of the input array.

Jump search

When we have an already sorted list, then another efficient algorithm to search for a value is jump search or block search. In jump search, it is not necessary to scan all the elements in the list to find the desired value. We just check an element, and if it is less than the desired value, then some of the elements following it are skipped by jumping ahead. After moving a little forward, the element is checked again. If the checked element is greater than the desired value, then we have a boundary, and we are sure that the desired value lies between the previously checked element and the currently checked element. However, if the checked element is less than the value being searched for, then we again make a small jump and repeat the process.

Once the boundary of the value is determined, a linear search is done to find the value and its position in the array. For example, consider an array **arr[]** = {11,12,13,14,15,16,17,18,19}. The length of the array is 9. If we have to find value 18, then the following steps are performed using the jump search technique:

1. The first three elements are checked. Since 3 is smaller than 8, we will have to make a jump ahead, shown as follows:

11	12	13	14	15	16	17	18	19

2. The next three elements are checked. Since 6 is smaller than 8, we will have to make a jump ahead.

11	12	13	14	15	16	17	18	19

3. The next three elements are checked. Since 9 is greater than 8, the desired value lies within the current boundary, illustrated as follows:

11	12	13	14	15	16	17	18	19	

4. A linear search is now done to find the value in the array.

Algorithm 4.4: Algorithm of jump search

```
JUMP_SEARCH (A, lower_bound, upper_bound, VAL, N)
Step 1: [INITIALIZE] SET STEP = sqrt(N), I = 0, LOW = lower_bound, HIGH =
upper_bound, POS = -1
Step 2: Repeat Step 3 while I < STEP
Step 3: IF VAL < A[STEP]
SET HIGH = STEP - 1
ELSE
SET LOW = STEP + 1
[END OF IF]
SET I = I + 1
[END OF LOOP]
Step 4: SET I = LOW
Step 5: Repeat Step 6 while I <= HIGH
Step 6: IF A[I] = Val
POS = I
PRINT POS
Go to Step 8
[END OF IF]
SET I = I + 1
[END OF LOOP]
Step 7: IF POS = -1
PRINT "VALUE IS NOT PRESENT IN THE ARRAY"
[END OF IF]
Step 8: EXIT
```

Advantages of jump search over linear search

Suppose we have a sorted list of 1000 elements where the elements have values 0, 1, 2, 3, 4, ..., 999, then a sequential search will find the value 674 in exactly 674 iterations. However, with a jump search, the same value can be found in 44 iterations. Hence, a jump search performs far better than a linear search on a sorted list of elements.

Advantages of jump search over binary search

Binary search is very easy to implement and has a complexity of *O(log n)*, but in the case of a list having a very large number of elements, jumping to the middle of the list to make comparisons is not a good idea because if the value being searched is at the beginning of the list, then one (or even more) large step(s) in the backward direction would have to be taken. In such cases, jump search performs better as we have to move a little backward, that too only once. Hence, when jumping back is slower than jumping forward, the jump search algorithm always performs better.

Choosing the step length

For the jump search algorithm to work efficiently, we must define a fixed size for the step. If the step size is 1, then the algorithm is the same as a linear search. Now, in order to find an appropriate step size, we must first try to figure out the relation between the size of the list (n) and the size of the step (k). Usually, k is calculated as √n.

Further optimization of jump search

Till now, we were dealing with lists having a small number of elements. But in real-world applications, lists can be very large. In such large lists, searching for the value from the beginning of the list may not be a good idea. A better option is to start the search from the kth element.

We can also improve the performance of the jump search algorithm by repeatedly applying jump search. For example, if the size of the list is 10,00,000 (n). The jump interval would then be $\sqrt{n} = \sqrt{1000000} = 1000$. Now, even the identified interval has 1000 elements and is again a large list. So, jump search can be applied again with a new step size of $\sqrt{1000} \approx 31$. Thus, every time we have a desired interval with a large number of values, the jump search algorithm can be applied again but with a smaller step. However, in this case, the complexity of the algorithm will no longer be $O(\sqrt{n})$ but will approach a logarithmic value.

Program 4.4: Implementation of jump search

```
#include <stdio.h>
#include<math.h>
#include <conio.h>
#define MAX 20
int jump_search(int a[], int low, int high, int val, int n)
{
int step, i;
step = sqrt(n);
for(i=0;i<step;i++)
```

```
{
if(val < a[step])
high = step - 1;
else
low = step + 1;
}
for(i=low;i<=high;i++)
{
if(a[i]==val)
return i;
}
return -1;
}
int main()
{
int arr[MAX], i, n, val, pos;
clrscr();
printf("\n Enter the number of elements in the array : ");
scanf("%d", &n);
printf("\n Enter the elements : ");
for(i = 0; i <n; i++)
scanf("%d", &arr[i]);
printf("\n Enter the value to be searched : ");
scanf("%d", &val);
pos = jump_search(arr, 0, n-1, val, n);
if(pos == -1)
printf("\n %d is not found in the array", val);
else
printf("\n %d is found at position %d", val, pos);
getche();
return 0;
}
```

Complexity of jump search algorithm

Jump search is another searching algorithm that operates on sorted arrays. Its complexity is as follows:

- **Time complexity**: The following is the complexity analysis:

  o **Worst-case scenario**: The worst-case scenario for jump search also occurs when the target element is not present in the array. In this case, the algorithm will perform a linear search through each block until it reaches the end of the array or finds a block where the target element could potentially exist. The number of comparisons in the worst-case scenario is also approximately $\sqrt{n}$, resulting in a time complexity of $O(\sqrt{n})$.

  o **Best-case scenario**: In the best-case scenario, the target element is found at the first position itself. This results in a time complexity of $O(1)$ as the algorithm only requires one comparison.

  o **Average-case scenario**: In an average-case scenario, the jump search algorithm divides the array into blocks of size $\sqrt{n}$, where n is the number of elements in the array. It then performs a linear search within each block to find the block containing the target element. Once the block is found, it performs a linear search within that block. On average, this results in approximately $\sqrt{n}$ comparisons. Hence, the average-case time complexity is $O(\sqrt{n})$.

- **Space complexity**: The space complexity of the jump search algorithm is $O(1)$, meaning it requires constant space regardless of the size of the input array.

Exponential search

Exponential search is a searching algorithm that aims to find the position of a target value within a sorted array. It works by first finding a range where the target element may lie using exponential increments, and then performing a binary search within that range. Exponential search is particularly useful when the array size is unknown or unbounded because it quickly narrows down the search space to a manageable size using exponentially increasing indices.

Phases of exponential search

The **first phase** finds the portion of x that contains z if it is present in the array. More specifically, the first phase finds the number j such that $x[2^j] <= z < x[2^{j-1}]$.

The idea is to partition x into sub-arrays of incremental sizes and check them consecutively until we find the one that can contain z. The boundary indices of those sub-arrays are powers of 2, hence the algorithm's name.

In the **second phase**, the algorithm looks for {z} using binary search in the following array:

$\{x[2^j : (2^{j+1}-1)] = [x[2^j], x[2^j + 1], x[2^j + 2], \ldots \ldots, x[2^{j+1} - 1]]\}$

We first check if *x[1]* <= *z* < *x[2]*, which simplifies to testing if *x[1]* = *z*. If the test fails, we check if *x[2]* <= *z* < *x[4]*. If that is not the case, we test if *x[4]* <= *z* < *x[8]*, then *x[8]* <= *z* < *x[16]*, *x[16]* <= *z* < *x[32]*, and so on until we find the boundaries that capture *z*: *x[2^j]* <= *z* < *x[2^{j+1}]*.

Afterward, we run binary search on *x[2^j : (2^{j+1}-1)]*. If it does not find *z*, then it is not an element of *x*. If it does, it will return the index of *z* in the sub-array as an integer from *1* to *2^j*. Adjust it to get the index of *z* in the entire array by adding the offset *2^j* (the starting index of the sub-array) and taking away *1*. The following figure shows the starting index of the sub-array:

1	2	3	4	5	6	7	8	9	10	11	12	13	14	15	16	17	18	19	...

Figure 4.1: Initialization of array with sub-array starting index

Algorithm 4.5: Algorithm of exponential search

```
int Exponential_Search (int arr[], int n, int x) {
    if (arr[0] == x) return 0;
    int i = 1;
    while (i < n && arr[i] <= x) i = i * 2;
    return Binary_Search (arr, i / 2, min(i, n - 1), x);
}
int Binary_Search (int arr[], int l, int r, int x)
{
    if (r >= l)
    {
        int mid = l + (r - l)/2;
        if (arr[mid] == x)
            return mid;
        if (arr[mid] > x)
            return Binary_Search (arr, l, mid-1, x);
        return Binary_Search (arr, mid+1, r, x);
    }
    return -1;
}
```

Program 4.5: Implementation of exponential search

```
#include <stdio.h>
#include <conio.h>
// Function to perform binary search within a sorted array
int binarySearch(int arr[], int left, int right, int target) {
```

```
    while (left <= right) {
        int mid = left + (right - left) / 2;
        if (arr[mid] == target)
            return mid;
        else if (arr[mid] < target)
            left = mid + 1;
        else
            right = mid - 1;
    }
    return -1; // Return -1 if the target is not found
}

// Function to perform exponential search
int exponentialSearch(int arr[], int size, int target) {
    if (arr[0] == target)
        return 0; // If the target is found at index 0
    // Find the range where the target may lie
    int i = 1;
    while (i < size && arr[i] <= target)
        i *= 2;
    // Perform binary search within the identified range
    return binarySearch(arr, i / 2, (i < size) ? i : size - 1, target);
}

int main() {
    int arr[] = {2, 3, 5, 8, 10, 15, 18};
    int size = sizeof(arr) / sizeof(arr[0]);
    int target = 10;
    int index = exponentialSearch(arr, size, target);
    if (index != -1)
        printf("Element %d found at index %d\n", target, index);
    else
        printf("Element %d not found in the array\n", target);
    return 0;
}
```

Complexity of exponential search algorithm

The time complexity of an exponential search can be analyzed in two steps, which are as follows:

1. **Finding the range where the target may lie**: This step involves iterating through indices exponentially until either the element at the current index exceeds the target value or the index exceeds the size of the array. Since the index is multiplied

by 2 in each iteration, the number of iterations required to find the range is $O(log\ n)$, where n is the size of the array.

2. **Performing binary search within the identified range**: After finding the range where the target may lie, a binary search is performed within that range. The time complexity of binary search is $O(log\ m)$, where m is the size of the range (which can be, at most, n elements).

Overall, the time complexity of exponential search is the sum of the time complexities of the preceding two steps, which is as follows:

$O(log\ n)$ (for finding the range) + $O(log\ m)$ (for binary search within the range)

Since m can be at most n, the overall time complexity of exponential search can be expressed as $O(log\ n)$ + $O(log\ n)$, which simplifies to $O(log\ n)$.

Fibonacci search

In the Fibonacci series, the first two terms are 0 and 1, and then each successive term is the sum of the previous two terms. In the following Fibonacci series, each number is called a Fibonacci number:

0, 1, 1, 2, 3, 5, 8, 13, 21, 34, 55, 89, …

The same series and concept can be used to search for a given value in a list of numbers. Such a search algorithm, which is based on Fibonacci numbers, is called **Fibonacci search** and was developed by *Kiefer* in 1953. The search follows a divide and conquer technique and narrows down possible locations with the help of Fibonacci numbers. Similar to jump search and exponential search, this algorithm does search by skipping through the indices of the input array.

Algorithm 4.6: Algorithm of Fibonacci search

1. `Find the smallest Fibonacci numbers, i.e., greater than or equal to the length of the array.`
2. `Initialize two pointers: left and right.`
   a. `Set left to 0.`
   b. `Set right to the smallest Fibonacci number greater than or equal to the length of the array.`
3. `While the target value is not found and the left is less than the length of the array:`
   a. `If the target value is greater than the value at index right, update left and right to move fib_(m-1) steps ahead.`
   b. `If the target value is less than the value at index right, update left and right to move fib_(m-2) steps ahead.`

    c. **If the target value is equal tc the value at index right, return right.**

    d. **Update m to m - 1 and recalculate the Fibonacci numbers accordingly.**

4. **If the target value is found, return the index of the target value.**

5. **If the target value is not found, return -1.**

Example 4.2: Imagine we need to find element 24 in a sorted array of {12, 14, 16. 17, 20, 24, 31, 43, 50, 62}, shown in *Figure 4.2*, using Fibonacci search:

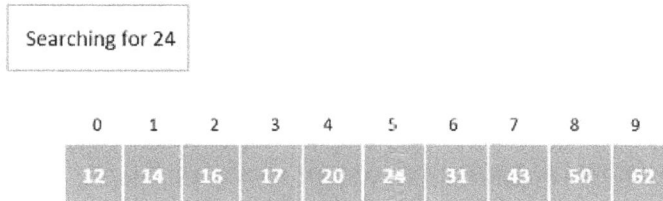

Figure 4.2: *Initialization of array in Fibonacci search*

1. The size of the input array is 10. The smallest Fibonacci number greater than 10 is 13. Therefore, $F_m = 13$, $F_{m-1} = 8$, $F_{m-2} = 5$.

We initialize *offset* = -1.

2. In the first iteration, compare it with the element at *index = minimum (offset + Fm-2, n – 1) = minimum (-1 + 5, 9) = minimum (4, 9) = 4*.

The fourth element in the array is 20, which is not a match and is less than the key element 24, shown as follows:

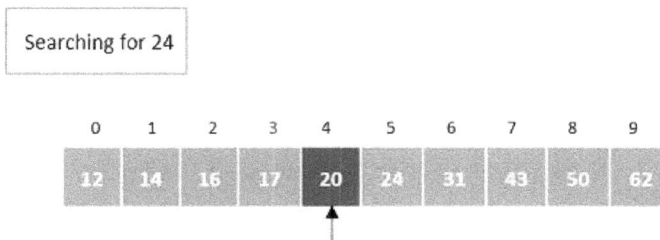

Figure 4.3: *First iteration compares at index 4*

3. In the second iteration, update the offset value and the Fibonacci numbers.

Since the key is greater, the offset value will become the index of the element, i.e., 4. Fibonacci numbers are updated as $F_m = F_{m-1} = 8$.

$F_{m-1} = 5$, $F_{m-2} = 3$.

Now, compare it with the element at *index = minimum (offset + F_{m-2}, n – 1) = minimum (4 + 3, 9) = minimum (7, 9) = 7*.

The element at seventh index of the array is 43, which is not a match and is also more than the key element 24, shown as follows:

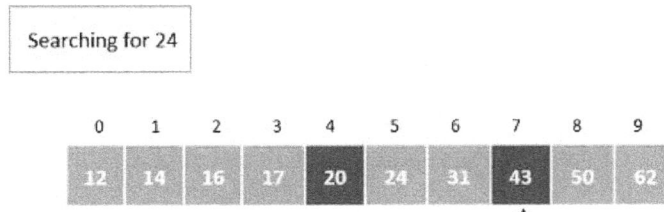

Figure 4.4: First iteration compares at index 7

4. We discard the elements after the seventh index, so $n = 7$, and the offset value remains 4.

Fibonacci numbers are pushed two steps backward, i.e., $F_m = F_{m-2} = 3$.

$F_{m-1} = 2, F_{m-2} = 1$.

Now, compare it with the element at *index = minimum (offset + Fm-2, n – 1) = minimum (4 + 1, 6) = minimum (5, 7) = 5*.

The element at the fifth index in the array is 24, which is our key element. The fifth index is returned as the output for this example array, shown as follows:

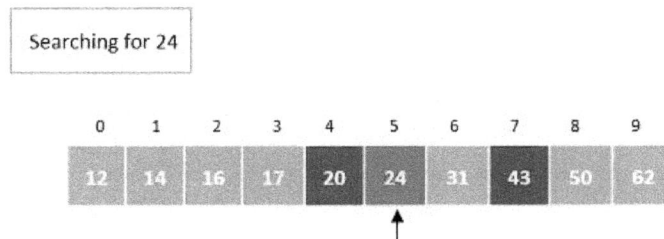

Figure 4.5: Output returned at index 5

The output is index 5.

Program 4.6: Implementation of Fibonacci search

```c
#include <stdio.h>
int min(int, int);
int fibonacci_search(int[], int, int);
int min(int a, int b){
    return (a > b) ? b : a;
}
int fibonacci_search(int arr[], int n, int key){
    int offset = -1;
```

```
    int Fm2 = 0;
    int Fm1 = 1;
    int Fm = Fm2 + Fm1;
    while (Fm < n) {
        Fm2 = Fm1;
        Fm1 = Fm;
        Fm = Fm2 + Fm1;
    }
    while (Fm > 1) {
        int i = min(offset + Fm2, n - 1);
        if (arr[i] < key) {
            Fm = Fm1;
            Fm1 = Fm2;
            Fm2 = Fm - Fm1;
            offset = i;
        } else if (arr[i] > key) {
            Fm = Fm2;
            Fm1 = Fm1 - Fm2;
            Fm2 = Fm - Fm1;
        } else
            return i;
    }
    if (Fm1 && arr[offset + 1] == key)
        return offset + 1;
    return -1;
}
int main(){
    int i, n, key, pos;
    int arr[10] = {6, 11, 19, 24, 33, 54, 67, 81, 94, 99};
    printf("Array elements are: ");
    int len = sizeof(arr) / sizeof(arr[0]);
    for(int j = 0; j<len; j++){
        printf("%d ", arr[j]);
    }
    n = 10;
    key = 67;
    printf("\nThe element to be searched: %d", key);
    pos = fibonacci_search(arr, n, key);
    if(pos >= 0)
```

```
        printf("\nThe element is found at index %d", pos);
    else
        printf("\nUnsuccessful Search");
}
```

Complexity of Fibonacci search algorithm

The **time complexity** of the Fibonacci search algorithm remains *O(log n)* for all cases, including the best, worst, and average cases. This is because the algorithm's efficiency is determined by the logarithmic reduction of the search space at each step, which is consistent across different scenarios.

The **space complexity** of the Fibonacci search algorithm is *O(1)*, which means it requires constant amount of additional space, regardless of the size of the input array.

Sublist search

One way to find a linked list within another linked list is through the sublist search algorithm. The goal is to find out if one list is in the other list, just like any basic pattern matching method. The algorithm iterates through the linked list, comparing the first element of one list with the first element of the second list. If a match is not found, it then compares the second element of the first list with the first element of the second list. This process persists until a match is encountered or it reaches the conclusion of a list.

As an illustration, let us examine two linked lists containing the following values: {14, 16, 17, 13, 18, 12} and {13, 18, 12}. Sublist search determines if the elements of the second list exist within the first linked list. The output is obtained as a binary result, represented by the Boolean values of either true or false. Due to the fact that a linked list is not an ordered data structure, it is unable to provide the position of the sub-list.

The output is true only if the second linked list is present in the first list in the exact same order, shown as follows:

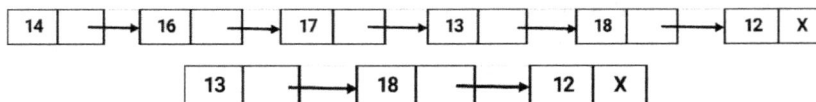

Figure 4.6: Output of sub-list 13, 18, 12

Algorithm 4.7: Algorithm of sublist search

The primary objective of this approach is to demonstrate that one linked list is a subset of another list. The search procedure in this algorithm is performed sequentially, examining each element of the linked list individually. If the result is true, it confirms that the second list is a sublist of the first linked list.

1. Utilize two pointers, with each pointer indicating a separate list. These pointers are utilized for navigating around the linked lists.

2. Examine the base cases of the linked lists as follows:

    a. If both linked lists are empty, then return TRUE.

    b. If the second list is not empty but the first list is empty, return FALSE.

    c. If the first list is not empty but the second list is empty, return FALSE.

3. After confirming that both lists are not empty, employ the pointers to sequentially navigate through the elements in the lists.

4. Compare the initial element of the first linked list with the initial element of the second linked list. If they are identical, update the pointers to point to the subsequent values in both lists.

5. If there is no match, maintain the pointer in the second list at the first entry, but advance the pointer in the first list. Reevaluate the components once more.

6. Repeat *Steps 4* and *5* until we reach the end of the lists.

7. If the final status is found, TRUE is returned and if not, FALSE.

Program 4.7: Implementation of sublist search

```
#include <stdio.h>
#include <stdlib.h>
#include <stdbool.h>
struct Node {
    int data;
    struct Node* next;
};
struct Node *newNode(int key){
    struct Node *val = (struct Node*)malloc(sizeof(struct Node));;
    val-> data= key;
    val->next = NULL;
    return val;
}
bool sublist_search(struct Node* list_ptr, struct Node* sub_ptr){
    struct Node* ptr1 = list_ptr, *ptr2 = sub_ptr;
    if (list_ptr == NULL && sub_ptr == NULL)
        return true;
    if ( sub_ptr == NULL || (sub_ptr != NULL && list_ptr == NULL))
        return false;
    while (list_ptr != NULL) {
```

```
        ptr1 = list_ptr;
        while (ptr2 != NULL) {
            if (ptr1 == NULL)
                return false;
            else if (ptr2->data == ptr1->data) {
                ptr2 = ptr2->next;
                ptr1 = ptr1->next;
            } else
                break;
        }
        if (ptr2 == NULL)
            return true;
        ptr2 = sub_ptr;
        list_ptr = list_ptr->next;
    }
    return false;
}
int main(){
    struct Node *list = newNode(2);
    list->next = newNode(5);
    list->next->next = newNode(3);
    list->next->next->next = newNode(3);
    list->next->next->next->next = newNode(6);
    list->next->next->next->next->next = newNode(7);
    list->next->next->next->next->next->next = newNode(0);
    struct Node *sub_list = newNode(3);
    sub_list->next = newNode(6);
    sub_list->next->next = newNode(7);
    bool res = sublist_search(list, sub_list);
    if (res)
        printf("Is the sublist present in the list? %d" , res);
}
```

Complexity of sublist search algorithm

The time complexity of the sublist search is contingent upon the quantity of elements contained in the linked lists being compared. The algorithm has a worst-case time complexity of $O(m*n)$, where m represents the number of entries in the first linked list and n represents the number of elements in the second linked list.

Conclusion

In this chapter, we discussed various searching algorithms. We also identified the time complexities of different cases and found the space complexity. So, the programmer can use any algorithm to find the element in the given array list. The list may be either in sorted or unsorted order. According to the requirement, the user can apply a suitable algorithm to find the element with its exact location.

In the next chapter, readers will explore the divide and conquer method, which represents a strong algorithmic framework that resolves difficulties using small modular problems. The algorithm operates through three fundamental steps, which include splitting the problem into areas, along with the recursive execution of these parts to deliver the outcome. Studying merge sort alongside quick sort and binary search within this chapter will offer students comprehensive skills to create efficient recursive solutions to boost system performance scalability for many computational issues.

Exercise

1. We are given an array list having elements {22, 45, 34, 67, 54, 88, 73, 12, 33}. Search element 88 in the array list using linear search method and return the index value where 88 is found.

2. In the previous question, consider data elements, sort the elements, and find the index of value 54 using the binary search method.

3. We are given a list of numbers, Arr[] = {15, 18, 21, 27, 39, 41, 43, 55, 57, 59}. Search for value 41 using the interpolation search technique.

4. Consider the data element from the previous question and search element 43 using jump search and exponential search and return the status.

5. What do you mean by Fibonacci search? How do we search and element in Fibonacci search?

6. Write a short note on sublist search and also mention the time complexity of this algorithm.

Join our Discord space

Join our Discord workspace for latest updates, offers, tech happenings around the world, new releases, and sessions with the authors:

https://discord.bpbonline.com

CHAPTER 5
Divide and Conquer

Introduction

This chapter will introduce the divide and conquer concept within the field of computer science. Divide and conquer is an algorithmic paradigm in which a problem is dissected into smaller, more easily handled sub-problems. These sub-problems are then solved recursively, and their solutions are amalgamated to resolve the initial problem. Widely applied in computer science and mathematics, this approach aids in crafting efficient algorithms for diverse problem sets. The typical divide and conquer strategy involves three primary steps: divide, conquer, and combine. The initial problem is partitioned into more manageable subproblems, a critical step in simplifying the overall complexity by breaking it down into simpler components. In the next step, every subproblem is addressed recursively, employing the divide and conquer strategy until they reach a level of simplicity where direct solutions are feasible. Recursive solutions are commonly implemented through function calls in this process. In the final step, the resolutions of the subproblems are subsequently consolidated to derive the solution to the original problem. This step entails combining or merging the outcomes from the smaller subproblems into a comprehensive solution for the overarching problem.

The divide and conquer methodology proves highly efficient in addressing problems characterized by overlapping subproblems and optimal substructure. Overlapping subproblems refer to the recurrence of solving the same subproblems multiple times, while optimal substructure indicates that the optimal solution to the original problem can be constructed from the optimal solutions of its subproblems.

Structure

The chapter covers the following topics:

- The general method
- Binary search
- Find maximum and minimum in number sequence
- Merge sort
- Quick sort
- Strassen's matrix multiplication
- Karatsuba multiplication
- Closest pair of points
- Maximum subarray sum
- Merge-based inversion count

Objectives

The chapter provides readers with extensive knowledge about divide and conquer, along with its vital role in designing algorithms. Students will master the process of reducing complex issues into smaller parts that they solve recursively in order to achieve efficient computation. The section presents several advantages, which include superior performance along with interchangeable solutions, as well as well-maintained code and simultaneous execution capabilities. Throughout the chapter, readers will examine practical algorithm implementations in different subject domains while developing more effective problem-solving abilities. Students will develop the ability to create efficient, modular, and scalable algorithms through the divide and conquer methodology.

In essence, the aim of the divide and conquer approach is to effectively address intricate problems by dissecting them into smaller, more manageable components. These components are addressed independently, and their solutions are then integrated to attain the resolution for the original problem.

The general method

The divide and conquer method adhere to a standard pattern, encompassing three fundamental steps: divide, conquer, and combine. A more comprehensive delineation of the overarching divide and conquer algorithmic approach is as follows:

- **Divide**

  o **Problem segmentation**: Fragment the primary problem into smaller, more digestible subproblems, entailing the division of the input data or problem instance into two or more smaller components.

  o **Recursion application**: Employ the divide and conquer strategy iteratively on each of the subproblems. This entails resolving the subproblems by reiterating the division step until they attain a level of simplicity suitable for direct solutions.

- **Conquer**

  o **Subproblem resolution**: Address the subproblems produced during the divide step. Frequently, this involves employing the same divide and conquer approach, iteratively applying the algorithm to the subproblems until reaching base cases.

  o **Base case definition**: Establish base cases that denote the smallest instances of the problem capable of being solved without additional division. These base cases act as termination conditions for the recursive process.

- **Combine**

  o **Solution integration**: Merge the solutions of the subproblems to derive the solution for the original problem. This encompasses consolidating or combining the outcomes obtained from the conquer step.

  o **Final result output**: Present the ultimate solution to the original problem derived from the amalgamated solutions of the subproblems.

This general method is systematically applied until the base cases are attained. Upon reaching the base cases, the algorithm computes and directly returns the solution without further subdivision. The efficacy of divide and conquer algorithms often hinges on minimizing redundant computations and leveraging the solutions of subproblems to prevent unnecessary recalculations.

It is crucial to emphasize that the success of the divide and conquer approach is contingent on the problem manifesting two key properties: overlapping subproblems and optimal substructure. Overlapping subproblems indicate the recurrence of solving the same subproblems multiple times, while optimal substructure signifies that the optimal solution to the original problem can be constructed from the optimal solutions of its subproblems. These properties facilitate the efficient reuse of solutions and contribute to the effectiveness of the divide and conquer strategy.

The process of the divide and conquer approach is shown in the following figure:

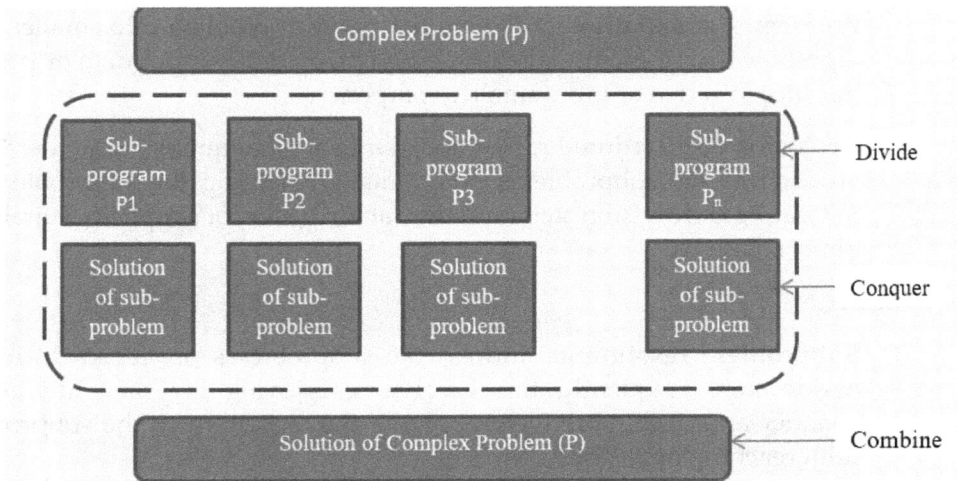

Figure 5.1: *Process of divide and conquer approach*

Binary search

Binary search stands as a timeless algorithm employed for locating an element in a sorted array or list. Employing the divide and conquer strategy, it exhibits high efficiency, boasting a time complexity of *O(log n)*. The fundamental concept involves iteratively halving the search space until either the target element is discovered or the search space becomes empty.

Algorithm 5.1: Binary search

```
binarySearch(arr, target)
   low = 0
   high = length(arr) - 1

   while low <= high
      mid = (low + high) / 2

      if arr[mid] equals target
         return mid   // Target found at index mid

      else if arr[mid] < target
         low = mid + 1   // Search the right half

      else
         high = mid - 1   // Search the left half

   return -1   // Target not found
```

Program 5.1: Implementation in C++

```cpp
#include <iostream>
#include <vector>

int binarySearch(const std::vector<int>& arr, int target) {
    int low = 0;
    int high = arr.size() - 1;

    while (low <= high) {
        int mid = low + (high - low) / 2;

        if (arr[mid] == target) {
            return mid;   // Target found
        } else if (arr[mid] < target) {
            low = mid + 1;   // Search the right half
        } else {
            high = mid - 1;   // Search the left half
        }
    }

    return -1;   // Target not found
}

int main() {
    std::vector<int> arr = {1, 2, 3, 4, 5, 6, 7, 8, 9, 10};
    int target = 5;
    int result = binarySearch(arr, target);

    if (result != -1) {
        std::cout << "Element found at index " << result << std::endl;
    } else {
        std::cout << "Element not found" << std::endl;
    }

    return 0;
}
```

Example 5.1: Consider the sorted array {1, 3, 5, 7, 9, 11, 13, 15}. Find the index of the target element 9.

Solution: Let us find the index of the target element 9 using binary search:

- **Initial**: $low = 0$, $high = 7$
- **Iteration 1**: $mid = 3$, $arr[mid] = 7 < 9$, so update $low = mid + 1$
- **Iteration 2**: $mid = 5$, $arr[mid] = 11 > 9$, so update $high = mid - 1$
- **Iteration 3**: $mid = 4$, $arr[mid] = 9$, target found at index 4

Complexity analysis

The complexity analysis is as follows:

- **Time complexity**: It is calculated as *O(log n)*. Binary search reduces the search space by half in each iteration.

- **Space complexity**: It is calculated as *O(1)*. Binary search utilizes a constant amount of additional space.

Applications

Binary search, renowned for its efficiency in locating elements within sorted datasets, finds application across various fields and domains. Some prevalent areas where binary search is employed encompass the following:

- **Computer science and programming**: Binary search is extensively used in computer science and programming for searching elements in arrays, lists, or other sorted data structures. It serves as a fundamental algorithm taught in introductory computer science courses.

- **Databases**: In databases, binary search is a common technique employed to search for records based on indexed columns, facilitating swift location and retrieval of specific data from extensive datasets.

- **Information retrieval**: Information retrieval systems utilize binary search to efficiently search and locate documents or records that match specific criteria.

- **Sorting algorithms**: Binary search is integral to various sorting algorithms. For instance, in merge sort or quick sort, it is employed to divide the dataset into smaller parts.

- **Networking**: Applied in networking protocols and routing algorithms, binary search efficiently locates and routes information through a network.

- **Game development**: In game development, binary search is employed for tasks such as searching for items in a sorted list, finding positions, or optimizing decision-making processes.

- **Genomics and bioinformatics**: In genomics and bioinformatics, binary search is utilized for tasks like searching and comparing DNA sequences or identifying patterns in extensive datasets.

- **Mathematics**: Binary search finds applications in mathematical tasks, including finding roots of equations or optimizing mathematical functions.

- **Economics and finance**: In finance and economics, binary search can be employed for tasks such as searching for specific financial data or optimizing investment portfolios.

- **Robotics**: In robotics, binary search is applied for efficient path planning and navigation algorithms.

Binary search stands as a foundational algorithm, laying the groundwork for more advanced algorithms and data structures.

Find maximum and minimum in number sequence

The task of finding the maximum and minimum elements in a sequence of numbers can be efficiently solved using a divide and conquer approach. This technique involves breaking down the problem into smaller subproblems, solving them independently, and then combining the results to obtain the final solution.

Algorithm 5.2: Find maximum and minimum

```
findMinMax(arr, low, high)
   if low equals high
      // Only one element in the array
      return {arr[low], arr[low]}

   else if high equals low + 1
      // Two elements in the array
      return {min(arr[low], arr[high]), max(arr[low], arr[high])}

   else
      mid = (low + high) / 2

      // Recursively find min and max in the left half
      leftResult = findMinMax(arr, low, mid)

      // Recursively find min and max in the right half
      rightResult = findMinMax(arr, mid + 1, high)

      // Combine the results
      return {min(leftResult.min, rightResult.min), max(leftResult.max,
rightResult.max)}
```

Program 5.2: Implementation in C++

```cpp
#include <iostream>
#include <vector>

struct MinMax {
    int min;
    int max;
};
```

```cpp
MinMax findMinMax(const std::vector<int>& arr, int low, int high) {
    MinMax result;

    // Base case: If the sequence has only one element
    if (low == high) {
        result.min = result.max = arr[low];
        return result;
    }

    // If the sequence has more than one element, divide and conquer
    int mid = (low + high) / 2;
    MinMax leftResult = findMinMax(arr, low, mid);
    MinMax rightResult = findMinMax(arr, mid + 1, high);

    // Combine the results
    result.min = std::min(leftResult.min, rightResult.min);
    result.max = std::max(leftResult.max, rightResult.max);

    return result;
}

int main() {
    std::vector<int> arr = {3, 1, 4, 1, 5, 9, 2, 6, 5, 3, 5};
    int n = arr.size();

    MinMax result = findMinMax(arr, 0, n - 1);

    std::cout << "Minimum element: " << result.min << std::endl;
    std::cout << "Maximum element: " << result.max << std::endl;

    return 0;
}
```

Example 5.2: Consider the sequence {3, 1, 4, 1, 5, 9, 2, 6, 5, 3, 5}.

Solution: The algorithm divides the sequence into two halves, recursively finds the minimum and maximum in each half, and then combines the results. The final output will be the minimum element (1) and the maximum element (9) in the sequence.

Complexity analysis

The complexity analysis is performed as follows:

- **Time complexity**: It is depicted as $O(n)$, where n is the number of elements in the sequence. Each element is examined once during the divide and conquer process.

- **Space complexity**: It is depicted as $O(log\ n)$ due to the recursive call stack.

Applications

This divide and conquer approach for finding the maximum and minimum is often used in algorithms where the goal is to efficiently search for both the maximum and minimum values simultaneously. It is employed in various applications, such as computational geometry, image processing, and optimization algorithms where identifying extreme values is a common requirement. Additionally, it serves as a building block in more complex algorithms and data structures.

Merge sort

Merge sort is a popular sorting algorithm that uses the divide and conquer paradigm. It divides the input array into two halves, recursively sorts each half, and then merges the sorted halves to produce a fully sorted array. Merge sort is known for its stability and guarantees $O(n \log n)$ time complexity, making it efficient for large datasets.

Algorithm 5.3: Merge sort

```
mergeSort(arr, low, high)
   if low < high
      mid = (low + high) / 2
      mergeSort(arr, low, mid)
      mergeSort(arr, mid + 1, high)
      merge(arr, low, mid, high)

merge(arr, low, mid, high)
   n1 = mid - low + 1
   n2 = high - mid

   // Create temporary arrays
   leftArray[1...n1], rightArray[1...n2]

   // Copy data to temporary arrays leftArray[] and rightArray[]
   for i = 1 to n1
      leftArray[i] = arr[low + i - 1]
   for j = 1 to n2
      rightArray[j] = arr[mid + j]

   // Merge the temporary arrays back into arr[low...high]
   i = 1
   j = 1
   k = low

   while i <= n1 and j <= n2
      if leftArray[i] <= rightArray[j]
         arr[k] = leftArray[i]
```

```
      i++
   else
      arr[k] = rightArray[j]
      j++
   k++

// Copy the remaining elements of leftArray[], if there are any
while i <= n1
   arr[k] = leftArray[i]
   i++
   k++

// Copy the remaining elements of rightArray[], if there are any
while j <= n2
   arr[k] = rightArray[j]
   j++
   k++
```

Program 5.3: Implementation in C++

```cpp
#include <iostream>
#include <vector>

void merge(std::vector<int>& arr, int left, int mid, int right) {
    int n1 = mid - left + 1;
    int n2 = right - mid;

    // Create temporary arrays
    std::vector<int> L(n1), R(n2);

    // Copy data to temporary arrays L[] and R[]
    for (int i = 0; i < n1; i++)
        L[i] = arr[left + i];
    for (int j = 0; j < n2; j++)
        R[j] = arr[mid + 1 + j];

    // Merge the temporary arrays back into arr[left..right]
    int i = 0, j = 0, k = left;
    while (i < n1 && j < n2) {
        if (L[i] <= R[j]) {
            arr[k] = L[i];
            i++;
        } else {
            arr[k] = R[j];
            j++;
        }
```

```
        k++;
    }

    // Copy the remaining elements of L[], if there are any
    while (i < n1) {
        arr[k] = L[i];
        i++;
        k++;
    }

    // Copy the remaining elements of R[], if there are any
    while (j < n2) {
        arr[k] = R[j];
        j++;
        k++;
    }
}

void mergeSort(std::vector<int>& arr, int left, int right) {
    if (left < right) {
        // Same as (left+right)/2, but avoids overflow
        int mid = left + (right - left) / 2;

        // Sort first and second halves
        mergeSort(arr, left, mid);
        mergeSort(arr, mid + 1, right);

        // Merge the sorted halves
        merge(arr, left, mid, right);
    }
}

int main() {
    std::vector<int> arr = {38, 27, 43, 3, 9, 82, 10};
    int n = arr.size();

    std::cout << "Original array: ";
    for (int num : arr) {
        std::cout << num << " ";
    }
    std::cout << std::endl;

    mergeSort(arr, 0, n - 1);

    std::cout << "Sorted array: ";
    for (int num : arr) {
```

```
        std::cout << num << " ";
    }
    std::cout << std::endl;

    return 0;
}
```

Example 5.3: Consider the array {38, 27, 43, 3, 9, 82, 10}.

Solution: The solution includes the following steps:

1. **Initial state**: The array is divided into two halves, and the **mergeSort** function is called recursively on each half.

2. **Recursive calls**: The array is further divided until individual elements are reached.

3. **Merge steps**: The merging process begins. The subarrays {38} and {27} are merged to form {27, 38}. Similarly, {43} and {3} are merged to form {3, 43}, and so on.

4. **Final merge**: The two halves {3, 27, 38, 43} and {9, 10, 82} are merged to produce the fully sorted array {3, 9, 10, 27, 38, 43, 82}.

Complexity analysis

The complexity analysis is as follows:

*   **Time complexity**: It is calculated as $O(n \log n)$. The array is repeatedly divided into halves log n times, and each level requires linear time for merging.

*   **Space complexity**: It is calculated as $O(n)$. Additional space is required for creating temporary arrays during the merging process.

Applications

Merge sort is widely used in scenarios where stability and predictable performance are important. The following list includes some common use cases:

*   **External sorting**: Merge sort is efficient for sorting large datasets that do not fit into memory because it minimizes the number of comparisons needed.

*   **Sorting linked lists**: Merge sort's divide and conquer approach is suitable for sorting linked lists, where random access is not as efficient as with arrays.

*   **Parallel computing**: Merge sort can be parallelized, making it suitable for parallel computing environments.

*   **Inversion counting**: Merge sort can be modified to count the number of inversions in an array, which has applications in areas like finance and data analysis.

Quick sort

Quick sort is a widely used sorting algorithm that employs the divide and conquer paradigm. It works by selecting a *pivot* element from the array and partitioning the other elements into two sub-arrays according to whether they are less than or greater than the pivot. The sub-arrays are then recursively sorted. Quick sort is known for its efficiency and often outperforms other sorting algorithms, especially for large datasets.

Algorithm 5.4: Quick sort

```
quickSort(arr, low, high)
   if low < high
      pi = partition(arr, low, high)
      quickSort(arr, low, pi - 1)
      quickSort(arr, pi + 1, high)

partition(arr, low, high)
   pivot = arr[high]
   i = low - 1

   for j = low to high - 1
      if arr[j] < pivot
         i++
         swap(arr[i], arr[j])

   swap(arr[i + 1], arr[high])
   return i + 1
```

Program 5.4: Implementation in C++

```cpp
#include <iostream>
#include <vector>

// Function to partition the array and return the pivot index
int partition(std::vector<int>& arr, int low, int high) {
    int pivot = arr[high];
    int i = low - 1;

    for (int j = low; j < high; j++) {
        if (arr[j] < pivot) {
            i++;
            std::swap(arr[i], arr[j]);
        }
    }

    std::swap(arr[i + 1], arr[high]);
```

```
        return i + 1;
}

// Function to perform Quick Sort
void quickSort(std::vector<int>& arr, int low, int high) {
    if (low < high) {
        int pi = partition(arr, low, high);

        // Recursively sort the sub-arrays
        quickSort(arr, low, pi - 1);
        quickSort(arr, pi + 1, high);
    }
}

int main() {
    std::vector<int> arr = {38, 27, 43, 3, 9, 82, 10};
    int n = arr.size();

    std::cout << "Original array: ";
    for (int num : arr) {
        std::cout << num << " ";
    }
    std::cout << std::endl;

    quickSort(arr, 0, n - 1);

    std::cout << "Sorted array: ";
    for (int num : arr) {
        std::cout << num << " ";
    }
    std::cout << std::endl;

    return 0;
}
```

Example 5.4: Consider the array {38, 27, 43, 3, 9, 82, 10}.

Solution: The following steps are involved:

1. **Initial state**: The function **quickSort** is called with the entire array. A **pivot** is selected, and the **partition** function is called to rearrange elements such that elements smaller than the **pivot** are on the left, and elements greater than the **pivot** are on the right.

2. **Recursive calls**: The array is divided into two sub-arrays based on the pivot. The **quickSort** function is recursively called on the left and right sub-arrays.

3. **Final result**: The process continues until each sub-array has one or zero elements. The final result is a fully sorted array.

Complexity analysis

The complexity analysis is as follows:

1. **Time complexity**: Time complexity is calculated based on the following cases:

   o **Best case**: *O(n log n)*

   o **Average case**: *O(n log n)*

   o **Worst case**: *O(n^2)*

   The pivot selection and partitioning steps dominate the time complexity. In the average case, the pivot is often close to the median, leading to efficient partitioning.

- **Space complexity**: It is calculated as *O(log n)* and is the space required for the recursive call stack.

Applications

Quick sort is widely used in practice due to its efficiency and is the default sorting algorithm in many programming languages and libraries. Some common use cases include:

- **General-purpose sorting**: Quick sort is used for sorting large datasets efficiently and is often preferred over other sorting algorithms.

- **System libraries**: Many system libraries and programming languages use quick sort as their default sorting algorithm.

- **Data deduplication**: Quick sort's in-place nature makes it suitable for tasks like data deduplication, where rearranging elements is acceptable.

- **Sorting in database systems**: Quick sort is used in sorting records and indexes in database systems.

- **Parallel computing**: Quick sort can be parallelized, making it suitable for parallel computing environments.

Despite the worst-case time complexity, quick sort is often faster in practice than other algorithms, making it a popular choice for sorting applications.

Strassen's matrix multiplication

Strassen's algorithm is an efficient divide and conquer method for matrix multiplication. It reduces the number of multiplications from 8 to 7 by using a set of recursive formulas. This reduction in the number of multiplications leads to a more efficient algorithm, especially for large matrices. Strassen's algorithm is based on the idea of dividing each matrix into submatrices and applying a set of mathematical formulas to compute the product.

Algorithm 5.5: Strassen's matrix multiplication

```
strassenMatrixMultiply(A, B)
    if size of A is 1
        return A * B  // Standard matrix multiplication for 1x1 matrices

    // Divide matrices into submatrices
    A11, A12, A21, A22 = submatrices of A
    B11, B12, B21, B22 = submatrices of B

    // Compute products of submatrices using Strassen's formulas
    P1 = strassenMatrixMultiply(A11 + A22, B11 + B22)
    P2 = strassenMatrixMultiply(A21 + A22, B11)
    P3 = strassenMatrixMultiply(A11, B12 - B22)
    P4 = strassenMatrixMultiply(A22, B21 - B11)
    P5 = strassenMatrixMultiply(A11 + A12, B22)
    P6 = strassenMatrixMultiply(A21 - A11, B11 + B12)
    P7 = strassenMatrixMultiply(A12 - A22, B21 + B22)

    // Compute submatrices of the result
    C11 = P1 + P4 - P5 + P7
    C12 = P3 + P5
    C21 = P2 + P4
    C22 = P1 - P2 + P3 + P6
    // Construct the result matrix
    result = constructMatrix(C11, C12, C21, C22)
    return result
```

Program 5.5: Implementation

```cpp
#include <iostream>
#include <vector>

using namespace std;

vector<vector<int>> addMatrices(const vector<vector<int>>& A, const
vector<vector<int>>& B) {
    int n = A.size();
    vector<vector<int>> result(n, vector<int>(n, 0));

    for (int i = 0; i < n; i++) {
        for (int j = 0; j < n; j++) {
            result[i][j] = A[i][j] + B[i][j];
        }
    }
```

```
        return result;
}

vector<vector<int>> subtractMatrices(const vector<vector<int>>& A, const
vector<vector<int>>& B) {
    int n = A.size();
    vector<vector<int>> result(n, vector<int>(n, 0));

    for (int i = 0; i < n; i++) {
        for (int j = 0; j < n; j++) {
            result[i][j] = A[i][j] - B[i][j];
        }
    }

    return result;
}

vector<vector<int>> strassenMatrixMultiply(const vector<vector<irt>>& A,
const vector<vector<int>>& B) {
    int n = A.size();

    if (n == 1) {
        // Base case: standard matrix multiplication for 1x1 matrices
        vector<vector<int>> result(1, vector<int>(1, 0));
        result[0][0] = A[0][0] * B[0][0];
        return result;
    }

    // Divide matrices into submatrices
    int mid = n / 2;
    vector<vector<int>> A11(mid, vector<int>(mid)), A12(mid,
vector<int>(mid)), A21(mid, vector<int>(mid)), A22(mid, vector<int>(mid));
    vector<vector<int>> B11(mid, vector<int>(mid)), B12(mid,
vector<int>(mid)), B21(mid, vector<int>(mid)), B22(mid, vector<int>(mid));

    for (int i = 0; i < mid; i++) {
        for (int j = 0; j < mid; j++) {
            A11[i][j] = A[i][j];
            A12[i][j] = A[i][j + mid];
            A21[i][j] = A[i + mid][j];
            A22[i][j] = A[i + mid][j + mid];
```

```
                B11[i][j] = B[i][j];
                B12[i][j] = B[i][j + mid];
                B21[i][j] = B[i + mid][j];
                B22[i][j] = B[i + mid][j + mid];
            }
        }

        // Compute products of submatrices using Strassen's formulas
        vector<vector<int>> P1 = strassenMatrixMultiply(addMatrices(A11, A22),
    addMatrices(B11, B22));
        vector<vector<int>> P2 = strassenMatrixMultiply(addMatrices(A21, A22),
    B11);
        vector<vector<int>> P3 = strassenMatrixMultiply(A11,
    subtractMatrices(B12, B22));
        vector<vector<int>> P4 = strassenMatrixMultiply(A22,
    subtractMatrices(B21, B11));
        vector<vector<int>> P5 = strassenMatrixMultiply(addMatrices(A11, A12),
    B22);
        vector<vector<int>> P6 = strassenMatrixMultiply(subtractMatrices(A21,
    A11), addMatrices(B11, B12));
        vector<vector<int>> P7 = strassenMatrixMultiply(subtractMatrices(A12,
    A22), addMatrices(B21, B22));

        // Compute submatrices of the result
        vector<vector<int>> C11 = subtractMatrices(addMatrices(P1, P4),
    addMatrices(P5, P7));
        vector<vector<int>> C12 = addMatrices(P3, P5);
        vector<vector<int>> C21 = addMatrices(P2, P4);
        vector<vector<int>> C22 = addMatrices(subtractMatrices(P1, P2),
    addMatrices(P3, P6));

        // Construct the result matrix
        vector<vector<int>> result(n, vector<int>(n, 0));
        for (int i = 0; i < mid; i++) {
            for (int j = 0; j < mid; j++) {
                result[i][j] = C11[i][j];
                result[i][j + mid] = C12[i][j];
                result[i + mid][j] = C21[i][j];
                result[i + mid][j + mid] = C22[i][j];
            }
        }
```

```
        return result;
}

int main() {
    // Example usage
    vector<vector<int>> A = {{1, 2}, {3, 4}};
    vector<vector<int>> B = {{5, 6}, {7, 8}};

    cout << "Matrix A:\n";
    for (const auto& row : A) {
        for (int elem : row) {
            cout << elem << " ";
        }
        cout << endl;
    }

    cout << "Matrix B:\n";
    for (const auto& row : B) {
        for (int elem : row) {
            cout << elem << " ";
        }
        cout << endl;
    }

    vector<vector<int>> result = strassenMatrixMultiply(A, B);

    cout << "Resultant Matrix:\n";
    for (const auto& row : result) {
        for (int elem : row) {
            cout << elem << " ";
        }
        cout << endl;
    }

    return 0;
}
```

Example 5.5: Consider two matrices:

$$A = \begin{bmatrix} 1 & 2 \\ 3 & 4 \end{bmatrix} \quad \text{and} \quad B = \begin{bmatrix} 5 & 6 \\ 7 & 8 \end{bmatrix}$$

Solution: Perform the following steps:

1. **Divide**: The matrices are divided into submatrices as follows:

$$A_{11} = [1]$$
$$A_{12} = [2]$$
$$A_{21} = [3]$$
$$A_{22} = [4]$$

$$B_{11} = [5]$$
$$B_{12} = [6]$$
$$B_{21} = [7]$$
$$B_{22} = [8]$$

2. **Conquer**: The recursive calls are made to compute products of submatrices using Strassen's formulas.

3. **Combine**: The submatrices of the result are computed using the products obtained from the recursive calls.

The final result is shown as follows:

$$Result = \begin{bmatrix} 19 & 22 \\ 43 & 50 \end{bmatrix}$$

Complexity analysis

The time complexity and space complexity are calculated as follows:

- **Time complexity**: $O(n^{\log_2 7}) \approx O(n^{2.81})$
- **Space complexity**: $O(n^{\log_2 7}) \approx O(n^{2.81})$

Strassen's algorithm is more efficient than the standard matrix multiplication algorithm for large matrices due to the reduction in the number of multiplications. However, its practical advantage is limited because of the overhead associated with the extra additions and subtractions.

Applications

Strassen's algorithm is primarily used in scenarios where large matrix multiplications need to be performed efficiently, such as in numerical simulations, scientific computing, and certain machine learning algorithms. Despite its theoretical efficiency, in practice, more optimized algorithms like the Coppersmith–Winograd algorithm or specialized linear algebra libraries (e.g., **Basic Linear Algebra Subprograms (BLAS)**, **Linear Algebra Package (LAPACK**)) are often used for large-scale matrix operations.

Karatsuba multiplication

Karatsuba multiplication is an efficient algorithm for multiplying two numbers. It employs a divide and conquer strategy to break down the multiplication problem into smaller subproblems and reduce the overall number of multiplications required. Karatsuba multiplication has a better asymptotic complexity compared to the standard multiplication algorithm, especially for large numbers.

Algorithm 5.6: Karatsuba multiplication

```
karatsuba(x, y)
   if x or y is a single-digit number
      return x * y

   n = max(length(x), length(y))
   m = ceil(n / 2)

   // Divide x and y into two halves
   a, b = split(x, m)
   c, d = split(y, m)

   // Recursively compute three products
   ac = karatsuba(a, c)
   bd = karatsuba(b, d)
   adbc = karatsuba((a + b), (c + d)) - ac - bd

   // Combine the results to obtain the final product
   result = ac * 10^(2m) + adbc * 10^m + bd
   return result
```

Karatsuba multiplication using divide and conquer

Karatsuba multiplication is an efficient algorithm for multiplying two numbers. It employs a divide and conquer strategy to break down the multiplication problem into smaller subproblems and reduce the overall number of multiplications required. Karatsuba multiplication has a better asymptotic complexity compared to the standard multiplication algorithm, especially for large numbers.

Consider the following pseudo-code:

```
karatsuba(x, y)
   if x or y is a single-digit number
      return x * y

   n = max(length(x), length(y))
   m = ceil(n / 2)
```

```
// Divide x and y into two halves
a, b = split(x, m)
c, d = split(y, m)

// Recursively compute three products
ac = karatsuba(a, c)
bd = karatsuba(b, d)
adbc = karatsuba((a + b), (c + d)) - ac - bd

// Combine the results to obtain the final product
result = ac * 10^(2m) + adbc * 10^m + bd
return result
```

Program 5.6: Implementation in C++

```cpp
#include <iostream>
#include <cmath>
#include <string>

using namespace std;

// Function to split a number into two halves
pair<string, string> split(const string& num, int m) {
    int len = num.length();
    string left = num.substr(0, len - m);
    string right = num.substr(len - m, m);
    return {left, right};
}

// Function to pad a number with zeros
string padZeros(const string& num, int count) {
    string result = num;
    result.insert(result.begin(), count, '0');
    return result;
}

// Function to perform Karatsuba multiplication
string karatsuba(const string& x, const string& y) {
    if (x.length() == 1 || y.length() == 1) {
        // Base case: Single-digit multiplication
        int result = stoi(x) * stoi(y);
        return to_string(result);
    }

    int n = max(x.length(), y.length());
    int m = ceil(n / 2);
```

```
    // Divide x and y into two halves
    auto [a, b] = split(x, m);
    auto [c, d] = split(y, m);

    // Recursively compute three products
    string ac = karatsuba(a, c);
    string bd = karatsuba(b, d);
    string adbc = karatsuba(to_string(stoi(a) + stoi(b)), to_string(stoi(c)
+ stoi(d))) - ac - bd;

    // Combine the results to obtain the final product
    string result = ac + padZeros(adbc, m) + bd;
    return result;
}
int main() {
    // Example usage
    string x = "1234";
    string y = "5678";

    cout << "Number 1: " << x << endl;
    cout << "Number 2: " << y << endl;

    string result = karatsuba(x, y);

    cout << "Product: " << result << endl;

    return 0;
}
```

Example 5.6: Consider multiplying two numbers:

- x=1234
- y=5678

Solution: Complete the following steps:

1. **Divide**: The numbers are divided into two halves:

    a=12, b=34

    c=56, d=78

2. **Recursive calls**: Three recursive calls are made to compute three products:

$$ac=12\times56$$

$$bd=34\times78$$

$$adbc=(12+34)\times(56+78)-ac-bd$$

3. **Combine**: The results are combined to obtain the final product:

$$ac \times 10^{2m} + adbc \times 10^m + bd$$

The final product is:

1234×5678=7006652

Complexity analysis

The time complexity and space complexity are calculated as follows:

- **Time complexity**: $O(n^{\log_2 3}) \approx O(n^{1.585})$
- **Space complexity**: $O(n^{\log_2 3}) \approx O(n^{1.585})$

Karatsuba multiplication has a better time complexity compared to the standard multiplication algorithm, especially for large numbers. It reduces the number of multiplications required, leading to improved performance.

Applications

Karatsuba multiplication is used in scenarios where efficient multiplication of large numbers is required, such as cryptography, signal processing, and polynomial multiplication in algebraic algorithms. It serves as a building block for more advanced algorithms and applications where large integer or polynomial multiplications are common.

Closest pair of points

The closest pair of points problem involves finding the pair of points with the smallest distance among a set of points in a 2D plane. The divide and conquer approach is commonly used to efficiently solve this problem. The idea is to recursively divide the set of points into smaller subsets, find the closest pairs in each subset, and then combine the results to determine the overall closest pair.

Algorithm 5.7: Closest pair of points

```
closestPair(points)
    // Sort points by x-coordinate
    sort(points)

    // Call the recursive function
    return closestPairRec(points)

closestPairRec(points)
    n = number of points

    // Base case: if there are only two or three points, brute force
```

```
   if n <= 3
      return closestPairBruteForce(points)

   // Divide the points into two halves
   mid = n / 2
   leftPoints = points[0...mid-1]
   rightPoints = points[mid...n-1]

   // Recursively find the closest pairs in each half
   leftClosest = closestPairRec(leftPoints)
   rightClosest = closestPairRec(rightPoints)

   // Find the minimum distance between the two halves
   minDistance = min(leftClosest, rightClosest)

   // Merge the results from the two halves
   strip = pointsWithinStrip(points, mid, minDistance)
   return min(minDistance, closestPairStrip(strip, minDistance))

pointsWithinStrip(points, mid, minDistance)
   // Extract points within the strip of width 2*minDistance around the middle
line
   strip = empty list

   for each point in points
      if abs(point.x - points[mid].x) < minDistance
         append point to strip

   // Sort points in the strip by y-coordinate
   sort(strip, compare by y-coordinate)

   return strip

closestPairStrip(strip, minDistance)
   // Find the closest pair of points within the strip
   n = size of strip

   // Initialize the minimum distance to the given minDistance
   minDistance = minDistance

   for i from 0 to n-1
      for j from i+1 to min(i+7, n-1)
         distance = distanceBetween(strip[i], strip[j])
         minDistance = min(minDistance, distance)

   return minDistance
```

Program 5.7: Implementation in C++

```cpp
#include <iostream>
#include <vector>
#include <algorithm>
#include <cmath>
#include <limits>

using namespace std;

struct Point {
    double x, y;
};

bool compareByX(const Point& p1, const Point& p2) {
    return p1.x < p2.x;
}

bool compareByY(const Point& p1, const Point& p2) {
    return p1.y < p2.y;
}

double distanceBetween(const Point& p1, const Point& p2) {
    return sqrt(pow(p1.x - p2.x, 2) + pow(p1.y - p2.y, 2));
}

double closestPairBruteForce(const vector<Point>& points) {
    int n = points.size();
    double minDistance = numeric_limits<double>::max();

    for (int i = 0; i < n - 1; i++) {
        for (int j = i + 1; j < n; j++) {
            double distance = distanceBetween(points[i], points[j]);
            minDistance = min(minDistance, distance);
        }
    }

    return minDistance;
}

double closestPairStrip(const vector<Point>& strip, double minDistance) {
    int n = strip.size();
    double minStripDistance = minDistance;

    for (int i = 0; i < n; i++) {
        for (int j = i + 1; j < min(i + 7, n); j++) {
```

```
            double distance = distanceBetween(strip[i], strip[j]);
            minStripDistance = min(minStripDistance, distance);
        }
    }

    return minStripDistance;
}

double closestPairRec(vector<Point>& points) {
    int n = points.size();

    if (n <= 3) {
        // Base case: Use brute force for small number of points
        return closestPairBruteForce(points);
    }

    // Divide the points into two halves
    int mid = n / 2;
    vector<Point> leftPoints(points.begin(), points.begin() + mid);
    vector<Point> rightPoints(points.begin() + mid, points.end());

    // Recursively find the closest pairs in each half
    double leftClosest = closestPairRec(leftPoints);
    double rightClosest = closestPairRec(rightPoints);

    // Find the minimum distance between the two halves
    double minDistance = min(leftClosest, rightClosest);

    // Merge the results from the two halves
    vector<Point> strip = pointsWithinStrip(points, mid, minDistance);
    return min(minDistance, closestPairStrip(strip, minDistance));
}

vector<Point> pointsWithinStrip(const vector<Point>& points, int mid,
double minDistance) {
    vector<Point> strip;

    for (const Point& point : points) {
        if (abs(point.x - points[mid].x) < minDistance) {
            strip.push_back(point);
        }
    }

    sort(strip.begin(), strip.end(), compareByY);

    return strip;
```

```
}

double closestPair(vector<Point>& points) {
    // Sort points by x-coordinate
    sort(points.begin(), points.end(), compareByX);

    // Call the recursive function
    return closestPairRec(points);
}

int main() {
    // Example usage
    vector<Point> points = {{0, 0}, {1, 1}, {2, 2}, {3, 3}, {4, 4}, {5, 5},
{6, 6}, {7, 7}, {8, 8}, {9, 9}};

    double minDistance = closestPair(points);

    cout << "Closest Pair Distance: " << minDistance << endl;

    return 0;
}
```

Example 5.7: Consider the set of points:

$\{(0,0),(1,1),(2,2),(3,3),(4,4),(5,5),(6,6),(7,7),(8,8),(9,9)\}$

Solution: To solve, follow these steps:

1. **Divide**: The points are sorted by x-coordinate, and the recursive function **closestPairRec** is called.

2. **Base case**: Since there are more than three points, the set is divided into two halves, shown as follows:

    $\{(0,0),(1,1),(2,2),(3,3),(4,4)\}$ and $\{(5,5),(6,6),(7,7),(8,8),(9,9)\}$

3. **Recursive calls**: The recursive calls are made on the left and right halves.

4. **Merge**: The minimum distance between the two halves is found to be 1.4142.

5. **Strip**: Points within the strip of width 2×1.4142 around the middle line are extracted:

    $\{(4,4),(5,5),(6,6)\}$

6. **Closest pair in strip**: The closest pair within the strip is found to be as follows:

    (4,4) and (5,5) with a distance of 1.4142

7. **Final result**: The overall closest pair is determined to be (5,5) with a distance of 1.4142.

Complexity analysis

The complexity analysis is as follows:

- **Time complexity**: The time complexity of the divide and conquer approach for the closest pair of points problem $O(n\log n)$.

- **Space complexity**: The space required for storing the sorted points and intermediate results is $C(n)$.

Applications

The closest pair of points problem has applications in computational geometry, computer graphics, pattern recognition, and robotics. The efficient divide and conquer algorithm is widely used in various applications where finding the closest pair of points is crucial, such as collision detection in computer graphics or robotics path planning.

Maximum subarray sum

The maximum subarray sum problem involves finding the contiguous subarray with the largest sum within a given array of numbers. The divide and conquer approach is commonly employed to efficiently solve this problem. The idea is to recursively divide the array into smaller subarrays, find the maximum subarray sum in each subarray, and then combine the results to determine the overall maximum subarray sum.

Algorithm 5.8: Maximum subarray sum

```
maxSubarraySum(arr, low, high)
   if low equals high
      return arr[low]

   mid = (low + high) / 2

   // Find the maximum subarray sum in the left subarray
   leftMax = maxSubarraySum(arr, low, mid)

   // Find the maximum subarray sum in the right subarray
   rightMax = maxSubarraySum(arr, mid + 1, high)

   // Find the maximum subarray sum crossing the midpoint
   crossMax = maxCrossingSubarraySum(arr, low, mid, high)

   // Return the maximum of the three sums
   return max(leftMax, rightMax, crossMax)

maxCrossingSubarraySum(arr, low, mid, high)
   // Find the maximum subarray sum in the left of the midpoint
```

```
    leftSum = -infinity
    sum = 0
    for i from mid downto low
        sum = sum + arr[i]
        leftSum = max(leftSum, sum)

    // Find the maximum subarray sum in the right of the midpoint
    rightSum = -infinity
    sum = 0
    for i from mid+1 to high
        sum = sum + arr[i]
        rightSum = max(rightSum, sum)

    // Return the sum of the maximum subarray sum in the left and right
    return leftSum + rightSum
```

Program 5.8: Implementation in C++

```cpp
#include <iostream>
#include <limits>

using namespace std;

int maxCrossingSubarraySum(int arr[], int low, int mid, int high) {
    int leftSum = numeric_limits<int>::min();
    int sum = 0;

    for (int i = mid; i >= low; i--) {
        sum += arr[i];
        leftSum = max(leftSum, sum);
    }

    int rightSum = numeric_limits<int>::min();
    sum = 0;

    for (int i = mid + 1; i <= high; i++) {
        sum += arr[i];
        rightSum = max(rightSum, sum);
    }

    return leftSum + rightSum;
}

int maxSubarraySum(int arr[], int low, int high) {
    if (low == high) {
        return arr[low];
```

```
    }

    int mid = (low + high) / 2;

    int leftMax = maxSubarraySum(arr, low, mid);
    int rightMax = maxSubarraySum(arr, mid + 1, high);
    int crossMax = maxCrossingSubarraySum(arr, low, mid, high);

    return max({leftMax, rightMax, crossMax});
}

int main() {
    // Example usage
    int arr[] = {-2, -3, 4, -1, -2, 1, 5, -3};
    int n = sizeof(arr) / sizeof(arr[0]);

    int result = maxSubarraySum(arr, 0, n - 1);

    cout << "Maximum Subarray Sum: " << result << endl;

    return 0;
}
```

Example 5.8: Consider the array: [-2, -3, 4, -1, -2, 1, 5, -3]

Solution: The following steps are involved:

1. **Divide**: The array is divided into two halves: [-2, -3, 4, -1] and [-2, 1, 5, -3].

2. **Recursive calls**: The recursive calls are made to find the maximum subarray sums in the left and right halves.

   Left half: [-2, -3, 4, -1] has a maximum subarray sum of 4.

   Right half: [-2, 1, 5, -3] has a maximum subarray sum of 6.

3. **Combine**: The maximum subarray sum crossing the midpoint is found. The subarray [4, -1, -2, 1, 5] has a sum of 7.

4. **Final result**: The overall maximum subarray sum is the maximum of the left, right, and crossing sums, which is 7.

Complexity analysis

The complexity analysis is as follows:

- **Time complexity**: The time complexity of the divide and conquer approach for the maximum subarray sum problem is $O(n \log n)$.

- **Space complexity**: The space required for recursive function calls is $O(\log n)$.

Applications

The maximum subarray sum problem has applications in various fields, including finance, signal processing, and data analysis. It is commonly used in algorithms for financial portfolio optimization, audio signal processing, and in the analysis of time-series data. Efficient algorithms for finding the maximum subarray sum are essential in solving optimization problems related to resource allocation and signal processing.

Merge-based inversion count

Inversion count refers to the number of pairs of elements in an array that are out of order. The merge-based inversion count algorithm uses a divide and conquer approach to efficiently count inversions in an array. By recursively dividing the array into halves, counting inversions within each half, and then merging the results, this algorithm determines the total number of inversions.

Algorithm 5.9: Inversion count

```
inversionCount(arr, low, high)
   count = 0

   if low < high
      mid = (low + high) / 2

      // Recursively count inversions in the left half
      count += inversionCount(arr, low, mid)

      // Recursively count inversions in the right half
      count += inversionCount(arr, mid + 1, high)

      // Merge the two halves and count inversions
      count += mergeAndCount(arr, low, mid, high)

   return count

mergeAndCount(arr, low, mid, high)
   leftSize = mid - low + 1
   rightSize = high - mid

   // Create temporary arrays for the left and right halves
   leftArr[leftSize], rightArr[rightSize]

   // Copy data to temporary arrays
   for i from 0 to leftSize - 1
      leftArr[i] = arr[low + i]

   for j from 0 to rightSize - 1
```

```
        rightArr[j] = arr[mid + 1 + j]

    i = 0, j = 0, k = low
    count = 0

    // Merge the two halves while counting inversions
    while i < leftSize and j < rightSize
        if leftArr[i] <= rightArr[j]
            arr[k] = leftArr[i]
            i++
        else
            arr[k] = rightArr[j]
            j++
            count += leftSize - i

        k++

    // Copy the remaining elements of leftArr, if any
    while i < leftSize
        arr[k] = leftArr[i]
        i++
        k++

    // Copy the remaining elements of rightArr, if any
    while j < rightSize
        arr[k] = rightArr[j]
        j++
        k++

    return count
```

Program 5.9: Implementation in C++

```cpp
#include <iostream>
#include <vector>

using namespace std;

long long mergeAndCount(vector<int>& arr, int low, int mid, int high) {
    int leftSize = mid - low + 1;
    int rightSize = high - mid;

    // Create temporary arrays for the left and right halves
    vector<int> leftArr(leftSize);
    vector<int> rightArr(rightSize);

    // Copy data to temporary arrays
```

```
    for (int i = 0; i < leftSize; i++)
        leftArr[i] = arr[low + i];

    for (int j = 0; j < rightSize; j++)
        rightArr[j] = arr[mid + 1 + j];

    int i = 0, j = 0, k = low;
    long long count = 0;

    // Merge the two halves while counting inversions
    while (i < leftSize && j < rightSize) {
        if (leftArr[i] <= rightArr[j]) {
            arr[k] = leftArr[i];
            i++;
        } else {
            arr[k] = rightArr[j];
            j++;
            count += leftSize - i;
        }
        k++;
    }

    // Copy the remaining elements of leftArr, if any
    while (i < leftSize) {
        arr[k] = leftArr[i];
        i++;
        k++;
    }

    // Copy the remaining elements of rightArr, if any
    while (j < rightSize) {
        arr[k] = rightArr[j];
        j++;
        k++;
    }

    return count;
}

long long inversionCount(vector<int>& arr, int low, int high) {
    long long count = 0;

    if (low < high) {
        int mid = (low + high) / 2;

        // Recursively count inversions in the left half
```

```
        count += inversionCount(arr, low, mid);

        // Recursively count inversions in the right half
        count += inversionCount(arr, mid + 1, high);

        // Merge the two halves and count inversions
        count += mergeAndCount(arr, low, mid, high);
    }

    return count;
}

int main() {
    // Example usage
    vector<int> arr = {1, 20, 6, 4, 5};

    long long result = inversionCount(arr, 0, arr.size() - 1);

    cout << "Inversion Count: " << result << endl;

    return 0;
}
```

Example 5.9: Consider the array: [1, 20, 6, 4, 5]

Solution: Perform these steps:

1. **Divide**: The array is divided into two halves: [1, 20] and [6, 4, 5].

2. **Recursive calls**: The recursive calls are made to find the inversion count in the left and right halves.

   Left half: [1, 20] has no inversions.

   Right half: [6, 4, 5] has two inversions: (6, 4) and (6, 5).

3. **Merge**: The two halves are merged while counting inversions. The merging step identifies an inversion (20, 6).

4. **Final result**: The overall inversion count is the sum of inversions in the left, right, and merging steps, which is $0 - 2 + 1 = 3$.

Complexity analysis

The complexity analysis is as follows:

- **Time complexity**: The time complexity of the merge-based inversion count algorithm is *O(n logn)*.

- **Space complexity**: The space required for temporary arrays during merging is *O(n)*.

Applications

Inversion count algorithms have applications in various fields, including data analysis, social network analysis, and optimization problems. They are used in scenarios where understanding the degree of disorder or the number of pairwise conflicts is important. For example, in sorting algorithms, inversion count can provide insights into the complexity of sorting an array, and it is also used in applications related to ranking and preference analysis.

Conclusion

The divide and conquer methodology serve as an efficient solution for complex problems because it transforms them into smaller workable components. Through this approach, the algorithm became more efficient and reusable because it maintained the system better while supporting parallel processing. Substructure optimization that uses recursion enables developers to build scalable products that function throughout different domains and application areas. This approach creates an organized framework, which enhances the computational execution as well as algorithm design effectiveness for problem-solving.

Exercise

1. Given an array of 16 elements, how many comparisons are needed to find both the maximum and minimum values using the divide and conquer approach?

2. For two 4×4 matrices, how many multiplications and additions are required using Strassen's matrix multiplication algorithm?

3. Consider an array of size n sorted in descending order and sorted using quick sort with the last element as the pivot.

   a) Derive the recurrence relation for the worst-case time complexity.

   b) Solve for T(n) using the recurrence method.

4. We are going to play the game of smaller, bigger. The goal is to guess a number between 1 and n (integer). We consider that the algorithm takes as input the value of n and the number x to guess, and that it returns the number of moves to find this number.

   a) State the problem more formally.

   b) Write the iterative algorithm solving this problem.

   c) Write the algorithm recursive solving this problem.

   d) Compare complexities.

CHAPTER 6
Greedy Algorithms

Introduction

In this chapter of the book, we will discuss greedy algorithms and their utility in the field of computer science engineering. The basic idea behind greedy algorithms is to make the best choice at each step without considering the overall consequences or future steps. This means that at each decision point, the algorithm selects the option that appears to be the best choice at that moment, without considering the potential impact on future decisions. Despite their limitations, greedy algorithms are widely used in various applications such as scheduling, minimum spanning trees, shortest path algorithms, and more, due to their simplicity and efficiency. Therefore, greedy algorithms make locally optimal choices at each step to construct a globally optimal solution. While they do not guarantee the absolute best solution, they are often used when finding an optimal solution is either computationally expensive or unnecessary.

Structure

The greedy algorithm chapter covers the following topics:

- Introduction to greedy algorithms
- General method
- Fractional knapsack problem
- Minimum cost spanning tree via Kruskal algorithm

- Minimum cost spanning tree via Prim's algorithm
- Huffman coding
- Optimal merge pattern
- Interval scheduling
- Activity selection problem
- Job scheduling problem

Objectives

The primary objective of a greedy algorithm is to find an optimal solution to an optimization problem by making a series of locally optimal choices at each step, with the aim of eventually reaching a globally optimal solution. This entails selecting the best possible choice available at each decision point without considering the consequences of those choices on future steps. The goal is to iteratively build up a solution that incrementally improves upon the previous ones, ultimately leading to a solution that is optimal or close to optimal for the entire problem. Greedy algorithms prioritize immediate gains and rely on the hope that these locally optimal choices will culminate in the best possible outcome. However, it is important to note that while greedy algorithms are often efficient and simple to implement, they do not guarantee an optimal solution for all problems, and careful consideration is necessary to ensure their effectiveness in specific contexts.

Introduction to greedy algorithms

Greedy algorithms are a class of algorithms used for solving optimization problems. Unlike dynamic programming, which may solve the problem by considering all possible solutions and choosing the best one, greedy algorithms make a series of choices at each step with the hope that these locally optimal choices will lead to a globally optimal solution. One of the key characteristics of greedy algorithms is that they are generally efficient and simple to implement. However, they do not always guarantee an optimal solution for every problem. In some cases, a greedy algorithm may produce a suboptimal solution that is close to the optimal solution but not exactly the best one. Therefore, it is important to carefully analyze the problem and ensure that the greedy approach is appropriate and yields the desired results.

Thus, a choice made at each step in the greedy method should be:

- **Feasible**: Choice should satisfy problem constraints.

- **Locally optimal**: The best solution from all feasible solutions at the current stage should be selected.

- **Irrevocable**: Once the choice is made, it cannot be altered, i.e., if a feasible solution is selected (rejected) in step 1, it cannot be rejected (selected) in subsequent stages.

Characteristics of greedy algorithms

Problems that can be solved using the greedy method generally possess the following two properties:

- **Greedy choice property**: The global optimal solution is found by selecting locally optimal choices, or the ones that appear to be the best at the time. If the choice is feasible, include it in the solution set and reduce the problem by the same amount. The current decision may be influenced by prior decisions, but it is independent of future decisions.

- **Optimal substructure**: We say that the given problem exhibits optimal substructure if the optimal solution to the given problem contains the optimal solution to its sub-problems too. In a problem that possesses the optimal substructure, the next best choice always leads to an optimal solution.

General method

The general method of a greedy algorithm involves making the locally optimal choice at each step with the hope that it will lead to a globally optimal solution.

Algorithm 6.1: Algorithm of the general approach for the greedy method

1. **Initialization**: Begin with an empty solution set or an initial solution.

2. **Selection**: At each step, choose the best available option without considering the consequences of this choice on future steps. This choice is based on a specific criterion or heuristic.

3. **Feasibility check**: Ensure that the chosen option does not violate any constraints or rules.

4. **Acceptance**: If the chosen option meets the criteria or improves the solution, add it to the solution set.

5. **Termination**: Repeat steps 2 to 4 until a solution is found or the problem is solved satisfactorily.

6. **Optimization (optional)**: Sometimes, additional steps are taken to optimize the solution further if needed.

The key characteristic of greedy algorithms is that they make decisions based solely on the current state of the problem without considering future consequences. This can lead to suboptimal solutions in some cases, but in many situations, greedy algorithms are efficient and provide acceptable solutions.

Fractional knapsack problem

In the context of a collection of items characterized by weight and profit values, the objective is to optimize the cumulative profit by strategically choosing items to fit into a knapsack, considering its constrained capacity. Unlike the conventional knapsack dilemma, where entire items must be selected, the fractional knapsack conundrum allows for breaking items into fractions to enhance the total value achieved.

Working of the fractional knapsack problem

The working of the fractional knapsack problem is as follows:

- **Given**: A list of items, each item represented as a pair of (profit, weight). Additionally, the capacity of the knapsack (W) is known.

- **Goal**: Optimize the selection of items to maximize the cumulative profit while ensuring that the total weight does not surpass W.

- **Greedy strategy**: Compute the profit-to-weight ratio for each item and arrange the items in descending order based on this ratio.

- **Process**:
    1. Begin with an empty knapsack.
    2. For every item in the sorted sequence:
        a. If the item's weight fits within the remaining capacity, include it entirely.
        b. Otherwise, add a fraction of the item to occupy the remaining capacity.
    3. Continue until the knapsack reaches full capacity or all items are considered.

- **Result**: The total profit attained.

Arrange the packages in descending order based on their unit cost *(vi/wi)*, shown as follows:

$$\frac{v_1}{w_1} \geq \frac{v_2}{w_2} \geq \cdots \geq \frac{v_n}{w_n}$$

Sequentially examine the arranged packages; place the current package into the knapsack if the remaining capacity allows it (ensuring that the combined weight of the already placed packages and the weight of the current package does not surpass the knapsack's capacity).

Selection of the packages

To select the packages, review the array of unit costs and opt for packages based on decreasing unit costs, shown as follows:

$$C = \left(\frac{v_1}{w_1}, \dots, \frac{v_n}{w_n}\right)$$

Let us assume you found a temporary solution: $(x1, \dots, xi)$.

The value of the knapsack is obtained as follows:

$$\text{TotalValue} = \sum_{j=1}^{i} x_j\, v_j = TotalValue + x_j v_j$$

Corresponding to the weight of packages that have been put into the knapsack, the total weight is calculated as follows:

$$\text{TotalWeight} = \sum_{j=1}^{i} x_j\, w_j = TotalWeight + x_j w_j$$

Therefore, the remaining weight limit of the knapsack is:

$$M - \text{TotalWeight} = M - \sum_{j=1}^{i} x_j\, w_j$$

Procedure

The steps involved are as follows:

1. The root node denotes the knapsack's initial state, where no packages have been selected yet.

    TotalValue = 0.

    The upper bound of the root node, *UpperBound,* equals M multiplied by the maximum unit cost.

2. The root node will generate child nodes corresponding to the option of selecting the package with the highest unit cost. For each node, recalculations are made for the parameters as follows:

    a. *TotalValue = Previous TotalValue + number of selected packages * value of each package*

    b. *M = Previous M - number of selected packages * weight of each package*

    c. *UpperBound = TotalValue + New M * The unit cost of the next package to be considered*

3. In the child nodes, priority is given to branching from the node with the higher upper bound. The child nodes of this branch correspond to selecting the next

package with the highest unit cost. The parameters *TotalValue*, *M*, and *UpperBound* must be recalculated for each node using the formula mentioned in *Step 2*.

4. *Step 3* is repeated with the caveat that nodes with upper bounds lower than or equal to the temporary maximum cost of an option found do not need further branching.

5. If all nodes are branched or cut off, the most valuable option is identified.

Algorithm 6.2: Algorithm of fractional knapsack using greedy method

```
Initialize an array called "cost" with the same size as V.
For i from 1 to the size of V, calculate cost[i] = V[i] / W[i].
Sort the array "cost" in descending order.
Initialize a variable i to 1.
While i is less than or equal to the size of V:
    a. If W[i] is less than or equal to M:
        - Decrease M by W[i].
        - Add V[i] to the total.
    b. If W[i] is greater than M, move to the next index (i = i + 1).
```

Example 6.1: Let us consider data items having the following parameter values:

I1: Profit is 60, and weight is 10

I2: Profit is 100, and weight is 20

I3: Profit is 120, and weight is 30

Additionally, the capacity of the knapsack is 50.

Solution: Perform these steps:

1. Sort the given data according to the profit-to-weight ratio.

2. Completely add I1, having a weight of 10, and I2, having a weight of 20.

3. Now, examine the remaining knapsack capacity. It is 20, so add 2/3 portion of I3, i.e., 20 units.

4. Final profit is $= 60 + 100 + 120*(2/3) = 240$

Program 6.1: Implementation of fractional knapsack

```cpp
#include <bits/stdc++.h>
using namespace std;
struct Item {
    int profit, weight;
    Item(int p, int w) {
        profit = p;
        weight = w;
```

```
    }
};
static bool cmp(struct Item a, struct Item b) {
    double r1 = (double)a.profit / (double)a.weight;
    double r2 = (double)b.profit / (double)b.weight;
    return r1 > r2;
}
double fractionalKnapsack(int W, struct Item arr[], int N) {
    sort(arr, arr + N, cmp);
    // Rest of the implementation...
    // Return the maximum profit achieved.
    :
// Example usage:
int main() {
    Item items[] = {{60, 10}, {100, 20}, {120, 30}};
    int knapsackCapacity = 50;
    double result = fractionalKnapsack(knapsackCapacity, items, 3);
    cout << "Maximum profit: " << result << endl;
    return 0;
}
```

Complexity of the fractional knapsack problem

The time complexity of the fractional knapsack problem hinges on the choice of sorting algorithm employed to arrange items by their value-to-weight ratios. Typically, common sorting algorithms like quick sort or heap sort are utilized, both boasting an average time complexity of *O(n log n)*, where *n* represents the number of items.

Following the sorting process, the greedy approach is applied to pick items based on their value-to-weight ratios until the knapsack reaches its capacity. This greedy strategy entails iterating through the sorted list of items once, resulting in a time complexity of *O(n)*.

Consequently, the overall time complexity of the fractional knapsack problem is chiefly determined by the sorting algorithm's time complexity, yielding an overall complexity of *O(n log n)*.

Minimum cost spanning tree via Kruskal algorithm

This algorithm serves as a fundamental technique within graph theory aimed at discovering a minimum-weight spanning tree for a weighted, connected, undirected graph. A **minimum spanning tree (MST)** is a tree encompassing all vertices of the graph while minimizing the cumulative sum of edge weights. Kruskal's algorithm adopts a greedy strategy to progressively construct the MST. The operational sequence is as follows:

1. **Sorting edges**: Commence by arranging all edges of the given graph in ascending order based on their weights. This step ensures the initiation with edges possessing the smallest weights.

2. **Adding edges to MST**: Initialize an empty MST. Continuously append edges and nodes to the MST if the newly included edge does not create a cycle. If the edge results in a cycle, discard it.

3. **Iterate**: Iterate through this procedure until the spanning tree comprises (*V-1*) edges, where *V* denotes the number of vertices in the graph.

4. **Union-find algorithm**: Kruskal's algorithm employs the union-find data structure to identify cycles. The union-find algorithm aids in determining whether the addition of an edge would lead to a cycle in the MST.

5. **Greedy choice**: At each step, Kruskal's algorithm makes a locally optimal selection to derive the overall optimal solution. It chooses the edge with the smallest weight that avoids creating a cycle in the constructed MST thus far.

Example 6.2: Let us assume the input graph having 9 V and 12 E as per the following table:

Weight value	Source node	Destination
1	7	6
2	8	2
2	6	5
4	0	1
4	2	5
6	8	6
7	7	8
8	0	7
9	3	4
10	5	4
11	1	7
14	3	5

Table 6.1: Table contains weights of edges from source to destination

Solution: The MST formed will comprise eight edges, as indicated by the equation (*9 - 1 = 8*). Let us proceed through the following steps:

1. **Select edge 7-6**: No cycle detected, so it is included.

2. **Choose edge 8-2**: No cycle detected, so it is included.

3. **Opt for edge 6-5**: No cycle detected, so it is included.

4. **Select edge 0-1**: No cycle detected, so it is included.

5. **Opt for edge 2-5**: No cycle detected, so it is included.

6. **Choose edge 8-6**: It forms a cycle, so it is discarded. Instead, pick edge 2-3: Include it.

7. **Select edge 7-8**: It forms a cycle, so it is discarded. Instead, pick edge 0-7: Include it.

8. **Choose edge 1-2**: It forms a cycle, so it is discarded. Instead, pick edge 3-4: Include it.

The resulting MST comprises the following edges: 7-6, 8-2, 6-5, 0-1, 2-5, 2-3, 0-7, and 3-4. It is important to note that the number of edges included in the MST equals (*V-1*), where *V* represents the number of vertices in the graph. Kruskal's algorithm efficiently identifies the minimum cost spanning tree, rendering it a valuable tool in network design, transportation planning, and various other applications.

Algorithm 6.3: Kruskal's algorithm for MST

```
Initialize with parameters (E, cost, n, t)
Let E be the set of edges in graph G, which consists of n vertices. The
cost[u, v] represents the cost of edge (u, v), and 't' denotes the set of
edges in the minimum-cost spanning tree. The function returns the final cost
as follows:
{
Create a heap from the edge costs using heapify;
for i := 1 to n do parent[i] := -1; // Assign each vertex to a different
set.
i := 0;
mincost := 0.0;
while ((i < n - 1) and (heap is not empty)) do
{
Remove a minimum-cost edge (u, v) from the heap and re-heapify using
Adjust;
j := Find(u);
k := Find(v);
if (j ≠ k) then
{
i := i + 1;
t[i, 1] := u;
t[i, 2] := v;
```

```
mincost := mincost + cost[u, v];
Union(j, k);
}
}
if (i ≠ n-1) then
write("no spanning tree");
else
return mincost;
}
```

Program 6.2: Implementation of Kruskal's algorithm for MST

```cpp
#include <iostream>
#include <vector>
#include <algorithm>
using namespace std;
// Structure to represent an edge
struct Edge {
    int src, dest, weight;
};
// Structure to represent a graph
class Graph {
public:
    int V, E;
    vector<Edge> edges;
    Graph(int V, int E) {
        this->V = V;
        this->E = E;
    }
    // Add an edge to the graph
    void addEdge(int src, int dest, int weight) {
        Edge edge;
        edge.src = src;
        edge.dest = dest;
        edge.weight = weight;
        edges.push_back(edge);
    }
    // Find operation for disjoint set
    int find(vector<int>& parent, int i) {
        if (parent[i] == -1)
```

```
                return i;
            return find(parent, parent[i]);
    }
    // Union operation for disjoint set
    void Union(vector<int>& parent, int x, int y) {
        int xset = find(parent, x);
        int yset = find(parent, y);
        parent[xset] = yset;
    }
    // Kruskal's algorithm to find MST
    void KruskalMST() {
        vector<Edge> result; // This will store the MST
        int i = 0; // Index used to pick next edge
        // Step 1: Sort all the edges in non-decreasing order of their
weight
        sort(edges.begin(), edges.end(), [](const Edge& a, const Edge& b) {
            return a.weight < b.weight;
        });
        // Allocate memory for creating V subsets
        vector<int> parent(V, -1);
        // Number of edges to be taken is equal to V-1
        while (result.size() < V - 1 && i < E) {
            Edge next_edge = edges[i++];
            int x = find(parent, next_edge.src);
            int y = find(parent, next_edge.dest);
            // If including this edge does not cause cycle, include it
            if (x != y) {
                result.push_back(next_edge);
                Union(parent, x, y);
            }
        }
        // Print the contents of result[] to display the built MST
        cout << "Edges in MST:\n";
        for (i = 0; i < result.size(); ++i)
            cout << result[i].src << " - " << result[i].dest << "  Weight:
" << result[i].weight << endl;
    }
};
int main() {
```

```
    // Example usage
    int V = 4; // Number of vertices
    int E = 5; // Number of edges
    Graph graph(V, E);
    // Adding edges to the graph
    graph.addEdge(0, 1, 10);
    graph.addEdge(0, 2, 6);
    graph.addEdge(0, 3, 5);
    graph.addEdge(1, 3, 15);
    graph.addEdge(2, 3, 4);
    // Finding minimum spanning tree
    graph.KruskalMST();
    return 0;
}
```

Complexity of Kruskal's algorithm

The time complexity of Kruskal's algorithm is primarily influenced by the sorting of edges and the operations performed on the disjoint-set data structure. The breakdown is as follows:

- **Sorting edges**: Sorting all edges takes $O(E \log E)$ time, where E is the number of edges in the graph.

- **Disjoint-set operations**:

  o Initializing the disjoint-set data structure takes $O(V)$ time, where V is the number of vertices.

  o Each find operation (to find the representative element of a set) and union operation (to merge two sets) takes nearly constant time. However, due to path compression and union by rank optimizations, the amortized time complexity for each of these operations is close to $O(1)$.

- **Iteration through edges**: Iterating through sorted edges and performing disjoint-set operations takes $O(E)$ time in the worst case.

Overall, the time complexity of Kruskal's algorithm is dominated by the sorting step, resulting in $O(E \log E)$ time complexity. Since E is typically upper-bounded by $O(V^2)$ in a dense graph and $O(V)$ in a sparse graph, the time complexity can be expressed as $O(E \log V)$ or $O(V^2 \log V)$ depending on the graph's characteristics.

The space complexity is dominated by the disjoint-set data structure, requiring $O(V)$ space for storing parent and rank arrays. Additionally, the sorted list of edges may require $O(E)$ space. Therefore, the total space complexity is $O(V + E)$.

Minimum cost spanning tree via Prim's algorithm

Prim's algorithm, a greedy approach utilized for discovering the MST within a connected, weighted graph, operates as follows:

1. **Initialization**:

    a. Commence with an empty spanning tree.

    b. Select an arbitrary vertex as the starting point.

2. **Core procedure**:

    a. While there remain vertices not yet encompassed in the MST (referred to as fringe vertices):

    b. Identify edges linking any tree vertex with the fringe vertices.

    c. Choose the edge with the minimum weight from these connections.

    d. Incorporate the selected edge into the MST if it doesn't create a cycle.

Iterate through step 2 until the complete spanning tree is obtained.

The advantages of Prim's algorithm are as follows:

- Ensures the discovery of the MST in a connected, weighted graph.

- Demonstrates a time complexity of $O(E \log V)$ when employing a binary heap or Fibonacci heap, where E represents the number of edges and V signifies the number of vertices.

Algorithm 6.4: Prim's algorithm for MST

```
Initialize with parameters (E, cost, n, t)
// Let E denote the set of edges in graph G. The cost [1: n, 1: n]
represents the cost adjacency matrix of an n-vertex graph, where cost [i,
j] is either a positive real number or infinity if no edge (i, j) exists.
A minimum spanning tree is calculated and stored as a set of edges in the
array t [1: n-1, 1: 2]. Each entry (t [i, 1], t [i, 2]) represents an edge
in the minimum-cost spanning tree. The final cost is then returned.
{
Let (k, 1) be an edge of minimum cost in E;
mincost := cost [k, 1];
t [1, 1] := k;
t [1, 2] := 1;
for i := 1 to n do // Initialize near
{
if (cost [i, 1] < cost [i, k]) then
```

```
near [i] := 1;
else
near [i] := k;
near [k] := near [l] := 0;
}
for i := 2 to n - 1 do // Find n - 2 additional edges for t.
{
Let j be an index such that near [j] != 0 and cost [j, near [j]] is
minimum;
t [i, 1] := j;
t [i, 2] := near [j];
mincost := mincost + cost [j, near [j]];
near [j] := 0;
}
for k := 1 to n do // Update near[].
{
if ((near [k] != 0) and (cost [k, near [k]] > cost [k, j])) then
near [k] := j;
}
return mincost;
}
```

Program 6.3: Implementation of Prim's algorithm for MST

```cpp
#include <cstring>
#include <iostream>
using namespace std;
#define INF 9999999
// number of vertices in graph
#define V 5
// create a 2d array of size 5x5
//for adjacency matrix to represent graph
int G[V][V] = {
  {0, 9, 75, 0, 0},
  {9, 0, 95, 19, 42},
  {75, 95, 0, 51, 66},
  {0, 19, 51, 0, 31},
  {0, 42, 66, 31, 0}};
int main() {
  int no_edge;  // number of edge
  // create a array to track selected vertex selected will become true
otherwise false
  int selected[V];
```

```
  // set selected false initially
  memset(selected, false, sizeof(selected));
  // set number of edge to 0
  no_edge = 0;
  // the number of egde in minimum spanning tree will be always less than
(V -1), where V is number of vertices in graph
  // choose 0th vertex and make it true
  selected[0] = true;
  int x;  //  row number
  int y;  //  col number
  // print for edge and weight
  cout << "Edge' << " : "<< "Weight";
  cout << endl;
  while (no_edge < V - 1) {
    //For every vertex in the set S, find the all-adjacent vertices,
calculate the distance from the vertex selected at step 1.
    // if the vertex is already in the set S, discard it otherwise choose
another vertex nearest to selected vertex  at step 1.
    int min = INF;
    x = 0;
    y = 0;
    for (int i = 0; i < V; i++) {
      if (selected[i]) {
        for (int j = 0; j < V; j++) {
          if (!selected[j] && G[i][j]) {  // not in selected and there is
an edge
            if (min > G[i][j]) {
              min = G[i][j];
              x = i;
              y = j;
            }
          }
        }
      }
    }
    cout << x << " - " << y << " :   " << G[x][y];
    cout << endl;
    selected[y] = true;
    no_edge++;
  }
  return 0;
}
```

Complexity of Prim's algorithm

The time complexity of Prim's algorithm varies depending on the data structures utilized for implementation and their respective implementations. Primarily, it can be implemented using either a priority queue or an adjacency matrix/adjacency list combined with arrays or heaps. The analysis is as follows:

- **Priority queue implementation**: In this approach, each vertex is added to the priority queue at most once, and each edge is processed at most once. Inserting and updating the priority queue operations take $O(log\ V)$ time, where V is the number of vertices. Thus, the time complexity using a priority queue *is* $O((V + E)\ log\ V)$, where E is the number of edges.

- **Arrays or heaps implementation**: Using arrays or heaps for maintaining the priority queue, updating the priorities might take $O(V)$ or $O(log\ V)$ time, respectively. Consequently, the overall time complexity using this approach would be $O(V^2)$ or $O(V\ log\ V)$, depending on the data structure chosen.

- **Adjacency matrix representation**: If the graph is represented using an adjacency matrix, finding the minimum weight edge adjacent to each vertex takes $O(V^2)$ time. Therefore, the total time complexity would be dominated by this step, resulting in $O(V^2)$.

- **Adjacency list with heap implementation**: When the graph is represented using an adjacency list and a heap (priority queue), finding the minimum weight edge adjacent to each vertex can be accomplished in $O(log\ V)$ time (assuming a binary heap). Since each edge is processed exactly once, the overall time complexity would be $O((V + E)\ log\ V)$.

In summary, the time complexity of Prim's algorithm is generally $O((V + E)\ log\ V)$ if a priority queue is used and $O(V^{\wedge}2)$ or $O(V\ log\ V)$ if arrays or heaps are employed, respectively. The choice of data structures significantly influences the algorithm's performance.

Regarding space complexity, it typically ranges from $O(V)$ to $O(V^{\wedge}2)$, contingent on the selected data structures and graph representation.

Huffman coding

Another utilization of the greedy algorithm manifests in file compression.

Consider a scenario where we possess a file containing only the characters a, e, i, s, t, spaces, and newline characters. The frequencies of appearance for these characters are as follows: 10 occurrences of a, 15 occurrences of e, 12 occurrences of i, 3 occurrences of s, 4 occurrences of t, 13 spaces, and 1 newline.

Utilizing a standard coding scheme, wherein 3 bits are allocated for each character, the file containing 58 characters necessitates 174 bits for representation. This encoding scheme is delineated in the following table:

Character	Code	Frequency	Total bits
A	000	10	30
E	001	15	45
I	010	12	36
S	011	3	9
T	100	4	12
Space	101	13	39
Newline	110	1	3

Table 6.2: Encoding scheme of characters

Expressed through a binary tree structure, the binary code corresponding to each alphabet is outlined as follows:

To determine the representation of each character, commence at the root and record the pathway. Employ a 0 to denote the left branch and a 1 to denote the right branch. If a character, denoted as ci, exists at a depth di and appears fi times, the code's cost is equivalent to the summation of *di* multiplied by *fi* ($\sum di\, fi$).

Consequently, with this representation, the total number of bits sums up to *3x10 + 3x15 + 3x12 + 3x3 + 3x4 + 3x13 + 3x1 = 174.*

An improved code can be achieved with the subsequent representation:

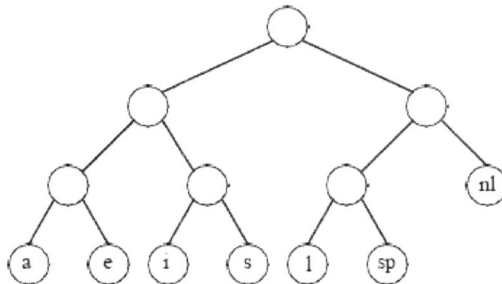

Figure 6.1: Binary tree structure

Algorithm 6.5: Huffman's algorithm using the greedy approach

Huffman's algorithm can be outlined as follows:

- A forest of trees is preserved, where each tree's weight equals the total frequency sum of its leaves.

- When the total number of characters is c, this process is iterated *c-1* times.

- During each iteration, the two trees, T1 and T2, with the smallest weights are selected, and a new tree is constructed incorporating these two subtrees.

- By continuously repeating this process, we eventually attain an optimal Huffman coding tree.

Example 6.3: Let us assume the initial forest with the weight value of each tree is as follows:

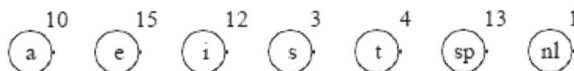

Figure 6.2: Initial forest with weight value

Solution: After merging the two trees with the least weight, a forest is formed. Following the initial merge in the Huffman algorithm, where a new root, denoted as T1, is created, the process is as follows: The total weight of the resulting tree equals the combined weights of the original trees, shown as follows:

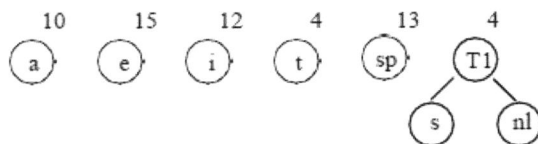

Figure 6.3: T1 tree structure

Once more, we pick the two trees with the lowest weights. In this case, these are T1 and t, which are then combined into a fresh tree having T2 as its root and a weight of 8, shown as follows:

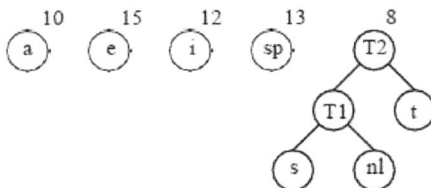

Figure 6.4: T2 tree structure

In the subsequent step, we merge T2 and a to form T3, with a weight of *10+8=18*. The outcome of this operation is shown in the following figure:

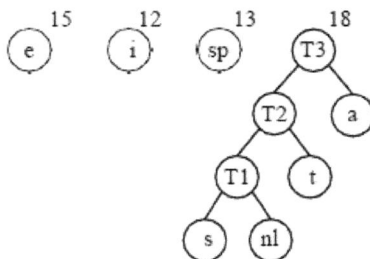

Figure 6.5: T3 tree structure

Following the third merge, the two trees with the lowest weights are the individual node trees representing i and the blank space, as shown in the following figure; these trees are combined to form a new tree with the root denoted as T4:

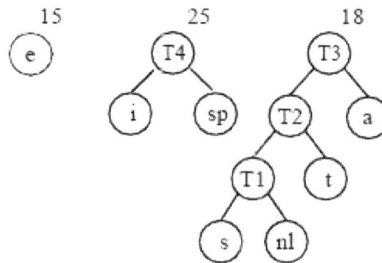

Figure 6.6: T4 tree structure

The fifth step involves merging the trees with roots e and T3. The outcome of this step is as follows:

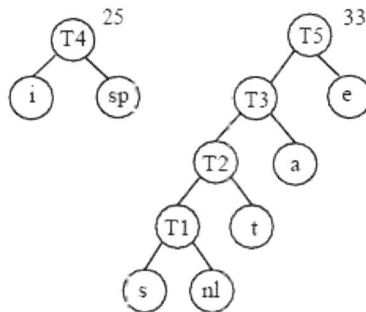

Figure 6.7: T5 tree structure

Ultimately, the optimal tree is achieved by merging the two remaining trees. The optimal tree, with root denoted as T6, is depicted in the following figure:

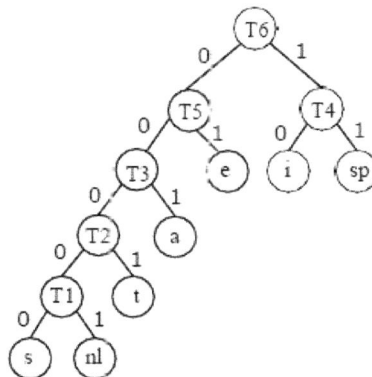

Figure 6.8: Final Huffman tree structure

Table 6.3 shows the final encoding schemes for these characters. The complete binary tree with the lowest total cost, where all characters are found in the leaves, requires only 146 bits.

Character	Code	Frequency	Total bits (Code bits X frequency)
A	001	10	30
E	01	15	30
I	10	12	24
S	00000	3	15
T	0001	4	16
Space	11	13	26
New line	00001	1	5
Total:		146	

Table 6.3: Final encoding scheme of characters

Complexity of the Huffman coding algorithm

The time and space complexities of Huffman coding are influenced by various factors, such as the length of the input text, character distribution, and implementation specifics. A general insight into its complexity is as follows:

- **Time complexity**:
  - **Building the Huffman tree**: This involves iterating through the frequency map of characters and constructing a priority queue, which usually takes $O(n \log n)$ time, where n represents the number of unique characters in the text.

  - **Generating Huffman codes**: Traversing the Huffman tree to derive Huffman codes for each character requires $O(n)$ time, where n is the count of unique characters.

  - **Encoding and decoding**: Performing encoding and decoding for each character in the input text using Huffman codes consumes $O(m)$ time, where m denotes the length of the input text.

  In total, the time complexity of Huffman coding stands at $O(n \log n + m)$, where n denotes the count of unique characters and m signifies the length of the input text.

- **Space complexity**:
  - **Building the Huffman tree**: The priority queue utilized for constructing the Huffman tree occupies $O(n)$ space, where n denotes the number of unique characters.

o **Huffman tree**: The space requirement for storing the Huffman tree relies on its size, which is proportional to the number of characters in the input text.

o **Huffman codes**: The space needed to store Huffman codes for each character varies based on the code lengths, typically ranging from $O(1)$ to $O(\log n)$, where n represents the count of unique characters.

Overall, the space complexity of Huffman coding amounts to $O(n + m)$, where n represents the count of unique characters and m signifies the length of the input text.

Optimal merge pattern

When presented with n sorted files, numerous methods exist to merge them pairwise into a single sorted file. Since various pairings entail different computational time requirements, our aim is to identify an optimal approach, specifically, one necessitating the fewest comparisons, to pairwise merge n sorted files. This process is commonly referred to as a 2-way merge pattern. Combining an n-record file with an m-record file may involve up to $n + m$ record movements. The straightforward strategy involves merging the two smallest files together at each step. These 2-way merge patterns can be depicted using binary merge trees.

Algorithm 6.6: Generation of 2-way merge tree

```
struct tree_node
{
tree_node * lchild; tree_node * rchild;
};
Algorithm TREE (n)
// list is a global of n single node binary trees
{
for i := 1 to n - 1 do
{
pt ß new tree_node
(pt -> lchild) ß least (list); // merge two trees with smallest lengths
(pt -> rchild) ß least (list);
(pt -> weight) ß ((pt -> lchild) -> weight) + ((pt -> rchild) -> weight);
insert (list, pt);
}
return least (list); // The tree left in list is the merge tree
}
```

Example 6.4: Let us consider three sorted files, denoted as X1, X2, and X3, containing 30, 20, and 10 records, respectively.

Solution: The merging of these files can proceed as outlined in the following table:

S. No.	First merging	Record moves in the first merging	Second merging	Record moves in the second merging	Total no. of records moves
1.	X1 and X2 = T1	50	T1 and X3	60	50 + 60 = 110
2.	X2 and X3 = T1	30	T1 and X1	60	30 + 60 = 90

Table 6.4: Merging of files using optimal merge pattern

The second case is optimal.

Example 6.5: Given five files (X1, X2, X3, X4, X5) with sizes (20, 30, 10, 5, 30), employ the greedy rule to determine the optimal method for pairwise merging, resulting in an optimal solution represented by a binary merge tree.

Solution: *Figure 6.9* represents the initial case of file records with their size in the nodes.

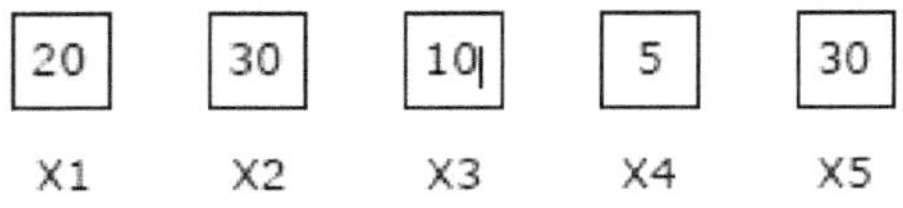

Figure 6.9: Initial case of files

Merge X4 and X3 to get 15 record moves. Call this Z1, illustrated as follows:

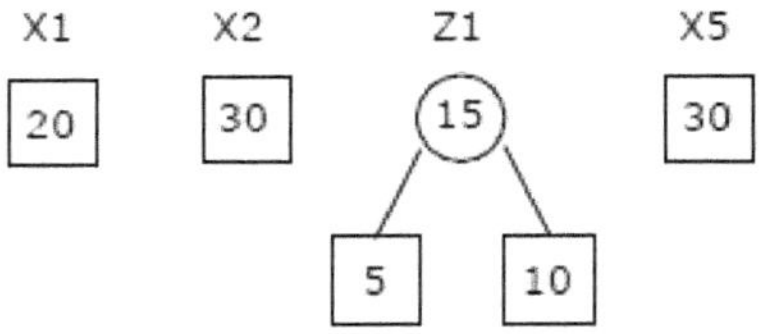

Figure 6.10: Merging of files in iteration 1

Merge Z1 and X1 to get 35 record moves. Call this Z2, as shown in the following figure:

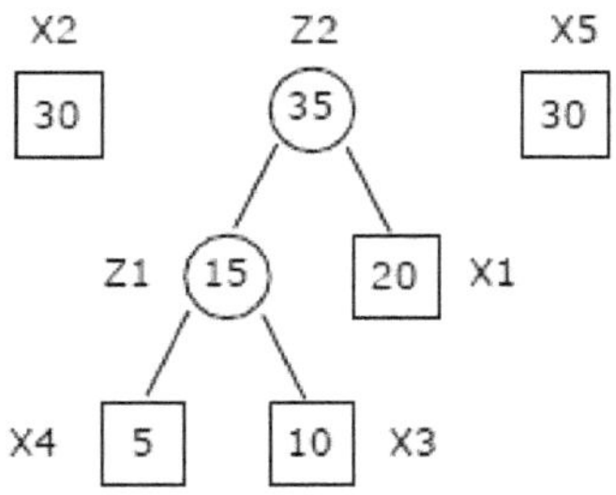

Figure 6.11: Merging of files in iteration 2

Merge X2 and X5 to get 60 record moves. Call this Z3, depicted in the following figure:

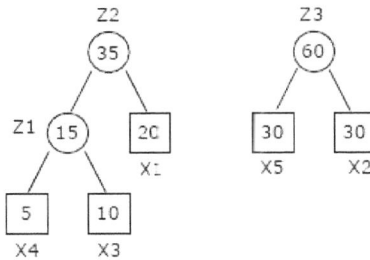

Figure 6.12: Merging of files in iteration 3

Merge Z2 and Z3 to get 95 record moves. This is the answer. Call this Z4, shown as follows:

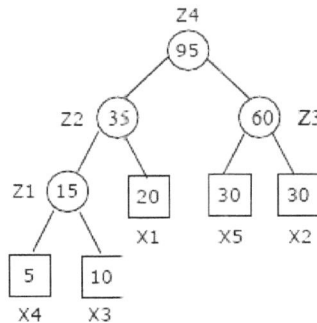

Figure 6.13: Final optimal merge pattern

Therefore, the total number of record moves is $15 + 35 + 60 + 95 = 205$. This is an optimal merge pattern for the given problem.

Program 6.4: Implementation of the optimal merge pattern

```
#include <iostream>
#include <queue>
#include <vector>
using namespace std;
// Function to find the minimum computations required to merge sorted arrays
int optimalMergePattern(vector<int>& arr) {
    // Create a priority queue to store the sizes of the sorted arrays
    priority_queue<int, vector<int>, greater<int>> pq(arr.begin(), arr.
end());
    int totalComputations = 0;
    // Merge the sorted arrays until there's only one array left
    while (pq.size() > 1) {
        // Extract the two smallest arrays
```

```
        int first = pq.top();
        pq.pop();
        int second = pq.top();
        pq.pop();
        // Merge the two arrays and update the total computations
        int mergedSize = first + second;
        totalComputations += mergedSize;
        // Add the merged array back to the priority queue
        pq.push(mergedSize);
    }

    return totalComputations;
}
int main() {
    // Example usage
    vector<int> arr = {4, 3, 2, 6};
    int minComputations = optimalMergePattern(arr);
    cout << "Minimum computations required: " << minComputations << endl;
    return 0;
}
```

Complexity of the optimal merge pattern algorithm

The time and space complexities of the optimal merge pattern algorithm are contingent on the implementation specifics, particularly the method employed for the merging process. The following is a breakdown of the complexity:

- **Time complexity**:

  o **Building the priority queue**: The initial construction of the priority queue from the input vector of array sizes demands $O(n \log n)$ time, where n represents the number of arrays.

  o **Merging arrays**: Within each iteration of the while loop, two arrays of minimum sizes are extracted from the priority queue and merged. Given the use of a priority queue, extracting the two minimum elements and inserting the merged array back into the priority queue necessitates $O(\log n)$ time, where n denotes the count of arrays in the priority queue.

  Overall, the time complexity of the algorithm is chiefly influenced by the sorting phase, resulting in $O(n \log n)$ time complexity, where n signifies the number of arrays.

- **Space complexity**:

  o **Priority queue**: The space allocation required for storing the priority queue depends on the count of arrays, amounting to $O(n)$.

  Overall, the space complexity of the algorithm is $O(n)$.

Interval scheduling

Provided a collection of N events, each characterized by its start and end times, our objective is to devise a schedule that accommodates the maximum number of events. However, the caveat lies in the fact that we cannot choose an event partially; it is an all-or-nothing proposition.

There exist several greedy algorithms capable of addressing this challenge. Let us explore a few of them.

Algorithm 6.7.1: Choosing the shortest events

The primary concept involves selecting the shortest events initially.

Nonetheless, this strategy does not consistently produce the optimal solution. For instance, contemplate the subsequent events:

- **Event A**: Commences at 1 and concludes at 5.
- **Event B**: Commences at 3 and concludes at 6.
- **Event C**: Commences at 4 and concludes at 7.

If we opt for the shortest events, we would only select one (either A or B), thereby overlooking the opportunity to select both B and C.

Algorithm 6.7.2: Selecting the earliest start time

Another method involves consistently choosing the subsequent event that begins at the earliest possible time.

Although effective in certain scenarios, this approach falters in others. Consider the following instance:

- **Event D**: Commences at 1 and concludes at 4.
- **Event E**: Commences at 3 and concludes at 6.
- **Event F**: Commences at 5 and concludes at 7.

Adhering to this strategy would lead to selecting only D, thereby overlooking both E and F.

Algorithm 6.7.3: Opt for the earliest end time (optimal)

The most efficient greedy algorithm entails selecting the subsequent event that concludes at the earliest possible time.

This strategy unfailingly yields an optimal solution.

Contemplate the outcome of selecting an event that concludes later than the earliest-ending event, in such a case:

- We would have an equal number of choices for the subsequent event.

- Consequently, opting for an event with a later conclusion time can never result in an improved solution.

Hence, this greedy algorithm guarantees an optimal schedule.

Note: Keep in mind that these algorithms serve as tools within our problem-solving repertoire. Depending on the particular context and constraints, we can select the most appropriate approach.

Program 6.5: Implementation of the interval scheduling algorithm

```cpp
#include <iostream>
#include <vector>
#include <algorithm>
using namespace std;
// Structure to represent an interval
struct Interval {
    int start;
    int end;
};
// Comparison function to sort intervals by their end times
bool compareIntervals(const Interval& a, const Interval& b) {
    return a.end < b.end;
}
// Function to find the maximum number of non-overlapping intervals
int intervalScheduling(vector<Interval>& intervals) {
    // Sort intervals by their end times
    sort(intervals.begin(), intervals.end(), compareIntervals);
    int count = 1; // Count of non-overlapping intervals
    int currentEnd = intervals[0].end;
    // Iterate through the sorted intervals
    for (int i = 1; i < intervals.size(); ++i) {
        // If the start time of the current interval is after the end time
of the previous interval,
        // it can be included in the schedule
        if (intervals[i].start >= currentEnd) {
            ++count;
            currentEnd = intervals[i].end;
```

```
        }
    }

    return count;
}

int main() {
    // Example usage
    vector<Interval> intervals = {{1, 3}, {2, 4}, {3, 6}, {5, 7}, {8, 10},
{9, 11}};
    int maxNonOverlapping = intervalScheduling(intervals);
    cout << "Maximum number of non-overlapping intervals: " <<
maxNonOverlapping << endl;
    return 0;
}
```

Complexity of the interval scheduling algorithm

The interval scheduling problem revolves around selecting the maximum number of non-overlapping intervals from a given set. This problem can be effectively tackled using the greedy algorithm, characterized by the following time and space complexities:

- **Time complexity**:
  - **Sorting**: If the intervals are not pre-sorted, the initial step typically involves sorting them based on their end times. This sorting operation generally consumes $O(n \log n)$ time, where n denotes the count of intervals.
  - **Greedy selection**: Following sorting, the greedy algorithm traverses through the sorted intervals once At each iteration, it chooses the interval that concludes earliest and avoids overlapping with previously selected intervals. This process demands $O(n)$ time, as each interval is scrutinized once.

  Overall, the time complexity of the greedy algorithm for interval scheduling is predominantly governed by the sorting phase, resulting in $O(n \log n)$ time complexity.

- **Space complexity**: The space complexity of the greedy algorithm for interval scheduling amounts to $O(n)$ since it necessitates storing the sorted intervals in memory.

Activity selection problem

Overall, the time complexity of the greedy algorithm for interval scheduling is predominantly.

The activity selection problem represents a renowned optimization challenge that can be efficiently resolved employing a greedy algorithm. Let us delve deeper into its intricacies:

- **Problem description**: You are provided with 'n' activities, each characterized by its start time and end time. The objective is to choose the highest number of non-overlapping activities feasible for execution by either an individual or a machine within a stipulated timeframe. It is assumed that an individual or machine can solely engage in one activity concurrently.

- **Greedy algorithm strategy**: The key greedy selection in this scenario involves consistently selecting the subsequent activity with the earliest finish time among the remaining activities, provided its start time is later than or equal to the finish time of the previously chosen activity.

Adhering to this approach guarantees the maximization of non-conflicting activities.

Example 6.6: Let us illustrate the activity selection problem with the given parameters:

Activities: A, B, and C

Start time: [10, 12, 20]

Finish time: [20, 25, 30]

Solution: The greedy algorithm unfolds as follows:

Choose activity A (10-20).

Activity B overlaps with A; therefore, it is skipped.

Select activity C (20-30).

The maximum set of activities that can be executed is {A, C}.

Applications of greedy algorithms

Greedy algorithms find utility in optimization problems where solutions are gradually constructed, selecting each component to provide the most immediate benefit.

Some common algorithms employing the greedy approach include:

- **Kruskal's minimum spanning tree (MST)**: Opting for edges with the smallest weight that avoid forming cycles.

- **Prim's MST**: Establishing connections between vertices via the smallest weight edge.

- **Dijkstra's shortest path**: Constructing the shortest-path tree by incrementally adding edges.

- **Huffman coding**: Assigning variable-length bit codes to characters based on their frequencies.

- **Approximation for challenging optimization problems**: For instance, the traveling salesman problem can be tackled by greedily selecting the nearest unvisited city at each stage.

Program 6.6: Implementation of the activity selection problem

```cpp
// C++ program for activity selection problem.
// The following implementation assumes that the activities
// are already sorted according to their finish time
#include <bits/stdc++.h>
using namespace std;
// Prints a maximum set of activities that can be done by a
// single person, one at a time.
void printMaxActivities(int s[], int f[], int n)
{
    int i, j;
    cout << 'Following activities are selected" << endl;
    // The first activity always gets selected
    i = 0;
    cout << i << " ";
    // Consider rest of the activities
    for (j = 1; j < n; j++) {
        // If this activity has start time greater than or
        // equal to the finish time of previously selected
        // activity, then select it
        if (s[j] >= f[i]) {
            cout << j << " ";
            i = j;
        }
    }
}
int main()
{
    int s[] = { 1, 3, 0, 5, 8, 5 };
    int f[] = { 2, 4, 6, 7, 9, 9 };
    int n = sizeof(s) / sizeof(s[0]);
    // Function call
    printMaxActivities(s, f, n);
    return 0;
}
```

Complexity of the activity selection problem

The time complexity of the greedy algorithm for the activity selection problem is generally $O(n \log n)$, where n represents the number of activities. This complexity arises primarily from the sorting step, which typically requires $O(n \log n)$ time if the activities are not already sorted. After sorting, the greedy selection of activities usually takes linear time, $O(n)$, since each activity is examined once. Therefore, the overall time complexity is dominated by the sorting step.

Job scheduling problem

The goal of the job scheduling problem is to assign jobs to resources in such a way that optimizes an objective while satisfying the constraints. The procedure of job sequencing with deadlines is given as follows:

When presented with a set of n jobs, each job i is associated with a deadline $di > 0$ and a profit $Pi > 0$. The profit Pi is earned only if the job is completed by its respective deadline. With only one machine available for processing jobs, the objective is to determine an optimal solution, defined as the feasible solution that maximizes profit.

First, the jobs are sorted in non-decreasing order by their deadlines. This sorting process creates an array d of size n to store the deadlines in accordance with their associated profit values.

To verify the feasibility of adding a new job i to the set of jobs J, we simply insert i into J while preserving the deadline ordering. Subsequently, we ensure that the deadlines of the jobs in J satisfy the condition $d[J[r]] \leq r$ for $1 \leq r \leq k+1$.

Example 6.7 Let us consider the example for job scheduling problem using greedy approach, $n = 4$, $(P1, P2, P3, P4,) = (100, 10, 15, 27)$ and $(d1\ d2\ d3\ d4) = (2, 1, 2, 1)$.

Solution: The feasible solutions and their values are as shown in the following table:

Serial number	Feasible solution	Procuring sequence	Value	Remarks
1	1,2	2,1		110
2	1,3	1,3 or 3,1		115
3	1,4	4,1	127	Optimal
4	2,3	2,3		25
5	3,4	4,3		42
6	1	1		100
7	2	2		10
8	3	3		15
9	4	4		27

Table 6.5: Job scheduling solution

Algorithm 6.8: Job scheduling using the greedy approach

The algorithm builds an optimal set J comprising jobs that can be completed within their respective deadlines.

```
Algorithm GreedyJob (d, J, n)
// J represents a set of jobs that meet their deadlines.
{
J := {1};
for i := 2 to n do
{
if (all jobs in J union {i} can be completed by their deadlines) then J :=
J union {i};
}
}
```

Program 6.7: Implementation of the job scheduling problem

```cpp
#include <iostream>
#include <algorithm>
#include <vector>
using namespace std;
// Structure to represent a job
struct Job {
    char id;     // Job ID
    int deadline; // Deadline of job
    int profit; // Profit associated with the job
};
// Function to compare jobs based on their profit
bool compare(Job a, Job b) {
    return (a.profit > b.profit);
}
// Function to find the maximum profit by scheduling jobs
void findMaxProfit(Job arr[], int n) {
    // Sort jobs based on profit in decreasing order
    sort(arr, arr + n, compare);
    vector<int> result(n, -1); // To store result (Sequence of jobs)
    vector<bool> slot(n, false); // To keep track of free time slots
    // Iterate through all given jobs
    for (int i = 0; i < n; i++) {
        // Find a free slot for this job (Note that we start from the last
possible slot)
```

```
            for (int j = min(n, arr[i].deadline) - 1; j >= 0; j--) {
                // Free slot found
                if (slot[j] == false) {
                    result[j] = i; // Add this job to result
                    slot[j] = true; // Make this slot occupied
                    break;
                }
            }
        }
    }
    // Print the sequence of jobs
    cout << "The sequence of jobs with maximum profit is: ";
    for (int i = 0; i < n; i++) {
        if (result[i] != -1)
            cout << arr[result[i]].id << " ";
    }
    cout << endl;
}
int main() {
    // Example jobs
    Job arr[] = { {'a', 2, 100}, {'b', 1, 19}, {'c', 2, 27}, {'d', 1, 25},
{'e', 3, 15} };
    int n = sizeof(arr) / sizeof(arr[0]);
    // Find the maximum profit
    findMaxProfit(arr, n);
    return 0;
}
```

Complexity of the job scheduling problem

The time complexity of the job scheduling problem solved using the greedy approach is $O(n \log n)$, where n denotes the number of jobs. A breakdown of the complexity is as follows:

- **Sorting the jobs by profit**: Sorting n jobs by their profit typically requires $O(n \log n)$ time complexity, as efficient sorting algorithms like quicksort or merge sort are commonly employed.

- **Iterating through the sorted jobs**: After sorting, iterating through the sorted jobs takes linear time, $O(n)$.

In summary, the sorting step dominates the time complexity, resulting in $O(n \log n)$ overall time complexity for solving the job scheduling problem using the greedy approach.

Conclusion

By maximizing the most advantageous decision at every stage, greedy algorithms provide a strong and natural way to solve optimization challenges. Their efficiency and simplicity make them perfect for a wide range of applications, particularly when the issue shows the greedy choice property and optimum substructure. Although they do not always provide the best solution, particularly in complicated situations like the traveling salesman problem, their performance in real-world uses like Dijkstra's algorithm, Prim's and Kruskal's MST algorithms, and Huffman coding highlights their value. Though they have shortcomings, greedy approaches are nonetheless crucial for algorithm designers. Using their strengths means knowing when and how to use them properly.

In the next chapter, the reader will examine a method called **dynamic programming** (**DP**), which resembles the divide and conquer strategy by decomposing the problem into smaller subproblems.

Exercise

1. Write the algorithm for the general greedy method. Compare how it is better than the traditional approach.

2. Explain the Huffman coding algorithm using the greedy method with a suitable example.

3. Explain how Kruskal's algorithm can be used to find the MST.

4. Explain how Prim's algorithm can be used to find the MST.

5. For the activity selection problem, consider the following set of activities with their start and end times:

Activity	Start time	End time
A	1	3
B	2	5
C	3	6
D	5	7
E	1	8

Using a greedy approach, determine the maximum number of activities that can be selected without overlapping. Additionally, provide the sequence of selected activities.

206 ■ *Mastering Algorithms*

6. You are given a set of jobs, each with a unique ID, a deadline by which it must be completed, and the profit gained upon completion. The goal is to schedule these jobs in a way that maximizes the total profit. Using a greedy approach, how would you determine the sequence of jobs to schedule, and what would be the resulting maximum profit for the following set of jobs?

Job ID	Deadline	Profit
A	2	100
B	1	19
C	2	27
D	1	25
E	3	15

Join our Discord space

Join our Discord workspace for latest updates, offers, tech happenings around the world, new releases, and sessions with the authors:

https://discord.bpbonline.com

CHAPTER 7

Dynamic Programming

Introduction

In this chapter, we will explore a technique known as **dynamic programming** (**DP**), which shares similarities with the divide and conquer approach, as it breaks down the problem into smaller subproblems. However, unlike divide and conquer, these subproblems are not solved independently. Instead, the results of these smaller subproblems are stored and utilized for similar or overlapping subproblems. This chapter also introduces various algorithms, including the 0/1 knapsack problem, the subset sum problem, edit distance (Levenshtein distance), optimal binary search tree, matrix chain multiplication, longest common subsequence problem, and the traveling salesman problem.

Structure

The chapter covers the following topics:

- Dynamic programming
- 0/1 knapsack problem
- Subset sum problem
- Levenshtein distance or edit distance
- Optimal binary search tree

- Matrix chain multiplication
- Longest common subsequence problem
- Traveling salesperson problem

Objectives

The objective of DP is to optimize the use of computational resources by breaking down complex problems into smaller, overlapping subproblems and solving each subproblem only once. By storing the results of these subproblems in a memory structure such as an array or a table, DP eliminates redundant calculations, thereby improving efficiency. This approach significantly reduces the time complexity of algorithms compared to naive recursive methods. DP is particularly useful for solving optimization problems where the goal is to find the best possible solution while minimizing computational effort. It is widely applied in areas such as graph algorithms, sequence alignment, and resource allocation.

Dynamic programming

DP is a powerful algorithmic technique utilized in computer science and mathematics to address problems efficiently. It involves breaking down intricate problems into smaller, interconnected subproblems and storing their solutions to avoid redundant calculations. This method is particularly advantageous for optimization challenges, as it allows for the creation of optimal solutions based on the optimal outcomes of these smaller subproblems.

DP encompasses the following three primary stages:

1. **Identification of overlapping subproblems**: Divide the primary problem into smaller subproblems that exhibit overlapping or recurrence.

2. **Establishment of a recurrence relation**: Formulate a recursive formula expressing the solution to the primary problem in terms of solutions to its subproblems.

3. **Memorization or tabulation**: Store solutions to subproblems in a structured data format (either through memorization or tabulation) to avoid redundant calculations and facilitate efficient solution retrieval.

Algorithm 7.1: Dynamic programming

```
// Function for solving the problem utilizing dynamic programming
int dynamicProgramming(int problem) {
    // Set up data structures for storing interim outcomes.
    int dp[SIZE][SIZE];
    // Initialization of base cases
    initializeBaseCases(dp);
    // Calculate and store the optimal solutions for subproblems.
```

```
    for (int i = 0; i < SIZE; i++) {
        for (int j = 0; j < SIZE; j++) {
            dp[i][j] = computeOptimalSolution(i, j, dp);
        }
    }
    // Retrieve and return the ultimate solution.
    return extractFinalSolution(dp);
}
// Function for initializing base cases.
void initializeBaseCases(int dp[SIZE][SIZE]) {
    // Establish the base cases in the dynamic programming table according
to the constraints of the problem.
}
// Function to calculate the optimal solution for a specific subproblem.
int computeOptimalSolution(int i, int j, int dp[SIZE][SIZE]) {
    // Compute the optimal solution for the given subproblem using previously
computed solutions
    return dp[i-1][j-1] + dp[i-1][j]; // Example of recurrence relation
}
// Function to retrieve the final solution.
int extractFinalSolution(int dp[SIZE][SIZE]) {
    // Retrieve the ultimate solution from the DP table according to the
specifications of the problem.
}
int main() {
    int solution = dynamicProgramming(problem);
    // Subsequent processing or output of the solution
    return 0;
}
```

In this algorithm, the variable **SIZE** denotes the size of the problem or the dimensions of the DP table. The **dynamicProgramming()** function is responsible for initializing the DP table, computing optimal solutions for subproblems, and extracting the final solution. The **initializeBaseCases()** function establishes the base cases in the DP table, **computeOptimalSolution()** calculates the optimal solution for each subproblem, and **extractFinalSolution()** retrieves the final solution from the DP table. Ultimately, the **main()** function invokes the **dynamicProgramming()** function to solve the problem utilizing DP techniques.

The **dynamicProgramming** function serves as the main entry point for solving the problem using DP. The following list follows the process of **dynamicProgramming()**:

1. It initializes a DP table (**dp**) to store intermediate results.

2. Base cases are initialized in the DP table to handle the simplest cases of the problem.

3. It iteratively computes optimal solutions for subproblems and stores them in the DP table.

4. Finally, it extracts the final solution from the DP table and returns it.

5. Each step (initialization, base case handling, solution computation, and final solution extraction) is represented by a separate function for clarity and modularity.

Detailed examples of DP span various domains and problem types. Some common examples include the following:

*   **Fibonacci sequence**: Computing Fibonacci numbers using DP can greatly reduce the time complexity compared to a naive recursive approach.

*   **Shortest path problems**: DP algorithms, such as Floyd-Warshall and Bellman-Ford, are used to find the shortest path between all pairs of vertices in a weighted graph.

*   **Longest common subsequence (LCS)**: Finding the longest subsequence that is common to two sequences is a classic example of a problem solved using DP.

*   **Knapsack problem**: DP can be used to find the most valuable combination of items that can be included in a knapsack of limited capacity.

*   **Matrix chain multiplication**: Optimally parenthesizing matrix multiplication to minimize the number of scalar multiplications can be achieved using DP.

These examples illustrate the versatility and effectiveness of DP in solving a wide range of problems efficiently.

0/1 knapsack problem

The 0/1 knapsack problem is a classic optimization problem in computer science and mathematics. In this problem, a set of items is given, each with a weight and a value, and one has to determine the number of each item to include in a knapsack so that the total weight is less than or equal to a given limit and the total value is maximized. The 0/1 in the problem name signifies that an item can only be selected either entirely or not at all.

Working of 0/1 knapsack

For each $i \leq n$ and each $w \leq W$, solve the knapsack problem for the first i objects when the capacity is w. This will work because solutions to larger subproblems can be built up easily from solutions to smaller ones. We construct a matrix $V[0 \ldots n, 0 \ldots W]$. For $1 \leq i \leq n$, and $0 \leq j \leq W$, $V[i, j]$ will store the maximum value of any set of objects $\{1, 2, \ldots, i\}$ that can fit into a knapsack of weight j. $V[n,W]$ will contain the maximum value of all n objects that can fit into the entire knapsack of weight W.

To compute entries of V, we will use an inductive approach. As a basis, $V[0, j] = 0$ for $0 . j . W$.

If we have no items, then we have no value. We consider the following two cases:

- **Leave object i**: If we choose not to take object i, then the optimal value will come about by considering how to fill a knapsack of size j with the remaining objects $\{1, 2, \ldots, i - 1\}$. This is just $V[i - 1, j]$.

- **Take object i**: If we take object i, then we gain a value of vi. But we use up w_i of the capacity. With the remaining $j - w_i$ capacity in the knapsack, we can fill it in the best possible way with objects $\{1, 2, \ldots, i - 1\}$. This is $vi + V[i - 1, j - w_i]$. This is only possible if $w_i \leq j$.

This leads to the following recursive formulation:

$$V[i, j] = -\infty; \, if \, j < 0$$

$$V[i, j] = 0; \, if \, j \geq 0$$

$$V[i, j] = \{V[i - 1, j]; \, if \, w_i > j \, \{V[i - 1, j], v_i + V[i - 1, j - w_i]\} \, ; \, if \, w_i \leq j$$

A naive evaluation of this recursive definition is exponential. So, as usual, we avoid recomputation by making a table.

DP is a powerful technique for solving optimization problems like the knapsack problem. In the case of the 0/1 knapsack problem, DP works by building a table where each cell represents the maximum value that can be obtained using a certain subset of items and a certain weight limit. The table is filled iteratively, considering each item and each possible weight limit and determining whether it is beneficial to include the item or not based on its weight and value.

Algorithm 7.2: 0/1 knapsack

```
function knapsack(values[], weights[], capacity, n):
    let dp be a 2D array of size (n+1) x (capacity+1)
        for i from 0 to n:
        for w from 0 to capacity:
            if i = 0 or w = 0:
                dp[i][w] = 0
            else if weights[i-1] <= w:
                dp[i][w] = max(values[i-1] + dp[i-1][w-weights[i-1]], dp[i-
1][w])
            else:
                dp[i][w] = dp[i-1][w]
        return dp[n][capacity]
```

Program 7.1: Implementation in C++

```cpp
#include <iostream>
#include <vector>
using namespace std;
int knapsack(vector<int>& values, vector<int>& weights, int capacity) {
    int n = values.size();
    vector<vector<int>> dp(n + 1, vector<int>(capacity + 1, 0));
    for (int i = 1; i <= n; ++i) {
        for (int w = 1; w <= capacity; ++w) {
            if (weights[i - 1] <= w) {
                dp[i][w] = max(values[i - 1] + dp[i - 1][w - weights[i -
1]], dp[i - 1][w]);
            } else {
                dp[i][w] = dp[i - 1][w];
            }
        }
    }
    return dp[n][capacity];
}
int main() {
    vector<int> values = {10, 15, 40};
    vector<int> weights = {1, 2, 3};
    int capacity = 6;
    cout << "Maximum value: " << knapsack(values, weights, capacity) <<
endl;
    return 0;
}
```

Example 7.1: Suppose we have the following items:

- **Item 1**: Weight = 2, Value = 6
- **Item 2**: Weight = 2, Value = 10
- **Item 3**: Weight = 3, Value = 12

The knapsack capacity is 5.

Solution: We will create a table to store the solutions to subproblems. Each cell *DP[i]* *[w]* will represent the maximum value that can be obtained using the first *I* items and a knapsack with capacity *w*.

1. **Initialization**: Create a 2D array with dimensions *(n+1) x (W+1)*, where n is the number of items and *W* is the knapsack capacity. Initialize all cells to 0. The following table shows the initialization of the table for the 0/1 knapsack problem:

	0	1	2	3	4	5
0	0	0	0	0	0	0
1	0					
2	0					
3	0					

Table 7.1: Table initialization

2. **Fill the table**: The table is filled for each item as follows:

Item 1 (Weight = 2, Value = 6):

- For each capacity from 0 to 5:
    - When capacity is 0, we cannot take any item. So, the value remains 0.
    - For capacities 1 and 2, we cannot take item 1, so the value remains 0.
    - When capacity is 3, we can take item 1 (Weight = 2) as it fits, so the maximum value is 6.
    - For capacities 4 and 5, we can take item 1 (Weight = 2) as it fits, so the maximum value is 6.

Table 7.2 shows the filling entries when item 1 is selected, having weight=2 and value=6.

	0	1	2	3	4	5
0	0	0	0	0	0	0
1	0	0	0	6	6	6
2	0					
3	0					

Table 7.2: Filling table for item 1

The next phase fills the table with the parameters for item number 2.

Item 2 (Weight = 2, Value = 10):

- For each capacity from 0 to 5:
    - When capacity is 0, we cannot take any item. So, the value remains 0.
    - For capacities 1 and 2, we cannot take item 2, so the value remains 6 (the value from the previous row).
    - When capacity is 3, we can either exclude item 2 or include it. Excluding it gives us the value of 6 (value from the previous row). Including it,

we get a total value of 10 (value of item 2) + value from the remaining capacity (3 - 2 = 1), which is 0. So, the maximum value is 10.

- o For capacities 4 and 5, we can take item 2 (Weight = 2) as it fits, so the maximum value is 10.

Table 7.3 shows the filling entries when item 1 is selected, having weight=2 and value=10.

	0	1	2	3	4	5
0	0	0	0	0	0	0
1	0	0	0	6	6	6
2	0	0	10	10	16	16
3	0					

Table 7.3: Filling table for item 2

The next phase fills the table with the parameters for item number 3.

Item 3 (Weight = 3, Value = 12):

- For each capacity from 0 to 5:

  - o When capacity is 0, we cannot take any item. So, the value remains 0.

  - o For capacities 1 and 2, we cannot take item 3, so the value remains 10 (the value from the previous row).

  - o When capacity is 3, we can either exclude item 3 or include it. Excluding it gives us the value of 10 (value from the previous row). Including it, we get a total value of 12 (value of item 3) + value from the remaining capacity (3 - 3 = 0), which is 0. So, the maximum value is 12.

  - o For capacities 4 and 5, we can either exclude item 3 or include it. Excluding it gives us the value of 16 (value from the previous row). Including it, we get a total value of 12 (value of item 3) + value from the remaining capacity (4 - 3 = 1), which is 6. So, the maximum value is 18.

Table 7.4 shows the filling entries when item 1 is selected, having weight=3 and value=12.

	0	1	2	3	4	5
0	0	0	0	0	0	0
1	0	0	0	6	6	6
2	0	0	10	10	16	16
3	0	0	12	12	16	18

Table 7.4: Filling table for item 3

3. **Retrieve optimal solution**: The maximum value that can be obtained is 18, which is in cell dp[3][5]. To retrieve the selected items, we backtrack from this cell to the first row:

- Starting from cell dp[3][5], we see that the value is different from the value in the cell, dp[2][5], above it. This means that item 3 (Weight = 3, Value = 12) was selected.

- We move diagonally up and left to cell dp[2][2]. The value here is different from the value in the cell, dp[1][2] above it. This means that item 2 (Weight = 2, Value = 10) was selected.

- We move diagonally up and left to cell dp[1][0]. The value here is the same as the value in the cell above it dp[0][0]. This means that item 1 (Weight = 2, Value = 6) was not selected

So, the selected items are items 2 and 3.

This completes the step-by-step solution of the 0/1 knapsack problem.

Complexity analysis

The time complexity of the DP solution for the 0/1 knapsack problem is *O(n*capacity)*, where n is the number of items and capacity is the maximum capacity of the knapsack.

Let us consider a few applications. The 0/1 knapsack problem has various real-world applications, such as resource allocation, portfolio optimization, and project selection. It is commonly used in fields like operations research, finance, and computer science for solving optimization problems involving resource constraints.

Subset sum problem

The subset sum problem is a classic algorithmic problem in computer science. Given a set of positive integers and a target sum, the task is to determine whether there exists a subset of the given set whose elements sum up to the target sum.

Algorithm 7.3: Subset sum problem

```
Function subsetSum(set[], n, target_sum):
    Create a 2D array dp[n+1][target_sum+1] and initialize it with false values.
    Set dp[0][0] = true, as an empty subset can sum up to 0.

    For i = 1 to n:
        For j = 0 to target_sum:
            If set[i-1] > j:
                Set dp[i][j] = dp[i-1][j] (current element cannot be included)
            Else:
                Set dp[i][j] = dp[i-1][j] OR dp[i-1][j-set[i-1]] (include
```

or exclude the current element)

Return dp[n][target_sum]

Program 7.2: Implementation in C++

```cpp
#include <iostream>
#include <vector>
using namespace std;

bool subsetSum(vector<int>& set, int target_sum) {
    int n = set.size();
    vector<vector<bool>> dp(n + 1, vector<bool>(target_sum + 1, false));

    // Base case: an empty subset can sum up to 0
    dp[0][0] = true;
    for (int i = 1; i <= n; ++i) {
        for (int j = 0; j <= target_sum; ++j) {
            if (set[i - 1] > j) {
                dp[i][j] = dp[i - 1][j]; // Exclude current element
            } else {
                dp[i][j] = dp[i - 1][j] || dp[i - 1][j - set[i - 1]]; //
Include or exclude current element
            }
        }
    }
    return dp[n][target_sum];
}
int main() {
    vector<int> set = {3, 34, 4, 12, 5, 2};
    int target_sum = 9;
    if (subsetSum(set, target_sum)) {
        cout << "Subset with the given sum exists." << endl;
    } else {
        cout << "Subset with the given sum does not exist." << endl;
    }
    return 0;
}
```

Example 7.2: Consider the set {3, 34, 4, 12, 5, 2} and the target sum 9. Check whether a subset with a given sum exists or not.

Solution: It involves the following steps:

1. **Initialization**: Create a 2D DP table with dimensions $(n + 1)$ x $(target\_sum + 1)$, where n is the number of elements in the set and **target_sum** is the given target sum, shown as follows:

Subset sum	0	1	2	3	4	5	6	7	8	9
{} (0)	T	F	F	F	F	F	F	F	F	F
3	T									
34	T									
4	T									
12	T									
5	T									
2	T									

Table 7.5: Initialization of the subset sum problem

2. **DP**: For each element in the set, we iterate over the target sum and update the DP table according to the recurrence relation.

For element 3:

When considering 3, we update the DP table as follows:

Subset sum	0	1	2	3	4	5	6	7	8	9
{} (0)	T	F	F	F	F	F	F	F	F	F
3	T	F	F	T	F	F	F	F	F	F
34	T									
4	T									
12	T									
5	T									
2	T									

Table 7.6: Subset sum for element 3

For element 34:

When considering 34, we update the DP table as follows:

Subset sum	0	1	2	3	4	5	6	7	8	9
{} (0)	T	F	F	F	F	F	F	F	F	F
3	T	F	F	T	F	F	F	F	F	F
34	T	F	F	T	F	F	F	F	F	F
4	T									
12	T									
5	T									
2	T									

Table 7.7: Subset sum for element 34

For element 4:

When considering 4, we update the DP table as follows:

Subset sum	0	1	2	3	4	5	6	7	8	9
{} (0)	T	F	F	T	F	F	F	F	F	F
3	T	F	F	T	F	F	F	F	F	F
34	T	F	F	T	F	F	F	F	F	F
4	T	F	F	T	T	F	F	F	F	F
12	T									
5	T									
2	T									

Table 7.8: Subset sum for element 4

For element 12:

When considering 12, we update the DP table as follows:

Subset sum	0	1	2	3	4	5	6	7	8	9
{} (0)	T	F	F	T	F	F	F	F	F	F
3	T	F	F	T	F	F	F	F	F	F
34	T	F	F	T	F	F	F	F	F	F
4	T	F	F	T	T	F	F	F	F	F
12	T	F	F	T	T	F	F	F	F	F
5	T									
2	T									

Table 7.9: Subset sum for element 12

For element 5:

When considering 5, we update the DP table as follows:

Subset sum	0	1	2	3	4	5	6	7	8	9
{} (0)	T	F	F	F	F	F	F	F	F	F
3	T	F	F	T	F	F	F	F	F	F
34	T	F	F	T	F	F	F	F	F	F
4	T	F	F	T	T	F	F	F	F	F
12	T	F	F	T	T	F	F	F	F	F
5	T	F	F	T	T	T	F	F	F	T
2	T									

Table 7.10: Subset sum for element 5

For the remaining elements in the set, repeat this process and update the table as follows:

Subset sum	0	1	2	3	4	5	6	7	8	9
{} (0)	T	F	F	F	F	F	F	F	F	F
3	T	F	F	T	F	F	F	F	F	F
34	T	F	F	T	F	F	F	F	F	F
4	T	F	F	T	T	F	F	F	F	F
12	T	F	F	T	T	F	F	F	F	F
5	T	F	F	T	T	T	F	F	F	T
2	T	F	T	T	T	T	T	F	F	T

Table 7.11: Subset sum for element 2

Traceback to find the subset:

- Start at dp[6][9] (which is True).
- Traceback through the table:

  Check if the value came from dp[i-1][j] or dp[i-1][j-arr[i-1]].

From the table:

- dp[6][9] is True because of dp[5][7].
- dp[5][7] is True because of dp[4][4].
- dp[4][4] is True because of dp[3][4].
- dp[3][4] is True because of dp[2][0].

So, the subset that gives the sum 9 is {3, 4, 2}.

Levenshtein distance or edit distance

Levenshtein distance, or edit distance, quantifies the similarity between two strings by determining the minimum number of single-character edits needed to transform one string into another. These edits may include insertions, deletions, or substitutions of characters.

DP is a widely adopted method for computing the Levenshtein distance efficiently. The process involves creating a matrix where each cell represents the distance between the substrings of the two strings being compared. It functions according to the following algorithm.

Algorithm 7.4: Levenshtein distance

1. **Initialize the matrix**: Create a matrix DP with dimensions *(m+1) x (n+1)*, where m is the length of the first string and n is the length of the second string.

2. **Set base cases**:

   a. dp[i][0] = i for all i from 0 to m (distance from string of length i to an empty string).

   b. dp[0][j] = j for all j from 0 to n (distance from an empty string to a string of length j).

   c. **Fill the matrix**: For each cell dp[i][j], compute the value based on the following rules:

      i. If the characters of the strings at positions i-1 and j-1 are the same, dp[i][j] = dp[i-1][j-1].

      ii. If the characters are different, compute the minimum cost of the three possible edits:

         • **Insertion**: dp[i][j-1] + 1

         • **Deletion**: dp[i-1][j] + 1

         • **Substitution**: dp[i-1][j-1] + 1

      iii. Set dp[i][j] to the minimum of these values.

   d. **Retrieve the result**: The value in the bottom-right cell of the matrix dp[m][n] is the Levenshtein distance between the two strings.

Program 7.3: Implementation in C++

```
#include <iostream>
#include <vector>
#include <algorithm>
using namespace std;

// Function to compute the Levenshtein Distance between two strings
int levenshteinDistance(const string& str1, const string& str2) {
    int m = str1.size();
    int n = str2.size();
    // Create a 2D vector to store the distances
    vector<vector<int>> dp(m + 1, vector<int>(n + 1));
    // Initialize the base cases
    for (int i = 0; i <= m; ++i) {
        dp[i][0] = i; // Distance from str1[0..i-1] to an empty str2
    }
    for (int j = 0; j <= n; ++j) {
        dp[0][j] = j; // Distance from an empty str1 to str2[0..j-1]
    }
```

```
    // Fill the rest of the dp matrix
    for (int i = 1; i <= m; ++i) {
        for (int j = 1; j <= n; ++j) {
            if (str1[i - 1] == str2[j - 1]) {
                dp[i][j] = dp[i - 1][j - 1]; // No change needed
            } else {
                dp[i][j] = min({
                    dp[i - 1][j] + 1,     // Deletion
                    dp[i][j - 1] + 1,     // Insertion
                    dp[i - 1][j - 1] + 1 // Substitution
                });
            }
        }
    }

    // The bottom-right cell contains the Levenshtein Distance
    return dp[m][n];
}
int main() {
    string str1 = "kitten";
    string str2 = "sitting";
    int distance = levenshteinDistance(str1, str2);
    cout << "The Levenshtein Distance between \"" << str1 << "\" and \"" <<
str2 << "\" is: " << distance << endl;
    return 0;
}
```

Example 7.3: Consider the strings *kitten* and *sitting*.

Solution: Initialization:

		s	i	t	t	i	n	g	
		0	1	2	3	4	5	6	7
k	1								
i	2								
t	3								
t	4								
e	5								
n	6								

Table 7.12: Kitten and sitting initialization

Base condition:

		s	i	t	t	i	n	g	
		0	1	2	3	4	5	6	7
k	1								
i	2								
t	3								
t	4								
e	5								
n	6								

Table 7.13: Base condition filling

Filling the matrix:

		s	i	t	t	i	n	g	
		0	1	2	3	4	5	6	7
k	1	1	2	3	4	5	6	7
i	2	2	1	2	3	4	5	6
t	3	3	2	1	2	3	4	5
t	4	4	3	2	1	2	3	4
e	5	5	4	3	2	2	3	4
n	6	6	5	4	3	3	2	3

Table 7.14: Matrix filling

Final matrix and result:

		s	i	t	t	i	n	g	
		0	1	2	3	4	5	6	7
k	1	1	2	3	4	5	6	7
i	2	2	1	2	3	4	5	6
t	3	3	2	1	2	3	4	5
t	4	4	3	2	1	2	3	4
e	5	5	4	3	2	2	3	4
n	6	6	5	4	3	3	2	3

Table 7.15: Resultant matrix

The Levenshtein distance between *kitten* and *sitting* is 3, which is the value in the bottom-right cell of the matrix. This means three edits are required to transform *kitten* into *sitting*:

- Substitute k with s
- Substitute ϵ with i
- Insert g at the end

Complexity analysis

The Levenshtein distance (edit distance) algorithm, implemented using DP, has specific computational complexities in terms of time and space. The following is a detailed analysis:

- **Time complexity**: The time complexity of the Levenshtein distance algorithm is determined by the number of operations performed to fill the DP table.

  - **Initialization**: Initializing the DP table requires $O(m + n)$ operations, where m is the length of the first string and n is the length of the second string.

  - **Filling the DP table**: The main computation involves filling a table of size $(m+1) \times (n+1)$.

    For each cell dp[i][j], a constant amount of work (comparing characters and taking the minimum of three values) is performed.

  Therefore, the total work done to fill the table is $O(m \times n)$.

  Combining these steps, the overall time complexity is $O(m \times n)$.

- **Space complexity**: The space complexity of the algorithm is determined by the amount of memory required to store the DP table.

  - The DP table requires $(m+1) \times (n+1)$ cells.

  - Each cell stores a single integer value, resulting in a space complexity of $O(m \times n)$.

  Optimized space complexity: In some implementations, it is possible to optimize the space complexity by using only two rows (or columns) of the DP table at any time because the calculation of each cell, $dp[i][j]$, only depends on the current and previous rows (or columns).

  Two-row optimization: By maintaining only two rows (or two columns) of the DP table at any time, the space complexity can be reduced to $O(min(m, n))$.

  This is particularly useful when one string is much shorter than the other.

Summary is as follows:

- **Time complexity**: $O(m \times n))$
- **Space complexity**: $O(m \times n)$ (can be optimized to $O(min(m, n))$)

Let us look at the detailed complexity analysis and break down the complexity further for clarity:

- **Time complexity analysis**
  - ○ **Initialization of the DP table**: $O(m + n)$

    Initialize the first row: $O(n)$

    Initialize the first column: $O(m)$
  - ○ **Filling the DP table**: $O(m \times n)$

    For each cell dp[i][j] (where $1 \le i \le m$ and $1 \le j \le n$):

    - Compare characters *str1[i-1]* and *str2[j-1]*.
    - Compute the minimum of the three values (insertion, deletion, substitution).

- **Space complexity analysis**
  - ○ **DP table storage**: $O(m \times n)$

    The table size is *(m+1) x (n+1)*.
  - ○ **Optimized storage (using two rows or columns)**: $O(min(m, n))$

    Only two rows (or columns) are maintained at any time.

Optimal binary search tree

Let us assume that the given set of identifiers is $\{a_1, \ldots, a_n\}$ with $a_1 < a_2 < \ldots < a_n$. Let $p(i)$ be the probability with which we search for ai. Let $q(i)$ be the probability that the identifier x being searched for is such that $a_i < x < a_{i+1}$, $0 < i < n$ (assume $a_0 = -\infty$ and $an+1 = +\infty$). We have to arrange the identifiers in a binary search tree in a way that minimizes the expected total access time.

In a binary search tree, the number of comparisons needed to access an element at depth d is $d + 1$, so if a_i is placed at depth d_i then we want to minimize:

$$\sum_{i=1}^{n} \Box\, P_i(1 + d_i)$$

Let $P(i)$ be the probability with which we shall be searching for a_i. Let $Q(i)$ be the probability of an unsuccessful search. Every internal node represents a point where a successful search may terminate. Every external node represents a point where an unsuccessful search may terminate.

The expected cost contribution for the internal node for a_i is:

$$P(i)^* \; level \; (a_i)$$

An unsuccessful search terminates with $i = 0$ (i.e., at an external node). Hence, the cost contribution for this node is:

$$Q(i) * level ((E_i) - 1)$$

The expected cost of the binary search tree is:

$$\sum_{i=1}^{n} P(i) * level (a_i) \sum_{i=0}^{n} Q(i) * level ((E_i) - 1)$$

The total time to evaluate all the c(i, j)'s and r(i, j)'s is therefore:

$$\sum_{1 \leq m \leq n} (mn - m^2) = O(n^3)$$

Example 7.4: Consider four elements a_1, a_2, a_3 and a_4 with $Q_0 = 1/8$, $Q_1 = 3/16$, $Q_2 = Q_3 = Q_4 = 1/16$ and $p_1 = 1/4$, $p_2 = 1/8$, $p_3 = p_4 = 1/16$. Construct an optimal binary search tree. Solving for C(0, n):

Solution: First, computing all C(i, j), such that $j - i = 1$; $j = i + 1$ and as $0 < i < 4$; $i = 0, 1, 2$ and 3; $i < k \leq J$. Start with $i = 0$; so $j = 1$; as $i < k \leq j$, so the possible value for $k = 1$

$$W (0, 1) = P (1) + Q (1) + W (0, 0) = 4 + 3 + 2 = 9$$

$$C (0, 1) = W (0, 1) + min \{C (0, 0) + C (1, 1)\} = 9 + [(0 + 0)] = 9$$

$$R (0, 1) = 1 \text{ (value of K that is minimum in the above equation)}$$

Next with $i = 1$; so, $j = 2$; as $i < k \leq j$, so the possible value for $k = 2$ W (1, 2) = P (2) + Q (2) + W (1, 1) = 2 + 1 + 3 = 6

$$C (1, 2) = W (1, 2) + min \{C (1, 1) + C (2, 2)\} = 6 + [(0 + 0)] = 6$$

$$R (1, 2) = 2$$

Next with $i = 2$; so, $j = 3$; as $i < k \leq j$, so the possible value for $k = 3$ W (2, 3) = P (3) + Q (3) + W (2, 2) = 1 + 1 + 1 = 3

$$C (2, 3) = W (2, 3) + min \{C (2, 2) + C (3, 3)\} = 3 + [(0 + 0)] = 3$$

$$R (2, 3) = 3$$

Next with $i = 3$; so, $j = 4$; as $i < k \leq j$, so the possible value for $k = 4$ W (3, 4) = P (4) + Q (4) + W (3, 3) = 1 + 1 - 1 = 3

$$C (3, 4) = W (3, 4) + min \{[C (3, 3) + C (4, 4)]\} = 3 + [(0 + 0)] = 3$$

$$R (3, 4) = 4$$

Second, computing all C (i, j), such that $j - i = 2$; $j = i + 2$ and as $0 < i < 3$; $i = 0, 1, 2$; $i < k \leq J$

Start with $i = 0$; so, $j = 2$; as $i < k \leq j$, so the possible values for $k = 1$ and 2. W (0, 2) = P (2) + Q (2) + W (0, 1) = 2 + 1 + 9 = 12

$$C(0, 2) = W(0, 2) + min\ \{(C(0, 0) + C(1, 2)), (C(0, 1) + C(2, 2))\}$$

$$= 12 + min\ \{(0 + 6, 9 + 0)\} = 12 + 6 = 18$$

$$R(0, 2) = 1$$

Next, with $i = 1$; so, $j = 3$; as $i < k \le j$, so the possible value for $k = 2$ and 3

$$W(1, 3) = P(3) + Q(3) + W(1, 2) = 1 + 1 + 6 = 8$$

$$C(1, 3) = W(1, 3) + min\ \{[C(1, 1) + C(2, 3)], [C(1, 2) + C(3, 3)]\}$$

$$= W(1, 3) + min\ \{(0 + 3), (6 + 0)\} = 8 + 3 = 11$$

$$R(1, 3) = 2$$

Next, with $i = 2$; so, $j = 4$; as $i < k \le j$, so the possible value for $k = 3$ and 4. $W(2, 4) = P(4) + Q(4) + W(2, 3) = 1 + 1 + 3 = 5$

$$C(2, 4) = W(2, 4) + min\ \{[C(2, 2) + C(3, 4)], [C(2, 3) + C(4, 4)]\}$$

$$= 5 + min\ \{(0 + 3), (3 + 0)\} = 5 + 3 = 8$$

$$R(2, 4) = 3$$

Third, computing all $C(i, j)$, such that $J - i = 3$; $j = i + 3$ and as $0 < i < 2$; $i = 0, 1$; $i < k \le J$. Start with $i = 0$; so, $j = 3$; as $i < k \le j$, so the possible values for $k = 1, 2$ and 3.

$$W(0, 3) = P(3) + Q(3) + W(0, 2) = 1 + 1 + 12 = 14$$

$$C(0, 3) = W(0, 3) + min\ \{[C(0, 0) + C(1, 3)], [C(0, 1) + C(2, 3)], [C(0, 2) + C(3, 3)]\}$$

$$= 14 + min\ \{(0 + 11), (9 + 3), (18 + 0)\} = 14 + 11 = 25$$

$$R(0, 3) = 1$$

Start with $i = 1$; so, $j = 4$; as $i < k \le j$, so the possible values for $k = 2, 3$ and 4. $W(1, 4) = P(4) + Q(4) + W(1, 3) = 1 + 1 + 8 = 10$

$$C(1, 4) = W(1, 4) + min\ \{[C(1, 1) + C(2, 4)], [C(1, 2) + C(3, 4)], [C(1, 3) + C(4, 4)]\}$$

$$= 10 + min\ \{(0 + 8), (6 + 3), (11 + 0)\} = 10 + 8 = 18$$

$$R(1, 4) = 2$$

Fourth, computing all $C(i, j)$ such that $J - i = 4$; $j = i + 4$ and as $0 < i < 1$; $i = 0$; $i < k \le J$. Start with $i = 0$; so, $j = 4$; as $i < k \le j$, so the possible values for $k = 1, 2, 3$ and 4.

$$W(0, 4) = P(4) + Q(4) + W(0, 3) = 1 + 1 + 14 = 16$$

$$C(0, 4) = W(0, 4) + min\ \{[C(0, 0) + C(1, 4)], [C(0, 1) + C(2, 4)], [C(0, 2) + C(3, 4)], [C(0, 3) + C(4, 4)]\}$$

$$= 16 + min\ [0 + 18, 9 + 8, 18 + 3, 25 + 0] = 16 + 17 = 33$$

$$R(0, 4) = 2$$

The table for recording $W(i, j)$, $C(i, j)$ and $R(i, j)$ is as follows:

Column row	0	1	2	3	4
0	2,0,0	1,0,0	1,0,0	1,0,0	1,0,0
1	9,9,1	6,6,2	3,3,3	3,3,4	
2	12,18,1	8,11,2	5,8,3		
3	14,25,2	11,18,2			
4	16,33,2				

Table 7.16: Recording table for variable W, C, R

From the preceding table, we see that $C(0, 4) = 33$ is the minimum cost of a binary search tree for (a_1, a_2, a_3, a_4).

The root of the tree T_{04} is a_2.

Hence, the left subtree is T_{01}, and the right subtree is T_{24}. The root of T_{01} is a_1, and the root of T_{24} is a_3.

The left and right subtrees for T_{01} are T_{00} and T_{11}, respectively. The root of T_{01} is a_1

The left and right subtrees for T_{24} are T_{22} and T_{34}, respectively. The root of T_{24} is a_3.

The root of T_{22} is null. The root of T_{34} is a_4.

The following figure shows the final structure of the optimal binary search tree:

Figure 7.1: Final optimal binary search tree

Matrix chain multiplication

It is a method under DP in which the previous output is taken as input for the next. Here, chain means one matrix's column is equal to the second matrix's row (always).

In general:

If $A = \lfloor a_{ij} \rfloor$ is a $p \times q$ matrix, $B = \lfloor b_{ij} \rfloor$ is a $q \times r$ matrix, $C = \lfloor c_{ij} \rfloor$ is a $p \times r$ matrix.

Then,

$$AB = C \;\; if \;\; C_{ij} = \sum_{k=1}^{q} a_{ik} \cdot b_{kj}$$

Given following matrices $\{A_1, A_2, A_3, ... A_n\}$ and we have to perform the matrix multiplication, which can be accomplished by a series of matrix multiplications:

$$A_1 \; x \; A_2 \; x, \; A_3 \; x.....x \; A_n$$

The matrix multiplication operation is **associative** rather than commutative in nature. By this, we mean that we have to follow the preceding matrix order for multiplication, but we are free to **parenthesize** the multiplication depending upon our needs.

In general, for $1 \leq i \leq p$ and $1 \leq j \leq r$:

$$C[i,j] = \sum_{k=1}^{q} A[i,k] \; B[k,j]$$

It can be observed that the total entries in matrix C is pr as the matrix is of dimension p x r. Also, each entry takes $O(q)$ time to compute. Thus, the total time to compute all possible entries for the matrix C, which is a multiplication of A and B, is proportional to the product of the dimensions p, q, and r.

It is also noticed that we can save the number of operations by reordering the parentheses.

Example 7.5: Let us have three matrices, A_1, A_2, A_3 of order *(10 x 100)*, *(100 x 5)* and *(5 x 50)* respectively.

Solution: Three matrices can be multiplied in two ways:

1. **A_1,(A_2,A_3):** First multiplying (A_2 and A_3) then multiplying and resultant with A_1.
2. **(A_1,A_2),A_3:** First multiplying (A_1 and A_2) then multiplying and resultant with A_3.

The number of scalar multiplication in case 1 will be:

$$(100 \; x \; 5 \; x \; 50) + (10 \; x \; 100 \; x \; 50) = 25000 + 50000 = 75000$$

The number of scalar multiplication in case 2 will be:

$$(100 \; x \; 10 \; x \; 5) + (10 \; x \; 5 \; x \; 50) = 5000 + 2500 = 7500$$

To find the best possible way to calculate the product, we could simply parenthesize the expression in every possible fashion and count each time how many scalar multiplications are required.

The matrix chain multiplication problem can be stated as finding the optimal parenthesization of a chain of matrices to be multiplied such that the number of scalar multiplication is minimized.

Number of ways for parenthesizing the matrices

There are numerous ways of parenthesizing these matrices. If there are n items, there are (n-1) ways in which the outermost pair of parentheses can be placed:

$(A_1) (A_2, A_3, A_4, \ldots \ldots \ldots A_n)$

Or $(A_1, A_2) (A_3, A_4 \ldots \ldots \ldots A_n)$

Or $(A_1, A_2, A_3) (A_4 \ldots \ldots \ldots A_n)$

Or $(A_1, A_2, A_3 \ldots \ldots \ldots A_{n-1}) (A_n)$

It can be observed that after splitting the kth matrices, we are left with two parenthesized sequences of matrices: one consists of *k* matrices, and another consists of *n-k* matrices.

Now there are L ways of parenthesizing the left sub-list and R ways of parenthesizing the right sub-list, then the total will be *L.R*:

$$p(n) = \begin{cases} 1 & \text{if } n = 1 \\ \sum_{k=1}^{n-1} p(k)p(n-k) & \text{if } n \geq 2 \end{cases}$$

Also, *p (n) = c (n-1)*, where *c (n)* is the nth **Catalan number**:

$$c(n) = \frac{1}{n+1} \binom{2n}{n}$$

On applying Stirling's formula, we have,

$$c(n) = \Omega\left(\frac{4^n}{n^{1.5}}\right)$$

This shows that 4^n grows faster, as it is an exponential function, than $n^{1.5}$.

The development of dynamic programming consists of the following steps:

1. Characterize the structure of an optimal solution.
2. Define the value of an optimal solution recursively.
3. Compute the value of an optimal solution in a bottom-up fashion.
4. Construct the optimal solution from the computed information.

Dynamic programming approach

Let $A_{i,j}$ be the result of multiplying matrices *i* through *j*. It can be seen that the dimension of $A_{i,j}$ is $p_{i-1} \times p_j$ matrix.

DP solution involves breaking up the problems into subproblems whose solutions can be combined to solve the global problem.

At the greatest level of parenthesization, we multiply two matrices, such that:

$$A_{1\ldots n} = A_{1\ldots k} \times A_{k+1\ldots n}$$

Thus, we are left with the following two questions:

1. How to split the sequence of matrices?

2. How to parenthesize the subsequence $A_{1....k}$ and $A_{k+1......n}$?

One possible answer to the first question for finding the best value of k is to check all possible choices of k and consider the best among them. It can be observed that checking all possibilities will lead to an exponential number of total possibilities. It can also be noticed that there exist only $O(n^2)$ different sequences of matrices. In this way, they do not reach exponential growth.

1. **Structure of an optimal parenthesization:** The first step in the dynamic paradigm is to find the optimal substructure and then use it to construct an optimal solution to the problem from an optimal solution to subproblems.

   Let $A_{i...j}$ where $i \leq j$ denotes the matrix that results from evaluating the product.

   $$A_i \, A_{i+1}....A_j$$

   If $i < j$, then any parenthesization of the product $A_i \, A_{i+1} ......A_j$ must split so that the product between A_k and A_{k+1} for some integer k is in the range $i \leq k \leq j$. That is for some value of k, we first compute the matrices $A_{i....k}$ and $A_{k+1...j}$ and then multiply them together to produce the final product $A_{i...j}$. The cost of computing $A_{i...k}$ plus the cost of computing $A_{k+1...j}$ plus the cost of multiplying them together is the cost of parenthesization.

2. **A recursive solution:** Let $m[i, j]$ be the minimum number of scalar multiplication needed to compute the matrix $A_{i...j}$.

   If $i=j$, the chain consists of just one matrix $A_{i...i} = A_i$ so no scalar multiplication is necessary to compute the product. Thus, $m[i, j] = 0$ for i= 1, 2, 3....n.

   If $i<j$, we assume that to optimally parenthesize the product, we split it between A_k and A_{k+1} where $i \leq k \leq j$. Then $m[i,j]$ equals the minimum cost for computing the subproducts $A_{i...k}$ and $A_{k+1...j}$ + *cost of multiplying* them together. We know A_i has dimension $p_{i-1} \times p_i$, so computing the product $A_{i...k}$ and $A_{k+1...j}$ takes $p_{i-1} \, p_k \, p_j$ scalar multiplication we obtain the following:

   $$m \, [i,j] = m \, [i, k] + m \, [k + 1, j] + pi\text{-}1 \ pk \ pj$$

   There are only $(j-1)$ possible values for k, namely $k = i, i+1.....j-1$. Since the optimal parenthesization must use one of these values for k, we only need to check them all to find the best.

   So, the minimum cost of parenthesizing the product $A_i \, A_{i+1}......A_j$ becomes:

   $$m[i,j] = \begin{cases} 0, & if \ i = j \\ \min \, \{m[i, k] + m[k + 1, j] + \, p_{i-1}p_kp_j\}, & if \ i < 1, \ i \leq k < j \end{cases}$$

To construct an optimal solution, let us define $s[i,j]$ to be the value of k at which we can split the product $A_i A_{i+1} \ldots A_j$ To obtain an optimal parenthesization, i.e., $s[i, j] = k$, such that:

$$m[i,j] = m[i, k] + m[k + 1, j] + p_{i-1}\ p_k\ p_j$$

MATRIX-CHAIN-ORDER (P)

1 $n = p.length - 1$

2 let $m[1 \ldots n, 1 \ldots n]$ and $s[1 \ldots n - 1, 2 \ldots n]$ be new tables

3 **for** $i = 1$ to n

4 $m[i, i] = 0$

5 **for** $l = 2$ to n　　// l is the chain length

6 　　　**for** $i = 1$ to $n - l + 1$

7 　　　$j = i + l - 1$

8 　　　$m[i, j] = \ldots.$

9 　　　**for** $k = i$ to $j - 1$

10 　　　　　　　　　$q = m[i, k] + m[k + 1, j] + Pi\text{-}1\ Pk\ Pj$

11 　　　　　　　　　**if** $q < m[i, j]$

12 　　　　　　　　　　　$m[i, j] = q$

13 　　　　　　　　　　　$s[i, j] = k$

14 **return** m and s

The following figure represents two different tables, where table m and table s are defined for the matrix chain having n=6:

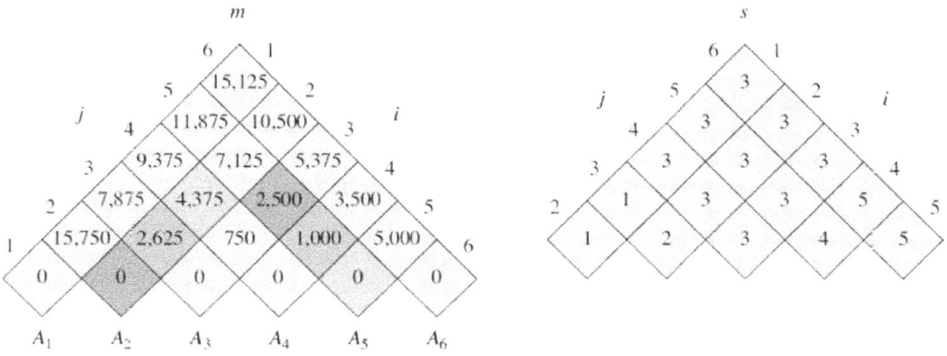

Figure 7.2: *Input matrix chain for n=6*

The *m* and *s* tables are computed by MATRIX-CHAIN-ORDER for *n* = 6, and the following matrix dimensions are calculated:

Matrix	A1	A2	A3	A4	A5		A6
Dimension	30 X 35	35 X 15		15 X 5	5 X 10	10 X 20	20 X 25

Table 7.17: Matrix dimensions calculation

The tables are rotated so that the main diagonal runs horizontally. The m table uses only the main diagonal and upper triangle, and the s table uses only the upper triangle. The minimum number of scalar multiplications needed to multiply the six matrices is $m[1, 6]$ = 15,125. On the darker entries, the pairs that have the same shading are taken together in line 10 when computing.

$$m[2,5] = min \begin{cases} m[2,2] + m[3,5] + p_1p_2p_5 = 0 + 2500 + 35.15.20 = 13,000, \\ m[2,3] + m[4,5] + p_1p_3p_5 = 2625 + 1000 + 35.5.20 = 7,125, \\ m[2,4] + m[5,5] + p_1p_4p_5 = 4375 + 0 + 35.10.20 = 11,375 \end{cases}$$

$$= 7125$$

PRINT-OPTIMAL_PARENS (s, i, j)

In the example, the call PRINT-OPTIMAL_PARENS (s, 1, 6) prints the parenthesization $((A_1(A_2A_3))\,((A_4A_5)\,A_6))$, calculated as follows:

```
1.  if i == j
2.  print "A" i
3.  else print "("
4.  PRINT-OPTIMAL_PARENS (s, i, s[i, j])
5.  PRINT-OPTIMAL_PARENS (s, s[i, j] + 1, j)
6.  print ")"
```

Example 7.6: We are given the sequence *{4, 10, 3, 12, 20, and 7}*. The matrices have size *4 x 10, 10 x 3, 3 x 12, 12 x 20, 20 x 7*. We need to compute *M [i,j], 0 ≤ i, j≤ 5*. We know *M [i, i] = 0 for all i*.

Solution: The initial case of matrix chain multiplication is mentioned in *Figure 7.3*:

Figure 7.3: Initial matrix with m[i,i]=0

Let us proceed with working away from the diagonal. We compute the optimal solution for the product of 2 matrices.

Figure 7.4 shows the sequence for the next step of multiplication:

Sequence: 4   10   3   12   20   7

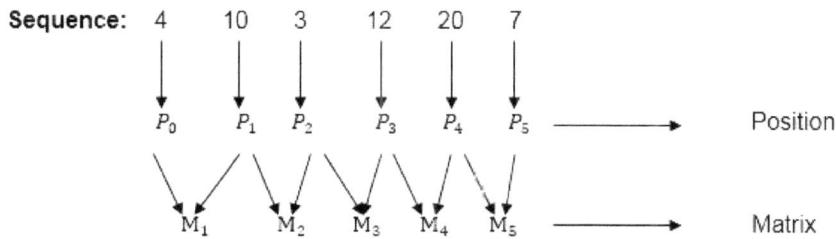

Figure 7.4: *Sequence for chaining multiplication*

Here, P_0 to P_5 are the positions, and M_1 to M_5 are the matrix of size (p_i to p_{i-1}).

On the basis of the sequence, we make the following formula:

For M_i p [i] as column

                               p[i-1] as row

In DP, the initialization of every method is done by 0. So, we initialize it by 0. It will sort out diagonally.

We have to sort out all the combinations, but the minimum output combination is taken into consideration.

Calculation of the product of two matrices is as follows:

1. m (1,2) = m_1 x m_2

    = 4 x 10 x 10 x 3

    = 4 x 10 x 3 = 120

2. m (2, 3) = m2 x m3

    = 10 x 3 x 3 x 12

    = 10 x 3 x 12 = 360

3. m (3, 4) = m3 x m4

    = 3 x 12 x 12 x 20

    = 3 x 12 x 20 = 720

4. m (4,5) = m4 x m5

    = 12 x 20 x 20 x 7

    = 12 x 20 x 7 = 1680

Figure 7.5 shows the multiplication result of 2 matrices:

1	2	3	4	5	
0	120				1
	0	360			2
		0	720		3
			0	1680	4
				0	5

Figure 7.5: *Product matrix of 2 matrices*

In the matrix:

- We initialize the diagonal element with equal i, j value with 0.

- After that, the second diagonal is sorted out, and we get all the values corresponding to it.

Now, the third diagonal will be solved in the same way.

Product of three matrices is as follows:

$$M [1, 3] = M_1 M_2 M_3$$

1. There are two cases by which we can solve this multiplication: $(M_1 \times M_2) + M_3$, $M_1 + (M_2 \times M_3)$

2. After solving both cases, we choose the case with the minimum output.

$$M[1,3] = min \begin{cases} m[1,2] + m[3,3] + p_0 p_2 p_3 = 120 + 0 + 4.3.12 = 264 \\ m[1,1] + m[2,3] + p_0 p_1 p_3 = 0 + 360 + 4.10.12 = 840 \end{cases}$$

$$M [1, 3] = 264$$

Comparing the outputs, 264 is the minimum in both cases, so we insert 264 in the table and $(M_1 \times M_2) + M_3$. This combination is chosen for the output making.

$$M [2, 4] = M_2 M_3 M_4$$

1. There are two cases by which we can solve this multiplication: $(M_2 \times M_3) + M_4$, $M_2 + (M_3 \times M_4)$

2. After solving both cases, we choose the case with the minimum output.

$$M[2, 4] = min \begin{cases} m[2,3] + m[4,4] + p_1 p_3 p_4 = 360 + 0 + 10.12.20 = 2760 \\ m[2,2] + m[3,4] + p_1 p_2 p_4 = 0 + 720 + 10.3.20 = 1320 \end{cases}$$

$$M [2, 4] = 1320$$

Comparing both the outputs, 1320 is the minimum in both cases, so we insert 1320 in the table and $M_2 + (M_3 \times M_4)$. This combination is chosen for the output making.

$$M [3, 5] = M_3 M_4 M_5$$

1. There are two cases by which we can solve this multiplication: $(M_3 \times M_4) + M_5, M_3 + (M_4 \times M_5)$

2. After solving both cases, we choose the case with the minimum output.

$$M[3,5] = min \begin{cases} m[3,4] + m[5,5] + p_2 p_4 p_5 = 720 + 0 + 3.20.7 = 1140 \\ m[3,3] + m[4,5] + p_2 p_3 p_5 = 0 + 1680 + 3.12.7 = 1932 \end{cases}$$

$$M[3,5] = 1140$$

Comparing both the outputs, *1140* is the minimum in both cases, so we insert 1140 in the table and $(M_3 \times M_4) + M_5$.This combination is chosen for the output making.

Figure 7.6 shows the multiplication result when we take three matrices as a chain:

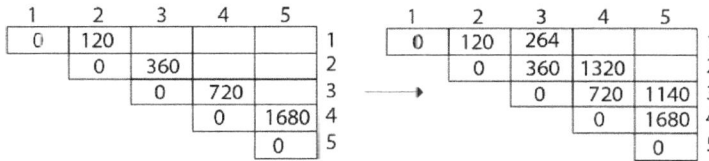

Figure 7.6: *Chain result up to 3 matrices*

Product of four matrices is as follows:

$$M[1, 4] = M_1 \, M_2 \, M_3 \, M_4$$

There are three cases by which we can solve this multiplication:

1. $(M_1 \times M_2 \times M_3) M_4$
2. $M_1 \times (M_2 \times M_3 \times M_4)$
3. $(M_1 \times M_2) \times (M_3 \times M_4)$

After solving these cases, we choose the case with the minimum output.

$$M[1,4] = min \begin{cases} M[1,3] + M[4,4] + p_0 p_3 p_4 = 264 + 0 + 4.12.20 = 1224, \\ M[1,2] + M[3,4] + p_0 p_2 p_4 = 120 + 720 + 4.3.20 = 1080, \\ M[1,1] + M[2,4] + p_0 p_1 p_4 = 0 + 1320 + 4.10.20 = 2120 \end{cases}$$

$$M[1, 4] = 1080$$

Comparing the output of different cases, *1080* is the minimum output, so we insert 1080 in the table, and $(M_1 \times M_2) \times (M_3 \times M_4)$ combination is taken out in output making.

$$M[2, 5] = M_2 \, M_3 \, M_4 \, M_5$$

There are three cases by which we can solve this multiplication:

1. $(M_2 \times M_3 \times M_4) \times M_5$

2. $M_2 \times (M_3 \times M_4 \times M_5)$

3. $(M_2 \times M_3) \times (M_4 \times M_5)$

After solving these cases, choose the case with the minimum output:

$$M[2,5] = min \begin{cases} M[2,4] + M[5,5] + p_1 p_4 p_5 = 1320 + 0 + 10.20.7 = 2720, \\ M[2,3] + M[4,5] + p_1 p_3 p_5 = 360 + 1680 + 10.12.7 = 2880, \\ M[2,2] + M[3,5] + p_1 p_2 p_5 = 0 + 1140 + 10.3.7 = 1350 \end{cases}$$

$$M[2, 5] = 1350$$

Comparing the output of different cases, *1350* is the minimum output, so we insert *1350* in the table, and $M_2 \times (M_3 \times M_4 \times M_5)$ combination is taken out in output making, shown as follows:

1	2	3	4	5			1	2	3	4	5	
0	120	264			1		0	120	264	1080		1
	0	360	1320		2			0	360	1320	1350	2
		0	720	1140	3	→			0	720	1140	3
			0	1680	4					0	1680	4
				0	5						0	5

Figure 7.7: Chain result up to 4 matrices

Product of five matrices is as follows:

$$M[1, 5] = M_1 M_2 M_3 M_4 M_5$$

There are five cases by which we can solve this multiplication:

1. $(M_1 \times M_2 \times M_3 \times M_4) \times M_5$

2. $M_1 \times (M_2 \times M_3 \times M_4 \times M_5)$

3. $(M_1 \times M_2 \times M_3) \times M_4 \times M_5$

4. $M_1 \times M_2 \times (M_3 \times M_4 \times M_5)$

After solving these cases, we choose the case with the minimum output, shown as follows:

$$M[1,5] = min \begin{cases} M[1,4] + M[5,5] + P_0 P_4 P_5 = 1080 + 0 + 4.20.7 = 1544 \\ M[1,3] + M[4,5] + P_0 P_3 P_5 = 264 + 1680 + 4.12.7 = 2016 \\ M[1,2] + M[3,5] + P_0 P_2 P_5 = 120 + 1140 + 4.3.7 = 1344 \\ M[1,1] + M[2,5] + P_0 P_1 P_5 = 0 + 1350 + 4.10.7 = 1630 \end{cases}$$

$$M[1, 5] = 1344$$

Comparing the output of the different cases, *1344* is the minimum output, so we insert *1344* in the table, and $M_1 \times M_2 \times (M_3 \times M_4 \times M_5)$ combination is taken out in output making.

The final output is as follows:

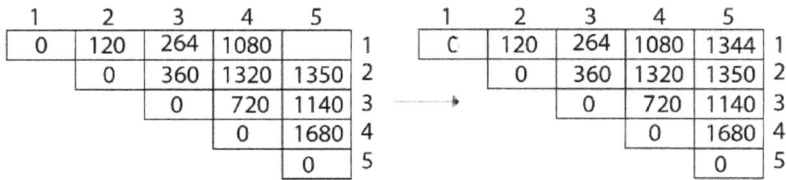

1	2	3	4	5			1	2	3	4	5	
0	120	264	1080		1		C	120	264	1080	1344	1
	0	360	1320	1350	2			0	360	1320	1350	2
		0	720	1140	3				0	720	1140	3
			0	1680	4					0	1680	4
				0	5						0	5

Figure 7.8: Chain result up to 5 matrices

Computing optimal costs

Let us assume that matrix A_i has dimension $p_{i-1} x p_i$ for $i=1, 2, 3....n$. The input is a sequence $(p_0, p_1,......p_n)$, where length $[p] = n+1$. The procedure uses an auxiliary table $m[1....n, 1.....n]$ for storing $m[i, j]$ costs and an auxiliary table $s[1.....n, 1.....n]$ that records which index of k achieved the optimal costs in computing $m[i, j]$.

The algorithm first computes $m[i, j] \leftarrow 0$ *for* $i=1, 2, 3.....n$, the minimum costs for the chain of length 1.

Longest common subsequence problem

The longest common subsequence problem is finding the longest sequence that exists in both the given strings.

Let us consider a sequence $S = <s_1, s_2, s_3, s_4, ...,s_r>$.

A sequence $Z = <z_1, z_2, z_3, z_4, ...,z_m>$ over S is called a subsequence of S, if and only if it can be derived from S deletion of some elements.

For the common subsequence, suppose X and Y are two sequences over a finite set of elements. We can say that Z is a common subsequence of X and Y, if Z is a subsequence of both X and Y.

Let us look at the longest common subsequence. If a set of sequences is given, the longest common subsequence problem is to find a common subsequence that is of the maximal length of all the sequences.

The longest common subsequence problem is a classic computer science problem, the basis of data comparison programs such as the diff-utility, and has applications in bioinformatics. It is also widely used by revision control systems, such as SVN and Git, for reconciling multiple changes made to a revision-controlled collection of files.

For the naïve method, let X be a sequence of length m and Y a sequence of length n. Check for every subsequence of X, whether it is a subsequence of Y, and return the longest common subsequence found.

There are 2^m subsequences of X. Testing if the sequences are a subsequence of Y takes $O(n)$ time. Thus, the naive algorithm would take $O(n2^m)$ time.

Dynamic programming

Let $X = <x_1, x_2, x_3, ..., x_m>$ and $Y = <y_1, y_2, y_3, ..., y_n>$ be the sequences. To compute the length of an element, the following algorithm is used:

In this procedure, table $C[m, n]$ is computed in row-major order, and another table $B[m,n]$ is computed to construct an optimal solution.

Algorithm 7.5: Longest common sequence

LCS-LENGTH (X, Y)

```
1.  m ← length [X]
2.  n ← length [Y]
3.  for i ← 1 to m
4.  do c [i,0] ← 0
5.  for j ← 0 to m
6.  do c [0,j] ← 0
7.  for i ← 1 to m
8.  do for j ← 1 to n
9.  do if xᵢ= yⱼ
10. then c [i,j] ← c [i-1,j-1] + 1
11. b [i,j] ← "↖"
12. else if c[i-1,j] ≥ c[i,j-1]
13. then c [i,j] ← c [i-1,j]
14. b [i,j] ← "↑"
15. else c [i,j] ← c [i,j-1]
16. b [i,j] ← "← "
17. return c and b
```

Example 7.7: Given two sequences $X[1...m]$ and $Y[1.....n]$. Find the longest common subsequences to both.

x: A	B	C	B	D	A	B
y: B	D	C	A	B	A	

Solution: Here, $X = (A,B,C,B,D,A,B)$ and $Y = (B,D,C,A,B,A)$

$m = length [X]$ and $n = length [Y]$

$m = 7$ and $n = 6$

Here, $x1 = x [1] = A$ $y1 = y [1] = B$

$$x2 = B \quad y2 = D$$
$$x3 = C \quad y3 = C$$
$$x4 = B \quad y4 = A$$
$$x5 = D \quad y5 = B$$
$$x6 = A \quad y6 = A$$
$$x7 = B$$

Now, fill the values of $c[i, j]$ in $m \times n$ table.

Initially, for $i=1$ to 7 $c[i, 0] = 0$

For $j = 0$ to 6 $c[0, j] = 0$

It is shown as follows:

j		0	1	2	3	4	5	6
i		y_i	B	D	C	A	B	A
0	X_i	0	0	0	0	0	0	0
1	A	0						
2	B	0						
3	C	0						
4	B	0						
5	D	0						
6	A	0						
7	B	0						

Figure 7.9: *Initial case of longest common sequence*

Now for $i=1$ and $j = 1$

$x1$ and $y1$ we get $x1 \neq y1$ i.e. $A \neq B$

And, $c[i-1, j] = c[0, 1] = 0$

$\qquad c[i, j-1] = c[1, 0] = 0$

That is, $c[i-1, j] = c[i, j-1]$ so $c[1, 1] = 0$ and $b[1, 1] = ' \uparrow '$

Now for $i=1$ and $j = 2$

$x1$ and $y2$ we get $x1 \neq y2$ i.e. $A \neq D$

$c[i-1, j] = c[0, 2] = 0$

$c[i, j-1] = c[1, 1] = 0$

That is, $c[i-1, j] = c[i, j-1]$ and $c[1, 2] = 0$ $b[1, 2] = ' \uparrow '$

Now for $i=1$ and $j = 3$

$x1$ and $y3$ we get $x1 \neq y3$ i.e. $A \neq C$

$c [i-1,j] = c [0, 3] = 0$

$c [i, j-1] = c [1,2] = 0$

So, $c [1,3] = 0$ $b [1,3] = ' \uparrow '$

Now for $i=1$ and $j = 4$

$x1$ and $y4$ we get $x1=y4$ i.e $A = A$

$c [1,4] = c [1-1,4-1] + 1$

$= c [0, 3] + 1$

$= 0 + 1 = 1$

$c [1,4] = 1$

$b [1,4] = ' \nwarrow '$

Now for $i=1$ and $j = 5$

$x1$ and $y5$ we get $x1 \neq y5$

$c [i-1,j] = c [0, 5] = 0$

$c [i, j-1] = c [1,4] = 1$

Thus, $c [i, j-1] > c [i-1,j]$, i.e., $c [1, 5] = c [i, j-1] = 1$. So $b [1, 5] = ' \leftarrow '$

Now for $i=1$ and $j = 6$

$x1$ and $y6$ we get $x1=y6$

$c [1, 6] = c [1-1,6-1] + 1$

$= c [0, 5] + 1 = 0 + 1 = 1$

$c [1,6] = 1$

$b [1,6] = ' \nwarrow '$

Figure 7.10 represents the table for 1st pass i = 1:

i	j	0	1 B	2 D	3 C	4 A	5 B	6 A
0	X	0	0	0	0	0	0	0
1	A	0	0	0	0	1	1	1
2	B	0						
3	C	0						
4	B	0						
5	D	0						
6	A	0						
7	B	0						

Figure 7.10: Longest common sequence table for i=1

Now for $i=2$ and $j = 1$

We get $x2$ and $y1$ $B = B$ i.e. $x2 = y1$

$c\,[2,1] = c\,[2-1,1-1] + 1$

$= c\,[1, 0] + 1$

$= 0 + 1 = 1$

$c\,[2, 1] = 1$ and $b\,[2, 1] = '\nwarrow '$

Similarly, we fill all the values of $c\,[i, j]$, and we get the following matrix:

i	j	0	1 B	2 D	3 C	4 A	5 B	6 A
0	X	0	0	0	0	0	0	0
1	A	0	0	0	0	1	1	1
2	B	0	1	1	1	1	2	2
3	C	0	1	1	2	2	2	2
4	B	0	1	1	2	2	3	3
5	D	0	1	2	2	2	3	3
6	A	0	1	2	2	3	3	4
7	B	0	1	2	2	3	4	4

Figure 7.11: Construction of matrix for remaining values of i

Construct an LCS. The initial call is **PRINT-LCS (b, X, X.length, Y.length)**

PRINT-LCS (b, x, i, j)

    1. **if i=0 or j=0**

2. **then return**
3. **if b [i,j] = ' ↖ '**
4. **then PRINT-LCS (b,x,i-1,j-1)**
5. **print x_i**
6. **else if b [i,j] = ' ↑ '**
7. **then PRINT-LCS (b,X,i-1,j)**
8. **else PRINT-LCS (b,X,i,j-1)**

Example 7.8: Determine the LCS of (1,0,0,1,0,1,0,1) and (0,1,0,1,1,0,1,1,0).

Solution: Let X = (1,0,0,1,0,1,0,1) and Y = (0,1,0,1,1,0,1,1,0).

$$c\,[i,j] = \begin{cases} 0 & if\ i = 0\ or\ j = 0 \\ c\,[i-1,j-1] + 1 & if\ i,j > 0\ and\ x_i = y_i \\ max(c[i,j-1],c[i-1,j]) & if\ i,j\ > 0\ and\ x_i \neq y_i \end{cases}$$

We are looking for *c [8, 9]*. The following table is built:

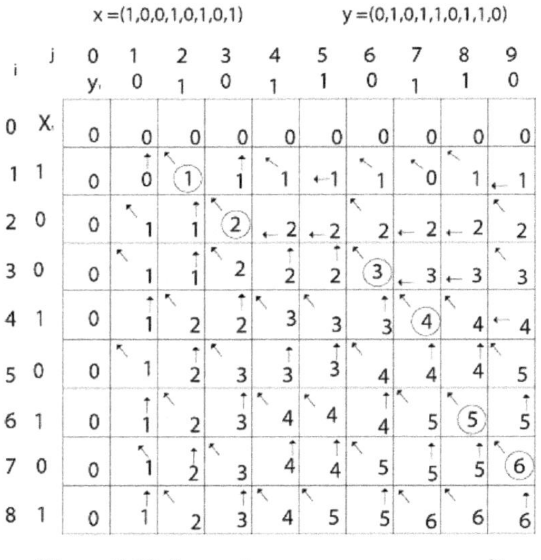

Figure 7.12: *Longest common sequence result*

From the table, we can deduce that *LCS = 6*. There are several such sequences, for instance, *(1,0,0,1,1,0) (0,1,0,1,0,1)* and *(0,0,1,1,0,1)*.

Example 7.9: In this example, we have two strings, *X = BACDB* and *Y = BDCB*, to find the longest common subsequence.

Solution: Following the algorithm LCS-Length-Table-Formulation (as stated previously), we have calculated Table C (shown on the left-hand side) and Table B (shown on the right-hand side) in *Figure 7.13*:

		0	1	2	3	4 =n
		B	D	C	B	
0		0	0	0	0	0
1	B	0	1	1	1	1
2	A	0	1	1	1	1
3	C	0	1	1	2	2
4	D	0	1	2	2	2
m=5	B	0	1	2	2	3

X = BACDB
Y = BDCB

		0	1	2	3	4 =n
		B	D	C	B	
0		0	0	0	0	0
1	B	0	1	1	1	1
2	A	0	1	1	1	1
3	C	0	1	1	2	2
4	D	0	1	2	2	2
m=5	B	0	1	2	2	3

LCS = BCB

start here

Figure 7.13: Length table formulation

In Table B, instead of *D*, *L*, and *U*, we are using the diagonal arrow, left arrow, and up arrow, respectively. After generating table B, the LCS is determined by function LCS-Print. The result is BCB.

Let us explore some applications. The longest common subsequence problem is a classic computer science problem, the basis of data comparison programs such as the diff-utility, and has applications in bioinformatics. It is also widely used by revision control systems, such as SVN and Git, for reconciling multiple changes made to a revision-controlled collection of files.

Traveling salesperson problem

The **traveling salesperson problem** (**TSP**) is a classic optimization problem in computer science and operations research. The objective is to find the shortest possible route such that the traveler visits each city exactly once and returns to the origin city. Using DP, we can solve TSP efficiently for a moderate number of cities.

Let us look at the problem definition. Given a set of n cities and a distance matrix dist where *dist[i][j]* represents the distance between city i and city j, the goal is to find the minimum distance tour that visits all cities exactly once and returns to the starting city.

Dynamic programming solution

To solve TSP using DP, we use a bitmask to represent subsets of cities and a DP table to store the minimum cost of visiting each subset of cities. The following steps are involved in the solution:

1. **State representation**: This step involves the following:

    a. dp[mask][i] represents the minimum cost of visiting the set of cities represented by mask, ending at city *i*.

    b. Mask is a bitmask of size *n*, where the *j*-th bit is *1* if city *j* is included in the subset.

2. **Initialization**: $dp[1 << i][i] = dist[0][i]$ for all i (starting from the first city).

3. **State transition**:

For each subset of cities represented by mask and each city i in the subset, update $dp[mask][i]$ using:

$$dp[mask][i]=min(dp[mask][i],dp[mask\setminus(1\ll i)][j]+dist[j][i])$$

Where j is any city in the subset mask except i.

4. **Final state**: The answer is the minimum cost of visiting all cities and returning to the starting city:

$$min(dp[(1\ll n)\text{-}1][i]+dist[i][0])$$

For all i.

Algorithm 7.6: Traveling salesperson problem

```
function tsp(dist)
    n = length(dist)  # Number of cities
    dp = array of size [2^n][n] initialized to infinity  # DP table

    # Initialize base cases
    for i from 0 to n-1
        dp[1 << i][i] = dist[0][i]

    # Iterate over all subsets of cities
    for mask from 0 to (1 << n) - 1
        for i from 0 to n-1
            if mask & (1 << i) != 0  # If city i is in the subset
represented by mask
                for j from 0 to n-1
                    if mask & (1 << j) != 0 and i != j  # If city j is also
in the subset and different from i
                        dp[mask][i] = min(dp[mask][i], dp[mask ^ (1 << i)]
[j] + dist[j][i])

    # Calculate the final answer
    answer = infinity
    for i from 1 to n-1  # Iterate over all cities except the starting city
        answer = min(answer, dp[(1 << n) - 1][i] + dist[i][0])

    return answer
```

Program 7.4: Implementation in C++

```cpp
#include <iostream>
#include <vector>
```

```cpp
#include <algorithm>
#include <limits.h>

using namespace std;

// Define the number of cities
const int N = 4;

// Define a large number representing infinity
const int INF = INT_MAX;

// Function to implement the Travelling Salesman Problem using dynamic
programming
int tsp(const vector<vector<int>>& dist) {
    int n = dist.size();
    int VISITED_ALL = (1 << n) - 1;

    // dp[mask][i] will store the minimum cost to visit all cities in mask
and end at city i
    vector<vector<int>> dp(1 << n, vector<int>(n, INF));

    // Initialize the base cases
    for (int i = 0; i < n; ++i) {
        dp[1 << i][i] = dist[0][i];
    }

    // Iterate over all subsets of cities
    for (int mask = 0; mask < (1 << n); ++mask) {
        for (int i = 0; i < n; ++i) {
            if (mask & (1 << i)) { // If city i is in the subset
represented by mask
                for (int j = 0; j < n; ++j) {
                    if ((mask & (1 << j)) && i != j) { // If city j is also
in the subset and different from i
                        dp[mask][i] = min(dp[mask][i], dp[mask ^ (1 << i)]
[j] + dist[j][i]);
                    }
                }
            }
        }
    }

    // Calculate the final answer
    int answer = INF;
    for (int i = 1; i < n; ++i) { // Iterate over all cities except the
starting city
```

```
        answer = min(answer, dp[VISITED_ALL][i] + dist[i][0]);
    }

    return answer;
}

int main() {
    // Define the distance matrix
    vector<vector<int>> dist = {
        {0, 10, 15, 20},
        {10, 0, 35, 25},
        {15, 35, 0, 30},
        {20, 25, 30, 0}
    };

    // Call the tsp function and print the result
    cout << "The minimum cost of visiting all cities and returning to the
start is: " << tsp(dist) << endl;

    return 0;
}
```

Example 7.10: Consider *Figure 7.14* as a connected graph where nodes represent cities and edge value shows the distance between cities. Find the optimal tour using the traveling salesman problem with dynamic programming.

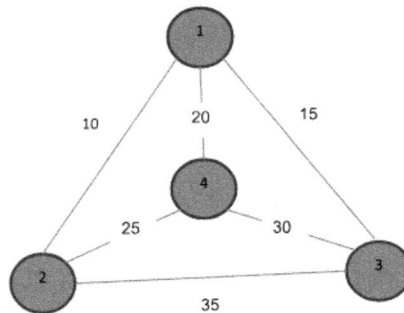

Figure 7.14: Connected graph between cities

Solution: Naive solution is as follows:

1. Consider city 1 as the starting and ending point.

2. Generate all *(n-1)!* permutations of cities.

3. Calculate the cost of every permutation and keep track of the minimum cost permutation.

4. Return the permutation with minimum cost.

$$n-1! = (4-1)! = 3 \times 2 \times 1 = 6$$
$$1,2,3,4,1 = 10+35+30+20 = 95$$
$$1,2,4,3,1 = 10+25+30+15 = 80$$
$$1,3,2,4,1 = 15+35+25+20 = 95$$
$$1,3,4,2,1 = 15+30+25+10 = 80$$
$$1,4,2,3,1 = 20+25+35+15 = 95$$
$$1,4,3,2,1 = 20+30+35+10 = 95$$

The distance matrix with respect to the preceding graph is as follows:

	1	2	3	4
1	0	10	15	20
2	10	0	35	25
3	15	35	0	30
4	20	25	30	0

Table 7.18: Distance matrix

Let us start from node 1:

$$C(4,\infty) = 20 \; ; \; C(3,\infty) = 15 \; ; \; C(2,\infty) = 10$$

$$C(2,\{3,4\}) = min(\, d(2,3)+C(3,\{4\}), \, d(2,4)+C(4,\{3\} \,)$$
$$C(3,\{2,4\}) = min(\, d(3,2)+C(2,\{4\}), \, d(3,4)+C(4,\{2\} \,)$$
$$C(4,\{2,3\}) = min(\, d(4,2)+C(2,\{3\}), \, d(4,3)+C(3,\{2\} \,)$$

$$C(2,\{3\}) = d(2,3)+C(3,phi) = 35 + 15 = 50$$
$$C(2,\{4\}) = d(2,4)+C(4,phi) = 25 + 20 = 45$$
$$C(3,\{2\}) = d(3,2)+C(2,phi) = 35 + 10 = 45$$
$$C(3,\{4\}) = d(3,4)+C(4,phi) = 30 + 20 = 50$$
$$C(4,\{2\}) = d(4,2)+C(2,phi) = 25 + 10 = 35$$
$$C(4,\{3\}) = d(4,3)+C(3,phi) = 30 + 15 = 45$$

$$C(2,\{3,4\}) = min(35+50), 25-45 \,) = min(85,70) = 70$$
$$C(3,\{2,4\}) = min(35+45), 30+35 \,) = min(80,65) = 65$$
$$C(4,\{2,3\}) = min(25+50), 30+45 \,) = min(75,75) = 75$$
$$C(1,\{2,3,4\}) = min(d(1,2)+ C(2,\{3,4\})), d(1,3) + C(3,\{2,4\},$$
$$d(1,4) + C(4,\{2,3\})$$

$$= min(10+70, 15+65, 20+75)$$

$$= min(80,80,95) = 80$$

The optimal tour for the graph has *length =80.*

The optimal tour is 1, 3, 4, 2, 1 or 1, 2, 4, 3, 1.

Complexity analysis

The time and space complexity of the traveling salesman problem using dynamic programming is as follows:

- **Time complexity**: $O(n^2 * 2^n)$ because we have 2^n subsets, and for each subset, we perform $O(n^2)$ operations.
- **Space complexity**: $O(n * 2^n)$ for storing the DP table.

The application is as follows:

The TSP has numerous practical applications across various industries. Its ability to optimize routes and reduce costs makes it an invaluable tool for businesses and services that rely on efficient routing and scheduling. By leveraging DP and other advanced algorithms, solutions to TSP can significantly enhance operational efficiency and resource management.

A comparison of divide and conquer and DP techniques is shown in the following table:

	Divide and conquer	Dynamic programming
Approach	It breaks down a problem into smaller independent subproblems.	It breaks down a problem into smaller subproblems, but subproblems may overlap.
Subproblems	Subproblems are solved independently.	The results of subproblems are stored and reused.
Memory	Does not store the results of subproblems.	Requires memory to store results of subproblems (usually in a table or array).
Usage	Typically used when subproblems do not overlap.	Used when subproblems overlap.
Examples	Merge sort, quick sort	Fibonacci series, knapsack problem, longest common subsequence

Table 7.19: Comparison of divide and conquer and dynamic programming

Comparison

Some major factors for the difference between the two methods mentioned in *Table 7.18* are described here:

- **Overlap of subproblems**: Divide and conquer solves each subproblem independently, while DP stores the results of overlapping subproblems.

- **Memory usage**: DP requires additional memory to store results, whereas divide and conquer does not.

- **Applicability**: Divide and conquer is more applicable when subproblems do not overlap, whereas DP is suitable when subproblems overlap and results can be reused.

- **Efficiency**: DP can be more efficient in terms of time complexity when compared to divide and conquer for problems with overlapping subproblems due to the reuse of results.

In summary, both techniques aim to break down problems into smaller subproblems, but DP optimizes by storing and reusing results of overlapping subproblems, which can lead to more efficient solutions for certain types of problems. However, regarding memory concerns, divide and conquer requires less space as compared to DP.

Conclusion

Dynamic programming is a powerful technique that enhances computational efficiency by breaking problems into smaller subproblems and storing their solutions to prevent redundant calculations. This approach significantly reduces time complexity compared to naive recursive methods, making it ideal for solving complex optimization problems. DP is widely used in various fields, including graph theory, sequence alignment, and resource allocation. By efficiently utilizing memory and computational resources, it helps in solving large-scale problems that would otherwise be infeasible. Its ability to provide optimal solutions while improving performance makes it a fundamental concept in computer science and algorithm design.

In the next chapter, the user will learn about backtracking algorithms and their utility in the field of computer science engineering. Furthermore, get knowledge about the complexity analysis in both ways, i.e., time and space complexity.

Exercise

1. What do you mean by the longest common subsequence? Explain.

2. Explain matrix chain multiplication with a suitable example.

3. Explain the traveling salesman problem using dynamic programming.

4. Write a short note on optimal binary search trees.

Join our Discord space

Join our Discord workspace for latest updates, offers, tech happenings around the world, new releases, and sessions with the authors:

https://discord.bpbonline.com

CHAPTER 8

Backtracking

Introduction

In this chapter of the book, we will discuss the various kinds of backtracking algorithms and their utility in the field of computer science engineering. Backtracking is a methodical algorithmic strategy that is utilized to solve problems by investigating all of the potential solutions through the process of exploration and experimentation. When you are faced with an issue in which you need to find one or more answers out of a huge number of options, it is especially effective. Puzzles, combinatorial optimization challenges, and constraint satisfaction issues are all examples of situations that frequently call for the application of backtracking.

Structure

The chapter covers the following topics:

- Overview of backtracking
- N-Queens problem
- Sudoku solver
- Graph coloring problem
- Constraints satisfaction problems

- Sum of subsets
- Hamiltonian cycles
- Solving crossword puzzles

Objectives

The objective of the chapter on backtracking algorithms is to provide a thorough understanding of this problem-solving technique commonly used in computer science and mathematics. The chapter begins by introducing the concept of backtracking and differentiating it from other algorithmic approaches. It then explores the fundamental principles of backtracking, including recursive exploration and systematic search. The chapter covers various aspects of problem-solving with backtracking, illustrating how it can be applied to solve combinatorial optimization problems, constraint satisfaction problems, and graph-related challenges. Implementation techniques for backtracking algorithms are also discussed, including recursive and iterative approaches, as well as strategies for pruning and optimization. Real-world examples and case studies are included throughout the chapter to demonstrate the practical application of backtracking algorithms in solving complex problems. By the end of the chapter, readers will have a solid grasp of backtracking algorithms, enabling them to analyze problems methodically, design efficient algorithms, and apply backtracking techniques effectively in problem-solving scenarios.

Overview of backtracking

Backtracking is a powerful algorithmic technique used to systematically search for solutions to combinatorial problems, constraint satisfaction problems, and optimization challenges. It is particularly useful when the problem space is large and exhaustive search methods become impractical. At its core, backtracking involves exploring all possible candidate solutions incrementally and abandoning a search path as soon as it is determined that the path cannot lead to a valid solution. This process of systematic exploration and pruning helps in efficiently navigating through the problem space, ultimately leading to the discovery of optimal or satisfactory solutions.

One of the defining characteristics of backtracking algorithms is their recursive nature, where decisions are made at each step to choose a candidate solution and explore further or backtrack and try a different path. This recursive exploration mimics a tree-like structure known as a decision tree, where each node represents a decision point, and each branch represents a possible choice. Backtracking algorithms are widely used in various domains, including artificial intelligence, operations research, algorithm design, and software development. They are especially suited for problems that involve searching for a feasible solution among a large number of possibilities, such as the N-Queens problem, Sudoku puzzles, and graph coloring problems.

General process of backtracking

In the process of backtracking, we initially take a step and then assess its correctness, determining whether it aligns with the desired outcome or not. Should it fail to yield the desired result, we backtrack and modify our initial step. Typically, this is achieved through recursion. Essentially, in backtracking, we commence with a partial sub-solution of the problem, which may or may not guide us towards the final solution. Subsequently, we evaluate whether we can proceed further based on this partial solution. If progress is not feasible, we backtrack and adjust the sub-solution before resuming the process. Hence, the typical steps involved in backtracking are as follows:

1. Begin with a sub-solution.

2. Evaluate if this sub-solution leads to the desired solution.

3. If not, backtrack and revise the sub-solution, then resume the process.

N–Queens problem

A classic illustration of backtracking involves arranging N queens on an *NxN* chessboard without any queen being able to attack another queen. Queens have the ability to strike horizontally, vertically, or diagonally. Similarly, the solution to this challenge follows a comparable approach. Initially, we position the first queen anywhere on the board, then proceed to place subsequent queens in safe positions. This sequence repeats until either all queens are placed (resulting in a solution) or no safe positions remain. In the latter scenario, where no safe positions are available, we adjust the placement of the previously positioned queen.

Algorithm 8.1: Algorithm of N-Queen using backtracking

1. Commence from the leftmost column.

2. If all queens are successfully placed, return true. Go to step 4.

3. Iterate through all rows in the current column. Perform the following steps for each row:

   a. Check if placing the queen in this row is safe.

   b. If safe, mark the position [row, column] as part of the solution and recursively check if placing the queen here leads to a valid solution.

   c. If placing the queen in [row, column] leads to a solution, return true.

   d. If placing the queen in [row, column] does not lead to a solution, unmark the position [row, column], backtrack, and try other rows.

   e. If no safe position is found in the current column, return false to initiate backtracking.

4. Exit.

The following figure shows the initial state of the 4-Queens problem:

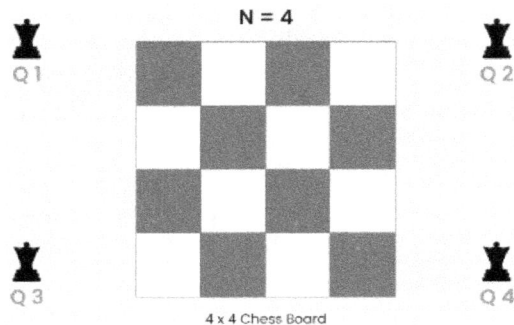

Figure 8.1: Initial state of the 4-Queens problem

Initial state

The N-Queens problem is one that involves the placement of N number of chess queens on a chessboard that is $N \times N$ in size, assuring that no two queens will attack each other.

The expected output is in the form of a matrix, with Qs representing the blocks in which queens are placed and periods (.) representing the empty spaces in the matrix. For instance, the output matrix for the 4-Queens solution described previously is presented in the following figure:

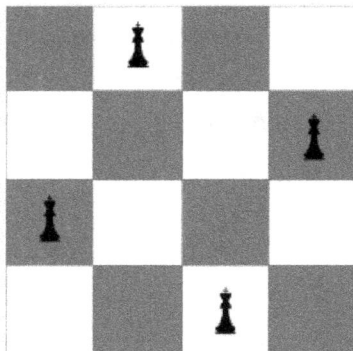

Figure 8.2: Goal state of the 4-Queens problem

Final state

```
_ Q _ _
_ _ _ Q
Q _ _ _
_ _ Q _
```

Program 8.1: Implementation of N-Queens problem

```
#include <bits/stdc++.h>
#define N 4
using namespace std;
// A utility function to print solution
void printSolution(int board[N][N])
{
        for (int i = 0; i < N; i++) {
                for (int j = 0; j < N; j++)
                if(board[i][j])
                        cout << "Q ";
                else cout<<". ";
                printf("\n");
        }
}
// A utility function to check if a queen can be placed on board[row][col].
// Note that this function is called when "col" queens are already placed in
// columns from 0 to col -1. So we need to check only left side for attacking
// queens
bool isSafe(int board[N][N], int row, int col)
{
        int i, j;
        // Check this row on left side
        for (i = 0; i < col; i++)
                if (board[row][i])
                        return false;
        // Check upper diagonal on left side
        for (i = row, j = col; i >= 0 && j >= 0; i--, j--)
                if (board[i][j])
                        return false;
        // Check lower diagonal on left side
        for (i = row, j = col; j >= 0 && i < N; i++, j--)
                if (board[i][j])
                        return false;
        return true;
}
// A recursive utility function to solve N Queen problem
bool solveNQUtil(int board[N][N], int col)
{
        // base case: If all queens are placed then return true
        if (col >= N)
                return true;
```

```
        // Consider this column and try placing this queen in all rows one
by one
        for (int i = 0; i < N; i++) {
                // Check if the queen can be placed on board[i][col]
                if (isSafe(board, i, col)) {
                        // Place this queen in board[i][col]
                        board[i][col] = 1;
                        // recur to place rest of the queens
                        if (solveNQUtil(board, col + 1))
                                return true;
                        // If placing queen in board[i][col] doesn't lead to a
solution, then remove queen from board[i][col]
                        board[i][col] = 0; // BACKTRACK
                }
        }
        // If the queen cannot be placed in any row in this column col then
return false
        return false;
}
// This function solves the N Queen problem using Backtracking. It mainly
uses solveNQUtil() to solve the problem. It returns false if queens cannot
be placed, otherwise, return true and prints placement of queens in the
form of 1s. Please note that there may be more than one solutions, this
function prints one of the feasible solutions.
bool solveNQ()
{
        int board[N][N] = { { 0, 0, 0, 0 },
        { 0, 0, 0, 0 },
        { 0, 0, 0, 0 },
        { 0, 0, 0, 0 } };
        if (solveNQUtil(board, 0) == false) {
                cout << "Solution does not exist";
                return false;
        }
        printSolution(board);
        return true;
}
// Driver program to test above function
int main()
{
        solveNQ();
        return 0;
}
```

Complexity of N-Queens problem

The time and space complexity of the N-Queens problem are as follows:

- **Time complexity**: The N-Queens problem is a combinatorial problem that involves finding a way to place N number of queens on an $N \times N$ chessboard such that no two queens threaten each other. The time complexity of the problem can be represented as $O(N!)$, where N is the size of the chessboard and also the number of queens to be placed. The factorial complexity arises from the number of possible permutations and combinations that need to be checked to find a valid solution.

- **Space complexity**: The space complexity of the N-Queens problem depends on the algorithm used to solve it. In the backtracking algorithm, which is commonly used to solve the N-Queen problem, the space complexity is $O(N^2)$ to represent the chessboard. This is because the algorithm typically uses a 2D array to represent the chessboard and keeps track of the queen placements.

Overall, the N-Queens problem is considered to have a high computational complexity, especially for larger values of N, due to its exponential time complexity in terms of the number of queens to be placed. Various optimization techniques, such as pruning and constraint propagation, can be applied to improve the performance of algorithms used to solve this problem.

Sudoku solver

Sudoku is a puzzle that involves logic and combinatorial techniques to place numbers correctly on a grid. The objective is to complete a 9×9 grid, represented as a 2D array grid [9][9], by filling the empty cells with digits from 1 to 9. The goal is to ensure that each row, column, and 3×3 sub-grid contains all digits from 1 to 9 exactly once.

Initial state of the puzzle

The initial state of the puzzle is as follows:

5	3			7				
6			1	9	5			
	9	8					6	
8				6				3
4			8		3			1
7				2				6
	6					2	8	
			4	1	9			5
				8			7	9

Figure 8.3: Initial state of the puzzle

Let us look at the solution:

- **Using the naïve approach:** The basic method involves generating every possible arrangement of numbers from 1 to 9 to fill in the empty cells. Each arrangement is then checked one by one until the correct one is discovered. Specifically, for each empty position, a number from 1 to 9 is assigned. Once all empty positions are filled, the matrix's safety is verified. If it is safe, it is printed; otherwise, the process recurs for other possibilities.

- **Using the backtracking approach:** In backtracking algorithms, you construct a solution incrementally, step by step. When it becomes evident at a certain step that the current path cannot lead to a solution, you backtrack to the previous step and explore an alternative path. In essence, you backtrack when you have exhausted all possibilities at a particular step. Backtracking is also termed as depth-first search.

Algorithm 8.2: Algorithm of the Sudoku solver using backtracking

1. Similar to other backtracking problems, Sudoku can be solved by sequentially assigning numbers to empty cells.

2. Before assigning a number, it is crucial to ensure that the number is not already present in the current row, the current column, and the current 3x3 sub-grid.

3. If the number is absent from the corresponding row, column, and sub-grid, proceed to assign that number. Then, recursively verify if this assignment contributes to a solution. If the assignment does not result in a solution, move on to the next number for the current empty cell. If none of the numbers from 1 to 9 lead to a solution, return false.

Final state of the puzzle

Figure 8.4 shows the goal state of the puzzle:

5	3	4	6	7	8	9	1	2
6	7	2	1	9	5	3	4	8
1	9	8	3	4	2	5	6	7
8	5	9	7	6	1	4	2	3
4	2	6	8	5	3	7	9	1
7	1	3	9	2	4	8	5	6
9	6	1	5	3	7	2	8	4
2	8	7	4	1	9	6	3	5
3	4	5	2	8	6	1	7	9

Figure 8.4: Goal state of puzzle

Program 8.2: Implementation of the Sudoku solver using backtracking

```cpp
#include <iostream>
using namespace std;
```

```cpp
// N is the size of the 2D matrix N*N
#define N 9
/* A utility function to print grid */
void print(int arr[N][N])
{
    for (int i = 0; i < N; i++)
    {
        for (int j = 0; j < N; j++)
            cout << arr[i][j] << " ";
        cout << endl;
    }
}
// Checks whether it will be legal to assign num to the given row, col
bool isSafe(int grid[N][N], int row, int col, int num)
{
    // Check if we find the same num in the similar row , we return false
    for (int x = 0; x <= 8; x++)
        if (grid[row][x] == num)
            return false;
    // Check if we find the same rum in the similar column , we return false
    for (int x = 0; x <= 8; x++)
        if (grid[x][col] == num)
            return false;
    // Check if we find the same num in the particular 3*3 matrix, we
    return false
    int startRow = row - row % 3,
            startCol = col - col % 3;
    for (int i = 0; i < 3; i++)
        for (int j = 0; j < 3; j++)
            if (grid[i + startRow][j + startCol] == num)
                return false;
    return true;
}
/* Takes a partially filled-in grid and attempts to assign values to all
unassigned locations in such a way to meet the requirements for Sudoku
solution (non-duplication across rows, columns, and boxes) */
bool solveSudoku(int grid[N][N], int row, int col)
{
    // Check if we have reached the 8th row and 9th column (0 indexed
```

```
matrix) , we are returning true to avoid further backtracking
        if (row == N - 1 && col == N)
                return true;
        // Check if column value becomes 9, we move to next row and column
start from 0
        if (col == N) {
                row++;
                col = 0;
        }
        // Check if the current position of the grid already contains value
>0, we iterate for next column
        if (grid[row][col] > 0)
                return solveSudoku(grid, row, col + 1);
        for (int num = 1; num <= N; num++)
        {
                // Check if it is safe to place the num (1-9) in the given row
,col ->we move to next column
                if (isSafe(grid, row, col, num))
                {
        /* Assigning the num in the current (row,col) position of the grid
and assuming  our assigned num in the position is correct */
                        grid[row][col] = num;
                        // Checking for next possibility with next column
                        if (solveSudoku(grid, row, col + 1))
                                return true;
                }
                // Removing the assigned num , since our assumption was wrong
, and we go for next assumption with diff num value
                grid[row][col] = 0;
        }
        return false;
}
int main()
{
        // 0 means unassigned cells
        int grid[N][N] = { { 5, 3, 0, 0, 7, 0, 0, 0, 0 },
                        { 6, 0, 0, 1, 9, 5, 0, 0, 0 },
                        { 0, 9, 8, 0, 0, 0, 0, 6, 0 },
                        { 8, 0, 0, 0, 6, 0, 0, 0, 3 },
```

```
                    { 4, 0, 0, 8, 0, 3, 0, 0, 1 },
                    { 7, 0, 0, 0, 2, 0, 0, 0, 6 },
                    { 0, 6, 0, 0, 0, 0, 2, 8, 0 },
                    { 0, 0, 0, 4, 1, 9, 0, 0, 5 },
                    { 0, 0, 0, 0, 8, 0, 0, 7, 9 } };
    if (solveSudoku(grid, 0, 0))
            print(grid);
    else
            cout << "no solution exists " << endl;
    return 0;
}
```

Complexity of the Sudoku solver algorithm

In a backtracking Sudoku solver, the time and space complexity can be analyzed as follows:

- **Time complexity**: In the worst-case scenario, a backtracking solver exhaustively tests all feasible number combinations for empty cells until it reaches a solution. This gives rise to a time complexity of $O(9^{(n^2)})$, where n represents the grid size (e.g., for a standard 9x9 Sudoku, $n=9$). Nevertheless, due to the backtracking method's ability to discard invalid options early in the process, the effective number of operations tends to be considerably lower than this worst-case estimate. Consequently, backtracking Sudoku solvers frequently exhibit fast solving times, particularly for puzzles possessing unique solutions and moderate difficulty levels.

- **Space complexity**: The space complexity of a backtracking Sudoku solver is contingent on its implementation methodology. The primary space utilization arises from the recursion stack, which retains the puzzle's state at each recursive invocation. In a conventional recursive backtracking setup lacking optimizations, the space complexity stands at $O(n^2)$, where n denotes the Sudoku grid's dimensions. This arises because the recursion depth correlates with the number of empty cells in the grid. However, certain optimizations can curtail space requirements. For instance, employing iterative backtracking or optimizing tail recursion can diminish the stack space demand. Moreover, if the solver adopts an explicit data structure to monitor empty cells and their feasible values, the space complexity might slightly escalate but typically remains manageable, often hovering around $O(n^2)$ or slightly higher.

Graph coloring problem

Consider a graph G and a positive integer m. We aim to determine if the nodes of G can be colored so that adjacent nodes have distinct colors, using at most m colors. This problem is known as the m-colorability decision problem. The m-colorability optimization problem seeks to find the smallest value of m that allows such coloring of graph G.

When coloring a map, only four colors are necessary to ensure that no adjacent regions share the same color. Historically, it was believed that five colors were always sufficient, but no map requiring more than four colors had been identified. This challenge persisted for centuries until a group of mathematicians, assisted by computer analysis, conclusively demonstrated that four colors are indeed adequate for planar graphs.

The m-coloring function initially converts the graph into its adjacency matrix and initializes an array **x[]** to zero. Colors are denoted by integers 1 through m, and a valid solution is represented by an n-tuple (x1, x2, ..., xn), where xi indicates the color of node i.

To implement a recursive backtracking algorithm for graph coloring, the process starts by calling the function **mcoloring(1)**.

Algorithm 8.3: Algorithm of graph coloring using backtracking

```
mcoloring(k) //It is an algorithm designed using a recursive backtracking
framework. It utilizes the Boolean adjacency matrix G[1:n, 1:n] to
represent the graph. The algorithm prints all assignments of integers from
1 to m to the graph's vertices, ensuring adjacent vertices are assigned
different integers. The parameter k signifies the index of the next vertex
to be colored.
{
Iterate until (false) {
// Generate all valid assignments for x[k].
NextValue(k); // Assign a valid color to x[k].
if (x[k] = 0) then return; // No new color is possible.
if (k = n) then // n vertices have been colored using at most m colors.
write(x[1: n]);
else
mcoloring(k+1);
}
}
```

Algorithm NextValue (k)

```
// x[1], ..., x[k-1] have been assigned integers within the range [1,
m], ensuring adjacent vertices have unique integers. A value for x[k] is
selected from the range [0, m], where x[k] is given the next highest number
that hasn't been used by adjacent vertices of vertex k. If such a color
isn't available, x[k] is set to 0.
{
Repeat
```

```
{
x[k] := (x[k] + 1) mod (m + 1); // Move to the next available color.
if (x[k] = 0)
then return; // All colors have been used.
for j := 1 to n do {
// Check if the color is distinct from adjacent colors.
if ((G[k, j] ≠ 0) and (x[k] = x[j])) then
{
// If (k, j) is an edge and adjacent vertices have the same color.
break;
}
}
if (j = n + 1) then
return; // A new distinct color has been found.
} until (false); // Otherwise, try finding another color.
}
```

Example 8.1: Color the following graph with the minimum number of colors by backtracking using the state space tree.

Solution: The following state space tree has been designed for all the possible solutions for given graph nodes:

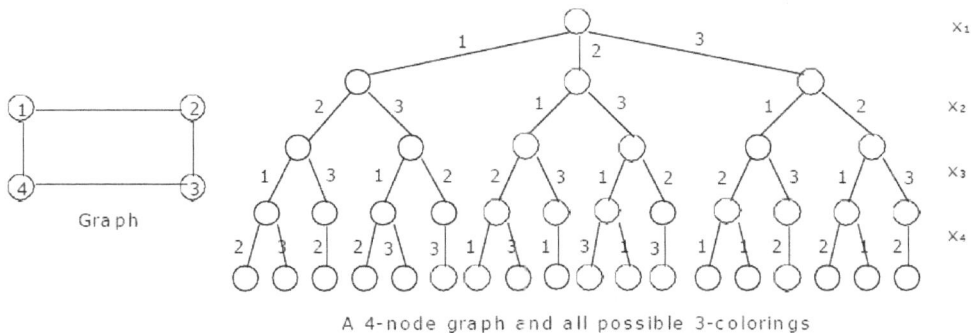

A 4-node graph and all possible 3-colorings

Figure 8.5: Graph with possible coloring

Program 8.3: Implementation of graph coloring problem using backtracking

```cpp
#include <bits/stdc++.h>
using namespace std;
#define V 4
void printSolution(int color[]);
bool isSafe(int v, bool graph[V][V], int color[], int c)
{
```

```
        for (int i = 0; i < V; i++)
            if (graph[v][i] && c == color[i])
                return false;
    return true;
}
// A recursive utility function to solve m coloring problem
bool graphColoringUtil(bool graph[V][V], int m, int color[], int v)
{
    // base case: If all vertices are assigned a color, then return true
    if (v == V)
        return true;
    // Consider this vertex v and try different colors
    for (int c = 1; c <= m; c++) {
        if (isSafe(v, graph, color, c)) {
            color[v] = c;
            if (graphColoringUtil(graph, m, color, v + 1) == true)
                return true;
            // If assigning color c doesn't lead to a solution then
remove it
            color[v] = 0;
            }
        }
        //If no color can be assigned to this vertex then return false
    return false;
}
/* This function solves the m Coloring problem using Backtracking. It
mainly uses graphColoringUtil() to solve the problem. It returns false
if the m colors cannot be assigned, otherwise return true and prints
assignments of colors to all vertices. Please note that there may be more
than one solutions, this function prints one of the feasible solutions.*/
bool graphColoring(bool graph[V][V], int m)
{
// Initialize all color values as 0. This initialization is needed correct
functioning of isSafe()
        int color[V];
        for (int i = 0; i < V; i++)
            color[i] = 0;
        // Call graphColoringUtil() for vertex 0
        if (graphColoringUtil(graph, m, color, 0) == false) {
            cout << "Solution does not exist";
```

```
            return false;
    }
    printSolution(color);
    return true;
}
// A utility function to print solution
void printSolution(int color[])
{
    cout << "Solution Exists:"
            << " Following are the assigned colors"
            << "\n";
    for (int i = 0; i < V; i++)
            cout << " " << color[i] << " ";
    cout << "\n";
}
int main()
{
    // Create following graph and test whether it is 3 colorable
    bool graph[V][V] = {
            { 0, 1, 1, 1 },
            { 1, 0, 1, 0 },
            { 1, 1, 0, 1 },
            { 1, 0, 1, 0 },
    };
    // Number of colors
    int m = 3;
    // Function call
    graphColoring(graph, m);
    return 0;
}
```

Complexity of graph coloring using backtracking

The complexity of graph coloring using backtracking is exponential due to the **nondeterministic polynomial time (NP)**-hard nature of the problem. The algorithm's time complexity increases with the number of vertices, edges, and available colors. It involves exploring a potentially large search space and checking constraints to ensure adjacent vertices have different colors. While heuristics can help, the fundamental challenge remains computationally intensive, especially for large or constrained graphs.

Constraints satisfaction problems

A constraint satisfaction problem, often known as a CSP, is a type of computational issue that requires the identification of a solution to a set of variables that are subject to conditions that have been established. To solve CSPs, one method that is frequently utilized is called backtracking. If you want to solve a CSP using backtracking, first determine the variables that are included in the complexity of the issue. It is possible for each variable to assign a value from a domain. Specify the potential values (domain) for each variable. This is the process of defining domains. In order to define constraints, you must first identify the constraints that restrict the potential combinations of variable values.

We can use the CSP strategy for solving the cryptarithmetic problem, the graph coloring problem, and the N-Queens problem. In this section, we will understand CSP for the cryptarithmetic problem.

Algorithm 8.4: CSP using backtracking search algorithm

```
Procedure Backtrack(assignment, csp):
// Returns a solution or failure
if assignment is complete:
        return assignment
var ← Select an unassigned variable from the CSP
for each value in the domain of var, respecting any ordering preferences,
based on assignment and CSP:
        if value is consistent with assignment:
                add { var = value } to assignment
                inferences ← Perform Inference(csp, var, value)
                    if inferences are not a failure:
                        add inferences to assignment
                result ← Backtrack(assignment, csp
            if result is not a failure:
                return result
        remove { var = value } and inferences from assignment
    return failure
```

Solution: If all variables are assigned values that satisfy the constraints, then a solution has been found.

Cryptarithmetic problem using CSP

Cryptarithmetic problems involve assigning digits to letters in an arithmetic expression such that the resulting equation holds true. For instance, in the problem *SEND + MORE = MONEY*, each letter represents a digit (from 0 to 9), and the goal is to find a valid assignment that satisfies the equation.

CSP contains the following components:

- **Variables**: These represent the unknowns in the problem. In cryptarithmetic, each letter corresponds to a variable.

- **Domains**: The domain of a variable consists of the possible values it can take. For cryptarithmetic, the domain is the set of digits (0-9).

- **Constraints**: Constraints define relationships between variables. In our case, constraints ensure that no two letters represent the same digit and that the equation remains valid.

Let us look at CSP representation. A CSP is defined by the following:

- A finite set of variables (V_1, V_2, ..., V_n).

- Non-empty domains for each variable (D_1, D_2, ..., D_n).

- A finite set of constraints (C_1, C_2, ..., C_m), where each constraint restricts the possible values for variables (e.g., $V_1 \neq V_2$).

Example 8.2: Solve the cryptarithmetic $TWO + TWO = FOUR$.

Solution:

$$
\begin{array}{r}
T\,W\,O \\
+\,T\,W\,O \\
\hline
F\,O\,U\,R
\end{array}
$$

Variables: F, T, U, W, R, O,   X1, X2, X3 (carry generated)

Domains: {0, 1, 2, 3, 4, 5, 6, 7, 8, 9} (same domain for all)

Sample constraints are given as follows:

All_different(F,T,U, W , R, O)

First, assign the value 5 to character O, so carry would be generated and forwarded to the next pair of characters. The value of carry is 1. R got the value 0. Next, we consider value 6 for W, we get carry, and the value for U is 3. Similarly, for character T, the value is 7. So, the resultant carry signifies 1 for character F.

$$
\begin{array}{rr}
T\,W\,O & 7\,6\,5 \\
+\,T\,W\,O & +\,7\,6\,5 \\
\hline
F\,O\,U\,R & 1\,5\,3\,0
\end{array}
$$

Program 8.4: Implementation of constraint satisfaction problem using backtracking

```
#include <iostream>
#include <vector>
```

```cpp
#include <algorithm>
using namespace std;
bool solveCryptarithmetic(vector<string>& words, string& resultWord) {
    string uniqueChars = "";
    for (string word : words) {
        for (char ch : word) {
            if (uniqueChars.find(ch) == string::npos)
                uniqueChars += ch;
        }
    }
    if (uniqueChars.size() > 10) return false; // Too many unique
characters for 0-9 digits
    sort(uniqueChars.begin(), uniqueChars.end());
    vector<int> mapping;
    do {
        if (uniqueChars.size() > 1 && mapping[0] == 0) continue; // Leading
zeros are not allowed
        int carry = 0, sum = 0;
        for (int i = resultWord.size() - 1; i >= 0; i--) {
            int digitSum = carry;
            for (string word : words) {
                if (word.size() > i)
                    digitSum += mapping[uniqueChars.find(word[i])];
            }
            carry = digitSum / 10;
            sum += (digitSum % 10) * pow(10, resultWord.size() - 1 - i);
        }
        if (carry == 0 && sum == 0) continue; // No leading zeros
        if (sum == 0) continue; // No leading zeros in result word
        int result = 0;
        for (char ch : resultWord)
            result = result * 10 + mapping[uniqueChars.find(ch)];
        if (sum == result) {
            for (char ch : uniqueChars)
                cout << ch << " = " << mapping[uniqueChars.find(ch)] << ",
";
            cout << endl;
            return true;
        }
    } while (next_permutation(mapping.begin(), mapping.end()));
    return false;
}
```

```
int main() {
    vector<string> words = {"TWO", "TWO"};
    string resultWord = "FOUR";
    vector<int> mapping;
    for (int i = 0; i < 10; i++)
        mapping.push_back(i);
    if (!solveCryptarithmetic(words, resultWord))
        cout << "No solution found!" << endl;
        return 0;
}
```

Complexity of CSP using backtracking

The time complexity of a CSP solved by backtracking is commonly exponential, denoted as $O(b^d)$, where:

- The branching factor, denoted as b, is the average number of possibilities available for each decision.

- The variable d represents the depth of the search tree, which is the greatest depth reached throughout the recursion process.

Sum of subsets

The subset sum problem involves identifying a subset of elements whose sum is equal to a specified number. In terms of the worst-case scenario, the backtracking strategy is capable of generating all permutations. However, it generally outperforms the recursive approach when it comes to solving the subset sum problem.

Let us consider one example to solve this problem.

Example 8.3: Given a set A consisting of n positive integers and a target value sum, determine whether there exists a subset of A whose elements add up to the target total. {9, 10, 1, 3, 2, 99}

Sum=4.

Solution: {1, 3} is the subset whose sum is 4.

For better understanding, we will use *Algorithm 8.5*.

In the backtracking process, as we traverse down the depth of the tree, we accumulate elements that we have encountered so far. If the sum of these elements satisfies the explicit criteria, we proceed to construct child nodes. Whenever the conditions are not satisfied, we cease generating more subtrees of that particular node and revert to the previous node in order to investigate the nodes that have not yet been examined. We must investigate the nodes throughout the width and depth of the tree. The generation of nodes along the width is regulated by a loop, whereas the generation of nodes along the depth is accomplished through recursion, specifically employing post-order traversal. An improved code can be achieved with the subsequent representation.

Algorithm 8.5: Sum of subset using backtracking

1. Begin with an empty subset.

2. Include the next element from the list in the subset.

3. If the subset achieves the sum M, terminate with that subset as the solution.

4. If the subset is infeasible or if the end of the list is reached, backtrack through the subset until you find the most appropriate value.

5. If the subset is feasible (sum of subset < M), proceed to step 2.

6. If all elements have been visited without discovering a suitable subset and no further backtracking is possible, halt without a solution.

Program 8.5: Implementation of the sum of subset problem using backtracking

```cpp
#include<iostream>
using namespace std;
   class Subset_Sum
   {
       public:
       void subsetsum_Backtracking(int Set[] , int pos, int sum, int
tmpsum, int size, bool & found)
       {
           if (sum == tmpsum)
               found = true;
               for (int i = pos; i < size; i++)
           {
            if (tmpsum + Set[i] <= sum)
               {
                   tmpsum += Set[i];
                   subsetsum_Backtracking(Set, i + 1, sum, tmpsum, size,
found);
                   tmpsum -= Set[i];
               }
           }
       }
   };
   int main()
   {
       int i, n, sum;
       Subset_Sum S;
```

```
cout << "Enter the number of elements in the set" << endl;
cin >> n;
int a[n];
cout << "Enter the values" << endl;
for(i=0;i<n;i++)
  cin>>a[i];
cout << "Enter the value of sum" << endl;
cin >> sum;
bool f = false;
S.subsetsum_Backtracking(a, 0, sum, 0, n, f);
if (f)
   cout << "subset with the given sum found" << endl;
else
   cout << "no required subset found" << endl;
return 0;
}
```

Complexity of sum of subset problem using backtracking

The time complexity of the sum of subset problem solved using backtracking is exponential, typically $O(2^n)$, where n is the number of elements in the set. However, this complexity can be reduced through optimization techniques like pruning and memorization, which help narrow down the search space and avoid redundant computations.

Hamiltonian cycles

Consider a connected graph G with n vertices, denoted as $G = (V, E)$. A Hamiltonian cycle, proposed by *William Hamilton*, is a closed path in graph G that traverses n edges, visits each vertex exactly once, and ends at the starting vertex. If the vertices of G are visited in the order v1, v2, ..., vn+1, then the edges $(vi, vi+1)$ are present in E, where $1 < i < n$. The vertices vi are distinct, except for v1 and vn+1, which are the same. In *Figure 8.5*, the graph G1 exhibits a Hamiltonian cycle consisting of the vertices 1, 2, 8, 7, 6, 5, 4, 3, and 1, while the graph G2 does not possess a Hamiltonian cycle:

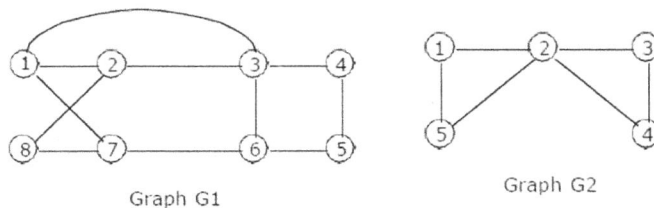

Graph G1   Graph G2

Figure 8.6: Connected graphs G1 and G2

The backtracking solution vector $(X1, \ldots X_n)$ is defined such that each xi represents the ith vertex visited in the proposed cycle. Given that $k = 1$, $X1$ can assume any of the n vertices. In order to prevent the repetition of the same cycle n times, it is necessary for $X1$ to be equal to 1. If $1 < k < n$, then Xk can be any vertex v that is different from $X1$, $X2$, ... , $Xk–1$, and v is next to kx-1. The vertex Xn must be the last remaining vertex, and it must be connected to both $Xn-1$ and $X1$.

The **NextValue** method can be used to specialize the recursive backtracking schema for finding all Hamiltonian cycles. The process begins by initializing the adjacency matrix $G[1: n, 1: n]$. Next, $X[2: n]$ is set to zero, and $X[1]$ is set to 1. Finally, the Hamiltonian (2) function is executed.

Algorithm 8.6: Hamiltonian cycle using backtracking

```
NextValue(k):
    repeat
        x[k]: = (x[k] + 1) mod (n + 1) // Get the next vertex
        if x[k] = 0 then
            return // If x[k] becomes 0, return
        if G[x[k-1], x[k]] ≠ 0 then // Check if there is an edge
            j: = 1
            while j <= k - 1 do
                if x[j] = x[k] then
                    break // Check for distinctness
                j := j + 1
            if j = k then
                if k < n or (k = n and G[x[n], x[1]] ≠ 0) then
                    return // If the vertex is distinct and meets
connectivity condition, return
    until false
```

```
Algorithm Hamiltonian(k):  //employs a recursive backtracking approach to
discover all Hamiltonian cycles within a graph. The graph, represented as
an adjacency matrix G[1:n, 1:n], is explored with cycles originating from
node 1.
{
repeat
{// Generate values for x[k].
NextValue(k); //Assign a valid next value to x[k]. If x[k] equals 0,
return.
if (k = n) then write (x[1: n]); else Hamiltonian(k + 1)
} until (false);
}
```

Program 8.6: Implementation of the Hamiltonian cycle using backtracking

This program prompts the user to enter the number of vertices and the adjacency matrix of the graph. Then, it checks whether a Hamiltonian cycle exists in the graph and prints the cycle if found.

```cpp
#include <iostream>
#include <vector>
using namespace std;
const int MAX = 10;
bool isSafe(int v, bool graph[MAX][MAX], vector<int>& path, int pos, int V)
{
    if (!graph[path[pos - 1]][v])
        return false;
    for (int i = 0; i < pos; i++)
        if (path[i] == v)
            return false;
    return true;
}
bool hamCycleUtil(bool graph[MAX][MAX], vector<int>& path, int pos, int V)
{
    if (pos == V) {
        if (graph[path[pos - 1]][path[0]])
            return true;
        else
            return false;
    }
    for (int v = 1; v < V; v++) {
        if (isSafe(v, graph, path, pos, V)) {
            path[pos] = v;
            if (hamCycleUtil(graph, path, pos + 1, V))
                return true;
            path[pos] = -1;
        }
    }
    return false;
}
void hamiltonianCycle(bool graph[MAX][MAX], int V) {
    vector<int> path(V, -1);
    path[0] = 0;
    if (hamCycleUtil(graph, path, 1, V)) {
        cout << "Hamiltonian cycle exists: ";
```

```
        for (int i = 0; i < V; i++)
            cout << path[i] << " ";
        cout << path[0] << endl;
    } else {
        cout << "No Hamiltonian cycle exists." << endl;
    }
}
int main() {
    int V;
    cout << "Enter the number of vertices: ";
    cin >> V;
    bool graph[MAX][MAX];
    cout << "Enter the adjacency matrix: " << endl;
    for (int i = 0; i < V; i++) {
        for (int j = 0; j < V; j++) {
            cin >> graph[i][j];
        }
    }
    hamiltonianCycle(graph, V);
    return 0;
}
```

Complexity of Hamiltonian cycle algorithm

The time complexity of the Hamiltonian cycle algorithm using backtracking is exponential, specifically $O(V!)$, where V is the number of vertices in the graph. This makes the algorithm impractical for large graphs due to its factorial growth in time complexity.

Solving crossword puzzles

A crossword puzzle comprises a grid, often square or rectangular, with white and black-shaded squares. The objective is to populate the white squares with letters, forming words or phrases according to the hints provided. Words are entered horizontally (across) and vertically (down) in languages that are read from left to right. Shaded squares separate the words or phrases.

The backtracking algorithm can be applied to solve a crossword puzzle in the following ways:

- **Naive approach**: The naive approach fills in the empty cells without any logic and then checks whether it was a valid placement. However, this can be inefficient and time-consuming.

- **Backtracking algorithm**: Backtracking is a form of a brute-force approach used when evaluating several options where we do not know which one is correct. We try to solve the problem using a trial-and-error method, making one decision at a time until we find the desired answer.

  The backtracking algorithm for solving a crossword puzzle traverses all the vacant cells, incrementally filling them with possible words retrieved from a dictionary file. The algorithm backtracks if a word filled does not comply with the constraint (the intersection point between horizontal and vertical words).

The following figure shows the crossword puzzle:

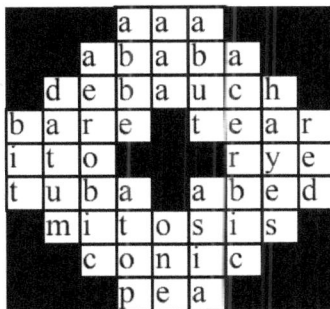

Figure 8.7: *Crossword puzzle*

Algorithm 8.7: Crossword puzzle problem using backtracking:

1. Begin by looking for a continuous row or column of empty cells.

2. Try to fill the continuous row or column with words retrieved from the dictionary file.

3. Examine the intersection point between the horizontal and vertical words for constraints before placing a word.

4. If a valid word can be placed, continue with the next continuous row or column of empty cells.

5. If none of the words can be placed, backtrack and alter the values for the cells visited previously.

Program 8.7: Implementation of crossword puzzle using backtracking algorithm

```
#include <iostream>
#include <vector>
#include <string>
#include <algorithm>
using namespace std;
const int GRID_SIZE = 10; // Change the grid size as needed
```

```cpp
// Structure to represent a word in the crossword
struct Word {
    string text;
    int row, col;
    bool isHorizontal;
    Word(string t, int r, int c, bool h) : text(t), row(r), col(c),
isHorizontal(h) {}
};
// Function to check if a word can be placed horizontally at the given
position
bool canPlaceHorizontal(const vector<string>& grid, const string& word, int
row, int col) {
    if (col + word.length() > GRID_SIZE) return false; // Check if word
exceeds grid boundary
    for (int i = 0; i < word.length(); ++i) {
        if (grid[row][col + i] != '-' && grid[row][col + i] != word[i]) {
            return false; // Check for conflicting letters
        }
    }
    return true;
}
// Function to check if a word can be placed vertically at the given
position
bool canPlaceVertical(const vector<string>& grid, const string& word, int
row, int col) {
    if (row + word.length() > GRID_SIZE) return false; // Check if word
exceeds grid boundary
    for (int i = 0; i < word.length(); ++i) {
        if (grid[row + i][col] != '-' && grid[row + i][col] != word[i]) {
            return false; // Check for conflicting letters
        }
    }
    return true;
}
// Function to place a word horizontally at the given position
void placeHorizontal(vector<string>& grid, const string& word, int row, int
col) {
    for (int i = 0; i < word.length(); ++i) {
        grid[row][col + i] = word[i];
    }
```

```
}
// Function to place a word vertically at the given position
void placeVertical(vector<string>& grid, const string& word, int row, int
col) {
    for (int i = 0; i < word.length(); ++i) {
        grid[row + i][col] = word[i];
    }
}
// Function to solve the crossword puzzle using backtracking
bool solveCrossword(vector<string>& grid, const vector<string>& words, int
index) {
    if (index == words.size()) return true; // Base case: all words are
placed
    for (int i = 0; i < GRID_SIZE; ++i) {
        for (int j = 0; j < GRID_SIZE; ++j) {
            if (grid[i][j] == '-' || grid[i][j] == words[index][0]) {
                if (canPlaceHorizontal(grid, words[index], i, j)) {
                    vector<string> tempGrid = grid;
                    placeHorizontal(tempGrid, words[index], i, j);
                    if (solveCrossword(tempGrid, words, index + 1)) {
                        grid = tempGrid;
                        return true;
                    }
                }
                if (canPlaceVertical(grid, words[index], i, j)) {
                    vector<string> tempGrid = grid;
                    placeVertical(tempGrid, words[index], i, j);
                    if (solveCrossword(tempGrid, words, index + 1)) {
                        grid = tempGrid;
                        return true;
                    }
                }
            }
        }
    }
    return false; // No solution found
}
// Function to display the crossword grid
void displayCrosswordGrid(const vector<string>& grid) {
```

```
    for (const string& row : grid) {
        cout << row << endl;
    }
}
int main() {
    vector<string> words = {"HELLO", "WORLD", "CROSSWORD", "PUZZLE"}; //
Words to place in the crossword
    sort(words.begin(), words.end(), [](const string& a, const string& b) {
return a.length() > b.length(); }); // Sort words by length
    vector<string> grid(GRID_SIZE, string(GRID_SIZE, '-')); // Initialize
the crossword grid with dashes
    if (solveCrossword(grid, words, 0)) {
        cout << "Crossword puzzle solved:" << endl;
        displayCrosswordGrid(grid);
    } else {
        cout << "No solution found." << endl;
    }
    return 0;
}
```

Complexity of crossword puzzle algorithm

The time and space complexity of the crossword puzzle problem using backtracking is as follows:

- **Time complexity**: Time complexity of the backtracking approach is $O((M * P)^D)$ where:

  N is the number of continuous rows or columns of empty cells (where a word is to be filled) in the grid.

  P is the list of possible words to be tested for the crossword constraint.

  For the backtracking function, the depth (D) of this recursive function will be equal to the crossword constraint.

  D = intersection point(s) between the horizontal and vertical words.

  M is the average length of a word.

- **Space complexity**: The space complexity is $O(L)$, where L is the length of the given word. This space is used for the recursion stack.

Conclusion

In this chapter, we explored various backtracking algorithms and their significance in solving complex computational problems. Backtracking provides an efficient way to navigate large solution spaces by systematically exploring and pruning possibilities. From classic problems like the N-Queens and Sudoku solver to constraint satisfaction and combinatorial challenges, backtracking proves to be a powerful tool in computer science. Its applications extend to graph problems, optimization, and even puzzle-solving. Understanding and implementing backtracking enhances problem-solving skills, making it a valuable approach in algorithm design and artificial intelligence.

In the next chapter, the user will learn about various kinds of branch and bound algorithms and their utility in the field of computer science engineering. Branch and bound is an algorithmic technique used to solve optimization problems by systematically exploring the solution space and pruning branches that cannot lead to an optimal solution.

Exercise

1. What is the N-Queens problem? Write a procedure to solve 8-Queens problem.

2. Explain the graph coloring problem using the backtracking technique.

3. Solve the cryptarithmetic SEND + MORE = MONEY using constraint satisfaction problem.

4. Find the subset from the given set whose sum is equal to 14. Use the backtracking strategy to solve the subset sum problem A = [2, 3, 5, 7, 10].

5. How can you solve a crossword puzzle problem using the constraint satisfaction mechanism? Justify your answer.

Join our Discord space

Join our Discord workspace for latest updates, offers, tech happenings around the world, new releases, and sessions with the authors:

https://discord.bpbonline.com

CHAPTER 9
Branch and Bound

Introduction

In this chapter of the book, we will discuss the various kinds of branch and bound algorithms and their utility in the field of computer science engineering. Branch and bound is an algorithmic technique used to solve optimization problems by systematically exploring the solution space and pruning branches that cannot lead to an optimal solution. It divides the problem into smaller subproblems and maintains bounds on the possible solutions within each subproblem. This chapter consists of detailed descriptions of various branch and bound algorithms with solved examples.

Structure

This chapter covers the following topics:

- Branch and bound approach
- 0/1 knapsack problem
- Traveling salesperson problem
- Resource allocation problem
- Quadratic assignment problem
- Job sequencing problem

Objectives

The objective of the chapter is to provide a systematic solution space search method. Like backtracking, boundary functions will prevent subtrees from being generated without a solution node. The branch and bound approach has two major differences from backtracking. First, the branching function of this system can use depth-first, breadth-first, or bounding functions. Secondly, the boundary function efficiently trims the search tree. The approach's primary goal is the optimal solution, the best optimization result. It assures the solution will be the highest or lowest value, depending on the problem. The branch and bound algorithm reduces the number of alternative solutions by methodically examining the solution space. By pruning fewer promising branches and favoring more promising ones, computational efficiency is improved. Bounding requires setting objective function upper and lower limits in subproblems. This technique eliminates branches that cannot produce better solutions than the best-known answer, narrowing the search. Since it can solve integer programming, the traveling salesman problem, the knapsack problem, and other combinatorial optimization problems, the branch and bound method is versatile.

Branch and bound approach

In computer science, there exist numerous optimization issues, some of which include finding the finite number of viable shortest paths in a graph or the least spanning trees. These problems can be addressed efficiently within polynomial time. Usually, these issues necessitate considering the most unfavorable outcome among all potential arrangements. The branch and bound algorithm generates alternative paths and constraints to get the optimal solution.

Using the branch and bound algorithm

Branch and bound is a highly efficient approach for solving some issues, as we have already mentioned. In this part, we will examine all instances in which branching and binding are suitable.

If the problem at hand involves discrete optimization, it is suitable to employ a branch and bound methodology. Discrete optimization pertains to issues when the variables are part of a discrete set. Some examples of these problems include 0-1 integer programming and network flow difficulties.

Branch and bound is an effective method for solving combinatory optimization problems. Combinatorial optimization is used to optimize an optimization problem by determining its maximum or lowest value, depending on its objective function. Combinatorial optimization challenges encompass Boolean satisfiability and integer linear programming.

The classification of branch and bound problems

It is based on the sequential order in which the state space tree is explored. There are three kinds of branch and bound methods, which are as follows:

- **FIFO** branch and bound is a search algorithm that explores the search space in a FIFO manner while using a bounding function to determine which branches to explore further.

- **LIFO** branch and bound is a method used in optimization problems to find the most efficient solution. It involves exploring the search space by prioritizing the nodes with the most potential for improvement.

- **Least cost-branch and bound**, which aims to minimize the cost of the solution by iteratively evaluating and refining the search space.

0/1 knapsack problem

Provided are two arrays, **V[ ]** and **W[ ]**, which represent the values and weights associated with n elements, respectively. Determine the subset with the highest value (maximum profit) from **V[ ]** such that the total weight of this subset is less than or equal to the knapsack capacity **W**.

Note: **The limitation in this scenario is that we can only place an item in the bag either in its entirety or not at all. It is not possible to partially place an item in the bag.**

Algorithm 9.1: Algorithm of 0/1 knapsack using branch and bound

1. Arrange all items in descending order based on their value-to-weight ratio to facilitate the computation of an upper limit using the greedy approach.

2. Begin by setting the maximum profit, **maxProfit**, to 0. Next, construct an empty queue called **Q**. Then, create a fake node for the decision tree and add it to the queue, **Q**. The dummy node has a profit and weight of 0.

3. Continue executing the following steps as long as **Q** is not empty:

   a. Retrieve an element from **Q**. Designate the extracted item as **u**.

   b. Calculate the profitability of the next level node. Update **maxProfit** if the profit exceeds the current **maxProfit**.

   c. Calculate the upper limit of the node in the following level. If the bound exceeds the maximum profit, then append the next level node to the **Q**.

   d. In this scenario, the next-level node is excluded from the solution. A node is added to the queue with the level set as the next level, but the weight and profit are calculated without taking into account the nodes at the next level.

Example 9.1: Let us take the following example: M is equal to *15*, *n* is equal to *4*, and we get the values $(P1, P2, P3, P4) = (10, 10, 12, 18)$ and $(w1, w2, w3, w4) = (2, 4, 6, 9)$.

Solution: You can use the branch and bound strategy to solve the 0/1 knapsack problem. This problem entails the calculation of both the lower limit and upper bound for each node.

Insert the initial item into the knapsack. The remaining weight of the knapsack is calculated by subtracting *2* from *15*, resulting in a value of *13*. Put the next item, $W2$, inside the backpack. The remaining weight of the knapsack is calculated as $13 - 4 = 9$. Put the next item, $W3$, into the knapsack. As a result, the remaining weight of the knapsack will be *3*, calculated by subtracting *6* from *9*. Fractions are prohibited in the calculation of the upper bound; hence, $W4$ cannot be included in the knapsack.

The total profit, denoted as P, is equal to the sum of three components: $P1$, $P2$, and $P3$. Specifically, $P1$ is *10*, $P2$ is *10*, and $P3$ is *12*. Therefore, the total profit is *32*.

The upper bound is equal to *32*.

To determine the lower bound, we can include item $W4$ in the knapsack, as the calculation of the lower bound allows for the consideration of fractional values.

The lower bound is calculated by adding *10*, *10*, *12*, and the product of *3* multiplied by *18*, which equals *32* plus *6*, resulting in a value of *38*.

$$Lower\ bound = 10 + 10 + 12 + ((3/9) \times 18) = 32 + 6 = 38$$

The knapsack problem is a maximization problem; however, the branch and bound technique can only be applied to minimization problems. To change a maximization problem into a minimization problem, we need to assign a negative sign to both the upper bound and lower bound.

Therefore, the *upper bound (U)* $= -32$

Lower bound (L) $= -38$

We select the route that has the smallest disparity between the upper limit and lower limit. If the difference is equal, we determine the path by comparing the upper bounds and eliminate the node with the highest upper bound, according to the following figure:

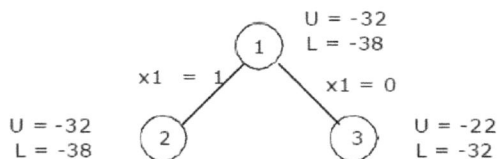

Figure 9.1: Branch and bound up to first level

Now, we will determine the upper bound and lower bound for nodes 2 and 3. For node 2, $x1 = 1$, which means we should place the first item in the knapsack.

$U = 10 + 10 + 12 = 32$, write it as -32.

$L = 10 + 10 + 12 + ((3/9) \times 18 = 32 + 6 = 38$, write it as -38.

For node 3, $x1 = 0$, which means we should not place the first item in the knapsack.

$U = 10 + 12 = 22$, write it as -22.

$L = 10 + 12 + ((5/9) \times 18 = 22 + 10 = 32$, write it as -32.

Next, we determine UB and LB for nodes 2 and 3.

Node2 $UB - LB = -32 + 38 = 6$

Node3 $UB - LB = -22 + 32 = 10$

Figure 9.2 represents a tree up to two levels:

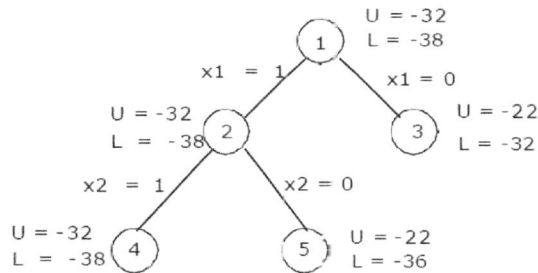

Figure 9.2: *Branch and bound up to the second level*

Select node 2 due to its lowest difference value, i.e., *6*.

Now, calculate LB and UB for node 4 and node 5 as follows:

For node 4, $UB - LB = -32 + 38 = 6$.

For node 5, $UB - LB = -22 + 36 = 14$.

Figure 9.3 represents a tree with up to three levels:

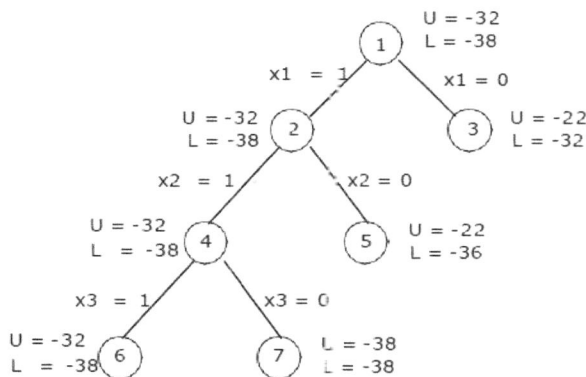

Figure 9.3: *Branch and bound up to the third level*

Select node 4, having the lowest difference value, i.e., 6.

Now, calculate LB and UB for node 6 and node 7.

For node 6, $UB - LB = -32 + 38 = 6$.

For node 7, $UB - LB = -38 + 38 = 0$.

Select node 7, having the lowest difference value, i.e., 0.

Figure 9.4 represents a tree up to four levels:

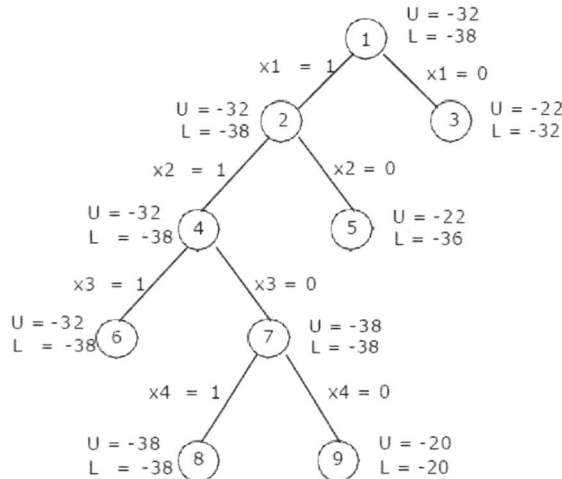

Figure 9.4: *Branch and bound up to the fourth level*

Now, we will calculate LB and UB of nodes 8 and 9. Calculate the difference of lower and upper bound of nodes 8 and 9.

For node 8, $UB - LB = -38 + 38 = 0$.

For node 9, $UB - LB = -20 + 20 = 0$.

For this particular instance, the difference is the same; hence, compare the upper bounds of nodes 8 and 9. The node that has the highest possible upper bound should be discarded. Choose node 8, and leave node 9 out of consideration because it has the highest possible upper bound.

Consider the path from $1 \to 2 \to 4 \to 7 \to 8$.

$$X1 = 1$$
$$X2 = 1$$
$$X3 = 0$$
$$X4 = 1$$

The final solution for $0/1$ knapsack problem is $(x1, x2, x3, x4) = (1, 1, 0, 1)$.

Maximum profit is as follows:

$$\sum P_i \, x_i = 10 \times 1 + 10 \times 1 + 12 \times 0 + 18 \times 1$$
$$= 10 + 10 + 18 = 38$$

Program 9.1: Implementation of 0/1 knapsack problem using branch and bound

```cpp
// C++ program to solve knapsack problem using branch and bound
#include <bits/stdc++.h>
using namespace std;
// Structure for Item which store weight and corresponding value of Item
struct Item
{
    float weight;
    int value;
};

// Node structure to store information of decision tree
struct Node
{
    // level --> Level of node in decision tree (or index in arr[]
    // profit --> Profit of nodes on path from root to this node (including
this node)
    // bound ---> Upper bound of maximum profit in subtree of this node/
    int level, profit, bound;
    float weight;
};

// Comparison function to sort Item according val/weight ratio
bool cmp(Item a, Item b)
{
    double r1 = (double)a.value / a.weight;
    double r2 = (double)b.value / b.weight;
    return r1 > r2;
}

// Returns bound of profit in subtree rooted with u. This function mainly
uses Greedy solution to find
// an upper bound on maximum profit.
int bound(Node u, int n, int W, Item arr[])
{
    // if weight overcomes the knapsack capacity, return 0 as expected
bound
    if (u.weight >= W)
```

```
            return 0;
    // initialize bound on profit by current profit
    int profit_bound = u.profit;
    // start including items from index 1 more to current item index
    int j = u.level + 1;
    int totweight = u.weight;
    // checking index condition and knapsack capacity condition
    while ((j < n) && (totweight + arr[j].weight <= W))
    {
        totweight += arr[j].weight;
        profit_bound += arr[j].value;
        j++;
    }

    // If k is not n, include last item partially for upper bound on profit
    if (j < n)
        profit_bound += (W - totweight) * arr[j].value / arr[j].weight;

    return profit_bound;
}

// Returns maximum profit we can get with capacity W
int knapsack(int W, Item arr[], int n)
{
    // sorting Item on basis of value per unit weight.
    sort(arr, arr + n, cmp);

    // make a queue for traversing the node
    queue<Node> Q;
    Node u, v;
    // dummy node at starting
    u.level = -1;
    u.profit = u.weight = 0;
    Q.push(u);

    // One by one extract an item from decision tree compute profit of all
children of extracted item and keep saving maxProfit
    int maxProfit = 0;
    while (!Q.empty())
    {
        // Dequeue a node
        u = Q.front();
        Q.pop();
        // If it is starting node, assign level 0
```

```
        if (u.level == -1)
            v.level = 0;
        // If there is nothing on next level
        if (u.level == n-1)
            continue;
        // Else if not last node, then increment level, and compute profit
of children nodes.
        v.level = u.level + 1;

        // Taking current level's item add current level's weight and value
to node u's weight and value
        v.weight = u.weight + arr[v.level].weight;
        v.profit = u.profit + arr[v.level].value;

        // If cumulated weight is less than W and profit is greater than
previous profit, update maxprofit
        if (v.weight <= W && v.profit > maxProfit)
            maxProfit = v.profit;

        // Get the upper bound on profit to decide whether to add v to Q or
not.
        v.bound = bound(v, n, W, arr);
        // If bound value is greater than profit, then only push into queue
for further consideration
        if (v.bound > maxProfit)
            Q.push(v);
        // Do the same thing, but Without taking the item in knapsack
        v.weight = u.weight;
        v.profit = u.profit;
        v.bound = bound(v, n, W, arr);
        if (v.bound > maxProfit)
            Q.push(v);
    }
    return maxProfit;
}
int main()
{
    int W = 10; // Weight of knapsack
    Item arr[] = {{2, 40}, {3.14, 50}, {1.98, 100}, {5, 95}, {3, 30}};
    int n = sizeof(arr) / sizeof(arr[0]);
    cout << "Maximum possible profit = " << knapsack(W, arr, n);
    return 0;
}
```

Complexity of 0/1 knapsack problem

The following explanations show how we determined the time and space complexity of the 0/1 knapsack problem using branch and bound.

- **Time complexity**: The time complexity of the 0/1 knapsack problem using the branch and bound technique is $O(2n \cdot n \cdot logn)$, where n is the number of items. This complexity arises due to the exponential nature of the branch and bound algorithm, which explores all possible subsets of items to find the optimal solution.

- **Space complexity**: Regarding the space complexity, the branch and bound approach for the 0/1 knapsack problem typically requires $O(n)$ space to store the current state of the problem during the search process. This space complexity is relatively lower compared to the time complexity, as it mainly involves storing information about the current state of the search rather than maintaining a large data structure.

Traveling salesperson problem

We can solve the problem by utilizing the dynamic programming approach, which has a time complexity of $O(n^2.2^n)$ for the worst-case scenario. The branch and bound strategy, which makes use of an efficient bounding function, can be used to tackle this problem. The temporal complexity of the traveling salesperson issue has been determined to be $O(n^2.2^n)$ when utilizing the **least cost** (**LC**) branch and bound algorithm. This indicates that there has been no change or reduction in complexity compared to the original method.

We begin at a specific node, travel to each node exactly once, and then return to the initial node with the least amount of expense.

Let $G = (V, E)$ be a connected graph. Let $C(i, J)$ be the cost of edge $<i, j>$. $c_{ij} = \infty$ if $<i, j> \not\in E$, and let $|V| = n$, the number of vertices. Every tour starts at vertex 1 and ends at the same vertex. So, the solution space is given by $S = \{1, \pi, 1 \mid \pi$ *is a permutation of* $(2, 3, \ldots, n)\}$ and $|S| = (n-1)!$. The size of S can be reduced by restricting S so that $(1, i_1, i_2, \ldots. i_{n-1}, 1) \in S$ if $<i_j, i_{j+1}> \in E, 0 <= j <= n - 1$ and $i_0 = i_n = 1$.

Algorithm 9.2: TSP algorithm

Refer to the following steps for the algorithm of the traveling salesperson problem using the branch and bound approach:

1. Reduce the cost matrix that has been provided. By reducing each row and column of a matrix, the matrix is said to be reduced. When a row or column contains at least one zero and all of the other entries are non-negative, we say that the row or column has already been reduced. The following is how this can be accomplished:

   a. First, take the minimum element from the first row and subtract it from all of the items in the first row. Next, take the minimum element from the second row and subtract it from the second row. In the same manner, apply the same process to each and every row.

b. Determine the total number of components that were removed without being added to rows.

c. The matrix that was obtained following the row reduction should then have column reductions applied to it.

Taking the minimum element from the first column and subtracting it from all of the items in the first column is the first step in the column reduction process. Next, pick the minimum element from the second column and remove it from the second column. In the same manner, apply the same approach to each and every column.

d. Determine the total number of components that were removed from the sections of the table.

e. Determine the total amount in which row-wise reduction and column-wise reduction have been added together.

Cumulative reduced *sum* = *row-wise* reduction *sum* + *column-wise* reduction sum.

Associate the cumulative reduced sum to the starting state as lower bound and ∞ as upper bound.

2. Determine the reduced cost matrix for each node R. Let A represent the cost matrix that has been lowered for node R. Consider a child node S of the node R, where the tree edge (R, S) represents the inclusion of the edge $<i, j>$ in the tour. To acquire the reduced cost matrix for S, it is necessary to check if S is a leaf node. If S is not a leaf node, the reduced cost matrix can be produced using the following method:

a. Replace all elements in row i and column j of matrix A with the symbol ∞.

b. Set the element $A(j, 1)$ to infinity.

c. Eliminate all rows and columns in the resultant matrix except for the rows and columns that contain only infinity (∞). Let r represent the total amount deducted to reduce the matrix.

d. The equation $c(S) = c(R) + A(i, j) + r$ calculates the cost function $c(S)$, where r represents the total amount deducted to reduce the matrix. $c(R)$ represents the lower bound of the ith node in the (i, j) path.

3. Repeat step number 2 until all nodes are traversed.

Example 9.2: Let us take the following example. Calculate the LC branch and bound solution for the traveling salesperson problem whose cost matrix is as follows:

$$Cost\ matrix = \begin{bmatrix} \infty & 20 & 30 & 10 & 11 \\ 15 & \infty & 16 & 4 & 2 \\ 3 & 5 & \infty & 2 & 4 \\ 19 & 6 & 18 & \infty & 3 \\ 16 & 4 & 7 & 16 & \infty \end{bmatrix}$$

Solution: The solution is as follows:

1. Calculate the reduced cost matrix as follows:

    Subtract 10 (which is the minimum) from all values in the 1st row.

    Subtract 2 (which is the minimum) from all values in the 2nd row.

    Subtract 2 (which is the minimum) from all values in the 3rd row.

    Subtract 3 (which is the minimum) from all values in the 4th row.

    Subtract 4 (which is the minimum) from all values in the 5th row.

$$Reduced\ cost\ matrix = \begin{bmatrix} \infty & 10 & 20 & 0 & 1 \\ 13 & \infty & 14 & 2 & 0 \\ 1 & 3 & \infty & 0 & 2 \\ 16 & 3 & 15 & \infty & 0 \\ 12 & 0 & 3 & 12 & \infty \end{bmatrix}$$

Now, row-wise reduction $sum = 10 + 2 + 2 + 3 + 4 = 21$.

Apply column reduction for resultant matrix.

Subtract 1 (which is the minimum) from all values in the 1st column.

Subtract 3 (which is the minimum) from all values in the 3rd column.

$$Reduced\ cost\ matrix = \begin{bmatrix} \infty & 10 & 17 & 0 & 1 \\ 12 & \infty & 11 & 2 & 0 \\ 0 & 3 & \infty & 0 & 2 \\ 15 & 3 & 12 & \infty & 0 \\ 11 & 0 & 0 & 12 & \infty \end{bmatrix}$$

Now, column wise reduction $sum = 1 + 0 + 3 + 0 + 0 = 4$.

Cumulative reduced sum = row reduction sum + column reduction sum

$$= 21 + 4 = 25$$

This is the cost of a root, i.e., node 1, because this is the initially reduced cost matrix. The lower bound for the node is 25, and the upper bound is ∞. Starting from node 1, we can next visit the vertices 2, 3, 4, and 5. So, consider exploring paths (1, 2), (1, 3), (1, 4), and (1, 5).

After step 1, the tree structure would be as follows, where variable i denotes the next node to visit:

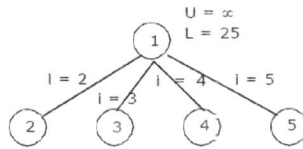

Figure 9.5: *Branch and bound tree after phase 1*

2. Let us pick up path (1, 2):

Change all entries of row 1 and column 2 of the matrix to ∞ and also set $A(2, 1)$ to ∞.

$$\text{Reduced cost matrix } (A) = \begin{bmatrix} \infty & \infty & \infty & \infty & \infty \\ \infty & \infty & 11 & 2 & 0 \\ 0 & \infty & \infty & 0 & 2 \\ 15 & \infty & 12 & \infty & 0 \\ 11 & \infty & 0 & 12 & \infty \end{bmatrix}$$

Apply row and column reduction for the rows and columns that are not completely ∞.

$$\text{Resultant cost matrix } (A) = \begin{bmatrix} \infty & \infty & \infty & \infty & \infty \\ \infty & \infty & 11 & 2 & 0 \\ 0 & \infty & \infty & 0 & 2 \\ 15 & \infty & 12 & \infty & 0 \\ 11 & \infty & 0 & 12 & \infty \end{bmatrix}$$

Row reduction sum $= 0 + 0 + 0 + 0 = 0$

Column reduction sum $= 0 + 0 + 0 + 0 = 0$

Cumulative reduction $(r) = 0 + 0 = 0$

That is why, $c(S) = c(R) + A(1, 2) + r$

$$C(S) = 25 + 10 + 0 = 35$$

Now, pick up path (1, 3):

Change all entries of row 1 and column 3 of the matrix to ∞ and also set $A(3, 1)$ to ∞.

$$\text{Reduced cost matrix } (A) = \begin{bmatrix} \infty & \infty & \infty & \infty & \infty \\ 12 & \infty & \infty & 2 & 0 \\ \infty & 3 & \infty & 0 & 2 \\ 15 & 3 & \infty & \infty & 0 \\ 11 & 0 & \infty & 12 & \infty \end{bmatrix}$$

Apply row and column reduction for the rows and columns that are not completely ∞.

$$
\text{Reduced cost matrix (A)} = \begin{bmatrix}
\infty & \infty & \infty & \infty & \infty \\
1 & \infty & \infty & 2 & 0 \\
\infty & 3 & \infty & 0 & 2 \\
4 & 3 & \infty & \infty & 0 \\
0 & 0 & \infty & 12 & \infty
\end{bmatrix}
$$

Row reduction sum = $0 + 0 + 0 + 0 = 0$

Column reduction sum = $11 + 0 + 0 + 0 = 11$

Cumulative reduction (r) = $0 + 11 = 11$

That is why, $c(S) = c(R) + A(1, 3) + r$

$$C(S) = 25 + 17 + 11 = 53$$

Now, pick up path (1, 4):

Change all entries of row 1 and column 4 of the matrix to ∞ and also set A(4, 1) to ∞.

$$
\text{Reduced cost matrix (A)} = \begin{bmatrix}
\infty & \infty & \infty & \infty & \infty \\
12 & \infty & 11 & \infty & 0 \\
0 & 3 & \infty & \infty & 2 \\
\infty & 3 & 12 & \infty & 0 \\
11 & 0 & 0 & \infty & \infty
\end{bmatrix}
$$

Apply row and column reduction for the rows and columns that are not completely ∞.

$$
\text{Reduced cost matrix (A)} = \begin{bmatrix}
\infty & \infty & \infty & \infty & \infty \\
12 & \infty & 11 & \infty & 0 \\
0 & 3 & \infty & \infty & 2 \\
\infty & 3 & 12 & \infty & 0 \\
11 & 0 & 0 & \infty & \infty
\end{bmatrix}
$$

Row reduction sum = $0 + 0 + 0 + 0 = 0$

Column reduction sum = $0 + 0 + 0 + 0 = 0$

Cumulative reduction (r) = $0 + 0 = 0$

That is why, $c(S) = c(R) + A(1, 4) + r$

$$C(S) = 25 + 0 + 0 = 25$$

Now, pick up path (1, 5):

Change all entries of row 1 and column 5 of the matrix to ∞ and also set A(5, 1) to ∞.

Reduced cost matrix (A) =
$$\begin{bmatrix} \infty & \infty & \infty & \infty & \infty \\ 12 & \infty & 11 & 2 & \infty \\ 0 & 3 & \infty & 0 & \infty \\ 15 & 3 & 12 & \infty & \infty \\ \infty & 0 & 0 & 12 & \infty \end{bmatrix}$$

Apply row and column reduction for the rows and columns that are not completely ∞.

Reduced cost matrix (A) =
$$\begin{bmatrix} \infty & \infty & \infty & \infty & \infty \\ 10 & \infty & 9 & 0 & \infty \\ 0 & 3 & \infty & 0 & \infty \\ 12 & 0 & 9 & \infty & \infty \\ \infty & 0 & 0 & 12 & \infty \end{bmatrix}$$

Row reduction sum = 2 + 0 + 3 + 0 = 5

Column reduction sum = 0 + 0 + 0 + 0 = 0

Cumulative reduction (r) = 5 + 0 = 5

That is why, $c(S) = c(R) + A(1, 5) + r$

$$C(S) = 25 + 1 + 5 = 31$$

The tree structure after step 2 is as follows:

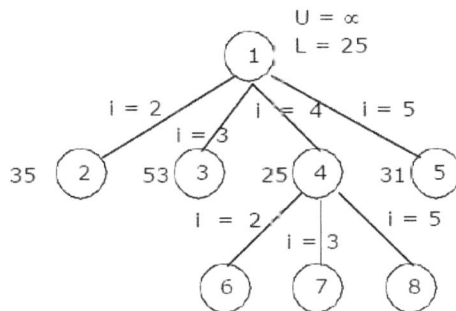

Figure 9.6: Branch and bound tree after phase 2

The cost of the paths between *(1, 2) = 35, (1, 3) = 53, (1, 4) = 25,* and *(1, 5) = 31.* The cost of the path between (1, 4) is minimum. Hence, the matrix obtained for path (1, 4) is considered as the reduced cost matrix.

Cost matrix $(A) =$
$$\begin{bmatrix} \infty & \infty & \infty & \infty & \infty \\ 12 & \infty & 11 & \infty & 0 \\ 0 & 3 & \infty & \infty & 2 \\ \infty & 3 & 12 & \infty & 0 \\ 11 & 0 & 0 & \infty & \infty \end{bmatrix}$$

The new available paths are (4, 2), (4, 3), and (4, 5).

3. Consider the path (4, 2):

    Change all entries of row 4 and column 2 of A to ∞ and also set A(2, 1) to ∞.

Reduced cost matrix $(A) =$
$$\begin{bmatrix} \infty & \infty & \infty & \infty & \infty \\ \infty & \infty & 11 & \infty & 0 \\ 0 & \infty & \infty & \infty & 2 \\ \infty & \infty & \infty & \infty & \infty \\ 11 & \infty & 0 & \infty & \infty \end{bmatrix}$$

Apply row and column reduction for the rows and columns that are not completely ∞.

Resultant reduced cost matrix (A) $=$
$$\begin{bmatrix} \infty & \infty & \infty & \infty & \infty \\ \infty & \infty & 11 & \infty & 0 \\ 0 & \infty & \infty & \infty & 2 \\ \infty & \infty & \infty & \infty & \infty \\ 11 & \infty & 0 & \infty & \infty \end{bmatrix}$$

Row reduction sum $= 0 + 0 + 0 + 0 = 0$

Column reduction sum $= 0 + 0 + 0 + 0 = 0$

Cumulative reduction $(r) = 0 + 0 = 0$

That is why, $c(S) = c(R) + A(4, 2) + r$

$C(S) = 25 + 3 + 0 = 28$

Consider the path (4, 3):

Change all entries of row 4 and column 3 of A to ∞ and also set A(3, 1) to ∞.

Reduced cost matrix $(A) =$
$$\begin{bmatrix} \infty & \infty & \infty & \infty & \infty \\ 12 & \infty & \infty & \infty & 0 \\ \infty & 3 & \infty & \infty & 2 \\ \infty & \infty & \infty & \infty & \infty \\ 11 & 0 & \infty & \infty & \infty \end{bmatrix}$$

Apply row and column reduction for the rows and columns that are not completely ∞.

$$Resultant\ cost\ matrix\ (A) = \begin{bmatrix} \infty & \infty & \infty & \infty & \infty \\ 1 & \infty & \infty & \infty & 0 \\ \infty & 1 & \infty & \infty & 0 \\ \infty & \infty & \infty & \infty & \infty \\ 0 & 0 & \infty & \infty & \infty \end{bmatrix}$$

Row reduction sum = 2

Column reduction sum = 11

Cumulative reduction (r) = 2 + 11 = 13

That is why, c(S) = c(R) + A(4, 3) + r

$$C(S) = 25 + 12 + 13 = 50$$

Consider the path (4, 5):

Change all entries of row 4 and column 5 of A to ∞ and also set A(5, 1) to ∞.

$$Reduced\ cost\ matrix\ (A) = \begin{bmatrix} \infty & \infty & \infty & \infty & \infty \\ 12 & \infty & 11 & \infty & \infty \\ 0 & 3 & \infty & \infty & \infty \\ \infty & \infty & \infty & \infty & \infty \\ \infty & 0 & 0 & \infty & \infty \end{bmatrix}$$

Apply row and column reduction for the rows and columns that are not completely ∞.

$$Resultant\ cost\ matrix\ (A) = \begin{bmatrix} \infty & \infty & \infty & \infty & \infty \\ 1 & \infty & 0 & \infty & \infty \\ 0 & 3 & \infty & \infty & \infty \\ \infty & \infty & \infty & \infty & \infty \\ \infty & 0 & 0 & \infty & \infty \end{bmatrix}$$

Row reduction sum = 11

Column reduction sum = 0

Cumulative reduction (r) = 11 + 0 = 11

That is why, c(S) = c(R) + A(4, 5) + r

$$C(S) = 25 + 0 + 11 = 36$$

After step 3, the tree structure is as follows:

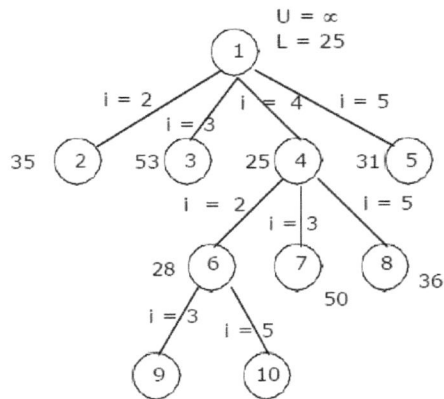

Figure 9.7: Branch and bound tree after phase 3

The cost of the paths between $(4, 2) = 28$, $(4, 3) = 50$, and $(4, 5) = 36$. The cost of the path between $(4, 2)$ is minimum. Hence, the matrix obtained for path $(4, 2)$ is considered as the reduced cost matrix.

$$
\text{Cost matrix } (A) = \begin{bmatrix} \infty & \infty & \infty & \infty & \infty \\ \infty & \infty & 11 & \infty & 0 \\ 0 & \infty & \infty & \infty & 2 \\ \infty & \infty & \infty & \infty & \infty \\ 11 & \infty & 0 & \infty & \infty \end{bmatrix}
$$

The new possible paths are $(2, 3)$ and $(2, 5)$.

4. Consider the path $(2, 3)$.

   Change all entries of row 2 and column 3 of A to ∞ and also set $A(3, 1)$ to ∞.

$$
\text{Reduced cost matrix } (A) = \begin{bmatrix} \infty & \infty & \infty & \infty & \infty \\ \infty & \infty & \infty & \infty & \infty \\ \infty & \infty & \infty & \infty & 2 \\ \infty & \infty & \infty & \infty & \infty \\ 11 & \infty & \infty & \infty & \infty \end{bmatrix}
$$

Apply row and column reduction for the rows and columns whose rows and columns are not completely ∞.

$$\text{Resultant cost matrix } (A) = \begin{bmatrix} \infty & \infty & \infty & \infty & \infty \\ \infty & \infty & \infty & \infty & \infty \\ \infty & \infty & \infty & \infty & 0 \\ \infty & \infty & \infty & \infty & \infty \\ 0 & \infty & \infty & \infty & \infty \end{bmatrix}$$

Row reduction sum = 2

Column reduction sum = 11

Cumulative reduction $(r) = 2 + 11 = 13$

That is why, $c(S) = c(R) + A(4, 5) + r$

$$C(S) = 28 + 11 + 13 = 52$$

Take the next path (2, 5).

Change all entries of row 2 and column 5 of A to ∞ and also set A(5, 1) to ∞.

$$\text{Reduced cost matrix } (A) = \begin{bmatrix} \infty & \infty & \infty & \infty & \infty \\ \infty & \infty & \infty & \infty & \infty \\ 0 & \infty & \infty & \infty & \infty \\ \infty & \infty & \infty & \infty & \infty \\ \infty & \infty & 0 & \infty & \infty \end{bmatrix}$$

Apply row and column reduction for the rows and columns that are not completely ∞.

$$\text{Resultant cost matrix } (A) = \begin{bmatrix} \infty & \infty & \infty & \infty & \infty \\ \infty & \infty & \infty & \infty & \infty \\ 0 & \infty & \infty & \infty & \infty \\ \infty & \infty & \infty & \infty & \infty \\ \infty & \infty & 0 & \infty & \infty \end{bmatrix}$$

Row reduction sum = 0

Column reduction sum = 0

Cumulative reduction $(r) = 0 + 0 = 0$

That is why, $c(S) = c(R) + A(2, 5) + r$

$$C(S) = 28 + 0 + 0 = 28$$

After step 4, the tree structure is as follows:

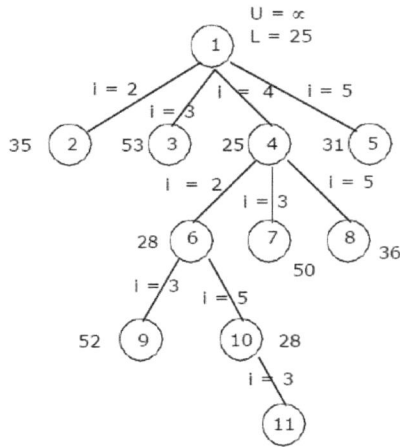

Figure 9.8: *Branch and bound tree after phase 4*

The cost of the paths between $(2, 3) = 52$ and $(2, 5) = 28$. The cost of the path between $(2, 5)$ is minimum. Hence, the matrix obtained for path $(2, 5)$ is considered as the reduced cost matrix.

$$\text{Cost matrix } (A) = \begin{bmatrix} \infty & \infty & \infty & \infty & \infty \\ \infty & \infty & \infty & \infty & \infty \\ 0 & \infty & \infty & \infty & \infty \\ \infty & \infty & \infty & \infty & \infty \\ \infty & \infty & 0 & \infty & \infty \end{bmatrix}$$

The new possible path is $(5, 3)$.

Let us consider this new path,

Change all entries of row 5 and column 3 of A to ∞ and also set $A(3, 1)$ to ∞. Apply row and column reduction for the rows and columns that are not completely ∞.

$$\text{Resultant cost matrix } (A) = \begin{bmatrix} \infty & \infty & \infty & \infty & \infty \\ \infty & \infty & \infty & \infty & \infty \\ \infty & \infty & \infty & \infty & \infty \\ \infty & \infty & \infty & \infty & \infty \\ \infty & \infty & \infty & \infty & \infty \end{bmatrix}$$

Row reduction sum = 0

Column reduction sum = 0

Cumulative reduction $(r) = 0 + 0 = 0$

That is why, $c(S) = c(R) + A(5, 3) + r$

$$C(S) = 28 + 0 + 0 = 28$$

The final tree structure will be as follows:

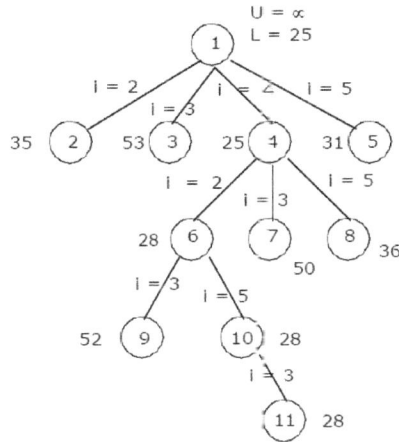

Figure 9.9: *Branch and bound tree after phase 5*

The path of the traveling salesperson problem is:

$1 - 4 - 2 - 5 - 3 - 1$

The minimum cost of the path is $10 + 6 + 2 + 7 + 3 = 28$.

Program 9.2: Implementation of TSP using branch and bound

```
#include <iostream>
#include <vector>
#include <queue>
#include <utility>
#include <limits>
using namespace std;
const int INF = numeric_limits<int>::max();
int n;
vector<vector<int>> cost;
vector<bool> visited;
vector<int> path;
int minCost = INF;

struct Node {
    vector<int> path;
    int cost;
    int level;
```

```
        Node(vector<int> p, int c, int l) : path(p), cost(c), level(l) {}
};
int reducedMatrix(vector<vector<int>>& matrix) {
    int n = matrix.size();int cost = 0;
    for (int i = 0; i < n; i++) {
        int minVal = *min_element(matrix[i].begin(), matrix[i].end());
        if (minVal != 0) {
            cost += minVal;
            for (int j = 0; j < n; j++) {
                if (matrix[i][j] != INF) {
                    matrix[i][j] -= minVal;
                }
            }
        }
    }
    vector<int> minVals(n, INF);
    for (int i = 0; i < n; i++) {
        for (int j = 0; j < n; j++) {
            if (matrix[j][i] != INF && matrix[j][i] < minVals[i]) {
                minVals[i] = matrix[j][i];
            }
        }
    }
    for (int i = 0; i < n; i++) {
        if (minVals[i] != INF) {
            cost += minVals[i];
            for (int j = 0; j < n; j++) {
                if (matrix[j][i] != INF) {
                    matrix[j][i] -= minVals[i];
                }
            }
        }
    }
    return cost;
}
int bound(Node& node) {
    int n = node.path.size();
    vector<vector<int>> matrix(n, vector<int>(n, INF));
    for (int i = 0; i < n; i++) {
        for (int j = 0; j < n; j++) {
            matrix[i][j] = cost[node.path[i]][node.path[j]];
```

```
            }
        }
        int bound = node.cost + reducedMatrix(matrix);
        for (int i = 0; i < n; i++) {
            matrix[i][node.path.back()] = INF;
        }
        int temp = reducedMatrix(matrix);
        bound += temp;
        return bound;
}

void solve() {
    queue<Node> q;
    vector<int> path = {0};
    q.push(Node(path, 0, 0));
    while (!q.empty()) {
        Node node = q.front();
        q.pop();
        if (node.level == n) {
            if (cost[node.path.back()][0] != INF) {
                int totalCost = node.cost + cost[node.path.back()][0];
                if (totalCost < minCost) {
                    minCost = totalCost;
                    path = node.path;
                }
            }
        } else {
            for (int i = 1; i < n; i++) {
                if (find(node.path.begin(), node.path.end(), i) == node.
path.end() && cost[node.path.back()][i] != INF) {
                    vector<int> newPath = node.path;
                    newPath.push_back(i);
                    int newCost = node.cost + cost[node.path.back()][i];
                    Node newNode(newPath, newCost, node.level + 1);
                    int boundVal = bound(newNode);
                    if (boundVal < minCost) {
                        q.push(newNode);
                    }
                }
            }
        }
    }
```

```
        }
    }
}
int main() {
    cout << "Enter the number of cities: ";
    cin >> n;
    cost = vector<vector<int>>(n, vector<int>(n, INF));
    visited = vector<bool>(n, false);
    cout << "Enter the cost matrix:\n";
    for (int i = 0; i < n; i++) {
        for (int j = 0; j < n; j++) {
            cin >> cost[i][j];
        }    }
    solve();
    cout << "Minimum cost: " << minCost << endl;
    cout << "Optimal path: ";
    for (int city : path)
        cout << city + 1 << " ";
    cout << endl;        return 0;     }
```

Complexity of TSP using branch and bound

The following explanations outline the calculation of the time and space complexity of the traveling salesman problem using branch and bound:

- **Time complexity**: The time complexity of solving the traveling salesman problem with branch and bound is $O(n!)$ in the worst case, akin to brute force. Despite this, branch and bound can excel by efficiently pruning the search space using lower bounds, leading to improved practical performance, especially for smaller instances. The choice of bounding function is critical for effectiveness. In practice, branch and bound can outperform brute force due to its ability to discard unpromising branches, making it a valuable approach for optimizing TSP solutions.

- **Space complexity**: The space complexity of the branch and bound algorithm for TSP is $O(n)$, as it needs to store the current partial solution and the set of unvisited cities.

Resource allocation problem

The resource allocation problem is a classic example of an optimization problem. The objective of this problem is to determine the most effective way to distribute limited resources (such as personnel, machinery, or finances) among a number of different projects or activities. The purpose is often to achieve some other target while satisfying constraints, such as minimizing costs, maximizing earnings, or achieving some other objective.

There is a specific variation of this problem known as the **job assignment problem**, which can be handled by employing the branch and bound method.

Let us begin by looking at the problem, which is as follows:

Given N workers and N jobs, we want to assign each job to exactly one worker and each worker to exactly one job. Each assignment has an associated cost (or profit), and we want to find an assignment that minimizes the total cost (or maximizes the total profit).

In branch and bound, we intelligently explore the state space tree by considering promising nodes first. The key idea is to use an approximate cost function to guide the search. We choose a live node with the least cost (promising cost) to explore the next node in the list.

Two common approaches for the cost function are as follows:

1. **For each worker**, choose the job with the minimum cost from the list of unassigned jobs (minimum entry from each row).

2. **For each job**, choose the worker with the lowest cost for that job from the list of unassigned workers (minimum entry from each column).

We can significantly reduce the search space and improve efficiency by following this approach.

Algorithm 9.3: Algorithm of job assignment using branch and bound

```
/* The findMinCost function uses the Least() and Add() functions to manage
the list of live nodes. Least() retrieves and removes the live node with
the least cost from the list, returning it.  Add(x) computes the cost
of x and adds it to the list of live nodes. The list of live nodes is
implemented as a min-heap. */
// Node structure for the Search Space Tree
struct Node {
    int job_number;
    int worker_number;
    Node* parent;
    int cost;
};
// Input: Cost matrix for the Job Assignment problem, Output: Optimal cost
and job assignment
void findMinCost(int costMatrix[][]) {
// Initialize the list of live nodes (min-Heap) with the root of the search
tree, i.e., a dummy node
    while (true) {
        // Retrieve and remove the live node with the least estimated cost
        Node* E = Least();
        // Check if the retrieved node is a leaf node
        if (isLeafNode(E)) {
```

```
            printSolution();
            return;
        }
        // For each child node x of E
        for (each child x of E) {
            Add(x); // Add x to the list of live nodes
            x->parent = E; // Set the parent pointer to maintain the path
to the root
        }
    }
}
```

Example 9.3: Given the matrix for workers and jobs, we have to find the minimum cost to assign the job to the workers.

9	2	7	8
6	4	3	7
5	8	1	8
7	6	9	4

Table 9.1: Input matrix

Solution: Here, rows are mapped by A, B, C, and D, while columns denote jobs like J1, J2, J3, and J4. Value 8 means worker A will take eight units of time to complete job J4.

Let us consider job J2 is assigned to worker A, mark it as green. cost becomes 2, and job J2 and worker A become unavailable (marked in red) as follows:

9	2	7	8
6	4	3	7
5	8	1	8
7	6	9	4

Table 9.2: Matrix after pass 1

Now, we give job J3 to worker B because it has the lowest cost of the jobs that have not been given yet. The price goes up to 2 + 3 = 5, and job J3 and worker B are no longer available, which is shown as follows:

9	2	7	8
6	4	3	7
5	8	1	8
7	6	9	4

Table 9.3: Matrix after pass 2

The last job, job J4, is given to worker D because it is the only one left. Job J1 was given to worker C because it had the lowest cost of all the jobs that had not been assigned. *Final cost = 2 + 3 + 5 + 4 = 14.* The matrix is as follows:

9	2	7	8
6	4	3	7
5	8	1	8
7	6	9	4

Table 9.4: Matrix after pass 3

Program 9.3: Implementation of resource allocation using branch and bound

```
#include <bits/stdc++.h>
using namespace std;
#define N 4
struct Node
{
    Node* parent;
    int pathCost;
    int cost;
    int workerID;
    int jobID;
    bool assigned[N];
};
// Function to allocate a new search tree node, here Person x is assigned
to job y
Node* newNode(int x, int y, bool assigned[], Node* parent)
{
    Node* node = new Node;
    for (int j = 0; j < N; j++)
        node->assigned[j] = assigned[j];
    node->assigned[y] = true;
    node->parent = parent;
    node->workerID = x;
    node->jobID = y;
    return node;
}
// Function to calculate the least promising cost of node after worker x is
assigned to job y.
int calculateCost(int costMatrix[N][N], int x, int y, bool assigned[])
{
    int cost = 0;
    bool available[N] = {true};
```

```
    for (int i = x + 1; i < N; i++)
    {
        int min = INT_MAX, minIndex = -1;
        for (int j = 0; j < N; j++)
        {
            if (!assigned[j] && available[j] && costMatrix[i][j] < min)
            {
                minIndex = j;
                min = costMatrix[i][j];
            }   }
        cost += min;
        available[minIndex] = false;
    }
    return cost; }
struct comp
{
    bool operator()(const Node* lhs, const Node* rhs) const
    {
        return lhs->cost > rhs->cost;
    }
};
void printAssignments(Node *min)
{
    if(min->parent==NULL)
        return;
    printAssignments(min->parent);
    cout << "Assign Worker " << char(min->workerID + 'A') << " to Job " <<
min->jobID << endl;
}
int findMinCost(int costMatrix[N][N])
{
    // Create a priority queue to store live nodes of search tree;
    priority_queue<Node*, std::vector<Node*>, comp> pq;
    bool assigned[N] = {false};
    Node* root = newNode(-1, -1, assigned, NULL);
    root->pathCost = root->cost = 0;
    root->workerID = -1;
    pq.push(root);
    while (!pq.empty())
    {
        Node* min = pq.top();
        pq.pop();
      int i = min->workerID + 1;
```

```
    if (i == N)
    {
        printAssignments(min);
        return min->cost;
    }
    for (int j = 0; j < N; j++)
    {
      if (!min->assigned[j])
      {
        Node* child = newNode(i, j, min->assigned, min);
        child->pathCost = min->pathCost + costMatrix[i][j];
        child->cost = child->pathCost + calculateCost(costMatrix, i, j,
child->assigned);
        pq.push(child);
      }
    }
  }
}
int main()
{
    int costMatrix[N][N] = { {9, 2, 7, 8},
                             {6, 4, 3, 7},
                             {5, 8, 1, 8},
                             {7, 6, 9, 4}};
    cout << "\n Optimal Cost is " << findMinCost(costMatrix);
    return 0;
}
```

Complexity of resource allocation

$O(M*N)$ is the time complexity. This is because a double for loop is used to go through the M x N matrix over and over again.

We denote space for extras as $O(M+N)$ because it tracks applicants and jobs with two groups of size M and N.

Quadratic assignment problem

The objective is to identify the allocation that minimizes the overall cost or distance, considering both the distances and the flows. The quadratic assignment problem can be formulated as a quadratic objective function by utilizing the distance matrix, flow matrix, and restrictions that guarantee each facility is assigned to only one location and each location is assigned to only one facility.

The **quadratic assignment problem** (QAP) is a widely recognized instance of an NP-hard problem, implying that finding the optimal solution might be challenging for bigger instances. Consequently, numerous methods and heuristics have been developed to locate close approximations of solutions rapidly.

Algorithm 9.4: QAP using branch and bound algorithm

The steps of the algorithm are as follows:

1. Define the distance matrix (D) and the flow matrix (F).

    a. Set the initial bound (can be calculated using a heuristic or set to infinity).

    b. Initialize an empty solution and the best solution found so far.

2. At each node of the search tree, choose a facility-location pair to assign.

    a. Generate child nodes by assigning the facility to each unassigned location.

3. Calculate a lower bound for each node. This can be done using relaxation techniques or heuristics.

    a. If the lower bound of a node is greater than or equal to the current best-known solution, prune that branch.

4. Use a priority queue (or stack for depth-first search) to explore nodes based on their bounds.

    a. Update the best solution when a complete assignment with a lower cost is found.

5. The algorithm terminates when all nodes have been explored or pruned. The best solution at the end is the optimal solution.

Example 9.4: Considering four facilities (F1, F2, F3, F4) and four sites (L1, L2, L3, L4). Our cost matrix shows the pairwise distances, that is, costs, between facilities. We also have a flow matrix to show the interactions, that is, the flow between sites. Based on interconnections between facilities and sites, identify the project that reduces the overall cost. Every facility has to be allocated to exactly one location, and that location can only house one other facility.

The cost matrix is as follows:

	L1	L2	L3	L4
F1	0	2	3	1
F2	2	0	1	4
F3	3	1	0	2
F4	1	4	2	0

Table 9.5: Cost matrix

The flow matrix is as follows:

	L1	L2	L3	L4
F1	0	1	2	3
F2	1	0	4	2
F3	2	4	0	1
F4	3	2	1	0

Table 9.6: Flow matrix

Solution: The final solution of the preceding problem is as follows:

In order to determine the overall expense, we examine every combination of facilities denoted by (i, j) and their corresponding positions (location1, location2). The product of the cost of allocating facility1 to facility2 (facilities[facility1][facility2]) and the flow from location1 to location2 (locations[location1][location2]) is calculated. This procedure is carried out for every combination of facilities in the assignment, and the costs are aggregated.

The optimal assignment is *F1:L1, F3:L2, F2:L3, F4:L4*

The total cost is *44*.

Program 9.4: Implementation of QAP using branch and bound

```
#include <iostream>
#include <vector>
#include <algorithm>
using namespace std;
int calculateTotalCost(const vector<vector<int>>& facilities, const
vector<vector<int>>& locations, const vector<int>& assignment) {
        int totalCost = 0;
        int n = facilities.size();
        for (int i = 0; i < n; i++) {
                for (int j = 0; j < n; j++) {
                        int facility1 = assignment[i];
                        int facility2 = assignment[j];
                        int location1 = i;
                        int location2 = j;
                        totalCost += facilities[facility1][facility2] *
locations[location1][location2];
                }
        }
        return totalCost;
```

```
}
int main() {
      // Facilities cost matrix
      vector<vector<int>> facilities = {
            {0, 2, 3, 1},
            {2, 0, 1, 4},
            {3, 1, 0, 2},
            {1, 4, 2, 0}
      };
      // Flow matrix
      vector<vector<int>> locations = {
            {0, 1, 2, 3},
            {1, 0, 4, 2},
            {2, 4, 0, 1},
            {3, 2, 1, 0}
      };
      int n = facilities.size();
      // Generate initial assignment (0, 1, 2, 3)
      vector<int> assignment(n);
      for (int i = 0; i < n; i++) {
            assignment[i] = i;
      }
      // Calculate the initial total cost
      int minCost = calculateTotalCost(facilities, locations, assignment);
      vector<int> minAssignment = assignment;
      // Generate all permutations of the assignment
      while (next_permutation(assignment.begin(), assignment.end())) {
            int cost = calculateTotalCost(facilities, locations,
assignment);
            if (cost < minCost) {
                  minCost = cost;
                  minAssignment = assignment;
            }
      }
      // Print the optimal assignment and total cost
      cout << "Optimal Assignment: ";
      for (int i = 0; i < n; i++) {
            cout << "F" << (minAssignment[i] + 1) << "->L" << (i + 1) << "
";
      }
```

```
        cout << endl;
        cout << "Total Cost: " << minCost << endl;
        return 0;
}
```

Complexity of QAP using branch and bound

The worst-case time complexity of QAP is $(O(n!))$ due to factorial growth in the number of possible assignments (permutations).

Job sequencing problem

One processor and n jobs are assigned to us. Every job i does corresponds with a three-tuples pi, di, ti. Job i need ti units of processing time. Should its processing not meet the deadline, di, a penalty, pi, results. The aim is to choose a subset J of the n jobs such that their deadlines allow every job in J to be finished. Consequently, a penalty might be paid just on those positions not under J. The subset J should be such that among all conceivable subsets J, the penalty obtained is minimum. Such J is optimal.

Example 9.5: Let us assume the following instances having n=4:

(p1, d1, t1) = (5, 1, 1),

(p2, d2, t2) = (10, 3, 2),

(p3, d3, t3) = (6, 2, 1),

(p4, d4, t4) = (3, 1, 1)

Solution: We will follow the FIFO approach to solve the problem.

The cost function c(x) for any circular node x is the minimum penalty corresponding to any node in the subtree with root x.

The value of $c(x) = \infty$ for a square node.

Let S_x be the subset of jobs selected for J at node x.

If $m = max \{i \mid i \in S_x \}$, then $Cx = \sum Pi$.

$S(2) = \{1\}$	$m=1$	$C(2) = \displaystyle\sum_{i<m,i\neq x} p_i = 0$
$S(3) = \{2\}$	$m=2$	$C(3) = \displaystyle\sum_{i<2} p_i = \sum_{i=1} p_i = 5$
$S(4) = \{3\}$	$m=3$	$C(4) = \displaystyle\sum_{i<3} p_i = \sum_{i=1,2} p_i = p_1 + p_2 = 5 + 10 = 15$

$S(5) = \{4\}$	$m=4$	$C(5) = \sum_{i<4} p_i = \sum_{i=1,2,3} p_i = p_1 + p_2 + p_3 = 5 + 10 + 6 = 21$
$S(6) = \{1, 2\}$	$m=2$	$C(6) = \sum_{i=1,2 \; i \in S_x} p_i = \sum_{i<1 \; i \neq S(6)} p_i = 0$
$S(7) = \{1, 3\}$	$m=3$	$C(7) = \sum_{i<3, \; i \neq S(7)} p_i = p_2 = 10$
$S(8) = \{1, 4\}$	$m=4$	$C(8) = \sum_{i<4, \; i \neq S(8)} p_i = p_2 + p_3 = 10 + 6 = 16$
$S(9) = \{2,3\}$	$m=3$	$C(9) = 5$
$S(10) = \{2, 4\}$	$m=3$	$C(10) = 11$
$S(11) = \{3, 4\}$	$m=4$	$C(11) = 15$

Table 9.7: *Job sequencing problem solution*

The calculation of the upper bound, $U(x) = \sum p_i$, where i does not belong to Sx.

$U(1) = 0$

$U(2) = P2 + P3 + P4 = 10 + 6 + 3 = 19$	job 1 eliminated
$U(3) = P1 + P3 + P4 = 5 + 6 + 3 = 14$	job 2 eliminated
$U(4) = P1 + P2 + P4 = 5 + 10 + 3 = 18$	job 3 eliminated
$U(5) = P1 + P2 + P3 = 5 + 10 + 6 = 21$	job 4 eliminated
$U(6) = P3 + P4 = 6 + 3 = 9$	jobs 1, 2 eliminated
$U(7) = P2 + P4 = 10 + 3 = 13$	jobs 1, 3 eliminated
$U(8) = P2 + P3 = 10 + 6 = 16$	jobs 1, 4 eliminated
$U(9) = P1 + P4 = 5 + 3 = 8$	jobs 2, 3 eliminated
$U(10) = P1 + P3 = 5 + 6 = 11$	jobs 2, 4 eliminated
$U(11) = P1 + P2 = 5 + 10 = 15$	jobs 3, 4 eliminated

Algorithm 9.5: Job sequencing using branch and bound

The algorithm steps for job sequencing using branch and bound are as follows:

1. **Sort jobs by profit**: Sort the jobs in decreasing order of profit because we want to maximize profit.

2. **State space tree**: The solution space is represented as a tree. Each node in the tree represents a partial solution (a subset of jobs scheduled up to that point).

3. **Bounding function**: For a node, compute an upper bound on the maximum profit that can be obtained from that node. If the upper bound is less than the best-known solution, prune that node.

4. **Branching**: For each node, generate child nodes by including or excluding the next job in the list.

5. **Pruning**: Use the bounding function to eliminate nodes that cannot yield a better solution than the current best.

Program 9.5: Implementation of job sequencing using branch and bound

```cpp
#include <iostream>
#include <vector>
#include <algorithm>
#include <queue>
using namespace std;
struct Job {
    int id;
    int deadline;
    int profit;
};
struct Node {
    vector<bool> job_schedule;
    int level;
    int profit;
    int bound;
};
// Comparison function to sort jobs according to their profits
bool jobComparator(Job a, Job b) {
    return (a.profit > b.profit);  }
// Function to calculate upper bound of profit in subtree rooted with 'u'
int calculateBound(Node u, int n, vector<Job>& jobs) {
    if (u.level >= n) return 0;
    int profit_bound = u.profit;
    int total_time = 0;
    for (int i = u.level; i < n; i++) {
        total_time += jobs[i].deadline;
        if (total_time <= jobs[i].deadline) {
            profit_bound += jobs[i].profit;
        }
    }   return profit_bound;
}
// Branch and Bound algorithm for Job Sequencing
void jobSequencing(vector<Job>& jobs, int n) {
    sort(jobs.begin(), jobs.end(), jobComparator);
    queue<Node> Q;
    Node u, v;
```

```cpp
    u.level = -1;
    u.profit = 0;
    u.job_schedule.resize(n, false);
    u.bound = calculateBound(u, n, jobs);
    Q.push(u);
    int max_profit = 0;
    vector<bool> best_schedule;
    while (!Q.empty()) {
        u = Q.front();
        Q.pop();
        if (u.level == -1) v.level = 0;
        if (u.level == n - 1) continue;
        v.level = u.level + 1;
        v.job_schedule = u.job_schedule;
        v.job_schedule[v.level] = true;
        v.profit = u.profit + jobs[v.level].profit;
        if (v.profit > max_profit) {
            max_profit = v.profit;
            best_schedule = v.job_schedule;
        }
        v.bound = calculateBound(v, n, jobs);
        if (v.bound > max_profit) Q.push(v);
        v.job_schedule[v.level] = false;
        v.profit = u.profit;
        v.bound = calculateBound(v, n, jobs);
        if (v.bound > max_profit) Q.push(v);
    }
    cout << "Scheduled Jobs: ";
    for (int i = 0; i < n; i++) {
        if (best_schedule[i]) {
            cout << jobs[i].id << " ";
        }
    }
    cout << "\n Max Profit: " << max_profit << endl;
}
int main() {
    vector<Job> jobs = {
        {1, 2, 100},
        {2, 1, 19},
        {3, 2, 27},
        {4, 1, 25},
        {5, 3, 15}
```

```
};
int n = jobs.size();
jobSequencing(jobs, n);
return 0;
}
```

Complexity of job sequencing using branch and bound

The time complexity and space complexity of the job sequencing problem using branch and bound approach is calculated as follows:

- **Time complexity**: The time complexity of the branch and bound algorithm for job sequencing depends on several factors, including the number of jobs n, the structure of the state space tree, and the efficiency of the bounding function. The following is a breakdown of the factors affecting the time complexity:

  o **State space tree size**: The state space tree can have up to 2^n nodes in the worst case, since each job can either be included or excluded from the schedule. Therefore, the size of the state space tree is $O(2^n)$.

  o **Bounding function**: For each node, we compute the bound, which in the worst case might require $O(n)$ operations (to calculate the remaining profit from unscheduled jobs). However, this bounding function can often be computed more efficiently with optimizations.

  o **Queue operations**: In the worst case, every node might be added to the queue, and each node might be processed once. Thus, the operations on the queue, such as insertion and extraction, can be $O(2^n)$.

  Considering these factors, the worst-case time complexity of the Branch and bound algorithm for job sequencing is $O(2^n . n)$. However, the actual complexity can be much lower in practice due to effective pruning by the bounding function, which reduces the number of nodes that need to be explored.

- **Space complexity**: The space complexity of the branch and bound algorithm is determined by the storage required for the queue and the state space tree nodes, as follows:

  o **Queue size**: In the worst case, the queue can hold up to $O(2^n)$ nodes. Each node contains information about the current state, including the job schedule (a Boolean vector of size n), profit, bound, and level.

  o **Auxiliary space**: Additional space is required for storing job information and intermediate calculations. Thus, the space complexity of the branch and bound algorithm for job sequencing is $O(2^n . n)$ in the worst case.

Conclusion

Branch and bound is an optimization method that breaks problems down into smaller problems and gets rid of non-optimal branches, which speeds up the search for solutions. This chapter discusses the applications of branch and bound in work scheduling, resource allocation, quadratic assignment, 0/1 knapsack, and traveling salesperson problems. Each of these problems shows how branch and bound can be used to solve difficult computer problems by keeping upper and lower solution bounds. Using heuristics and boundary functions is useful in computer science and engineering because it greatly reduces the amount of work that needs to be done on processing. Understanding these algorithms enables the development of superior solutions for various issues, including scheduling and logistics.

In the next chapter, the readers will learn about graph theory in computer science. Graph theory offers a versatile framework for representing relationships and connections between entities, making it essential for various applications across numerous fields.

Exercise

1. What do you mean by the branch and bound technique? Why is it better?

2. Find the solution using 0/1 knapsack problem, M is equal to 18, n is equal to 4, and we get the values (P1, P2, P3, P4) = (12, 10, 11, 16) and (w1, w2, w3, w4) = (3, 4, 7, 8).

3. What is the significance of branch and bound to solve the traveling salesman problem?

4. How can job sequencing be implemented using the branch and bound mechanism? Explain with a suitable example.

Join our Discord space

Join our Discord workspace for latest updates, offers, tech happenings around the world, new releases, and sessions with the authors:

https://discord.bpbonline.com

CHAPTER 10

Graph Algorithms

Introduction

This chapter will provide a concise overview of graph theory, a key area within computer science dedicated to solving problems related to graphs. Graph theory offers a versatile framework for representing relationships and connections between entities, making it essential for various applications across numerous fields. Graphs consist of nodes (or vertices) connected by edges (or links), and they can model many real-world systems. For example, in social networks, nodes represent individuals and edges represent friendships; in transportation networks, nodes represent cities and edges represent routes, and in biological networks, nodes and edges depict interactions between genes or proteins.

Structure

The chapter covers the following topics:

- Basic terminology and representation of graph
- Topological sort
- Strongly connected components
- Eulerian path and circuit
- Single-source shortest path algorithm

- All-pair shortest paths
- Max-flow min-cut

Objectives

This chapter aims to offer a thorough grasp of fundamental graph theory concepts and algorithms. Graph theory is a crucial discipline in computer science, providing effective tools for addressing intricate problems concerning networks, pathways, and connections. By engaging with this chapter, you will acquire the knowledge and skills necessary to model, analyze, and solve problems using graph-based approaches.

Basic terminology and representation of graph

A graph can be described as a collection of vertices and edges that connect these vertices. Unlike a tree structure, a graph allows for complex relationships between its vertices (nodes), rather than a strict parent-child hierarchy.

A graph G can be formally defined as an ordered pair $G(V,Es)$ where:

- $V(G)$ represents the set of vertices.
- $E(G)$ represents the set of edges that connect these vertices.

Consider a graph $G(V, E)$ with five vertices (A, B, C, D, E) and six edges: $(A, B), (B, C), (C, E), (E, D), (D, B), (D, A)$. This graph is illustrated in the following figure:

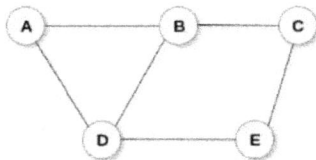

Figure 10.1: Graph

Directed and undirected graph

A graph can be either directed or undirected. In an undirected graph, edges do not have associated directions. *Figure 10.1* illustrates an undirected graph, where edges are not marked with any specific direction. For example, if there is an edge between vertex A and B, you can traverse from B to A as well as from A to B.

In a directed graph, edges are represented as ordered pairs. Each edge signifies a specific directed path from a vertex A to another vertex B. Node A is referred to as the initial node, while node B is the terminal node. *Figure 10.2* shows an example of a directed graph:

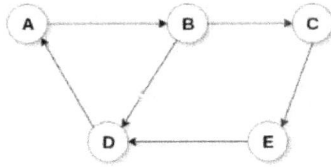

Figure 10.2: *Directed graph*

The following figure illustrates an undirected graph:

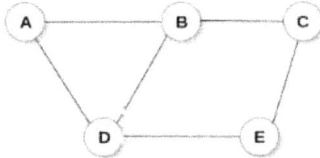

Figure 10.3: *Undirected graph*

Graph terminology

The following are important terms related to graphs:

- **Path**: A path is a sequence of nodes that are traversed in order to reach a terminal node V from an initial node U.

- **Closed path**: A path is called a closed path if the initial node is the same as the terminal node. A closed path is denoted as $V_0 = V_N$.

- **Simple path**: A simple path P is a path where all nodes are distinct, except possibly the initial and terminal nodes V_0 and V_N.

- **Cycle**: A cycle is a path that has no repeated edges or vertices, except that the first and last vertices are the same.

- **Connected graph**: A connected graph is one in which there is a path between every pair of vertices (u, v) in V. There are no isolated nodes in a connected graph.

- **Complete graph**: A complete graph is one in which every node is connected to all other nodes. A complete graph on n nodes contains $n(n-1)/2$ edges.

- **Weighted graph**: In a weighted graph, each edge is assigned some data, such as length or weight. The weight w(e) of an edge e is a positive value indicating the cost of traversing the edge.

- **Digraph**: A digraph (directed graph) is a graph in which each edge is associated with a direction, and traversal is allowed only in the specified direction.

- **Loop**: A loop is an edge that connects a vertex to itself.

- **Adjacent nodes**: Two nodes u and v are adjacent if they are connected by an edge e. They are also referred to as neighbors.

- **Degree of the node**: The degree of a node is the number of edges connected to that node. A node with degree 0 is called an isolated node.

Representation of graph

Graph representation refers to the method used to store a graph in a computer's memory. A graph is a data structure consisting of a set of vertices (also known as nodes) and edges. There are two primary methods to store graphs in a computer's memory:

- Sequential representation (or, adjacency matrix representation).
- Linked list representation (or, adjacency list representation).

In sequential representation, the graph is stored using an adjacency matrix. In a linked list representation, an adjacency list is used to store the graph.

Sequential representation

In sequential representation, an adjacency matrix is employed to depict the connections between vertices and edges within the graph. This matrix can be utilized to represent undirected graphs, directed graphs, weighted directed graphs, and weighted undirected graphs.

If $adj[i][j] = w$, it indicates that there exists an edge from vertex i to vertex j with weight w.

In the adjacency matrix representation of an undirected graph G, an entry A_{ij} will be 1, if an edge exists between vertices V_i and V_j. If an undirected graph G consists of n vertices, then its adjacency matrix A, denoted as a_{ij}, is an $n \times n$ matrix defined as:

$a_{ij} = 1$ {if there is a path that exists from V_i to V_j}

$a_{ij} = 0$ {otherwise}

In an adjacency matrix, 0 indicates no connection between nodes, while 1 indicates the presence of an edge between two nodes.

If the graph does not contain self-loops, the diagonal entries of the adjacency matrix will be 0.

Now, let us examine the adjacency matrix representation of an undirected graph:

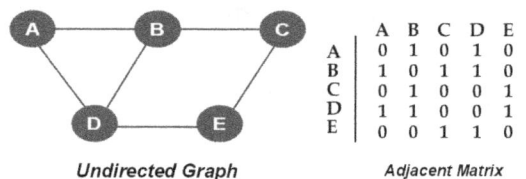

	A	B	C	D	E
A	0	1	0	1	0
B	1	0	1	1	0
C	0	1	0	0	1
D	1	1	0	0	1
E	0	0	1	1	0

Undirected Graph   *Adjacent Matrix*

Figure 10.4: *Adjacency matrix of an undirected graph*

In the aforementioned figure, an image illustrates the mapping among the vertices (A, B, C, D, E) using the adjacency matrix.

There are different adjacency matrices for directed and undirected graphs. In a directed graph, an entry A_{ij} will be 1 only when there is an edge directed from V_i to V_j.

Adjacency matrix for a directed graph

In a directed graph, edges represent a specific path from one vertex to another. If there is a path from vertex A to vertex B, it means that vertex A is the initial node and vertex B is the terminal node.

Consider the following directed graph and attempt to construct its adjacency matrix:

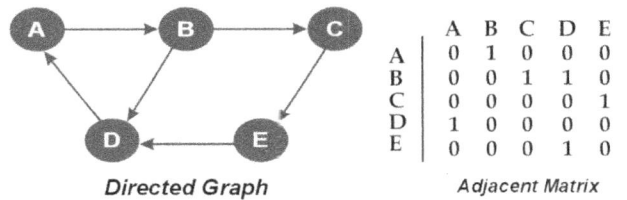

	A	B	C	D	E
A	0	1	0	0	0
B	0	0	1	1	0
C	0	0	0	0	1
D	1	0	0	0	0
E	0	0	0	1	0

Directed Graph   *Adjacent Matrix*

Figure 10.5: Adjacency Matrix of a directed graph

Adjacency matrix for a weighted directed graph

The adjacency matrix representation of a weighted directed graph is similar to that of a directed graph, with the difference that instead of using 1 to indicate the existence of a path, we use the weight associated with the edge. The weights of the graph edges are represented as the entries of the adjacency matrix. This can be illustrated with an example. Consider the graph below and its adjacency matrix representation, where the weights associated with the edges are shown as the entries in the adjacency matrix:

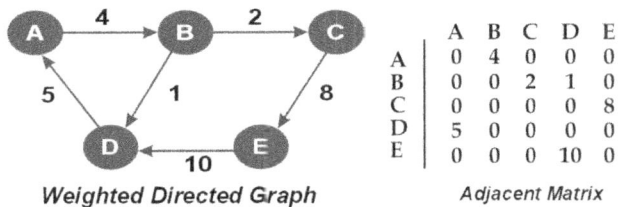

	A	B	C	D	E
A	0	4	0	0	0
B	0	0	2	1	0
C	0	0	0	0	8
D	5	0	0	0	0
E	0	0	0	10	0

Weighted Directed Graph   *Adjacent Matrix*

Figure 10.6: Adjacency matrix of a weighted directed graph

In *Figure 10.6*, observe that the adjacency matrix representation of the weighted directed graph differs from other representations. This variation arises from replacing non-zero values with the actual weights assigned to the edges. While an adjacency matrix is straightforward to implement and comprehend, it is more space-intensive. This matrix is beneficial for dense graphs with numerous edges. However, even for sparse graphs, the matrix occupies the same amount of space.

Linked list representation

In the linked list representation, an adjacency list is used to store the graph in the computer's memory. This method is efficient in terms of storage because we only need to store the values for edges. Let us understand the adjacency list representation of an undirected graph:

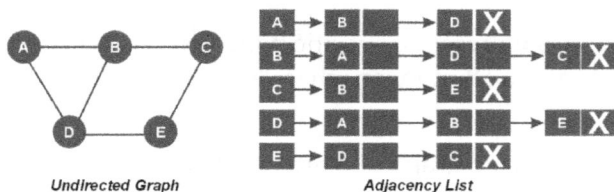

Figure 10.7: *Adjacency list of an undirected graph*

In *Figure 10.7*, we can observe that each node of the graph has a linked list or adjacency list associated with it. From vertex A, there are paths to vertices B and D. These nodes are linked to node A in the provided adjacency list. An adjacency list is maintained for each node in the graph, storing the node's value and a pointer to the next adjacent node. Once all adjacent nodes have been traversed, the pointer field of the last node in the list is set to NULL. The sum of the lengths of adjacency lists equals twice the number of edges present in an undirected graph.

Now, consider the directed graph, and let us examine its adjacency list representation:

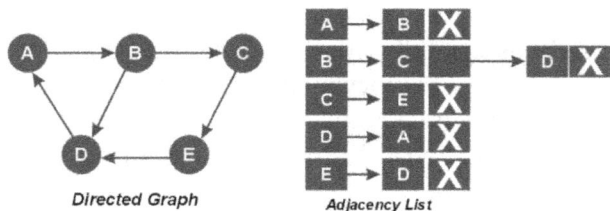

Figure 10.8: *Adjacency list of a directed graph*

In a directed graph, the sum of the lengths of adjacency lists equals the number of edges present in the graph. Now, let us consider a weighted directed graph and examine its adjacency list representation as shown in the following figure:

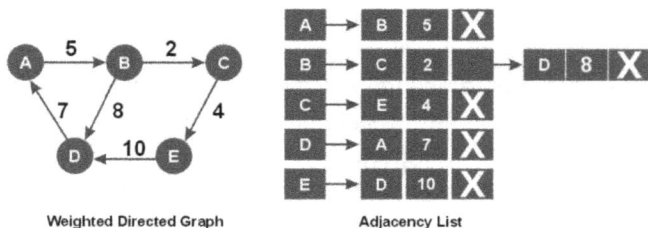

Figure 10.9: *Adjacency list of a directed graph*

In a weighted directed graph, each node includes an additional field called the weight of the node. Using an adjacency list makes it easy to add a vertex, and the use of linked lists also helps save space.

Topological sort

Topological sort is a graph theory technique used to order the vertices of a **directed acyclic graph (DAG)**. It ensures that for every directed edge from vertex A to vertex B, vertex A precedes vertex B in the ordering. This technique is particularly useful in scheduling problems where tasks must be performed in a specific sequence. The algorithm starts by selecting a vertex with no incoming edges, adding it to the ordering, and then removing all its outgoing edges. This process is repeated until all vertices are visited, resulting in a topological sort of the DAG.

Algorithm 10.1: Topological sort

```
function Topsort(G)
T ← empty list .
Z ← empty stack
in ← dictionary mapping all vertices to 0 .
for each v ∈ V do
for each u adjacent to v do
increment in[v]
for each v ∈ V do
if in[v] = 0 then
add v to Z
while S is not empty do
v ← Z.remove
append v to T
for each u adjacent to v do
decrement in[u]
if in[u] = 0 then
add u to Z
return T
```

Program 10.1: Implementation in C++

```cpp
#include <iostream>
#include <vector>
#include <queue>
using namespace std:
void topologicalSort(vector<vector<int>>& graph, int numVertices) {
    vector<int> inDegree(numVertices, 0):
```

```
queue<int> zeroInDegreeQueue:
vector<int> topoOrder:
// Calculate in-degrees of all vertices
for (int i = 0: i < numVertices: i++) {
    for (int j : graph[i]) {
        inDegree[j]++:
    }
}
// Enqueue vertices with zero in-degree
for (int i = 0: i < numVertices: i++) {
    if (inDegree[i] == 0) {
        zeroInDegreeQueue.push(i):
    }
}

while (!zeroInDegreeQueue.empty()) {
    int vertex = zeroInDegreeQueue.front():
    zeroInDegreeQueue.pop():
    topoOrder.push_back(vertex):
    // Decrease in-degree for all adjacent vertices
    for (int adjVertex : graph[vertex]) {
        inDegree[adjVertex]--:
        if (inDegree[adjVertex] == 0) {
            zeroInDegreeQueue.push(adjVertex):
        }
    }
}

// Check for a cycle
if (topoOrder.size() != numVertices) {
    cout << "Graph has a cycle, topological sort not possible." <<
endl:
    return:
}

// Print topological order
for (int vertex : topoOrder) {
    cout << vertex << " ":
}
cout << endl:
```

```
}
int main() {
    int numVertices = 6:
    vector<vector<int>> graph(numVertices):
    // Example graph (DAG)
    graph[5] = { 2, 0 }:
    graph[4] = { 0, 1 }:
    graph[2] = { 3 }:
    graph[3] = { 1 }:
    topologicalSort(graph, numVertices):
    return 0:
}
```

Example 10.1: Generate a topological ordering for the following directed graph:

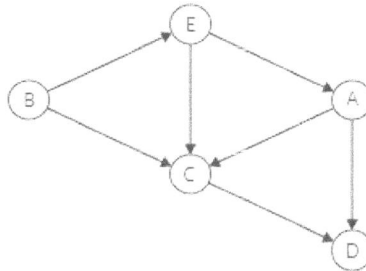

Figure 10.10: Directed graph for topological ordering

Solution: Identify the first node in the topological ordering. This node must have no incoming directed edges, meaning its in-degree is zero. Find a node with an in-degree of zero and add it to the topological ordering.

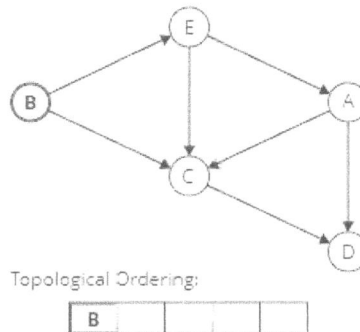

Figure 10.11: Topological ordering first step

Once a node is added to the topological ordering, remove the node and its outgoing edges from the graph:

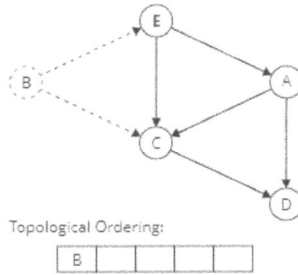

Figure 10.12: Topological ordering second step

Now, repeat:

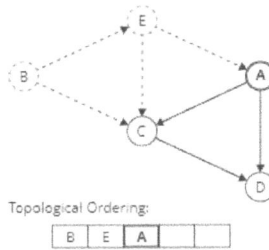

Figure 10.13: Topological ordering third step

Then, repeat:

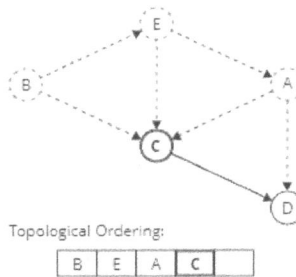

Figure 10.14: Topological ordering fourth step

Until we reach the last node:

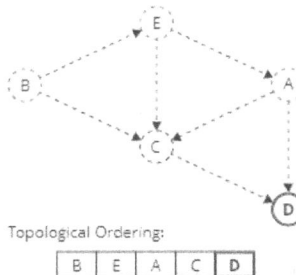

Figure 10.15: Topological ordering final step

Complexity analysis

The complexity analysis is as follows:

- **Time complexity**: The DFS-based method employs a depth-first search and utilizes a stack to maintain vertices in the order they complete processing. The complexity of both entries is mentioned below.

  - **DFS traversal**: Each vertex is visited once, and all its adjacent vertices are explored, resulting in $O(V+E)$ time complexity, akin to standard graph traversal.

  - **Stack operations**: Pushing and popping vertices from the stack totals $O(V)$ time.

    Consequently, the overall time complexity of the DFS-based method remains $O(V+E)$.

- **Space complexity**: Both methods necessitate additional space for data structures employed during the process.

  - **Adjacency list**: Storing the graph using an adjacency list requires $O(V + E)$ space.

  - **DFS-based method**: It uses a stack to store the topological order, requiring $O(V)$ space, and a visited array also taking $O(V)$ space.

Therefore, the space complexity for both methods is $O(V + E)$.

Applications

Some significant applications of topological sort include:

- Scheduling jobs based on dependencies among jobs
- Instruction scheduling
- Determining the order of compilation tasks in make files
- Data serialization

Strongly connected components

Strongly connected components (**SCCs**) in a directed graph are subsets of vertices where every vertex is reachable from every other vertex in the same subset. In simpler terms, within an SCC, there is a path from any vertex to every other vertex.

An SCC in a directed graph G is a maximal subgraph C such that for every pair of vertices u, $v \in C$, there exists both a path from u to v and a path from v to u in G.

An algorithm known as Kosaraju's Algorithm is used to identify strongly connected components.

Algorithm 10.2: Strongly connected component

```
procedure Kosaraju(G):
    Input: Directed graph G
    Output: List of strongly connected components (SCCs)
    n = number of vertices in G
    visited[n] = false
    stack = empty stack
    finishOrder = empty list

    // Step 1: Perform a DFS and record the finishing order
    procedure DFS1(v):
        visited[v] = true
        for each (v, u) in G.adjacentEdges(v):
            if not visited[u]:
                DFS1(u)
        stack.push(v)
        finishOrder.push(v)

    for each v in G.vertices():
        if not visited[v]:
            DFS1(v)

    // Step 2: Transpose the graph G
    G_transposed = G.transpose()

    // Step 3: Perform DFS on the transposed graph in the order of finishOrder
    procedure DFS2(v):
        visited[v] = true
        add v to current SCC
        for each (v, u) in G_transposed.adjacentEdges(v):
            if not visited[u]:
                DFS2(u)

    visited[n] = false
    SCCs = empty list

    while stack is not empty:
        v = stack.pop()
        if not visited[v]:
            create a new empty set for current SCC
            DFS2(v)
            add current SCC to SCCs
    return SCCs
```

Program 10.2: Implementation in C++

```cpp
#include <iostream>
#include <vector>
#include <stack>
#include <algorithm>
using namespace std:
class Graph {
    int V: // Number of vertices
    vector<vector<int>> adj: // Adjacency list
public:
    Graph(int V) : V(V) {
        adj.resize(V):
    }
    void addEdge(int u, int v) {
        adj[u].push_back(v):
    }

    void DFS1(int v, vector<bool>& visited, stack<int>& finishStack) {
        visited[v] = true:
        for (int u : adj[v]) {
            if (!visited[u]) {
                DFS1(u, visited, finishStack):
            }
        }
        finishStack.push(v):
    }

    void DFS2(int v, vector<bool>& visited, vector<int>& SCC) {
        visited[v] = true:
        SCC.push_back(v):
        for (int u : adj[v]) {
            if (!visited[u]) {
                DFS2(u, visited, SCC):
            }
        }
    }

    Graph transpose() {
        Graph transposed(V):
        for (int v = 0: v < V: ++v) {
            for (int u : adj[v]) {
                transposed.addEdge(u, v):
```

```
                }
            }
            return transposed:
        }

    vector<vector<int>> findSCCs() {
        vector<bool> visited(V, false):
        stack<int> finishStack:
        // Step 1: Fill finishStack in order of finish times
        for (int v = 0: v < V: ++v) {
            if (!visited[v]) {
                DFS1(v, visited, finishStack):
            }
        }

        // Step 2: Get the transposed graph
        Graph transposed = transpose():
        // Reset visited array
        fill(visited.begin(), visited.end(), false):
        // Step 3: Process vertices in order defined by finishStack
        vector<vector<int>> SCCs:
        while (!finishStack.empty()) {
            int v = finishStack.top():
            finishStack.pop():
            if (!visited[v]) {
                vector<int> SCC:
                transposed.DFS2(v, visited, SCC):
                SCCs.push_back(SCC):
            }
        }
        return SCCs:
    }
}:

int main() {
    Graph g(5): // Example graph with 5 vertices

    // Adding edges
    g.addEdge(0, 1):
    g.addEdge(1, 2):
    g.addEdge(2, 0):
    g.addEdge(1, 3):
    g.addEdge(3, 4):
```

```
// Finding Strongly Connected Components
vector<vector<int>> SCCs = g.findSCCs():
// Output SCCs
cout << "Strongly Connected Components:\n":
for (const auto& SCC : SCCs) {
    for (int v : SCC) {
        cout << v << " ":
    }
    cout << "\n":
}

return 0:
}
```

Example 10.2: Find SCC of the following graph:

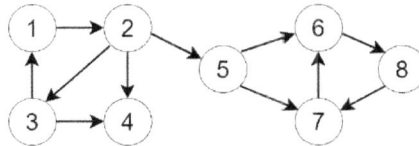

Figure 10.16: Strongly connected graph

Solution: To find SCC, follow these steps:

1. In the initial step, conduct a DFS traversal to establish the priorities of the vertices. Specifically, for each vertex, record when the DFS completes its processing. The vertices that are processed later have higher priorities. This step resembles topological sorting but is distinct because it is applicable to any directed graph, not just DAGs.

   The preceding section illustrates the outcome of executing this step for the graph. The process began with vertex 1 (though it could have started from any node). The priorities are indicated by the numbers outside the circles:

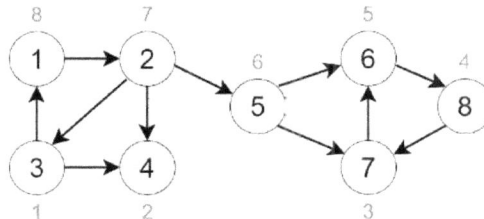

Figure 10.17: SCC step 1

During the DFS traversal, push the vertices onto a stack based on their priorities. At the end of the process, the stack will contain: [3, 4, 7, 8, 6, 5, 2, 1].

2. In the second step, we construct the transpose graph of G. The transpose graph TG has the same vertices as the original graph but with reversed edge directions:

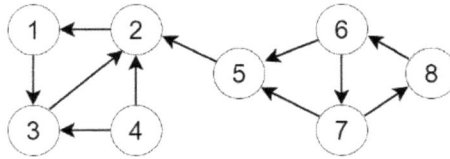

Figure 10.18: SCC step 2

Construct TG as a separate graph where the edge directions are inverted compared to G.

3. After completing step 2, vertex 1 has the highest priority. Therefore, we initiate the first DFS from vertex 1. During this DFS traversal, vertices 1, 3, and 2 are visited in that order, identifying one SCC:

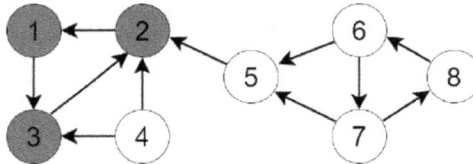

Figure 10.19: SCC step 3

The next vertex with the highest priority is 5, given that vertex 2 has already been visited. We execute DFS starting from node 5, identifying the second SCC, which contains only that node:

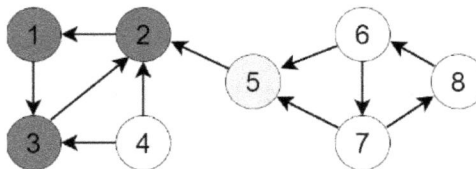

Figure 10.20: SCC step 4

Vertex 6 is the next vertex to be visited. During DFS, we traverse vertices 6, 7, and 8 in this order, resulting in:

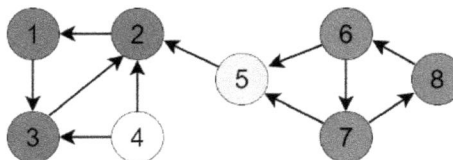

Figure 10.21: SCC step 5

Lastly, invoke DFS for vertex 4 and find the final SCC containing only that vertex:

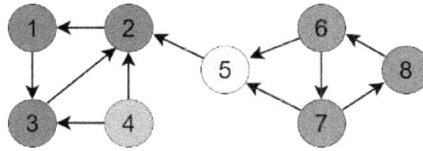

Figure 10.22: SCC step 6

At this point, all the SCCs are obtained, and the algorithm terminates.

Complexity analysis

In Kosaraju's algorithm, the adjacency list representation for G ensures that DFS runs in *O(N+M)* time. The algorithm consists of three steps, each depending on the variables N (number of vertices) and M (number of edges). Therefore, the algorithm's complexity is determined by the maximum complexity among these steps:

- Step 1 involves a DFS traversal of G, which runs in *O(N+M)*.

- Transposing G requires iterating over all vertices and edges, also operating in *O(N+M)* time.

- Step 3 is a DFS traversal of TG (the transposed graph), which similarly runs in *O(N+M)*.

Thus, the overall complexity of Kosaraju's algorithm is O(N+M).

Applications

This algorithm is used for vehicle routing applications, maps, and model-checking in formal verification.

Eulerian path and circuit

The Euler path is a route that allows us to traverse every edge exactly once, and vertices can be revisited multiple times. A Euler circuit is a specific type of Euler path where the starting vertex of the path is also connected to its ending vertex:

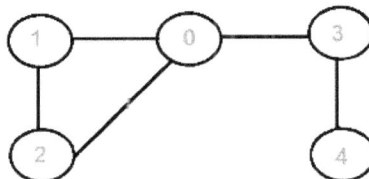

Figure 10.23: Connected graph for Eulerian path and circuit

The graph contains Eulerian paths, such as *4 3 0 1 2 0*, but lacks an Eulerian cycle. It is worth noting that two vertices, 4 and 0, have odd degrees:

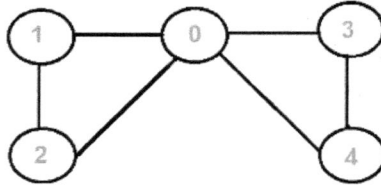

Figure 10.24: Eulerian path

The graph contains an Eulerian cycle, such as *2 1 0 3 4 0 2*, and all vertices have even degrees:

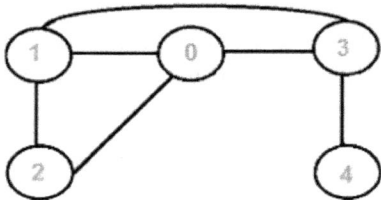

Figure 10.25: Eulerian cycle

The graph is not Eulerian because all vertices have odd degrees.

In an Eulerian path, each time we visit a vertex v, we traverse exactly two unvisited edges with one endpoint at v. Hence, all intermediate vertices in a Eulerian path must have an even degree. For an Eulerian cycle, any vertex can act as an intermediate vertex, so all vertices must have an even degree.

Single-source shortest path algorithm

For a weighted directed graph, the shortest path problem identifies the path with the lowest total weight between two vertices. The **single-source shortest path problem (SSSP)** seeks the shortest path from a single vertex (the source) to every other vertex in the graph.

Relaxation property

The single-source shortest paths rely on a technique called relaxation, which iteratively reduces an upper bound on the actual shortest path weight of each vertex until the upper bound equals the shortest path weight. For each vertex v in V, we maintain an attribute $d[v]$, which serves as an upper bound on the weight of the shortest path from source s to v. This attribute $d[v]$ is referred to as the shortest path estimate.

The following algorithm shows the SSSP process:

INITIALIZE - SINGLE - SOURCE (G, s)

1. for each vertex v ∈ V [G]

2. **do d [v] ← ∞**

3. **π [v] ← NIL**

4. **d [s] ← 0**

After initialization, $\pi [v] = NIL$ for all $v \in V$, $d [v] = 0$ for $v = s$, and $d [v] = \infty$ for $v \in V - \{s\}$.

The process of relaxing an edge (u, v) involves checking if we can enhance the shortest path to vertex v by passing through vertex u. If this is possible, we update $d[v]$, which represents the shortest path estimate to v, and $\pi[v]$, the predecessor field of v. This step may decrease the shortest path estimate $d[v]$ and update $\pi[v]$. In *Figure 10.26*, after the relaxation step, the value $d[v]$ decreases because $v.d > u.d + w(u, v)$ prior to the relaxation step:

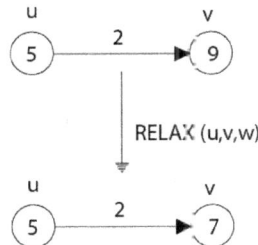

Figure 10.26: Relaxation for SSSP case 1

Figure 10.27 represents $v.d < u.d + w(u, v)$ before relaxing the edge, so the relaxation step leaves $v.d$ unchanged:

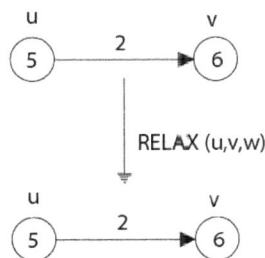

Figure 10.27: Relaxation for SSSP case 2

The following pseudo-code performs a relaxation step on edge (u, v):

RELAX (u, v, w)

1. If d [v] > d [u] + w (u, v)

2. then d [v] ← d [u] + w (u, v)

3. π [v] ← u

Dijkstra's algorithm

Dijkstra's algorithm is utilized to determine the shortest path between any two vertices within a graph. These two vertices may either be adjacent or at the graph's most distant points. The algorithm commences from the source vertex. Its inputs consist of the graph $G\{V, E\}$, where V represents the set of vertices and E the set of edges, along with the source vertex S. The output is the shortest path spanning tree.

Algorithm 10.3: Dijkstra's algorithm

The algorithm is as follows:

1. Initialize two arrays: **distance[]** to store distances from the source vertex to all other vertices in the graph, and **visited[]** to keep track of visited vertices.

2. Set **distance[S]** = **0**, where S is the source vertex, and **distance[v]** = ∞ for all other vertices v in the graph.

3. Add the source vertex S to the **visited[]** array.

4. Find the adjacent vertices of S that have the minimum distance.

5. Choose the adjacent vertex A with the minimum distance that is not yet visited. Add A to the **visited[]** array and update its distance from ∞ to its assigned distance **d1**, where $d1 < \infty$.

6. Repeat the process for the adjacent vertices of all visited vertices until the shortest path spanning tree is constructed.

Program 10.3: Implementation in C++

```
#include<stdio.h>
#include<limits.h>
#include<stdbool.h>
int min_dist(int[], bool[]):
void dijsktra(int[][6],int):
int min_dist(int dist[], bool visited[]){ // finding minimum dist
    int minimum=INT_MAX,ind:
    for(int k=0: k<6: k++) {
        if(visited[k]==false && dist[k]<=minimum) {
            minimum=dist[k]:
            ind=k:
        }
    }
    return ind:
}
```

```
void dijsktra(int graph[6][6],int src){
    int dist[6]:
    bool visited[6]:
    for(int k = 0: k<6: k++) {
        dist[k] = INT_MAX:
        visited[k] = false:
    }
    dist[src] = 0: // Source vertex dist is set 0
    for(int k = 0: k<6: k++) {
        int m=min_dist(dist,visited):
        visited[m]=true:
        for(int k = 0: k<6: k++) {

            // updating the dist of neighbouring vertex
            if(!visited[k] && graph[m][k] && dist[m]!=INT_MAX &&
dist[m]+graph[m][k]<dist[k])
                dist[k]=dist[m]+graph[m][k]:
        }
    }
    printf("Vertex\t\tdist from source vertex\n"):
    for(int k = 0: k<6: k++) {
        char str=65+k:
        printf(„%c\t\t\t%d\n", str, dist[k]):
    }
}
int main(){
    int graph[6][6]= {
        {0, 1, 2, 0, 0, 0},
        {1, 0, 0, 5, 1, 0},
        {2, 0, 0, 2, 3, 0},
        {0, 5, 2, 0, 2, 2},
        {0, 1, 3, 2, 0, 1},
        {0, 0, 0, 2, 1, 0}
    }:
    dijsktra(graph,0):
    return 0:
}
```

Example 10.3: Find the shortest path from the source node S in the following graph:

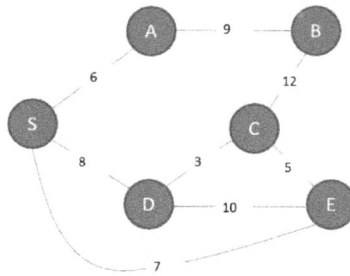

Figure 10.28: Connected graph for shortest path

Solution: To find the shortest path:

1. Initialize the distances of all vertices as infinity, except for the source node S:

Vertex	S	A	B	C	D	E
Distance	0	∞	∞	∞	∞	∞

Table 10.1: Distance table initialization

Now, source node S is a visited node, so add it in the visited array:

`visited={S}`

2. The vertex S has three adjacent vertices with different distances, and the vertex with the minimum distance among them all is A. Therefore, A is visited, and `dist[A]` is updated from ∞ to 6.

$S \rightarrow A = 6$

$S \rightarrow D = 8$

$S \rightarrow E = 7$

The values are updated in the table:

Vertex	S	A	B	C	D	E
Distance	0	6	∞	∞	8	7

Table 10.2: Updated distance table

visited = {S, A}, shown as follows:

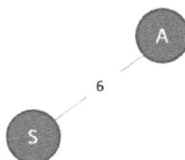

Figure 10.29: First edge visited {S, A}

3. Since there are two vertices already visited in the visited array, we need to check the adjacent vertices for both of them.

Vertex S still has two adjacent vertices to be visited: D and E. Vertex A has one adjacent vertex, B.

Calculate the distances from S to D, E, and B, and select the minimum distance:

$S \rightarrow D = 8$ and $S \rightarrow E = 7$.

$S \rightarrow B = S \rightarrow A + A \rightarrow B = 6 + 9 = 15$

The values are updated in the table:

Vertex	S	A	B	C	D	E
Distance	0	6	15	∞	8	7

Table 10.3: Distance table from S to D, E, B

$visited = \{S, A, E\}$, shown as follows:

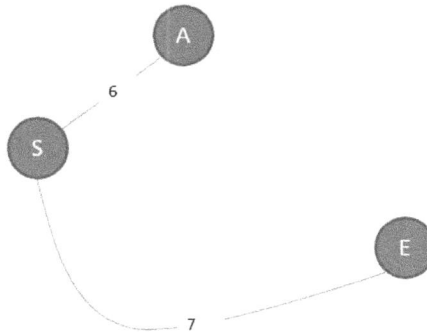

Figure 10.30: Visited nodes from S

4. Calculate the distances of the adjacent vertices, S, A, and E, from all the vertices in the visited array and select the vertex with the minimum distance:

$S \rightarrow D = 8$

$S \rightarrow B = 15$

$S \rightarrow C = S \rightarrow E + E \rightarrow C = 7 + 5 = 12$

The values are updated in the table:

Vertex	S	A	B	C	D	E
Distance	0	6	15	12	8	7

Table 10.4: Updated distance table from S to C

visited = {S, A, E, D}, illustrated as follows:

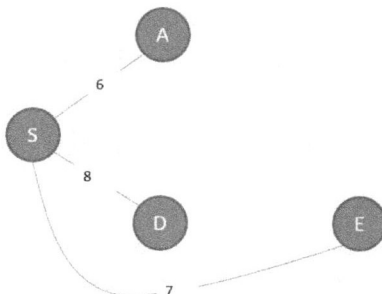

Figure 10.31: *Visited nodes A, D, E from S*

5. Recalculate the distances of unvisited vertices. If a new minimum distance is found, update the distance array accordingly:

$S \rightarrow C = S \rightarrow E + E \rightarrow C = 7 + 5 = 12$

$S \rightarrow C = S \rightarrow D + D \rightarrow C = 8 + 3 = 11$

dist[C] = minimum (12, 11) = 11

$S \rightarrow B = S \rightarrow A + A \rightarrow B = 6 + 9 = 15$

$S \rightarrow B = S \rightarrow D + D \rightarrow C + C \rightarrow B = 8 + 3 + 12 = 23$

dist[B] = minimum (15,23) = 15

The new distance array:

Vertex	S	A	B	C	D	E
Distance	0	6	15	11	8	7

Table 10.5: *Final distance table*

visited = { S, A, E, D, C}, as depicted in the following figure:

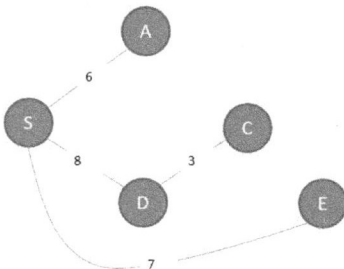

Figure 10.32: *Visited nodes A, D, E, C from S*

6. The remaining unvisited vertex in the graph is B, which has a minimum distance of 15, and it is added to the output spanning tree as shown in *Figure 10.33*:

$visited = \{S, A, E, D, C, B\}$

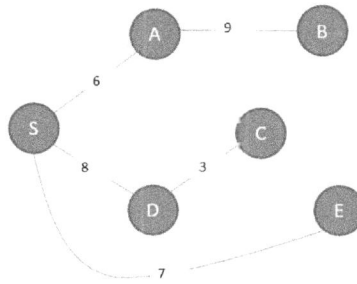

Figure 10.33: *Final shortest path spanning tree*

The shortest path spanning tree is generated as the output using Dijkstra's algorithm.

Complexity analysis

The complexity is calculated as:

- **Time complexity**: *O(E Log V)*, where E is the number of edges and V is the number of vertices.
- **Space complexity**: *O(V)*

Applications

The applications of this algorithm are:

- To determine the quickest route
- In applications for social networking
- Within a phone network
- To locate the places on the map

Bellman-Ford algorithm

The Bellman-Ford algorithm is a dynamic programming-based single-source shortest path algorithm. It starts from a vertex and calculates the shortest distance to other vertices in the graph.

The Bellman-Ford algorithm is a single-source shortest path algorithm based on the bottom-up approach of dynamic programming. It starts from a single vertex and calculates the shortest path from that vertex to all other nodes in a weighted graph. It is based on the *principle of relaxation*. Negative edge weights in the graph can create a negative cycle, which makes it challenging to find the shortest path using Dijkstra's algorithm and other methods. The Bellman-Ford algorithm resolves this issue by effectively handling graphs with negative edges.

Role of negative weight

The presence of negative edges in a weighted graph can create a negative cycle, which leads to incorrect results in shortest path algorithms like Dijkstra's. Dijkstra's algorithm may incorrectly find a shorter path due to the negative values in each cycle.

Negative weights in the graph must be handled carefully to avoid incorrect results.

The core concept behind the Bellman-Ford algorithm is to start from a single source and initially estimate the distance to each node as infinity. The algorithm then iteratively relaxes these paths by finding shorter paths, which is known as the **principle of relaxation**. To ensure the optimized result, the algorithm repeats these steps for all vertices. If a new shorter path is found for any vertex during this process, it means the previous result was not optimized.

Algorithm 10.4: Bellman-Ford algorithm

```
Bellmanford(G, S)
for each vertex V in G
dist[V] ←infinite
prev[V] ← NULL
dist[S] ← 0
for each vertex V in G
for each edge (U, V) in G
tempDist ← dist[U] + edge_weight(U, V)
if tempDist < dist[V]
dist[V] ← tempDist
prev[V] ← U
for each edge (U,V) in G
if dist[U] + edge_weight(U, V) < dist[V}
Error: Negative Cycle Exists
return dist[], prev[]
```

Program 10.4: Implementation in C++

```cpp
#include <iostream>
#include <vector>
#include <limits>
using namespace std:

struct Edge {
    int source, destination, weight:
}:
void BellmanFord(vector<Edge>& edges, int V, int E, int source) {
    vector<int> dist(V, numeric_limits<int>::max()):
    vector<int> prev(V, -1):
```

```
        dist[source] = 0:
        // Relax all edges |V| - 1 times
        for (int i = 1: i <= V - 1: ++i) {
            for (int j = 0: j < E: ++j) {
                int u = edges[j].source:
                int v = edges[j].destination:
                int weight = edges[j].weight:
                if (dist[u] != numeric_limits<int>::max() && dist[u] + weight <
dist[v]) {
                    dist[v] = dist[u] + weight:
                    prev[v] = u:
                }
            }
        }

        // Check for negative-weight cycles
        for (int i = 0: i < E: ++i) {
            int u = edges[i].source:
            int v = edges[i].destination:
            int weight = edges[i].weight:
            if (dist[u] != numeric_limits<int>::max() && dist[u] + weight <
dist[v]) {
                cout << "Error: Negative Cycle Exists" << endl:
                return:
            }
        }
        // Print the shortest paths
        cout << "Vertex Distance from Source:" << endl:
        for (int i = 0: i < V: ++i)
            cout << i << "\t\t" << dist[i] << endl:
}

int main() {
    int V = 5:  // Number of vertices in graph
    int E = 8:  // Number of edges in graph
    vector<Edge> edges = {
        {0, 1, -1}, {0, 2, 4}, {1, 2, 3}, {1, 3, 2},
        {1, 4, 2}, {3, 2, 5}, {3, 1, 1}, {4, 3, -3}
    }:
    int source = 0:  // Source vertex
    BellmanFord(edges, V, E, source):
    return 0:
}
```

Example 10.4: Find the shortest path from the source node 'S' in the graph provided:

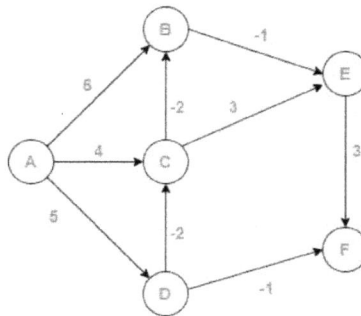

Figure 10.34: Directed graph for shortest path

Solution: Initially, the distance of each vertex from the source vertex is set to infinity, and the distance from the source to itself is zero. Let us consider vertex A as the source vertex:

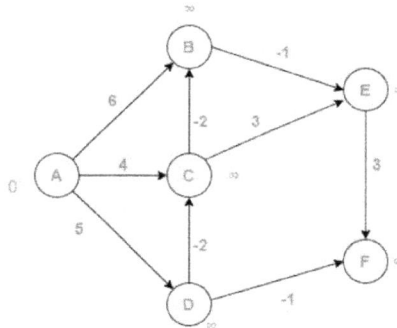

Figure 10.35: Graph initialization with infinity distance from S

Relax all edges for *n-1* iterations, where *n* is the number of vertices.

If, $[(d(u) + c(u, v) < d(v))]$

$$d(v) = d(u) + c(u, v)$$

So, for this problem, there will be a total of 5 iterations (6-1).

Enumerate all the edges in the graph.

(A, B), (A, C), (A, D), (B, E), (D, C), (D, F) (C, E), (C, B), (E, F)

First iteration:

Consider the edge (A, B), where *d(u)* is 0, *d(v)* is ∞, and *c(u, v)* is 6.

Applying the principle of relaxation:

If $0 + 6 < \infty$... True

So, $d(B) = 6$

Now, consider the edge (A, C):

Applying the principle of relaxation

$d(C) = 4$

Now, consider the edge (A, D):

Applying the principle of relaxation:

$d(D) = 5$

Now, consider the edge (B, E):

Applying the principle of relaxation:

If $6 + (-1) < \infty$... True

So, $d(E) = 5$

Now, consider the edge (C, E):

Applying the principle of relaxation:

If $4 + 3 < 5$ ... False

So, it is not updated.

Now, consider the edge (D, C):

Applying the principle of relaxation:

If $5 + (-2) < 4$ ... True

So, $d(C) = 3$

Now, consider the edge (D, F):

Applying the principle of relaxation:

If $5 + (-1) < \infty$... True

So, $d(F) = 4$

Now, consider the edge (E, F):

Applying the principle of relaxation:

If $5 + 3 < 4$ ... False

So, no update is made.

Now, consider the edge (C, B):

Applying the principle of relaxation:

If $3 + (-2) < 6$ ... True

So, $d(B) = 1$

The graph after the first iteration looks as follows:

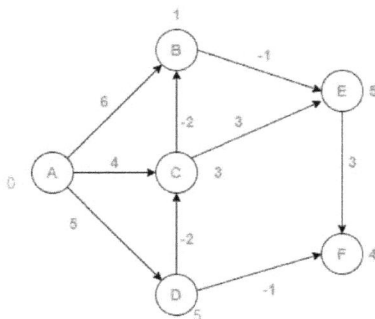

Figure 10.36: Directed graph after the first iteration

Second iteration:

Let us take (A, B):

Applying the principle of relaxation:

If *0 + 6 < 1 …* False

So, do not update.

Now, let us take (A, C):

Applying the principle of relaxation:

If *0 + 4 < 3 …* False

So, do not update.

Now, let us take (A, D):

Applying the principle of relaxation:

If *0 + 5 < 5…* False

So, do not update.

Now, let us take (B, E):

Applying the principle of relaxation:

If *1 + (-1) < 5 …* True

So, *d(E) = 0*

Now, let us take (C, E):

Applying the principle of relaxation:

If *3 + 3 < 0…* False

So, do not update.

Now, let us take (D, C):

Applying the principle of relaxation:

If $5 + (-2) < 3$ ... False

So, do not update.

Now, let us take (D, F):

Applying the principle of relaxation:

If $5 + (-1) < 4$ ... False

So, do not update.

Now, let us take (E, F):

Applying the principle of relaxation:

If $0 + 3 < 4$ ... True

So, $d(F) = 3$

Now, let us take (C, B):

Applying the principle of relaxation:

If $3 + (-2) < 6$ ... False

So, do not update.

The graph after the second iteration:

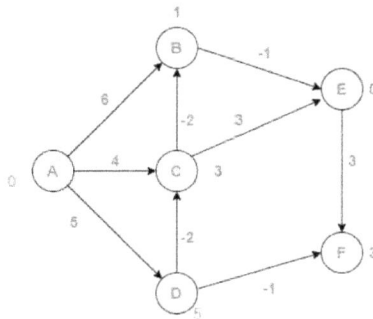

Figure 10.37: *Directed graph after the second iteration*

Third iteration:

Let us take (A, B):

Applying the principle of relaxation:

If $0 + 6 < 1$... False

So, do not update.

Now, let us take (A, C):

Applying the principle of relaxation:

If $0 + 4 < 3$ ... False

So, do not update.

Now, let us take (A, D):

Applying the principle of relaxation:

If $0 + 5 < 5$ ... False

So, do not update.

Now, let us take (B, E):

Applying the principle of relaxation:

If $1 + (-1) < 0$... False

So, do not update.

Now, let us take (C, E):

Applying the principle of relaxation:

If $3 + 3 < 0$ ... False

So, do not update.

Now, let us take (D, C):

Applying the principle of relaxation:

If $5 + (-2) < 3$... False

So, do not update.

Now, let us take (D, F):

Applying the principle of relaxation:

If $5 + (-1) < 3$ ... False

So, do not update.

Now, let us take (E, F):

Applying the principle of relaxation:

If $0 + 3 < 3$... False

So, do not update.

Now, let us take (C, B):

Applying the principle of relaxation:

If $3 + (-2) < 6$... False

So, do not update.

The graph after the third iteration is:

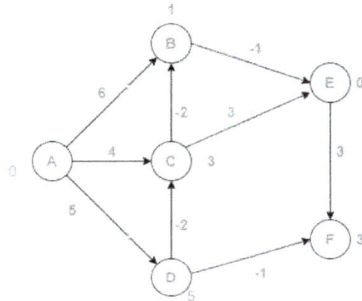

Figure 10.38: Directed graph after the third iteration

According to the relaxation condition, we need at most five iterations. As far as we can tell, the third iteration itself contains no updates or modifications. Therefore, we will stop here and document the shortest path for each vertex in A.

So, the cost for each vertex from A is:

A- A: 0

A- B: 1

A- C: 3

A- D: 5

A- E: 0

A- F: 3

Complexity analysis

The complexity analysis is as follows:

- **Time complexity**:
  - **Best case**: *O(E)*
  - **Average case**: *O(VE)*
  - **Worst case**: *O(VE)*
- **Space complexity**: *O(V)*

Here, V is the number of vertices and E is the number of edges.

Applications

The applications of Bellman-Ford algorithm are:

- **Network routing**: This algorithm is used to determine the shortest path in a network with negative weights, such as the internet.

- **Robot navigation**: It finds the shortest path for a robot to navigate in an environment with obstacles.

- **Resource allocation**: The algorithm optimally allocates resources, such as assigning tasks to workers in a factory.

- **Image processing**: This algorithm finds the shortest path between two points in an image, aiding in image segmentation and object recognition.

- **Game theory**: It determines the optimal strategy for players in a game, like chess.

- **Genetics**: The algorithm identifies the shortest path in a genetic network, useful for analyzing genetic interactions and identifying potential drug targets.

All-pair shortest paths

The all-pairs shortest path algorithm, also known as the **Floyd-Warshall algorithm**, is used to solve the problem of finding the shortest paths between all pairs of nodes in a given weighted graph. This algorithm produces a matrix representing the minimum distances from each node to every other node in the graph. It is a dynamic programming technique used to find the shortest paths in a weighted graph, even when the graph contains negative weight cycles. The algorithm determines the shortest route between every pair of vertices by utilizing a matrix of intermediate vertices to keep track of the best-known path at each step.

It is similar to Dijkstra's and Bellman-Ford's algorithms. However, while Dijkstra's and Bellman-Ford's algorithms are single-source shortest path algorithms, Floyd-Warshall is an all-pairs shortest path algorithm. This means it can compute the shortest path between every pair of vertices in the graph.

Algorithm 10.5: Floyd-Warshall algorithm

```
n = number of vertices
D = matrix of dimension n*n
for k = 1 to n
for i = 1 to n
for j = 1 to n
Dk[i, j] = min (Dk-1[i, j], Dk-1[i, k] + Dk-1[k, j])
return D
```

Program 10.5: Implementation in C++

```cpp
#include <iostream>
#include <vector>
#include <climits>
using namespace std:
// Number of vertices in the graph
#define V 4

// A function to print the solution matrix
void printSolution(const vector<vector<int>>& dist) {
    cout << "The following matrix shows the shortest distances between every pair of vertices:\n":
    for (int i = 0: i < V: i++) {
        for (int j = 0: j < V: j++) {
            if (dist[i][j] == INT_MAX)
                cout << "INF" << "      ":
            else
                cout << dist[i][j] << "      ":
        }
        cout << endl:
    }
}

// Function to implement Floyd-Warshall algorithm
void floydWarshall(vector<vector<irt>>& graph) {
    // Initialize the solution matrix same as input graph matrix
    vector<vector<int>> dist = graph:

    // Add all vertices one by one to the set of intermediate vertices
    for (int k = 0: k < V: k++) {
        // Pick all vertices as source one by one
        for (int i = 0: i < V: i++) {
            // Pick all vertices as destination for the above picked source
            for (int j = 0: j < V: j++) {
                // If vertex k is on the shortest path from i to j, then update the value of dist[i][j]
                if (dist[i][k] != INT_MAX && dist[k][j] != INT_MAX && dist[i][k] + dist[k][j] < dist[i][j])
                    dist[i][j] = dist[i][k] + dist[k][j]:
            }
        }
    }
```

```
    // Print the shortest distance matrix
    printSolution(dist):
}

int main() {
    vector<vector<int>> graph = { {0, 5, INT_MAX, 10},
                                            {INT_MAX, 0, 3, INT_
MAX},
                                            {INT_MAX, INT_MAX,
0, 1},
                                            {INT_MAX, INT_MAX,
INT_MAX, 0} }:
    // Function call
    floydWarshall(graph):
    return 0:
}
```

Example 10.5: The Floyd-Warshall algorithm is utilized to determine the shortest paths between all pairs of vertices in a weighted graph. The following is a step-by-step explanation of its functioning, accompanied by an example:

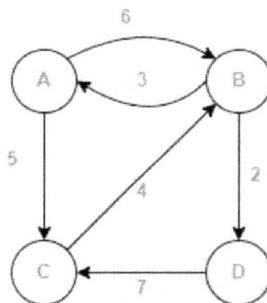

Figure 10.39: Graph for Floyd-Warshall algorithm

Solution: Make the distance matrix or graph matrix. Insert the distance value, and if the distance is unknown, fill that with ∞, shown as follows:

	A	B	C	D
A	0	6	5	∞
B	3	0	∞	2
C	∞	4	0	∞
D	∞	∞	7	0

D0=

Figure 10.40: Distance matrix

Now, calculating the distance of every pair via A:

	A	B	C	D
A	0	6	5	∞
B	3			
C	∞			
D	∞			

DA =

Figure 10.41: *Distance matrix for node A*

Applying Floyd-Warshall's algorithm:

$D0[B, C] = D0[B, A] + D0[A, C]$

$\infty > 3 + 5$

$\infty > 8$ \, (updating the distance)

$D0[B, C] = 8$

$D0[B, D] = D0[B, A] + D0[A, D]$

$2 > 3 + \infty$

$2 > \infty$, (no changes)

$D0[B, D] = 2$

$D0[C, B] = 8$

$D0[C, D] = D0[C, A] + D0[A, D]$

$\infty > \infty + \infty$

$\infty > \infty$, (no changes)

$D0[C, D] = \infty$

$D0[D, B] = D0[D, A] + D0[A, B]$

$\infty > \infty + \infty$

$\infty > \infty$, (no changes)

$D0[D, B] = \infty$

$D0[D, C] = 7$

Similarly, for all other vertices, the resulting matrix will look like:

DA =

	A	B	C	D
A	0	6	5	∞
B	3	0	8	2
C	∞	4	0	∞
D	∞	∞	7	0

Figure 10.42: *Distance matrix for all vertices from A*

Now, calculating the distance of every pair via B:

DB =

	A	B	C	D
A		6		
B	3	0	8	2
C		4		
D		∞		

Figure 10.43: *Distance matrix for vertex B*

After applying Floyd-Warshall formula, we get:

$D0 [A, C] = D0 [A, B] + D0 [B, C]$

$5 > 6 + ∞$...... False, No changes required.

$D0 [A, C] = 5$

$D0 [A, D] = D0 [A, B] + D0 [B, D]$

$∞ > 6 + 2$...... Update the value.

$D0 [A, D] = 8$

$D0 [C, A] = D0 [C, B] + D0 [B, C]$

$∞ > 4 + 3$...... Update the value.

$D0 [C, A] = 7$

$D0 [C, D] = D0 [C, B] + D0 [B, D]$

$∞ > 4 + 2$...... Update the value.

$D0 [C, D] = 6$

$D0 [D, A] = D0 [D, B] + D0 [B, A]$

$∞ > ∞ + 3$...... No changes are required.

$D0\ [C, A] = \infty$

$D0\ [D, C] = D0\ [D, B] + D0\ [B, C]$

$\infty > \infty + 2$...... No changes required.

$D0\ [C, D] = \infty$

	A	B	C	D
A	0	6	5	8
B	3	0	8	2
C	7	4	0	6
D	∞	∞	7	0

DB =

Figure 10.44: *Distance matrix for all vertices from B*

Now, calculating the distance of each path via C:

	A	B	C	D
A			5	
B			8	
C	7	4	0	6
D			7	

DC =

Figure 10.45: *Distance matrix for vertex C*

After applying Floyd-Warshall formula, we get:

$D0\ [A, B] = D0\ [A, C] + D0\ [C, B]$

$6 > 5 + 4$...... False, No changes required.

$D0\ [A, B] = 6$

$D0\ [A, D] = D0\ [A, C] + D0\ [C, D]$

$8 > 5 + 6$...... False, No changes required.

$D0\ [A, D] = 8$

$D0\ [B, A] = D0\ [B, C] + D0\ [C, A]$

$3 > 0 + 7$...... False, No changes required.

$D0\ [B, A] = 3$

$D0\ [B, D] = D0\ [B, C] + D0\ [C, D]$

$2 > \infty + 6$...... False, No changes required.

$D0 [B, D] = 2$

$D0 [D, A] = D0 [D, C] + D0 [C, A]$

$\infty > 7 + 7$...... Update the value.

$D0 [D, A] = 14$

$D0 [D, B] = D0 [D, C] + D0 [C, B]$

$\infty > 7 + 4$...... Update the value.

$D0 [D, B] = 11$

Figure 10.46 shows the distance matrix from vertex C:

	A	B	C	D
A	0	6	5	8
B	3	0	8	2
C	7	4	0	6
D	14	11	7	0

DC =

Figure 10.46: Distance matrix for all vertices from C

Similarly, if we calculate the shortest distance via D, no changes will be required.

Hence, the shortest path matrix using Floyd-Warshall algorithm is as follows:

	A	B	C	D
A	0	6	5	8
B	3	0	8	2
C	7	4	0	6
D	14	11	7	0

Figure 10.47: Distance matrix for all vertices from D

Complexity analysis

Time and space complexity for the shortest path using Floyd-Warshall algorithm are:

- **Time complexity**: There are three for loops in the pseudo-code of the algorithm, so the time complexity will be $O(n^3)$.

- **Space complexity**: The space complexity of Floyd-Warshall algorithm is $O(n^2)$.

Applications

The applications of Floyd-Warshall algorithm are:

- In routing data packets
- Calculating the inversion of the real matrix
- Calculating the transitive closure of directed graphs
- To check whether an undirected graph is bipartite
- To find the shortest path in a directed graph

Max-flow min-cut

In graph theory, a flow network is defined as a directed graph involving a source (S) and a sink (T) and several other nodes connected with edges. Each edge has an individual capacity, which is the maximum limit of flow that the edge could allow.

Flow in the network should follow these conditions:

- For any non-source and non-sink node, the input flow is equal to the output flow.
- For any edge (E_i) in the network, $0 \leq flow(E_i) \leq Capacity(E_i)$.
- Total flow out of the source node is equal to total flow into the sink node.
- Net flow in the edges follows skew symmetry, i.e., $F(u,v)=-F(v,u)$ where $F(v,u)$ is flow from node u to node v. This leads to a conclusion where you have to sum up all the flows between two nodes (either direction) to find the net flow between the nodes initially.

Ford-Fulkerson algorithm

It was developed by *L. R. Ford Jr.* and *D. R. Fulkerson* in 1956. Here is a pseudocode for this algorithm. The required inputs are the network graph G, source node S, and sink node T.

An augmenting path is a simple path from the source to the sink that does not include any cycles and passes only through edges with positive weights. A residual network graph indicates how much more flow is allowed in each edge in the network graph. If no augmenting paths are possible from S to T, then the flow is maximum. The maximum flow result will be the total flow out of the source node, which is also equal to the total flow into the sink node.

Max-flow min-cut theorem

A s-t-cut is a partition of the vertices of a flow network into two sets, such that a set includes the source s and the other one includes the sink t. The capacity of a s-t-cut is defined as the sum of the capacities of the edges from the source side to the sink side. According to Max-flow min-cut theorem, the capacity of the maximum flow has to be equal to the capacity of the minimum cut.

A minimum cut can be found after performing a maximum flow computation using the Ford-Fulkerson method. One possible minimum cut is the following: the set of all the vertices that can be reached from s in the residual graph (using edges with positive residual capacity), and the set of all the other vertices.

Figure 10.48 shows the sample residual graph, which is used for max-cut and min-cut theorem:

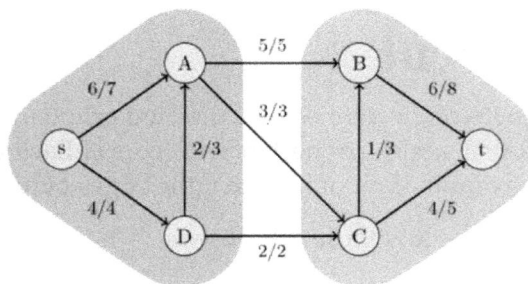

Figure 10.48: *Sample residual graph*

The capacity of the cut {s, A, D} and {B, C, t} is $5 + 3 + 2 = 10$, which matches the maximum flow we determined. Other cuts will have a higher capacity: for instance, the capacity between {s, A} and {B, C, D, t} is $4 + 3 + 5 = 12$.

Algorithm 10.6: Ford-Fulkerson algorithm

```
FordFulkerson(Graph G,Node S,Node T):
    Initialise flow in all edges to 0
    while (there exists an augmenting path(P) between S and T in residual
network graph):
        Augment flow between S to T along the path P
        Update residual network graph
    Return
```

Program 10.6: Implementation in C++

```cpp
#include <iostream>
#include <limits.h>
#include <queue>
#include <vector>
#include <cstring>
using namespace std:
#define V 6 // Number of vertices in the graph
```

```
// A utility function to perform BFS and find if there is a path from source
to sink
bool bfs(int rGraph[V][V], int s, int t, int parent[]) {
    // Create a visited array and mark all vertices as not visited
    bool visited[V]:
    memset(visited, 0, sizeof(visited)):
        // Create a queue for BFS
    queue<int> q:
    q.push(s):
    visited[s] = true:
    parent[s] = -1:
        // Standard BFS loop
    while (!q.empty()) {
        int u = q.front():
        q.pop():
        for (int v = 0: v < V: v++) {
            if (visited[v] == false && rGraph[u][v] > 0) {
                // If we find a connection to the sink, we return true
                if (v == t) {
                    parent[v] = u:
                    return true:
                }
                q.push(v):
                parent[v] = u:
                visited[v] = true:
            }
        }
    }

    // We didn't reach sink in BFS starting from source, so return false
    return false:
}

// Returns the maximum flow from s to t in the given graph
int fordFulkerson(int graph[V][V], int s, int t) {
    int u, v:
    // Create a residual graph and fill the residual graph with given
capacities in the original graph as residual capacities in residual graph
    int rGraph[V][V]:
    for (u = 0: u < V: u++)
        for (v = 0: v < V: v++)
```

```
            rGraph[u][v] = graph[u][v]:

    int parent[V]: // This array is filled by BFS and to store path
    int max_flow = 0: // There is no flow initially

    // Augment the flow while there is a path from source to sink
    while (bfs(rGraph, s, t, parent)) {
        // Find the maximum flow through the path found.
        int path_flow = INT_MAX:
        for (v = t: v != s: v = parent[v]) {
            u = parent[v]:
            path_flow = min(path_flow, rGraph[u][v]):
        }

        // update residual capacities of the edges and reverse edges along
the path
        for (v = t: v != s: v = parent[v]) {
            u = parent[v]:
            rGraph[u][v] -= path_flow:
            rGraph[v][u] += path_flow:
        }
        // Add path flow to overall flow
        max_flow += path_flow:
    }
    // Return the overall flow
    return max_flow:
}

int main() {
    // Create a graph given in the above diagram
    int graph[V][V] = { {0, 16, 13, 0, 0, 0},
                        {0, 0, 10, 12, 0, 0},
                        {0, 4, 0, 0, 14, 0},
                        {0, 0, 9, 0, 0, 20},
                        {0, 0, 0, 7, 0, 4},
                        {0, 0, 0, 0, 0, 0}
                      }:
    cout << "The maximum possible flow is " << fordFulkerson(graph, 0, 5):
    return 0:
}
```

Example 10.6: A demonstration of the working of the Ford-Fulkerson algorithm is shown with the help of figures.

The following figures show the input network graph G and the residual graph G_R:

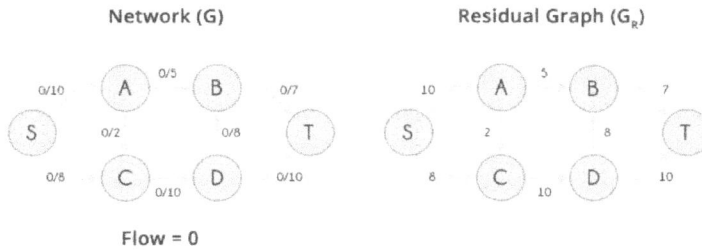

Figure 10.49: *Graph G and residual graph G_R*

Solution: Using these two graphs, we calculate path 1 and also find the flow of the network from source S:

Path 1:   S - C - D - B - T   →   Flow = Flow + 7

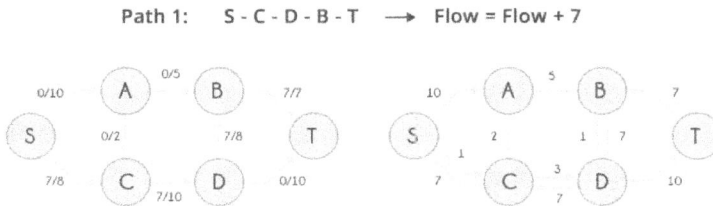

Figure 10.50: *Path 1 with flow*

Similarly, we find the path 2 with the updated flow:

Path 2:   S - C - D - T   →   Flow = Flow + 1

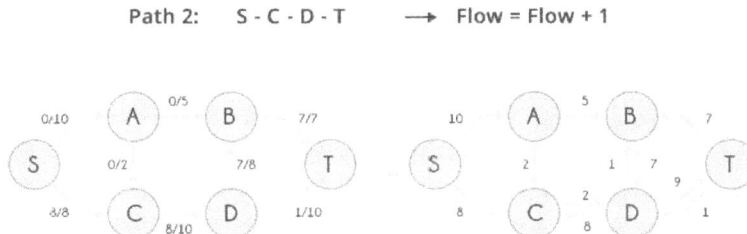

Figure 10.51: *Path 2 with flow*

In the next step, we find the path 3 and also update the flow value:

Path 3:   S - A - B - T   →   Flow = Flow + 5

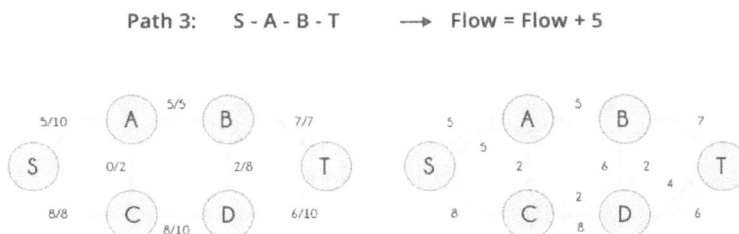

Figure 10.52: *Path 3 with flow*

As per the previous process, we find the next path 4 and update the value of flow:

Path 4:   S - A - C - D - T   ⟶   Flow = Flow + 2

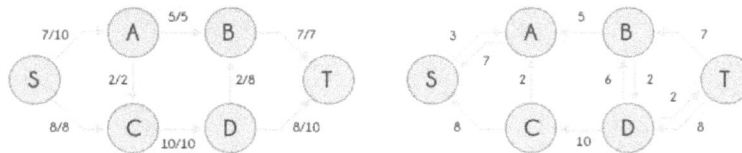

No More Paths Left

Max Flow = 15

Figure 10.53: Final path 4 with max flow

Complexity analysis

The time and space complexity of Ford Fulkerson's algorithm are as follows:

- **Time complexity**: $O(|V| * E^2)$, where E is the number of edges and V is the number of vertices.

- **Space complexity**: $O(V)$

Applications

The applications are:

- Water distribution pipeline.
- Bipartite matching problem.
- Circulation with demands.

Conclusion

This chapter provided an essential introduction to graph theory, highlighting its role in representing and analyzing relationships within various systems. Topics such as graph terminology, topological sorting, strongly connected components, shortest path algorithms, and flow networks were discussed to illustrate key principles and techniques. These graph-based methods are widely used in fields like communication, transportation, biology, and computing. Understanding these concepts allows learners to model and solve complex problems involving interconnected data. A solid grasp of graph theory also serves as a foundation for learning more advanced algorithms and systems.

The upcoming chapter will explore evaluating algorithm performance and understanding the theoretical boundaries of what can be computed efficiently.

Exercise

1. Write a function to compute the lengths of the shortest paths between all pairs of nodes for the given adjacency matrix:

$$\begin{pmatrix} 0 & 6 & 13 \\ 8 & 0 & 4 \\ 5 & \infty & 0 \end{pmatrix}$$

Figure 10.54: Matrix for calculating shortest path

2. Perform a depth first search and breadth first search on the following graph starting at A.

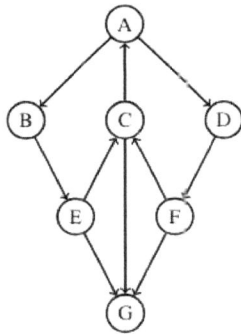

Figure 10.55: Calculating depth first and breadth first search

3. Illustrate the execution of the Ford Fulkerson algorithm in the flow network:

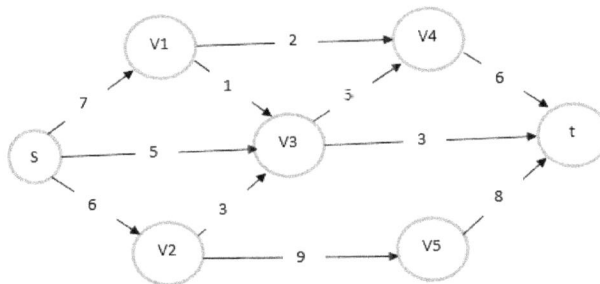

Figure 10.56: Flow network for Ford Fulkerson algorithm

4. Apply Floyd-Warshall algorithm for constructing the shortest path. Show the matrix $D^{(k)}$ that results each iteration.

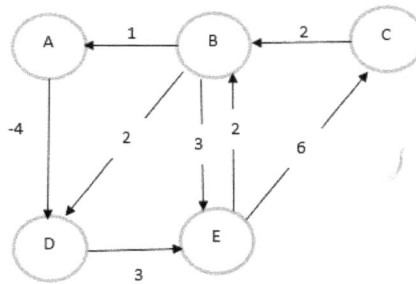

Figure 10.57: Applying Floyd-Warshall algorithm to construct the shortest path

5. For the graph shown as follows, obtain the following:

    a.   Kruskal's method

    b.   Prim's method

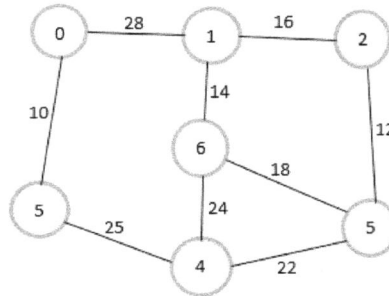

Figure 10.58: Applying Kruskal's method and Prim's method

Join our Discord space

Join our Discord workspace for latest updates, offers, tech happenings around the world, new releases, and sessions with the authors:

https://discord.bpbonline.com

CHAPTER 11
Computational Complexity

Introduction

This chapter offers a comprehensive overview of computational complexity, highlighting its most essential aspects. Each section can be elaborated with in-depth discussions, examples, and proofs to thoroughly illustrate the field's depth and scope. Computational complexity studies the resources, such as time and space, needed to solve computational problems. It assesses how efficiently algorithms use these resources as input size increases. This field aims to understand the inherent difficulty of various computational problems and classify them based on the resources required to solve them. By doing so, computational complexity provides insights into which problems can be solved efficiently and which are computationally hard or even infeasible within practical limits.

Structure

This chapter will cover the following topics:

- Key aspects
- P and NP-classes
- Proof of NP-hardness and NP-completeness
- Polynomial space
- Exponential time

- Reductions and completeness
- Approximation algorithms
- Probabilistic algorithms
- Bounded-error probabilistic polynomial time
- Randomized polynomial time
- Complement of randomized polynomial time

Objectives

The objective of this chapter is to learn computational complexity, understand the inherent difficulty of computational problems, and categorize them based on the resources required to solve them. Specifically, it aims to measure and analyze the time, space, and other resources (like parallelism and randomness) that algorithms need. Classify problems into complexity classes based on their resource requirements, such as P, NP, and PSPACE. Readers will be able to use reductions and completeness concepts to determine how the complexity of one problem relates to another, develop efficient algorithms, and understand the limits of algorithmic efficiency, and explore the theoretical limits of what can be computed efficiently, including proving lower bounds on resource requirements. Finally, readers will also be able to apply insights from complexity theory to practical computing tasks, cryptography, optimization, and other areas, and address significant unresolved questions in the field, such as the P vs. NP problem, to advance computational theory.

Key aspects

The analysis in computational complexity involves several key aspects:

- **Resource measurement**: This process involves quantifying the time (number of computational steps) and space (amount of memory) an algorithm needs to solve a problem. Other resources like parallelism (use of multiple processors) and randomness (use of random numbers) are also considered.

- **Complexity classes**: Problems are grouped into classes based on their resource requirements. For example, problems in class P can be solved in polynomial time by a deterministic Turing machine, while problems in NP can be verified in polynomial time by a deterministic Turing machine. Other classes include PSPACE, which involves problems solvable in polynomial space, and EXP, which involves problems solvable in exponential time.

- **Reductions and completeness**: To understand the relative difficulty of problems, computational complexity uses reductions, which transform one problem into another. If a problem can be reduced to another problem known to be hard, it indicates that the original problem is at least as hard. Completeness concepts, like NP-completeness, identify the most challenging problems within a class.

- **Algorithmic efficiency**: The field seeks to develop the most efficient algorithms possible and to understand the limits of what can be achieved. This involves proving lower bounds on the resources needed for specific problems, demonstrating that certain problems cannot be solved more efficiently than a given threshold.

- **Practical applications**: Insights from computational complexity are applied to real-world problems in areas such as cryptography, where the hardness of certain problems ensures security, and optimization, where efficient algorithms are crucial for practical applications.

- **Theoretical boundaries**: Computational complexity explores the boundaries of what can be computed efficiently. This includes investigating theoretical limits and understanding why some problems are inherently difficult to solve.

- **Open problems and research**: The field addresses significant unresolved questions, such as the famous P vs. NP problem, which asks whether every problem whose solution can be quickly verified can also be quickly solved. Solving these open problems would have profound implications for both theory and practice.

By categorizing problems and analyzing their resource requirements, computational complexity helps in understanding the feasibility of finding efficient solutions and guides the development of algorithms that can effectively tackle practical computational challenges.

Basic concepts of computational complexity

The basic concepts of computational complexity focus on understanding the resources required to solve computational problems. The key concepts are as follows:

- **Problem instances and input size**: Every computational problem has different instances, and the size of an instance is defined by the length of its input. For example, in sorting a list, the input size is the number of elements in it.

- **Algorithm efficiency**: Algorithms are evaluated based on how efficiently they use computational resources (time and space) to solve problem instances of varying sizes. Efficient algorithms typically have polynomial time complexity, meaning their running time is bounded by a polynomial function of the input size.

- **Complexity classes**: Problems are categorized into complexity classes based on the amount of resources (time or space) required to solve them. Common complexity classes include P (problems solvable in polynomial time), NP (problems for which a solution can be verified in polynomial time), and NP-hard or NP-complete (problems at least as hard as the hardest problems in NP).

- **Worst-case vs. average-case complexity**: Algorithms may perform differently depending on the input data. Worst-case complexity measures the maximum resources an algorithm requires for any input of a given size, while average-case complexity considers the average resource usage over all possible inputs.

- **Reduction**: Reductions are transformations that map one problem (source problem) into another (target problem) such that a solution to the target problem can be used to solve the source problem. Reductions are fundamental for proving the complexity of problems and classifying them into complexity classes like NP-complete.

- **Feasibility and intractability**: Some problems are inherently difficult to solve efficiently. NP-complete problems, for example, are problems in NP for which no polynomial-time algorithm is known, and if one exists for any of them, it would solve all NP problems in polynomial time.

P and NP-classes

Let us explore the concept of P and NP-classes:

- **Polynomial time (P)**: The class P includes all decision problems (problems with a yes/no answer) that can be solved by a deterministic Turing machine in polynomial time. Simply put, a problem belongs to P if an algorithm can solve it in polynomial time based on the size of its input.

  The characteristics are as follows:

  o **Efficiently solvable**: Problems in P can be solved within a reasonable timeframe for practical input sizes.

  o **Deterministic algorithms**: The solutions are computed using deterministic algorithms, where each step follows a specific, predictable sequence.

  Sorting algorithms are like merge sort, searching algorithms like binary search, and many basic arithmetic operations are in P because algorithms exist that solve these problems in polynomial time.

  For example:

  o **Decision problem**: Given a list of numbers, is there a number in the list greater than 100?

  o **Algorithm**: Traverse the list once, checking each number against 100. If such a number is found, return **yes**; otherwise, return **no**. This algorithm runs in linear time, $O(n)$, which is polynomial time for input size n.

- **Nondeterministic polynomial time (NP)**: The class NP consists of all decision problems for which a solution can be verified in polynomial time by a deterministic Turing machine. In other words, if someone provides a solution to an NP problem, we can check its correctness in polynomial time.

  The characteristics are as follows:

  o **Verification**: While finding a solution might be challenging, verifying a proposed solution is straightforward and efficient.

- o **Nondeterministic algorithms**: Conceptually, the verification process is performed by a nondeterministic algorithm that can guess the solution and verify it in polynomial time.

The **traveling salesperson problem (TSP)**, where the goal is to find the shortest route visiting all cities, is in NP because verifying that a given route is indeed the shortest can be done in polynomial time, though finding the shortest route is not known to be achievable in polynomial time.

For example:

- o **Decision problem**: Is there a route for the TSP that visits all cities and has a total length less than or equal to a given threshold?

- o **Algorithm**: A nondeterministic algorithm might guess a route and then verify in polynomial time that it visits all cities and has a total length within the threshold.

- o **P vs. NP Problem**: The central question in theoretical computer science is whether P equals NP. This unsolved millennium prize problem asks if every problem for which a solution can be verified in polynomial time can also be solved in polynomial time.

- o **Implications**:

    - If $P = NP$, it would mean that problems traditionally considered difficult, such as many combinatorial optimization problems, can be solved efficiently.

    - If $P \neq NP$, then there exist problems in NP that are inherently more difficult to solve than those in P.

- **NP-complete and NP-hard**

    - o **NP-complete**: These are problems in NP that are as hard as any problem in NP. If you can solve any NP-complete problem in polynomial time, you can solve all NP problems in polynomial time. NP-complete problems are both in NP and NP-hard.

    - o **NP-hard**: These are problems that are at least as difficult as the hardest problems in NP, but they may not be in NP themselves. This means they do not necessarily have polynomial-time verification.

P represents problems that are efficiently solvable, while NP includes problems where solutions can be verified efficiently. The relationship between P and NP is a fundamental open question in computer science with significant implications for cryptography, optimization, and artificial intelligence.

Proof of NP-hardness and NP-completeness

To understand NP-hardness and NP-completeness, we need to explore the concepts of reductions and how they are used in computational complexity theory to prove these properties for problems. Let us break down each concept and how proofs typically work.

NP-hardness

A problem is NP-hard if every problem in NP can be reduced to it in polynomial time. This means that if you can solve an NP-hard problem in polynomial time, you can solve all NP problems in polynomial time, making NP-hard problems among the most difficult in NP.

The proof technique is as follows:

- **Reduction**: To prove that a problem X is NP-hard, we reduce a known NP-hard problem Y to X. This reduction demonstrates that any algorithm that can solve X in polynomial time can also solve Y in polynomial time.

   Reduction steps:

   1. Assume we have a problem Y known to be NP-hard.

   2. Construct a polynomial-time reduction from Y to X, which transforms instances of Y into instances of X.

   3. Show that the reduction preserves the answer: if there is a solution to the transformed instance of X, there must also be a solution to the original instance of Y, and vice versa.

The conclusion is that by showing the reduction from a known NP-hard problem to X, we establish that X is NP-hard.

Consider the following example of NP-hardness proof:

- **Problem Y**: Vertex cover (Given a graph G and a number k, is there a set of k vertices that touches every edge in G?)

- **Problem X**: Dominating set (Given a graph G and a number k, is there a set of k vertices such that every vertex in G is either in the set or adjacent to a vertex in the set?)

The proof sketch is as follows:

- **Reduction**: To prove that dominating set (X) is NP-hard, reduce vertex cover (Y) to dominating set (X).

- **Transformation**: Given an instance of vertex cover (G, k), construct an instance of dominating set (G, k) where the transformation is straightforward (details depend on the exact reduction technique used).

- **Preservation**: Show that a solution to the transformed instance of dominating set corresponds to a solution of vertex cover, and vice versa.

- **Conclusion**: Since vertex cover is NP-hard and we have shown a polynomial-time reduction from vertex cover to dominating set, dominating set is also NP-hard.

NP-completeness

A problem is NP-complete if it is both NP-hard and in NP. NP-complete problems represent the hardest problems in NP for which a solution, if found, can be verified in polynomial time. Solving any NP-complete problem in polynomial time would imply $P = NP$.

To prove that a problem X is NP-complete, we follow these steps:

1. **NP-hardness**: First, prove that X is NP-hard using the reduction technique described earlier.

2. **Membership in NP**: Show that X belongs to NP by demonstrating that a proposed solution can be verified in polynomial time.

3. **Conclusion**: By proving both NP-hardness and membership in NP, we establish that X is NP-complete.

Consider the following example of NP-completeness proof:

- **Problem X**: Subset sum (Given a set of integers and a target sum, is there a subset of integers that sums to the target?)

The proof sketch is as follows:

- **NP-hardness**: Reduce a known NP-hard problem, such as 3SAT (Boolean satisfiability), to subset sum. This reduction shows that if we can solve subset sum in polynomial time, we c also solve 3SAT in polynomial time.

- **Membership in NP**: Show that a proposed subset that sums to the target can be verified in polynomial time (just add up the subset elements and check if they sum to the target).

- **Conclusion**: Since subset sum is both NP-hard and in NP, it is NP-complete.

Thus, it can be concluded that:

- **NP-hardness**: Proven by reducing a known NP-hard problem to the problem in question, demonstrating that a polynomial-time solution to the latter would imply a polynomial-time solution to all NP problems.

- **NP-completeness**: Proven by demonstrating both NP-hardness (via reduction) and membership in NP (efficient verification of solutions).

These proofs are foundational in computational complexity theory, helping to classify problems based on their inherent difficulty and the computational resources required for their solutions.

Polynomial space

Polynomial space (PSPACE) is a complexity class that focuses on the amount of memory (space) required by a Turing machine to solve problems. PSPACE consists of all decision problems that can be solved by either a deterministic or nondeterministic Turing machine using a polynomial amount of memory space relative to the size of the input.

The characteristics are as follows:

- **Memory usage**: Unlike the P and NP classes, which focus on time complexity, PSPACE is concerned with space complexity. A problem is in PSPACE if there exists an algorithm that solves it using a polynomial amount of space.

- **Deterministic vs. nondeterministic**: PSPACE includes problems solvable by both deterministic and nondeterministic Turing machines within polynomial space bounds.

Some examples of problems in PSPACE include:

- Solving games such as chess or Go on a game board of fixed size.

- Determining whether a given mathematical statement (e.g., a logical formula) is true or false within a specified range of integers.

Relationship to other complexity classes:

- **PSPACE vs. P and NP**: PSPACE includes P and NP as special cases:

- **PSPACE ⊇ P**: Problems that can be solved in polynomial time also require polynomial space, as time complexity inherently includes space complexity.

- **PSPACE ⊇ NP**: Problems with solutions that can be verified in polynomial time also have algorithms that are bounded by polynomial space.

- **PSPACE vs. NP-hard and NP-complete**: While PSPACE includes both P and NP, PSPACE-hard problems are not necessarily NP-hard, and vice versa. PSPACE-hardness pertains to the space complexity of problems rather than their time complexity.

Complexity theories and problems

PSPACE-complete problems are the most challenging problems within PSPACE; solving any PSPACE-complete problem in polynomial space would enable the solution of all problems in PSPACE. They are analogous to NP-complete problems in NP.

Similar to NP-complete problems, PSPACE-complete problems are the most difficult problems in the PSPACE complexity class. They are both in PSPACE and PSPACE-hard.

For examples, a well-known PSPACE-complete problem is the **quantified Boolean formula (QBF)**, which involves determining whether a given formula with quantifiers ($\forall$ and $\exists$) is true for all possible assignments.

SPACE is an essential complexity class that evaluates problems based on the memory resources needed to solve them. It broadens the focus from time complexity (as seen in the P and NP classes) to include problems that might require substantial memory but can still be solved within polynomial space limits. Understanding PSPACE aids in analyzing the memory requirements of algorithms and determining the theoretical limits of computation in terms of space usage.

Exponential time

Exponential time (EXP) is a complexity class that includes decision problems solvable by deterministic Turing machines within exponential time bounds. Here's a detailed exploration of EXP:

EXP encompasses all decision problems that a deterministic Turing machine can solve in 2poly(n) time, where poly(n) denotes a polynomial function of the input size n.

In contrast to polynomial time complexity classes such as P, NP, and PSPACE, which limit computation time to a polynomial function of the input size, EXP permits computations that increase exponentially with the input size.

The relationship to other complexity classes are as follows:

- **P vs. EXP**: P is contained within EXP because any problem solvable in polynomial time is also solvable in exponential time.
- **NP vs. EXP**: EXP is more powerful than NP because there exist problems that can be solved in exponential time but not in polynomial time. However, the relationship between NP and EXP is not fully understood; whether NP problems can be solved in exponential time is a major open question (related to the P vs. NP problem).

Complexity theories and problems

EXP-complete problems are the hardest problems in EXP; solving any EXP-complete problem in exponential time would solve all problems in EXP. Examples include certain problems in formal language theory and specific combinatorial optimization problems.

EXP is an important complexity class that captures problems solvable in exponential time. It represents a significant increase in computational difficulty compared to polynomial time classes (P, NP, PSPACE) and is used to classify problems based on their resource requirements. Understanding EXP helps in analyzing the inherent complexity of computational problems and exploring the theoretical limits of what can be feasibly computed within exponential time constraints.

Reductions and completeness

Reductions and completeness are foundational concepts in theoretical computer science, particularly in the study of computational complexity. Let us explore both concepts in detail.

Reductions

Reduction is a technique used to transform one problem into another. If problem A can be reduced to problem B, it means that any instance of problem A can be transformed into an instance of problem B in polynomial time. This transformation allows us to solve problem A using a solution to problem B. There are different types of reductions, such as:

- **Many-one reduction (Karp reduction)**: A problem A is many-one reducible to problem B (denoted as A $\leq_m$ B) if there is a polynomial-time computable function, f, such that for every instance x of A, x is a *yes* instance of A if and only if f(x) is a *yes* instance of B.

- **Turing reduction**: A problem A is Turing reducible to problem B if a solution to B can be used as an oracle to decide A in polynomial time. This means that we can solve A using an algorithm that is allowed to call a subroutine for solving B.

Completeness

Completeness is a concept that identifies the hardest problems within a complexity class. A problem is complete for a complexity class if it is among the most difficult problems in that class, and every problem in the class can be reduced to it. Here are the main types:

- **NP-completeness**: A problem is NP-complete if it is in NP and every problem in NP can be reduced to it in polynomial time. These problems are significant because if any NP-complete problem can be solved in polynomial time, then every problem in NP can also be solved in polynomial time (i.e., P = NP). Famous NP-complete problems include the TSP, the knapsack problem, and SAT (Boolean satisfiability problem).

- **P-completeness**: A problem is P-complete if it is in P and every problem in P can be reduced to it using a reduction that can be computed in logarithmic space. P-complete problems are the hardest problems in the class P under logarithmic space reductions.

- **PSPACE-completeness**: A problem is PSPACE-complete if it is in PSPACE (the class of problems solvable in polynomial space) and every problem in PSPACE can be reduced to it in polynomial time. An example of a PSPACE-complete problem is the QBF problem.

Consider the following examples of reductions and completeness:

- **SAT and 3-SAT**: The Boolean satisfiability problem (SAT) was the first problem proven to be NP-complete by *Stephen Cook*. The reduction from SAT to 3-SAT (a version of SAT where each clause has exactly three literals) is a classic example. SAT can be reduced to 3-SAT in polynomial time, showing that 3-SAT is also NP-complete.

- **Vertex cover and independent set**: The vertex cover problem can be reduced to the independent set problem. Given a graph G and an integer k, finding a vertex cover of size k can be transformed into finding an independent set of size $|V| - k$ in the same graph.

Understanding reductions and completeness helps us classify problems based on their computational difficulty and relationships, guiding the development of efficient algorithms and the understanding of computational intractability.

Approximation algorithms

Approximation algorithms are algorithms designed to find near-optimal solutions to optimization problems where finding the exact optimal solution is computationally infeasible (often due to the problem being NP-hard). These algorithms are particularly valuable when exact solutions are too costly in terms of time or resources. Here is a detailed look into approximation algorithms:

The key concepts are as follows:

- **Optimization problems**: Problems where the goal is to find the best solution according to some criteria. Examples include the TSP (minimize the travel cost) and the knapsack problem (maximize the total value of items without exceeding capacity).

- **Approximation ratio**: The performance of an approximation algorithm is measured by its approximation ratio. For a minimization problem, if is the cost of the solution produced by the algorithm and C* is the cost of the optimal solution, the approximation ratio α is defined as:

$$\alpha = \frac{C}{C^*}$$

For a maximization problem, it is:

$$\alpha = \frac{C}{C^*}$$

A lower ratio (closer to 1) indicates a better approximation for a minimization problem, and a higher ratio (closer to 1) indicates a better approximation for a maximization problem.

- **Polynomial-time approximation scheme (PTAS)**: A family of algorithms that can find a solution within $(1+\epsilon)$ times the optimal solution for any given $\epsilon > 0$. The running time of a PTAS is polynomial in the size of the input for fixed ϵ, but can become impractical as ϵ decreases.

- **Fully polynomial-time approximation scheme (FPTAS)**: A PTAS where the running time is polynomial in both the size of the input and $1/\epsilon$. FPTAS is more efficient than PTAS in terms of how running time depends on ϵ.

Consider the following examples of approximation algorithms:

- **Vertex cover**: For the vertex cover problem, a simple 2-approximation algorithm works as follows:

  o   Initialize an empty set C for the vertex cover.

  o   While there are edges left in the graph, pick any edge (u, v).

  o   Add both endpoints u and v to C, and remove all edges incident to u or v from the graph.

  o   Return C.

  This algorithm ensures that C is at most twice the size of the minimum vertex cover.

- **TSP**: For the metric TSP (where the distance between any two points satisfies the triangle inequality), a 2-approximation algorithm can be implemented using a **minimum spanning tree (MST)**:

  o   Compute an MST of the graph.

  o   Perform a preorder traversal of the MST to get a Hamiltonian cycle.

  o   Shortcut the Hamiltonian cycle to remove any repeated vertices (thanks to the triangle inequality, this doesn't increase the tour length).

  This algorithm produces a tour whose length is at most twice the optimal length.

- **Knapsack problem**: For the 0/1 knapsack problem, an FPTAS is available:

  o   Sort items by their value-to-weight ratio.

  o   Use dynamic programming to find the best combination of items up to a scaled and rounded version of their values.

  o   Adjust the dynamic programming approach to ensure the solution is within $(1+\epsilon)$ of the optimal value.

  o   The running time of this FPTAS is polynomial in both the number of items and $1/\epsilon$.

Importance and use cases

Approximation algorithms are critical in various fields such as:

- **Operations research**: Where finding exact solutions to large-scale optimization problems can be computationally infeasible.

- **Network design**: Where problems like network flow and connectivity must be optimized.

- **Bioinformatics**: For problems like sequence alignment and phylogenetic tree reconstruction.

- **Machine learning**: Where clustering and classification problems often rely on approximate solutions.

Approximation algorithms provide practical solutions for NP-hard optimization problems, balancing between solution quality and computational efficiency. They are essential tools in scenarios where exact solutions are impractical due to time or resource constraints.

Probabilistic algorithms

Probabilistic algorithms, also known as **randomized algorithms**, use random numbers to influence the steps or decisions made during computation. These algorithms can offer significant advantages in terms of simplicity, speed, and efficiency, especially for problems where deterministic algorithms might be too slow or complex. Here's an overview of probabilistic algorithms:

The following are the types of probabilistic algorithms:

- **Las Vegas algorithms**: These algorithms always produce a correct result, but their running time is a random variable.

  For example, randomized quicksort is a Las Vegas algorithm where the pivot is chosen randomly. This ensures that the algorithm avoids worst-case scenarios on average, leading to an expected $O(nlogn)$ running time.

- **Monte Carlo algorithms**: These algorithms have a fixed running time, but they may produce incorrect results with a certain probability.

  For example, the Monte Carlo algorithm for primality testing, such as the Miller-Rabin primality test, runs in polynomial time but has a small probability of incorrectly identifying a composite number as prime. The error probability can be reduced by increasing the number of iterations.

The examples of probabilistic algorithms are as follows:

- **Randomized quick sort algorithm**: In quick sort, the pivot element is chosen randomly. This randomization ensures that the expected running time remains $O(nlogn)$, making it less likely to encounter the worst-case scenario $O(n^2)$.

The advantage of randomized quick sort is the simplicity and good average-case performance.

- **Miller-Rabin primality test**: This algorithm tests whether a number is prime by using random bases and checking certain mathematical conditions. Each test reduces the probability of error.

  Its advantage is that it is fast and can handle very large numbers efficiently. The probability of error can be made arbitrarily small by running more iterations.

- **Randomized algorithms for graph problems**: For example, for the min-cut problem (finding the minimum cut in a graph), the Karger's algorithm repeatedly contracts random edges until only two vertices remain. This process is repeated multiple times to increase the probability of finding the minimum cut.

  It is simpler than deterministic counterparts and often faster.

- **Monte Carlo simulation**: It is used for numerical integration and optimization problems. Random samples are taken, and the results are averaged to approximate the solution.

  It is applicable to a wide range of problems where deterministic methods are infeasible.

The following are the benefits of probabilistic algorithms:

- **Simplicity**: Randomization can simplify the design and implementation of algorithms.

- **Speed**: Randomized algorithms can often be faster than their deterministic counterparts, especially for large input sizes.

- **Performance guarantees**: They often have good average-case performance and can avoid worst-case scenarios.

- **Versatility**: Applicable to a wide range of problems, including those in cryptography, numerical analysis, and optimization.

The limitations of probabilistic algorithms are as follows:

- **Uncertainty**: Monte Carlo algorithms can produce incorrect results, which might not be acceptable in all applications.

- **Dependence on randomness**: The performance of these algorithms can depend heavily on the quality of the random number generator used.

- **Complexity analysis**: Analyzing the performance and correctness of probabilistic algorithms can be more challenging than for deterministic ones.

Probabilistic algorithms leverage randomness to provide efficient and often simpler solutions to complex problems. While they introduce some uncertainty, their advantages in terms of speed and average-case performance make them valuable tools in many areas of computer science and beyond.

Bounded-error probabilistic polynomial time

Bounded-error probabilistic polynomial time (BPP) is a class of decision problems that can be solved by probabilistic algorithms in polynomial time with a bounded probability of error. It is a key concept in computational complexity theory, highlighting the power and limitations of probabilistic computation.

A language L belongs to the complexity class BPP if there exists a probabilistic Turing machine M such that:

- **Polynomial time**: M runs in polynomial time for all inputs.
- **Bounded error**: For any input x:
    - If $x \in L$, M accepts x with a probability of at least $2/3$.
    - If $x \notin L$, M rejects x with a probability of at least $2/3$.

The constants $2/3$ and $1/3$ are arbitrary and can be replaced by any values between $1/2$ and 1, as long as the difference is a constant. This error probability can be reduced further using techniques like majority voting or running the algorithm multiple times and taking the majority result.

The key characteristics of BPP are as follows:

- **Randomness**: BPP algorithms use randomness to make decisions during computation. The randomness allows the algorithm to potentially achieve better average-case performance or avoid worst-case scenarios.
- **Efficiency**: BPP algorithms run in polynomial time, making them efficient for practical use on large inputs.
- **Bounded error**: The probability of error is bounded away from $1/2$ by a constant. This ensures that the algorithm is highly likely to produce the correct result.

The examples of BPP algorithms are as follows:

- **Primality testing**: The Miller-Rabin primality test is a classic example of a BPP algorithm. It can determine whether a number is prime with high confidence, and the probability of error can be made arbitrarily small by running the test multiple times.
- **Graph properties**: Testing certain properties of graphs, such as connectivity or bipartiteness, can often be done using probabilistic algorithms that fall within BPP.
- **Approximate counting**: Estimating the number of solutions to certain combinatorial problems can be efficiently done using randomized algorithms that belong to BPP.

The following is BPP's relationship with other complexity classes:

- **P**: P is the class of problems solvable by deterministic algorithms in polynomial time. Clearly, P⊆BPP, as deterministic algorithms can be viewed as probabilistic algorithms with no randomness.

- **RP**: RP is a subclass of BPP where the algorithm has no false positives:
  - If x ∈ L, the algorithm accepts with a probability of at least ½ .
  - If $x \notin L$, the algorithm always rejects.

- **Co-RP**: The complement of RP, where the algorithm has no false negatives:
  - If $x \in L$, the algorithm always accepts.
  - If $x \notin L$, the algorithm rejects with a probability of at least ½.

- **Nondeterministic polynomial time (NP)**: The relationship between BPP and NP is not fully understood. It is known that P ⊆ BPP ⊆ PNP (P with an NP oracle).

The following is the significance of BPP:

- **Practical applications**: BPP algorithms are used in practical applications such as cryptography, randomized algorithms for network design, and machine learning, where deterministic algorithms might be too slow or complex.

- **Theoretical insights**: Studying BPP helps in understanding the power of randomness in computation and provides insights into the boundaries of efficient computation.

Reducing error probability

The error probability in BPP algorithms can be reduced by amplification techniques:

- **Repeated runs**: Run the algorithm multiple times and take the majority vote. For example, running a BPP algorithm k times and taking the majority result can reduce the error probability to $2-k$.

- **Chernoff bound**: This probabilistic bound can be used to show that the error probability decreases exponentially with the number of repetitions.

BPP represents problems that can be efficiently solved by probabilistic algorithms with a small, bounded error probability. It highlights the role of randomness in computation, providing powerful tools for solving complex problems and contributing to both practical applications and theoretical computer science.

Randomized polynomial time

Randomized polynomial time (RP) is a complexity class that characterizes decision problems that can be solved by probabilistic algorithms with one-sided error in polynomial time. This means that the algorithm may err on one side (either false positives or false negatives) but not both. Specifically, RP allows false negatives but not false positives.

A language L is in the complexity class RP if there exists a probabilistic Turing machine M such that:

- **Polynomial time**: M runs in polynomial time for all inputs.
- **One-sided error**:
  - If x ∈ L, the probability that M accepts x is at least ½.
  - If $x \notin L$, the probability that M accepts x is 0 (i.e., M always rejects x).

The following are the key characteristics of RP are as follows:

- **Randomness**: RP algorithms use randomness to make decisions during the computation.
- **Efficiency**: RP algorithms run in polynomial time, making them efficient.
- **One-sided error**: RP algorithms have no false positives. They only have false negatives, meaning they may fail to recognize a member of the language, but they will never incorrectly identify a non-member as a member.

Consider the following examples of RP algorithms:

- **Primality testing**: Before the discovery of deterministic polynomial-time algorithms for primality testing (such as the AKS primality test), the Miller-Rabin primality test was a common example of an RP algorithm. It can determine whether a number is composite with high confidence and no false positives (i.e., it never incorrectly identifies a composite number as prime).
- **Polynomial identity testing**: Given two polynomials, determine whether they are identical. The RP algorithm evaluates the polynomials at a randomly chosen point. If they differ at this point, they are not identical. If they are the same, the algorithm repeats the process to increase confidence.

The following is RP algorithm's relationship with other complexity classes:

- **P**: P is the class of problems solvable by deterministic algorithms in polynomial time. Clearly, P⊆RP, as deterministic algorithms can be viewed as probabilistic algorithms with no randomness and no error.
- **BPP**: BPP algorithms allow two-sided error, meaning they can have both false positives and false negatives but with bounded probability. It is known that RP ⊆ BPP.
- **Co-RP**: Co-RP is the class of problems where the complements are in RP. In Co-RP:
  - If x ∈ L, the algorithm always accepts.
  - If $x \notin L$, the algorithm rejects with a probability of at least ½.

- **Zero-error probabilistic polynomial time (ZPP)**: ZPP is the class of problems solvable by a randomized algorithm that always returns the correct answer or reports *I don't know* (in polynomial expected time). It is the intersection of RP and Co-RP, i.e., *ZPP=RP ∩ Co-RP*.

Reducing error probability

Amplification techniques can reduce the error probability in RP algorithms:

- **Repeated runs**: Run the algorithm multiple times. If the input x is in L, the probability that all runs fail to recognize x as a member decreases exponentially. For example, running an RP algorithm k times reduces the error probability to $(1/2)^k$.

The significance of RP is as follows:

- **Practical applications**: RP algorithms are used in various fields where it is crucial to avoid false positives, such as cryptographic protocols and probabilistic verification.

- **Theoretical insights**: Studying RP helps in understanding the boundaries of efficient computation with randomness and the impact of one-sided error on algorithm design.

RP represents problems that can be efficiently solved by probabilistic algorithms with one-sided error. These algorithms use randomness and guarantee no false positives, making them valuable for applications requiring high confidence in the correctness of positive instances. Understanding RP and its relationships with other complexity classes provides insights into the power and limitations of randomness in computation.

Complement of randomized polynomial time

Complement of randomized polynomial time (Co-RP) is a complexity class that characterizes decision problems that can be solved by probabilistic algorithms with one-sided error in polynomial time, where the error is on the opposite side compared to RP. Specifically, Co-RP algorithms may have false positives but not false negatives.

Let us look at the definition of Co-RP. A language L is in the complexity class Co-RP if there exists a probabilistic Turing machine M such that:

- **Polynomial time**: M runs in polynomial time for all inputs.
- **One-sided error**:
  - If $x \in L$, the probability that M accepts x is 1 (i.e., *M* always accepts x).
  - If $x \notin L$, the probability that M accepts x is at most ½.

Key characteristics of Co-RP are as follows:

- **Randomness**: Co-RP algorithms use randomness to make decisions during the computation.

- **Efficiency**: Co-RP algorithms run in polynomial time, making them efficient.

- **One-sided error**: Co-RP algorithms have no false negatives. They may incorrectly identify a non-member as a member of the language (false positives), but they will never fail to recognize a member of the language.

Let us look at some examples of Co-RP algorithms:

- **Polynomial identity testing**: Given two polynomials, determine whether they are identical. The Co-RP algorithm evaluates the polynomials at a randomly chosen point. If they differ at this point, they are not identical, and the algorithm rejects. If they are the same at this point, the algorithm accepts, potentially with some probability of error if they are not truly identical.

- **Minimum spanning tree verification**: Given a graph and a spanning tree, verify if the spanning tree is a minimum spanning tree. A Co-RP algorithm can probabilistically verify this by checking certain properties or performing random checks.

Relationship with other complexity classes is given in the following list:

- **P**: P is the class of problems solvable by deterministic algorithms in polynomial time. Clearly, $P \subseteq$ Co-RP, as deterministic algorithms can be viewed as probabilistic algorithms with no randomness and no error.

- **RP**: RP is the class of problems where the complements are in Co-RP. In RP:

  - If $x \in L$, the algorithm accepts with a probability of at least ½.

  - If $x \notin L$, the algorithm always rejects.

- **BPP**: BPP algorithms allow two-sided error, meaning they can have both false positives and false negatives but with bounded probability. It is known that Co-RP $\subseteq$ BPP.

- **ZPP**: ZPP is the class of problems solvable by a randomized algorithm that always returns the correct answer or reports *I don't know* (in polynomial expected time). It is the intersection of RP and Co-RP, i.e., ZPP = RP ∩ Co-RP.

Reducing error probability

The error probability in Co-RP algorithms can be reduced by amplification techniques:

- **Repeated runs**: Run the algorithm multiple times. If the input $x \notin L$, the probability that all runs incorrectly accept x as a member decreases exponentially. For example, running a Co-RP algorithm k times reduces the error probability to $(1/2)^k$.

Significance of Co-RP is as follows:

- **Practical applications**: Co-RP algorithms are used in various fields where it is crucial to avoid false negatives, such as verification of mathematical proofs and combinatorial property testing.

- **Theoretical insights**: Studying Co-RP helps in understanding the boundaries of efficient computation with randomness and the impact of one-sided error on algorithm design.

Co-RP represents problems that can be efficiently solved by probabilistic algorithms with one-sided error, where the error is only on the positive side (false positives). These algorithms use randomness and guarantee no false negatives, making them valuable for applications, requiring high confidence in the correctness of negative instances. Understanding Co-RP and its relationships with other complexity classes provides insights into the power and limitations of randomness in computation.

Conclusion

This chapter examined the fundamental ideas of computational complexity, focusing on how different problems are grouped according to the time and space required to solve them. It covered a range of topics from the distinction between P and NP problems to more complex subjects like NP-hardness, polynomial space, and probabilistic approaches. Through the study of reductions, approximations, and randomized techniques, the chapter demonstrated various strategies for managing problems that are difficult or impossible to solve exactly. Understanding these classifications enables learners to recognize which problems are computationally feasible and which present significant challenges.

In the next chapter, we will explore a variety of sophisticated algorithmic techniques designed to tackle demanding and large-scale computational tasks encountered in real-world applications.

Exercise

1. Define and differentiate between the complexity classes P and NP.
2. Explain the concept of polynomial-time reductions.
3. What does it mean for a problem to be NP-hard but not NP-complete?
4. Compare and contrast deterministic and probabilistic algorithms in the context of complexity classes.
5. Discuss the relevance and limitations of approximation algorithms for NP-hard problems.

CHAPTER 12

Other Advanced Algorithms

Introduction

This chapter explores advanced algorithms, organized into categories like cryptosystems, computational geometry, and complexity classes. It covers randomized algorithms and NP-completeness problems, providing a comprehensive look at each area. It also includes a variety of advanced algorithms, complete with detailed explanations and complexity analyses in both space and time formats.

Structure

The chapter covers the following topics:

- Randomized quick sort
- Graham's scan algorithm
- Jarvis's March algorithm
- Karger's minimum cut
- Fisher-Yates shuffles
- Travelling salesman approximation algorithm
- Euclid's algorithm for GCD
- Modulo arithmetic

- Chinese remainder theorem
- RSA public-key cryptosystem
- 3-CNF satisfiability
- The clique problem
- The vertex problem

Objectives

The goal of this chapter is to explore advanced algorithms, grouping them into areas such as cryptosystems, computational geometry, and complexity classes. It seeks to provide a clear and detailed understanding of topics like randomized algorithms and NP-completeness problems within these fields.

Randomized quick sort

Randomized quick sort is a variation of the quick sort algorithm that improves performance on average by randomly selecting the pivot element. It works as follows:

1. **Pick a random pivot:** Rather than always choosing the first or last element as the pivot, randomly select an element from the array.

2. **Partition the array:** Arrange the elements so that those less than the pivot is on the left and those greater than the pivot are on the right.

3. **Sort the subarrays:** Apply these steps recursively to the left and right subarrays.

This approach helps ensure that the algorithm performs well across different scenarios.

Algorithm 12.1: Randomized quick sort

```
RandomizedQuickSort(arr, low, high):
    IF low < high:
        pivot_index = RandomizedPartition(arr, low, high)
        RandomizedQuickSort(arr, low, pivot_index - 1)
        RandomizedQuickSort(arr, pivot_index + 1, high)

RandomizedPartition(arr, low, high):
    pivot_index = Random(low, high)
    Swap(arr[pivot_index], arr[high])
    RETURN Partition(arr, low, high)

Partition(arr, low, high):
    pivot = arr[high]
    i = low - 1
```

```
    FOR j = low TO high - 1:
        IF arr[j] <= pivot:
            i = i + 1
            Swap(arr[i], arr[j])
    Swap(arr[i + 1], arr[high])
    RETURN i + 1

Swap(a, b):
    temp = a
    a = b
    b = temp
```

Program 12.1: Implementation in C

```c
#include <stdio.h>
#include <stdlib.h>
#include <time.h>

// Function to swap two elements
void swap(int *a, int *b) {
    int temp = *a;
    *a = *b;
    *b = temp;
}

// Partition function
int partition(int arr[], int low, int high) {
    int pivot = arr[high];
    int i = (lcw - 1);
    for (int j = low; j <= high - 1; j++) {
        if (arr[j] <= pivot) {
            i++;
            swap(&arr[i], &arr[j]);
        }
    }
    swap(&arr[i + 1], &arr[high]);
    return (i + 1);
}

// Randomized Partition function
int randomizedPartition(int arr[], int low, int high) {
    int pivot_index = low + rand() % (high - low + 1);
    swap(&arr[pivot_index], &arr[high]);
```

```
        return partition(arr, low, high);
}

// Randomized QuickSort function
void randomizedQuickSort(int arr[], int low, int high) {
    if (low < high) {
        int pivot_index = randomizedPartition(arr, low, high);
        randomizedQuickSort(arr, low, pivot_index - 1);
        randomizedQuickSort(arr, pivot_index + 1, high);
    }
}

// Utility function to print an array
void printArray(int arr[], int size) {
    for (int i = 0; i < size; i++)
        printf("%d ", arr[i]);
    printf("\n");
}

// Main function to test the Randomized QuickSort
int main() {
    srand(time(0)); // Seed for random number generation
    int arr[] = {10, 7, 8, 9, 1, 5};
    int n = sizeof(arr) / sizeof(arr[0]);
    printf("Original array: \n");
    printArray(arr, n);
    randomizedQuickSort(arr, 0, n - 1);
    printf("Sorted array: \n");
    printArray(arr, n);
    return 0;
}
```

The following is the explanation of the preceding code:

- **swap:** This function swaps two elements in the array.

- **partition:** It rearranges the array based on the pivot, so elements less than the pivot end up on one side, and the elements greater than the pivot end up on the other.

- **randomizedPartition:** This function picks a random pivot, moves it to the end of the array, and then calls the partition function.

- **randomizedQuicksort:** The core recursive function that sorts the array using the randomized partitioning method.

- **printArray:** A helper function that prints out the array.

- **main:** Sets up the array, prints the original version, sorts it using `randomizedQuicksort`, and then prints the sorted result.

Complexity analysis

The time and space complexity of randomized quicksort are as follows:

- **Time complexity:** On average, randomized quick sort runs in $O(n \log n)$ time. Although it is quite rare, in the worst-case scenario, it can degrade to $O(n^2)$ if the randomization does not work out well.

- **Space complexity:** The space complexity is $O(\log n)$, which comes from the space needed for the recursive call stack.

The randomization in this algorithm helps ensure that the pivot element is more likely to split the array into two roughly equal parts, reducing the chances of encountering the worst-case performance.

Graham's scan algorithm

Graham's scan is an algorithm for finding the convex hull of a set of points on a plane. The convex hull is the smallest convex shape that can enclose all the given points.

The steps of Graham's scan algorithm are as follows:

1. **Identify the starting point:** Find the point with the lowest y-coordinate. If there are multiple such points, choose the one with the lowest x-coordinate. This point will be the pivot and is guaranteed to be on the convex hull.

2. **Sort the points:** The remaining points should be arranged in accordance with the angle that they create with the pivot. Whenever two points form the same angle, the one that is closer to the pivot should be selected.

3. **Build the convex hull:** The next step is to build the convex hull, which is done as follows:

   a. Start with the pivot and the point with the smallest angle.

   b. Go through the sorted points and check whether each point makes a left or right turn relative to the last two points in the hull.

   c. If a point makes a right turn, it is removed from the hull (it is not part of the convex hull).

   d. If it makes a left turn or is collinear, add it to the hull.

This approach ensures that you construct the convex hull efficiently and correctly.

Algorithm 12.2: Graham's scan algorithm

```
FUNCTION GrahamScan(points):
    pivot = FindLowestPoint(points)
    sorted_points = SortByPolarAngle(points, pivot)

    hull = Stack()
    PUSH(pivot, hull)
    PUSH(sorted_points[0], hull)

    FOR i = 1 TO LENGTH(sorted_points) - 1:
        WHILE SIZE(hull) > 1 AND ccw(NextToTop(hull), Top(hull), sorted_
points[i]) <= 0:
            POP(hull)
      PUSH(sorted_points[i], hull)

    RETURN hull

FUNCTION FindLowestPoint(points):
    lowest = points[0]
    FOR point IN points:
      IF point.y < lowest.y OR (point.y == lowest.y AND point.x < lowest.x):
          lowest = point
    RETURN lowest

FUNCTION SortByPolarAngle(points, pivot):
    SORT points BY (angle_with_pivot, distance_from_pivot)
    RETURN points

FUNCTION ccw(a, b, c):
    RETURN (b.x - a.x) * (c.y - a.y) - (b.y - a.y) * (c.x - a.x)
```

The following is the explanation of the algorithm:

- **FindLowestPoint:** This function finds the point with the lowest y-coordinate, which becomes the pivot for the convex hull.

- **SortByPolarAngle:** This function sorts the remaining points by the angle they make with the pivot.

- **ccw(counter-clockwise):** This function checks whether three points make a left turn, a right turn, or are collinear.

- **GrahamScan:** This function uses a stack to build the convex hull by adding points that make a left turn and removing those that make a right turn.

Program 12.2: Implementation in C

```c
#include <stdio.h>
#include <stdlib.h>

// Point structure
typedef struct Point {
    int x, y;
} Point;

// Function to swap two points
void swap(Point *a, Point *b) {
    Point temp = *a;
    *a = *b;
    *b = temp;
}

// Function to find the orientation of the triplet (p, q, r).
// The function returns the following values:
// 0 -> p, q and r are collinear
// 1 -> Clockwise
// 2 -> Counterclockwise
int orientation(Point p, Point q, Point r) {
    int val = (q.y - p.y) * (r.x - q.x) - (q.x - p.x) * (r.y - q.y);
    if (val == 0) return 0; // collinear
    return (val > 0) ? 1 : 2; // clock or counterclock wise
}

// Function to sort points by polar angle with the pivot
int compare(const void *vp1, const void *vp2) {
    Point *p1 = (Point *)vp1;
    Point *p2 = (Point *)vp2;

    int o = orientation(pivot, *p1, *p2);
    if (o == 0)
        return (p1->x - pivot.x) * (p1->x - pivot.x) + (p1->y - pivot.y) *
(p1->y - pivot.y) <
                (p2->x - pivot.x) * (p2->x - pivot.x) + (p2->y - pivot.y) *
(p2->y - pivot.y) ? -1 : 1;
    return (o == 2) ? -1 : 1;
}

// Function to return the next to top element of a stack
Point nextToTop(Point stack[], int *top) {
```

```
        return stack[*top - 1];
}

// Function to print the convex hull
void printConvexHull(Point points[], int n) {
    // Find the bottom-most point
    int ymin = points[0].y, min = 0;
    for (int i = 1; i < n; i++) {
        int y = points[i].y;
        if ((y < ymin) || (ymin == y && points[i].x < points[min].x))
            ymin = points[i].y, min = i;
    }

    // Place the bottom-most point at first position
    swap(&points[0], &points[min]);

    // Sort n-1 points with respect to the first point. A point p1 comes
before p2 in sorted output if p2
    // has a larger polar angle (in counterclockwise direction) than p1
    pivot = points[0];
    qsort(&points[1], n - 1, sizeof(Point), compare);

    // Create an empty stack and push first three points to it
    Point stack[n];
    int top = -1;
    stack[++top] = points[0];
    stack[++top] = points[1];
    stack[++top] = points[2];

    // Process remaining n-3 points
    for (int i = 3; i < n; i++) {
        // Keep removing top while the angle formed by points next-to-top,
top, and points[i] makes a non-left turn
        while (top > 0 && orientation(nextToTop(stack, &top), stack[top],
points[i]) != 2)
            top--;
        stack[++top] = points[i];
    }

    // Now stack has the output points, print contents of stack
    printf("The points in the convex hull are:\n");
    for (int i = 0; i <= top; i++)
        printf("(%d, %d)\n", stack[i].x, stack[i].y);
```

```
}

// Main function
int main() {
    Point points[] = {{0, 3}, {1, 1}, {2, 2}, {4, 4}, {0, 0}, {1, 2}, {3,
1}, {3, 3}};
    int n = sizeof(points) / sizeof(points[0]);
    printConvexHull(points, n);
    return 0;
}
```

The following is the explanation:

- **Point structure:** Defines a point with its x and y coordinates.

- **swap:** Switches the positions of two points.

- **orientation:** Determines how three points (p, q, r) are oriented relative to each other, whether they form a left turn, a right turn, or are collinear.

- **compare:** Sorts the points based on the angle they make with the pivot.

- **nextToTop:** Retrieves the second-to-last element from the stack.

- **printConvexHull:** Computes the convex hull of a set of points and displays it.

Complexity analysis

The time and space complexity of Graham's scan algorithm are as follows:

- **Time complexity:** The time complexity is calculated as follows:

    1. **Finding the lowest point:** This step involves going through all the points to find the one with the lowest y-coordinate, which takes $O(n)$ time.

    2. **Sorting the points:** Once the pivot is identified, the remaining points are sorted by their polar angle relative to the pivot. Sorting is the most time-consuming part and usually takes $O(n \log n)$ time using efficient algorithms like merge sort or quick sort.

    3. **Constructing the convex hull:** After sorting, the convex hull is built by going through the sorted points and using a stack. This step takes $O(n)$ time, as each point is added to and removed from the stack at most once.

    Overall, the time complexity of Graham's scan is dominated by the sorting step, making it $O(n \log n)$.

- **Space complexity:** The space complexity is as follows:

    ○ **Storage for points:** The algorithm needs $O(n)$ space to store the points.

    o   **Stack space:** It also requires $O(n)$ space for the stack used to build the convex hull in the worst-case scenario where all points are part of the hull.

In conclusion, Graham's scan is efficient with a time complexity of $O(n \log n)$ and a space complexity of $O(n)$, making it a solid choice for finding the convex hull of a set of points.

Jarvis's March algorithm

Jarvis's March, also known as the **gift wrapping algorithm,** is used to find the convex hull of a set of points on a plane. The convex hull is the smallest convex shape that can enclose all the given points.

The steps of Jarvis's March algorithm are as follows:

1. **Find the leftmost point:** Start by finding the point with the smallest x-coordinate. If there are ties, choose the one with the smallest y-coordinate. This point will definitely be part of the convex hull.

2. **Select the next point:** From your current point, find the next point such that all other points are to the right of the line drawn between the current point and this new point. Use the orientation function to check the direction of the turn.

3. **Repeat:** Continue this process, selecting the next point and checking the direction of the turn, until you loop back to the starting point.

This method effectively wraps around the set of points to form the convex hull.

Algorithm 12.3: Jarvis's March algorithm

```
FUNCTION JarvisMarch(points):
    hull = []
    # Find the leftmost point
    leftmost = points[0]
    FOR point IN points:
        IF point.x < leftmost.x OR (point.x == leftmost.x AND point.y <
leftmost.y):
            leftmost = point

    current = leftmost
    REPEAT:
        ADD current TO hull
        next_point = points[0]
        FOR point IN points:
            IF next_point == current OR orientation(current, next_point,
point) == -1:
                next_point = point
```

```
        current = next_point
    UNTIL current == leftmost
    RETURN hull

FUNCTION orientation(p, q, r):
    # Returns -1 if r is to the left of line pq
    # Returns 0 if p, q, r are collinear
    # Returns 1 if r is to the right of line pq
    val = (q.y - p.y) * (r.x - q.x) - (q.x - p.x) * (r.y - q.y)
    IF val == 0: RETURN 0
    IF val > 0: RETURN 1
    ELSE: RETURN -1
```

The explanation is as follows:

- **Orientation:** Using the three locations (p, q, and r), this function determines the direction of the turn that has been made. If r is to the left of the line produced by p and q, it returns -1; if all three points are on a straight line, it returns 0; and if r is to the right of that line, it returns to the right of that line.

- **JarvisMarch:** This function carries out Jarvis's March algorithm to find the convex hull. It starts at the leftmost point and repeatedly selects the next point such that all other points are on the right side of the line connecting the current point and the new point.

Program 12.3: Implementation in C

```c
#include <stdio.h>

typedef struct Point {
    int x, y;
} Point;

// Function to swap two points
void swap(Point *a, Point *b) {
    Point temp = *a;
    *a = *b;
    *b = temp;
}

// Function to find the orientation of the triplet (p, q, r).
// The function returns the following values:
// 0 -> p, q and r are collinear
// 1 -> Clockwise
// 2 -> Counterclockwise
```

```
int orientation(Point p, Point q, Point r) {
    int val = (q.y - p.y) * (r.x - q.x) - (q.x - p.x) * (r.y - q.y);
    if (val == 0) return 0; // collinear
    return (val > 0) ? 1 : 2; // clock or counterclock wise
}

// Function to print the convex hull
void printConvexHull(Point points[], int n) {
    // There must be at least 3 points
    if (n < 3) return;

    // Initialize Result
    Point hull[n];
    int hullSize = 0;

    // Find the leftmost point
    int leftmost = 0;
    for (int i = 1; i < n; i++) {
        if (points[i].x < points[leftmost].x)
            leftmost = i;
    }

    // Start from leftmost point, keep moving counterclockwise
    // until reach the start point again. This loop runs O(h)
    // times where h is number of points in result or output.
    int p = leftmost, q;
    do {
        // Add current point to result
        hull[hullSize++] = points[p];

        // Search for a point 'q' such that orientation(p, x,
        // q) is counterclockwise for all points 'x'. The idea
        // is to keep track of last visited most counterclock-
        // wise point in q. If any point 'i' is more counterclock-
        // wise than q, then update q.
        q = (p + 1) % n;
        for (int i = 0; i < n; i++) {
            // If i is more counterclockwise than current q, then
            // update q
            if (orientation(points[p], points[i], points[q]) == 2)
                q = i;
        }
```

```
        // Now q is the most counterclockwise with respect to p
        // Set p as q for next iteration, so that q is added to
        // result 'hull'
        p = q;

    } while (p != leftmost);   // While we don't come to first point

    // Print Result
    printf("The points in the convex hull are:\n");
    for (int i = 0; i < hullSize; i++)
        printf("(%d, %d)\n", hull[i].x, hull[i].y);
}

// Main functior
int main() {
    Point points[] = {{0, 3}, {1, 1}, {2, 2}, {4, 4}, {0, 0}, {1, 2}, {3,
1}, {3, 3}};
    int n = sizeof(points) / sizeof(points[0]);
    printConvexHull(points, n);
    return 0;
}
```

Let us look at the explanation. The preceding program consists of the following modules:

- **Point structure:** Defines a point with x and y coordinates.

- **swap:** Swaps the positions of two points.

- **orientation:** Checks the orientation of three points (p, q, r). It returns 0 if they are collinear, 1 if they form a clockwise turn, and 2 if they form a counterclockwise turn.

- **printConvexHull:** Uses the Jarvis's March algorithm to find and display the convex hull of a set of points.

- **main:** Sets up the points and calls printConvexHull to compute and show the convex hull.

Complexity analysis

The complexity analysis of Jarvis's March algorithm is as follows:

- **Time complexity:** The time complexity is calculated as follows:

    1. **Finding the leftmost point:** This step involves going through all the points to identify the one with the smallest x-coordinate. It takes $O(n)$ time to do this.

2. **Constructing the convex hull:** The core of Jarvis's March involves finding the next point for the convex hull by checking all points relative to the current one. In the worst-case scenario, this can mean checking every point each time, leading to a time complexity of $O(n^2)$. This inefficiency arises because each point may require a full scan to ensure it is correctly positioned relative to the convex hull.

So, Jarvis's March has an overall time complexity of $O(n^2)$, which can be slower compared to other algorithms like Graham's scan or QuickHull, especially with larger datasets.

- **Space complexity:** The space complexity is as follows:

  ○ **Storage for points:** The algorithm needs $O(n)$ space to store the points.

  ○ **Additional space:** It also requires a small amount of extra space for variables and the final result, but this is minimal compared to the space used for storing the points.

Overall, Jarvis's March has a space complexity of $O(n)$, making it suitable for smaller datasets despite its higher time complexity.

In summary, Jarvis' March is a straightforward and simple algorithm to build; yet, due to the fact that it has an $O(n2)$ time complexity, it may not be as effective for large datasets. It has a space complexity of $O(n)$, which is well within the realm of possibility for more compact point sets.

Karger's minimum cut

Karger's algorithm is a randomized method for finding the minimum cut of a connected graph. A cut splits the graph's vertex into two non-empty groups, and the cut size is the number of edges connecting these groups. The minimum cut is the one with the fewest edges. Karger's algorithm works by repeatedly contracting random edges until only two nodes are left, with the remaining edges between these two nodes representing the cut.

The following are the steps of Karger's minimum cut algorithm:

1. **Choose a random edge:** Pick a random edge (u, v) from the graph.

2. **Contract the edge:** Merge the two vertices, u and v, into a single vertex. Make sure to remove any self-loops created by this merge.

3. **Repeat:** Continue contracting edges until only two vertices are left. The edges between these two vertices then represent the minimum cut.

4. **Repeat multiple times:** To improve the chances of finding the true minimum cut, run the entire algorithm multiple times and keep track of the smallest cut found.

This approach leverages randomness to approximate the minimum cut, and repeating the process multiple times helps in finding a more accurate result.

Algorithm 12.4: Karger's minimum cut algorithm

```
FUNCTION KargerMinCut(graph):
    minCut = INFINITY
    REPEAT log(n) * n TIMES:
        copiedGraph = copy(graph)
        WHILE copiedGraph has more than 2 vertices:
            edge = randomEdge(copiedGraph)
            contract(copiedGraph, edge)
        currentCut = number of edges in copiedGraph
        IF currentCut < minCut:
            minCut = currentCut
    RETURN minCut

FUNCTION contract(graph, edge):
    u, v = edge
    merge vertices u and v into a single vertex
    remove self-loops
```

The explanation is as follows:

- **KargerMinCut:** This function runs the algorithm several times (usually *log(n)* * *n* times) to boost the chances of finding the true minimum cut. It tracks the smallest cut discovered during all these runs.

- **contract:** This function merges the two vertices connected by the chosen edge into a single vertex and removes any self-loops that result from this merge.

Program 12.4: Implementation in C

```c
#include <stdio.h>
#include <stdlib.h>
#include <limits.h>
#include <time.h>

// A structure to represent a graph
struct Graph {
    int V, E;
    int** edges;
};

// A utility function to create a graph with V vertices and E edges
struct Graph* createGraph(int V, int E) {
    struct Graph* graph = (struct Graph*)malloc(sizeof(struct Graph));
    graph->V = V;
    graph->E = E;
```

```c
    graph->edges = (int**)malloc(E * sizeof(int*));
    for (int i = 0; i < E; i++) {
        graph->edges[i] = (int*)malloc(2 * sizeof(int));
    }
    return graph;
}

// A utility function to find the subset of an element i
int find(int parent[], int i) {
    if (parent[i] == i)
        return i;
    return find(parent, parent[i]);
}

// A function that does union of two sets of x and y (uses union by rank)
void Union(int parent[], int rank[], int x, int y) {
    int xroot = find(parent, x);
    int yroot = find(parent, y);

    if (rank[xroot] < rank[yroot])
        parent[xroot] = yroot;
    else if (rank[xroot] > rank[yroot])
        parent[yroot] = xroot;
    else {
        parent[yroot] = xroot;
        rank[xroot]++;
    }
}

// A function to contract an edge (u, v) in the given graph
void contractEdge(struct Graph* graph, int u, int v) {
    for (int i = 0; i < graph->E; i++) {
        if (graph->edges[i][0] == v)
            graph->edges[i][0] = u;
        if (graph->edges[i][1] == v)
            graph->edges[i][1] = u;
    }
}

// A function to copy a graph
struct Graph* copyGraph(struct Graph* graph) {
    struct Graph* newGraph = createGraph(graph->V, graph->E);
    for (int i = 0; i < graph->E; i++) {
        newGraph->edges[i][0] = graph->edges[i][0];
```

```
        newGraph->edges[i][1] = graph->edges[i][1];
    }
    return newGraph;
}

// A function to count the number of edges in the graph
int countEdges(struct Graph* graph) {
    int count = 0;
    for (int i = 0; i < graph->E; i++) {
        if (graph->edges[i][0] != graph->edges[i][1])
            count++;
    }
    return count;
}

// Karger's minimum cut algorithm
int KargerMinCut(struct Graph* graph) {
    int minCut = INT_MAX;

    for (int i = 0; i < graph->V * graph->V; i++) {
        struct Graph* copiedGraph = copyGraph(graph);
        int vertices = graph->V;

        while (vertices > 2) {
            int randomEdge = rand() % copiedGraph->E;
            int u = copiedGraph->edges[randomEdge][0];
            int v = copiedGraph->edges[randomEdge][1];

            contractEdge(copiedGraph, u, v);
            vertices--;
        }

        int cutEdges = countEdges(copiedGraph);
        if (cutEdges < minCut)
            minCut = cutEdges;

        free(copiedGraph);
    }

    return minCut;
}

// Driver program to test above functions
int main() {
    srand(time(NULL));

    int V = 4;   // Number of vertices in graph
```

```
    int E = 5;   // Number of edges in graph
    struct Graph* graph = createGraph(V, E);

    // add edge 0-1
    graph->edges[0][0] = 0;
    graph->edges[0][1] = 1;

    // add edge 0-2
    graph->edges[1][0] = 0;
    graph->edges[1][1] = 2;

    // add edge 0-3
    graph->edges[2][0] = 0;
    graph->edges[2][1] = 3;

    // add edge 1-3
    graph->edges[3][0] = 1;
    graph->edges[3][1] = 3;

    // add edge 2-3
    graph->edges[4][0] = 2;
    graph->edges[4][1] = 3;

    printf("Minimum cut is %d\n", KargerMinCut(graph));

    return 0;
}
```

The explanation is as follows:

- **Graph structure:** Defines a graph with a set number of vertices (V) and edges (E).
- **createGraph:** Sets up the graph by allocating memory and initializing its components.
- **find:** Identifies the subset to which a particular element belongs.
- **Union:** Merges two sets into one.
- **contractEdge:** Merges the two vertices connected by a chosen edge into a single vertex and removes any self-loops that are created.
- **copyGraph:** Creates a duplicate of the given graph.
- **countEdges:** Counts how many edges are present in the graph.
- **KargerMinCut:** Runs Karger's minimum cut algorithm, repeating the edge contraction process multiple times to improve the chances of finding the minimum cut.
- **main:** Sets up the graph with a specified set of edges and calls **KargerMinCut** to find and display the minimum cut.

Complexity analysis

The time and space complexity of Karger's algorithm are as follows:

- **Time complexity:** The time complexity is calculated in the following manner:

  o **Single run of Karger's algorithm:** In each run, the algorithm contracts edges until only two vertices are left. This requires $O(E)$ operations, where E is the number of edges in the graph. Each contraction involves finding and merging sets, which can be efficiently handled with Union-Find data structures, taking nearly constant time for each operation.

    The contraction process involves iterating through and merging edges, and since each edge can be contracted once, the overall time complexity per run is $O(E)$.

  o **Number of runs:** To increase the probability of finding the true minimum cut, Karger's algorithm is typically run multiple times. The number of runs required to achieve a high probability of success is approximately $O(n^2 \log n)$, where n is the number of vertices. This is because the probability of finding the minimum cut in a single run is $1/n(n-1)$, and running the algorithm $O(n^2 \log n)$ times boosts the probability significantly.

  Therefore, the overall time complexity of running Karger's algorithm multiple times is $O(n^2 \log n * E)$, assuming each run takes $O(E)$ time.

- **Space complexity:** The space complexity is as follows:

  o **Graph storage:** The space needed to store the graph, including vertices and edges, is $O(V + E)$, where V is the number of vertices and E is the number of edges.

  o **Additional space:** Additional space is required for maintaining data structures like Union-Find to manage sets and handle edge contractions, which also requires $O(V)$ space in the worst case.

  Therefore, the overall space complexity is $O(V + E)$.

In summary, Karger's minimum cut algorithm has a time complexity of $O(n^2 \log n * E)$ when run multiple times to ensure a high probability of finding the minimum cut. Its space complexity is $O(V + E)$, making it suitable for moderate-sized graphs.

Fisher-Yates shuffles

The Fisher-Yates shuffle, also known as the **Knuth shuffle**, is a method for shuffling a list of items so that each possible arrangement of the items is equally likely. In other words, it is a fair way to shuffle.

Imagine you have a playlist of songs or a deck of cards that you want to mix up. The Fisher-Yates shuffle ensures that every possible order of the songs or cards could happen, making the shuffle truly random.

By following these steps, every card has an equal chance of ending up in any position, ensuring a fair shuffle:

1. **Start at the end:** Begin with the last card in the deck.

2. **Pick a random card:** Choose a random card from the whole deck.

3. **Swap the cards:** Swap the randomly chosen card with the last card in the deck.

4. **Move back:** Move to the second-last card in the deck, and repeat the process, pick a random card from the remaining unshuffled cards, and swap.

5. **Keep going:** Continue this process, working backward through the deck, until you have reached the first card. By the time you get there, the entire deck will be shuffled.

Algorithm 12.5: Fisher-Yates shuffle

```
FUNCTION FisherYatesShuffle(arr, n):
    FOR i FROM n - 1 DOWNTO 1:
        j = randomInt(0, i)
        SWAP arr[i] WITH arr[j]
```

The explanation is as follows:

- **randomInt(0, i):** This generates a random number between 0 and i, including both 0 and i. It is like rolling a die with (i + 1) sides and getting a random result.

- **SWAP arr[i] WITH arr[j]:** This means taking the element at position i in the list and swapping it with the element at position j. It is like trading places between two items in the list.

Program 12.5: Implementation in C

```c
#include <stdio.h>
#include <stdlib.h>
#include <time.h>

// Function to swap two elements
void swap(int *a, int *b) {
    int temp = *a;
    *a = *b;
    *b = temp;
}

// Function to perform the Fisher-Yates shuffle
```

```c
void fisherYatesShuffle(int arr[], int n) {
    // Seed the random number generator
    srand(time(NULL));

    for (int i = n - 1; i > 0; i--) {
        // Generate a random index j such that 0 <= j <= i
        int j = rand() % (i + 1);

        // Swap arr[i] with the element at random index
        swap(&arr[i], &arr[j]);
    }
}

// Function to print an array
void printArray(int arr[], int n) {
    for (int i = 0; i < n; i++) {
        printf("%d ", arr[i]);
    }
    printf("\n");
}

// Main function to test the Fisher-Yates shuffle
int main() {
    int arr[] = {1, 2, 3, 4, 5, 6, 7, 8, 9, 10};
    int n = sizeof(arr) / sizeof(arr[0]);

    printf("Original array:\n");
    printArray(arr, n);

    fisherYatesShuffle(arr, n);

    printf("Shuffled array:\n");
    printArray(arr, n);

    return 0;
}
```

The explanation is as follows:

- **swap:** This is a little helper function that switches the positions of two items in the list.

- **fisherYatesShuffle:** This is the main function that mixes up the list. It goes through the list from the end to the beginning, and for each item, it swaps it with a randomly chosen item that comes before it (or itself).

- **printArray:** This function just displays the items in the list.

- **main:** This function sets up the list, shows you what it looks like before shuffling, uses the **fisherYatesShuffle** to mix it up, and then shows you the shuffled list.

Complexity analysis

The complexity analysis of the Fisher-Yates shuffle is as follows:

- **Time complexity:** The Fisher-Yates shuffle algorithm is very efficient with time. It only needs to go through the list of items once, no matter how many items there are. This means if you have ten items, it takes roughly ten steps; if you have 100 items, it takes about 100 steps, and so on. We describe this efficiency as $O(n)$, where n is the number of items in the list.

- **Space complexity:** Moreover, the Fisher-Yates shuffle is particularly effective in terms of space utilization. With the exception of a few variables of a predetermined size, it does not require any additional space to do its function. In other words, regardless of the size of your list, it will only require a minimal amount of additional space that is consistent throughout. Therefore, this efficiency is described as $O(1)$.

Travelling salesman approximation algorithm

The TSP is a famous puzzle in computer science and operations research. Imagine a salesperson who needs to visit a list of cities and then return to the starting point. The challenge is to figure out the shortest route that visits each city exactly once and gets you back home.

Solving this problem perfectly is very hard and takes a lot of computing power (it is what we call NP-hard). However, there are smart shortcuts, known as approximation algorithms, that can find pretty good solutions much faster.

One of the most popular shortcuts is the Christofides algorithm. This algorithm can give you a route that is at most 1.5 times longer than the best possible route, but only if the distances between cities meet a specific condition (the triangle inequality, which means going from city A to city C is never shorter than going from A to B and then B to C).

So, while the exact solution to TSP might be tough to get, the Christofides algorithm helps you get a good-enough route in a reasonable amount of time.

The steps of the Christofides algorithm are as follows:

1. **Build a simple backbone (minimum spanning tree):** Start by creating a simple network (tree) that connects all cities with the shortest possible total distance without any loops.

2. **Find lonely connections (odd degree vertices):** In this tree, look for cities that have an odd number of connections.

3. **Pair up the odd ones (minimum weight perfect matching):** Match up these lonely cities in pairs, using the shortest possible paths.

4. **Combine paths (combine MST and matching):** Add these new shortest paths to your original tree. Now, you have a network where each city has an even number of connections.

5. **Create a loop (Eulerian circuit):** Use this network to create a path that visits each connection exactly once and returns to the starting city.

6. **Simplify the path (Hamiltonian circuit):** Convert this path into a final route by skipping any cities you have already visited, ensuring you visit each city exactly once.

Algorithm 12.6: Christofides algorithm

```
FUNCTION ChristofidesAlgorithm(graph):
    # Step 1: Find MST
    MST = findMST(graph)

    # Step 2: Find vertices with odd degree
    oddVertices = findOddDegreeVertices(MST)

    # Step 3: Find minimum weight perfect matching for odd degree vertices
    matching = findMinimumWeightPerfectMatching(graph, oddVertices)

    # Step 4: Combine MST and matching to form Eulerian multigraph
    multigraph = combineMSTAndMatching(MST, matching)

    # Step 5: Find Eulerian circuit in multigraph
    eulerianCircuit = findEulerianCircuit(multigraph)

    # Step 6: Convert Eulerian circuit to Hamiltonian circuit
    hamiltonianCircuit = convertToHamiltonianCircuit(eulerianCircuit)

    RETURN hamiltonianCircuit
```

The explanation is as follows:

- **findMST(graph):** This step uses a method like Prim's or Kruskal's algorithm to create a basic network (tree) that connects all the cities with the shortest total distance, without any loops.

- **findOddDegreeVertices(MST):** Here, we look at the tree and find the cities that have an odd number of connections. These cities need special attention because they do not fit perfectly into our current network.

- **findMinimumWeightPerfectMatching(graph, oddVertices):** Next, we find the shortest paths to pair up these odd cities. This way, we make sure that every city has an even number of connections.

- **combineMSTAndMatching(MST, matching):** We then merge the original tree with these new shortest paths. This creates a network where every city now has an even number of connections, which is what we need for the next step.

- **findEulerianCircuit(multigraph):** In this network, we create a route that visits each connection exactly once and returns to the starting city. This type of route is called an Eulerian circuit.

- **convertToHamiltonianCircuit(eulerianCircuit):** Finally, we take this route and adjust it so that we visit each city only once. We do this by skipping over any cities we have already visited in the route.

Program 12.6: Implementation in C

```c
#include <stdio.h>
#include <stdlib.h>
#include <limits.h>

// Define structure for a graph
struct Graph {
    int V;
    int** adjMatrix;
};

// Create a graph with V vertices
struct Graph* createGraph(int V) {
    struct Graph* graph = (struct Graph*) malloc(sizeof(struct Graph));
    graph->V = V;
    graph->adjMatrix = (int**) malloc(V * sizeof(int*));
    for (int i = 0; i < V; i++) {
        graph->adjMatrix[i] = (int*) malloc(V * sizeof(int));
    }
    return graph;
}

// Utility function to print the adjacency matrix of the graph
void printGraph(struct Graph* graph) {
    for (int i = 0; i < graph->V; i++) {
        for (int j = 0; j < graph->V; j++) {
            printf("%d ", graph->adjMatrix[i][j]);
        }
```

```
            printf("\n");
    }
}

// A utility function to find the vertex with minimum key value, from
// the set of vertices not yet included in MST
int minKey(int key[], int mstSet[], int V) {
    int min = INT_MAX, minIndex;

    for (int v = 0; v < V; v++)
        if (mstSet[v] == 0 && key[v] < min)
            min = key[v], minIndex = v;

    return minIndex;
}
// Function to construct and print MST for a graph represented using
adjacency matrix
void primMST(struct Graph* graph) {
    int V = graph->V;
    int parent[V];   // Array to store constructed MST
    int key[V];      // Key values used to pick minimum weight edge in cut
    int mstSet[V];   // To represent set of vertices included in MST

    // Initialize all keys as INFINITE
    for (int i = 0; i < V; i++)
        key[i] = INT_MAX, mstSet[i] = 0;

    // Always include first 1st vertex in MST.
    key[0] = 0;      // Make key 0 so that this vertex is picked as first
vertex
    parent[0] = -1; // First node is always root of MST

    // The MST will have V vertices
    for (int count = 0; count < V - 1; count++) {
        // Pick the minimum key vertex from the set of vertices not yet
included in MST
        int u = minKey(key, mstSet, V);

        // Add the picked vertex to the MST Set
        mstSet[u] = 1;

        // Update key value and parent index of the adjacent vertices of
the picked vertex.
        for (int v = 0; v < V; v++)
            if (graph->adjMatrix[u][v] && mstSet[v] == 0 && graph-
```

```
>adjMatrix[u][v] < key[v])
                parent[v] = u, key[v] = graph->adjMatrix[u][v];
    }

    // Print the constructed MST
    printf("Edge \tWeight\n");
    for (int i = 1; i < V; i++)
        printf("%d - %d \t%d \n", parent[i], i, graph->adjMatrix[i]
[parent[i]]);
}

int main() {
    int V = 5;
    struct Graph* graph = createGraph(V);
    graph->adjMatrix[0][1] = 2;
    graph->adjMatrix[0][2] = 3;
    graph->adjMatrix[0][3] = 1;
    graph->adjMatrix[0][4] = 4;
    graph->adjMatrix[1][2] = 1;
    graph->adjMatrix[1][3] = 5;
    graph->adjMatrix[1][4] = 3;
    graph->adjMatrix[2][3] = 2;
    graph->adjMatrix[2][4] = 1;
    graph->adjMatrix[3][4] = 6;

    // Since the graph is undirected, fill the other half of the matrix
    for (int i = 0; i < V; i++) {
        for (int j = i; j < V; j++) {
            graph->adjMatrix[j][i] = graph->adjMatrix[i][j];
        }
    }

    printf("Adjacency Matrix of the graph:\n");
    printGraph(graph);

    printf("Minimum Spanning Tree (MST) using Prim's Algorithm:\n");
    primMST(graph);

    return 0;
}
```

The explanation is as follows:

- **Graph structure:** Think of this as a way to represent a network of cities (or nodes) and the connections between them using a table (adjacency matrix).

- **createGraph:** This step sets up the network, creating space in memory to store information about the cities and their connections, and then fills in the initial details.

- **printGraph:** This function simply displays the table that shows how all the cities are connected to each other.

- **minKey:** This function finds the city with the smallest connection cost that has not been added to the network yet. It is like picking the cheapest city to add to your growing network.

- **primMST:** Here is where we use Prim's algorithm to build a minimum spanning tree, a way to connect all the cities with the shortest total connection cost. This function also shows the connections (edges) and their costs.

- **main:** This is the main setup where we create our network of cities, show the connection details, and then use Prim's algorithm to find and display the minimum spanning tree.

Complexity analysis

The complexity analysis is calculated as follows:

- **Time complexity:** $O(n^3)$

  This algorithm is much faster than the brute-force method. It gives you a solution that is close to the best possible route, within 1.5 times the optimal length. The reason it works relatively quickly is that it handles the problem in a few key steps, finding a minimum spanning tree, matching up some connections, and creating a path that covers all the cities. Each of these steps involves calculations that are manageable within $O(n3)$ time, meaning it is feasible for larger numbers of cities compared to the exhaustive approach.

- **Space complexity:** $O(n^2)$

  The amount of extra space the Christofides algorithm needs mainly comes from storing the graph's connections. Specifically, it uses an adjacency matrix, which is a big table showing how each city is connected to every other city. This table needs space proportional to $n2$, where n is the number of cities.

Euclid's algorithm for GCD

Euclid's algorithm is a clever way to find the **greatest common divisor (GCD)** of two numbers. The GCD is the largest number that can evenly divide both the original numbers without leaving any remainder.

For example, if you want to find the GCD of 12 and 15, Euclid's algorithm helps you figure out the biggest number that divides both 12 and 15 evenly, which in this case is 3. This method is efficient and quick, making it easy to handle even for larger numbers.

Euclid's algorithm is a simple and efficient way to find the GCD of two numbers. It works as follows:

1. **Start with two numbers:** Begin with two numbers, a and b, where a is the larger number or at least equal to b.

2. **Repeat the process:** Repeat the following steps:

    a. **Check if b is 0:** If b is 0, then the GCD is a because any number divided by 0 is itself.

    b. **Update the numbers:** If b is not 0, replace a with b, and replace b with the remainder when a is divided by b (this is written as a mod b).

    c. **Repeat:** Keep doing this until b becomes 0.

3. **Get the result:** When b is 0, the remaining value of a is the GCD of the original two numbers.

In simple terms, keep swapping and reducing the numbers until one of them becomes 0, and the non-zero number is the greatest number that can evenly divide both of the original numbers.

Algorithm 12.7: Euclid's algorithm

```
FUNCTION EuclidGCD(a, b):
    WHILE b != 0:
        temp = b
        b = a % b
        a = temp
    RETURN a
```

The explanation is as follows:

- **temp = b:** First, save the value of b in a temporary spot so you do not lose it.

- **b = a % b:** Next, update b to be the remainder when a is divided by b. This gives you the part of a that does not fit evenly into b.

- **a = temp:** Then, set a to be the old value of b (which you saved in step 1).

- **Repeat:** Keep doing these steps and updating a and b as described until b becomes 0.

- **Return:** When b is 0, the value of a is the GCD of the original numbers.

Program 12.7: Implementation in C

```c
#include <stdio.h>

// Function to calculate GCD using Euclid s algorithm
int euclidGCD(irt a, int b) {
    while (b != 0) {
        int temp = b;
        b = a % b;
        a = temp;
    }
    return a;
}

// Main function to test the GCD function
int main() {
    int a = 56;
    int b = 98;

    printf("The GCD of %d and %d is %d\n", a, b, euclidGCD(a, b));

    return 0;
}
```

The explanation is as follows:

- **euclidGCD:** This function uses Euclid's algorithm to find the GCD of two numbers, a and b. It works by repeatedly swapping a and b with b and the remainder of a divided by b, until b becomes 0. At that point, a holds the GCD.

- **main:** This part of the code tests the euclidGCD function with some example numbers and prints out the result, showing you the GCD of those numbers.

Complexity analysis

The following is the time and space complexity of Euclid's algorithm:

- **Time complexity:** The time complexity is $O(logmin(a,b))$. It is very efficient due to the rapid reduction in problem size.

- **Space complexity:** There is a space complexity of $O(1)$. Only a modest and consistent amount of additional space is required for it.

Modulo arithmetic

Modulo arithmetic is like working with a clock where you only care about the time on the face, not the actual number of hours that have passed. For example, on a standard clock, if you add three hours to 10 o'clock, you end up at 1 o'clock, not 13 o'clock.

In the same way, modulo arithmetic takes large numbers and wraps them around a fixed value, called the modulus. So, if you are working with modulo 12, adding 7 to 8 would bring you back to 3 (because 15 hours is the same as three hours on a 12-hour clock).

This kind of math is useful for simplifying problems in computer science, cryptography, and other fields, where dealing with huge numbers or repeating patterns is common.

Basic concepts

Imagine you are dividing a number by another number and only caring about the remainder. For example, if you divide 17 by 5, you get a remainder of 2 (because $17=3\times5+2$). In modular arithmetic, we say that 17 is congruent to 2 modulo 5, which we write as follows:

$$17 \equiv 2 \ (mod \ 5)$$

This means both 17 and 2 leave the same remainder when divided by 5.

Properties

The following list of operations is used with modulo operations:

- **Addition:** Adding numbers and then taking the remainder is the same as taking the remainder of each number first, then adding them, and taking the remainder again. For example, $(17+7)\%5=24\%5=4$, which is the same as $[(17\%5)+(7\%5)]\%5=(2+2)\%5=4$.

- **Subtraction:** Subtracting numbers and then taking the remainder works similarly. For instance, $(17-7)\%5=10\%5=0$, and $[(17\%5)-(7\%5)]\%5=(2-2)\%5=0$.

- **Multiplication:** Multiplying numbers and then taking the remainder is the same as taking the remainders first, multiplying them, and then taking the remainder. For example, $(17\times7)\%5=119\%5=4$, which is the same as $[(17\%5)\times(7\%5)]\%5=(2\times2)\%5=4$.

- **Division:** This is a more difficult one. The process of dividing in modular arithmetic frequently includes locating a unique integer, which is referred to as the modular inverse, that enables the division to be performed.

Applications

Modulo arithmetic has applications in the following fields:

- **Cryptography:** In secure communication, like encrypting messages, modular arithmetic helps keep data safe. It is used in algorithms like **Rivest–Shamir–Adleman (RSA)** to ensure that only the right people can read the message.

- **Computer science**: It helps in various tasks like creating unique identifiers (hashes), generating random numbers, and more.

- **Mathematics:** It is useful for solving certain types of mathematical problems and understanding number properties.

Program 12.8: Implementation in C

```c
#include <stdio.h>

// Function to perform addition modulo
int modAdd(int a, int b, int m) {
    return (a % m + b % m) % m;
}

// Function to perform subtraction modulo
int modSub(int a, int b, int m) {
    return (a % m - b % m + m) % m; // Add m to ensure non-negative result
}

// Function to perform multiplication modulo
int modMul(int a, int b, int m) {
    return (a % m * b % m) % m;
}

// Function to perform division modulo using modular inverse (only valid
for prime m)
int modDiv(int a, int b, int m) {
    // Compute modular inverse of b modulo m using Fermat's Little Theorem
    int inverse = 1;
    int exponent = m - 2; // For prime m, a^(m-1) ≡ 1 (mod m) => a^(m-2) ≡
a^(-1) (mod m)
    int base = b % m;

    while (exponent > 0) {
        if (exponent % 2 == 1) {
            inverse = (inverse * base) % m;
        }
        base = (base * base) % m;
        exponent /= 2;
    }
    return (a % m * inverse) % m;
}

int main() {
    int a = 17, b = 5, m = 7;
```

```
    printf("Addition: (%d + %d) %% %d = %d\n", a, b, m, modAdd(a, b, m));
    printf("Subtraction: (%d - %d) %% %d = %d\n", a, b, m, modSub(a, b, m));
    printf("Multiplication: (%d * %d) %% %d = %d\n", a, b, m, modMul(a, b, m));
    printf("Division: (%d / %d) %% %d = %d\n", a, b, m, modDiv(a, b, m));

    return 0;
}
```

The explanation is as follows:

- **modAdd:** This is like adding two numbers as usual, but then taking the result and seeing what is left if you only care about a fixed range. For example, if you add 8 and 9 in a system that wraps around after 10, you get 17. Since we are only interested in numbers from 0 to 9, you would end up with 7 (because 17 minus 10 leaves a remainder of 7).

- **modSub:** This works similarly to addition, but for subtraction. If you subtract one number from another and get a negative result, this function adjusts it so you still end up with a positive number within the desired range. For instance, subtracting 5 from 3 in a system where you wrap around after 10 would give you -2, but adjusting it to be within 0 to 9 would give you 8 (because -2 plus 10 equals 8).

- **modMul:** This involves multiplying two numbers and then finding out what is left if you divide by the modulus. For example, multiplying 4 by 6 and then taking the result modulo 7 gives you 24. Since 24 divided by 7 leaves a remainder of 3, you get 3.

- **modDiv:** Dividing in modular arithmetic is a bit trickier. It involves finding a special number (called the modular inverse) that helps you perform the division. This method usually works only when the modulus is a prime number. Essentially, it is like finding a number that, when multiplied by your original number, gives you the result you are looking for under the modulus.

Complexity analysis

The complexity analysis is as follows:

- **Addition, subtraction, multiplication modulo:** The complexity is $O(1)$ as these operations are direct and efficient.

- **Division modulo:** The complexity is $O(\log m)$ as computing modular inverses introduces logarithmic complexity due to the algorithms involved.

- **Exponentiation modulo:** Due to the fact that efficient methods for exponentiation ensure that this operation is still manageable even with large exponents, it is calculated as $O(\log e)$.

Chinese remainder theorem

The **chinese remainder theorem** (**CRT**) is a mathematical tool that helps solve problems where you have several equations with remainders. If you have different clocks (or moduli) that do not share common factors (they are pairwise coprime), CRT lets you figure out a single number that fits all these clocks simultaneously. For example, imagine you have two clocks: one that ticks every three hours and another that ticks every five hours. If you know a number has specific remainders when divided by 3 and 5, CRT can help you find cut exactly what that number is.

This theorem is handy in various fields, such as the following:

- **Cryptography:** It helps in making encryption and decryption faster.
- **Computer science:** It is used in algorithms and computations involving large numbers.
- **Algebra:** It aids in solving equations and understanding number patterns.

In short, CRT simplifies complex problems involving multiple modular conditions, making it easier to work with in different applications.

Example 12.1: You have a set of equations like this:

$$\{x \equiv a_1 \ (mod \ m_1) \ x \equiv a_2 \ (mod \ m_2) \ \overline{\ \vdots \ } \ x \equiv a_n \ (mod \ m_n)$$

Where each m_i is a different modulus, and they are all pairwise coprime (meaning no two of them share any common factors except 1).

Solution: The steps to find the solution are as follows:

1. **Calculate the product of moduli:** Multiply all the moduli together to get MMM. For example, if your moduli are 3, 4, and 5, then $M=3\times4\times5=60$.

2. **Compute partial products:** For each modulus m_i, calculate M_i by dividing M by m_i. So, for $m_1=3$, $M_1=60/3=20$; for $m_2=4$, $M_2=60/4=15$; for $m_3=5$, $m_3=60/5=12$.

3. **Find modular inverses:** For each M_i, find a number N_i such that when M_i is multiplied by N_i, the result is 1 modulo m_i. This number N_i is the modular inverse. For and $M_1=20$ and $m_1=3$, you find N_1 such that $20\times N_1\equiv1$ *(mod 3)*. The inverse N_1 is 2 because $20\times2\equiv1$ *(mod 3)* or 20×2 *(mod 3) = 1*.

4. **Calculate the solution:** Combine everything using the following formula:

$$x = \sum_{i=1}^{n} \square \, a_i * M_i * N_i (mod \ M)$$

For each congruence, multiply the remainder a_i by its partial product M_i and its modular inverse N_i, then sum these values and take the result modulo M.

For our example, the calculation would be as follows:

$$x=(2\times20\times2)+(3\times15\times3)+(2\times12\times3) \ (mod \ 60)$$

$$x=(80)+(135)+(72) \ (mod \ 60)$$

$$x=287 \ (mod \ 60)=47$$

So, the unique solution that fits all the given congruences is as follows:

$$x=47 \ modulo \ 60$$

Program 12.9: Implementation in C

```c
#include <stdio.h>
// Function to compute the modular inverse of a modulo m
int modInverse(int a, int m) {
    int m0 = m, t, q;
    int x0 = 0, x1 = 1;
    if (m == 1) return 0;
    while (a > 1) {
        q = a / m;
        t = m;
        // m is remainder now, process same as Euclid's algo
        m = a % m, a = t;
        t = x0;
        // Update x0 and x1
        x0 = x1 - q * x0;
        x1 = t;
    }

    // Make x1 positive
    if (x1 < 0) x1 += m0;
    return x1;
}
// Function to solve the system of congruences using CRT
int chineseRemainderTheorem(int num[], int rem[], int k) {
    int prod = 1;
    for (int i = 0; i < k; i++)
        prod *= num[i];
    int result = 0;
    for (int i = 0; i < k; i++) {
        int pp = prod / num[i];
```

```
        result += rem[i] * modInverse(pp, num[i]) * pp;
    }
    return result % prod;
}
// Main function to test the CRT function
int main() {
    int num[] = {3, 4, 5}; // Moduli
    int rem[] = {2, 3, 2}; // Remainders
    int k = sizeof(num) / sizeof(num[0]);
    int result = chineseRemainderTheorem(num, rem, k);
    printf("x = %d\n", result);
    return 0;
}
```

The explanation is as follows:

- **modInverse:** This function finds a special number called the modular inverse. Imagine you need to find a number that, when multiplied by another specific number, gives you a remainder of 1 when divided by a given modulus. The extended Euclidean algorithm is a method used to find this modular inverse efficiently.

- **chineseRemainderTheorem:** This function is where the magic happens. It takes a set of equations with remainders and moduli and finds a single number that satisfies all those equations at once. It uses the CRT algorithm, which combines the remainders and moduli in a clever way to find the unique solution.

- **main:** This part of the code is like a test run. It uses the CRT function with a specific set of moduli and remainders to demonstrate how the algorithm works. It is like checking if everything is functioning correctly by giving it some example problems to solve.

RSA public-key cryptosystem

RSA is a method of encrypting and decrypting messages so that only the intended recipient can read them. It was invented by three mathematicians, *Ron Rivest, Adi Shamir,* and *Leonard Adleman,* in 1977. RSA relies on the mathematical properties of large prime numbers to create secure keys.

The working of RSA involves the following steps:

1. **Key generation:** For a key to be generated, the following steps must be completed:

   a. **Choose two large prime numbers:** The security of RSA comes from the difficulty of factoring large numbers, so two large prime numbers (let us call them p and q) are chosen

b. **Calculate their product:** Multiply these primes to get $n=p \times q$. This number n is part of both the public and private keys.

c. **Compute Euler's Totient function:** Calculate $\varphi(n)=(p-1) \times (q-1)$. This value is used to create the keys.

d. **Generate public key:** Choose a number e (the public exponent) that is coprime with $\varphi(n)$ (typically, e=65537 is used).

e. **Generate private key:** Calculate d (the private exponent) such that $e \times d \equiv 1$ *(mod $\varphi(n)$)*. The number d is kept secret.

2. **Encryption:** The sender uses the recipient's public key (n and e) to encrypt the message. If m is the message, the encrypted message c is calculated as $c=m^e$ *(mod n)*.

3. **Decryption:** The recipient uses their private key (n and d) to decrypt the message. The original message m is recovered by calculating $m=c^d$ *(mod n)*.

The applications of RSA are as follows:

- **Secure data transmission:** Ensures that only the intended recipient can read the message.

- **Digital signatures:** Verifies the authenticity and integrity of a message or document.

The security of RSA is based on the fact that while it is easy to multiply two large primes, it is extremely difficult to reverse the process (i.e., factor the product back into the original primes). This difficulty ensures that even if someone has the public key, they cannot easily determine the private key. Thus, RSA is a cornerstone of modern encryption, allowing secure data exchange and authentication across the internet.

Consider the following example:

- Choose $p = 3$ and $q = 11$

- Compute $n = p * q = 3 * 11 = 33$

- Compute $\phi(n) = (p - 1) * (q - 1) = 2 * 10 = 20$

- Choose e such that $1 < e < \phi(n)$ and e and $\phi(n)$ are coprime. Let $e = 7$

- Compute a value for d such that $(d * e) \% \phi(n) = 1$. One solution is $d = 3$ [(3 * 7) % 20 = 1]

- Public key is $(e, n) => (7, 33)$

- Private key is $(d, n) => (3, 33)$

- The encryption of $m = 2$ is $c = 2^7 \% 33 = 29$

- The decryption of $c = 29$ is $m = 29^3 \% 33 = 2$

Program 12.10: Implementation in C

```c
#include <stdio.h>
#include <math.h>

// Function to compute (base^exp) % mod using modular exponentiation
long long modExp(long long base, long long exp, long long mod) {
    long long result = 1;
    base = base % mod;
    while (exp > 0) {
        if (exp % 2 == 1) // If exp is odd
            result = (result * base) % mod;
        exp = exp >> 1; // Divide exp by 2
        base = (base * base) % mod;
    }
    return result;
}

// Function to compute gcd of a and b
long long gcd(long long a, long long b) {
    if (b == 0)
        return a;
    return gcd(b, a % b);
}

// Function to find modular inverse of a with respect to mod
long long modInverse(long long a, long long mod) {
    long long m0 = mod, t, q;
    long long x0 = 0, x1 = 1;

    if (mod == 1)
        return 0;

    while (a > 1) {
        q = a / mod;
        t = mod;

        mod = a % mod;
        a = t;
        t = x0;

        x0 = x1 - q * x0;
        x1 = t;
    }
```

```
    if (x1 < 0)
        x1 += m0;

    return x1;
}

int main() {
    long long p = 61, q = 53;
    long long n = p * q;
    long long phi = (p - 1) * (q - 1);
    long long e = 17;
    long long d = modInverse(e, phi);

    printf("Public Key: (%lld, %lld)\n", e, n);
    printf("Private Key: (%lld, %lld)\n", d, n);

    long long message = 65;
    long long encrypted = modExp(message, e, n);
    long long decrypted = modExp(encrypted, d, n);

    printf("Original Message: %lld\n", message);
    printf("Encrypted Message: %lld\n", encrypted);
    printf("Decrypted Message: %lld\n", decrypted);

    return 0;
}
```

Complexity analysis

The complexity analysis is as follows:

- **Key generation:** $O(k^4)$ for finding primes and $O(k^3)$ for computing d.
- **Encryption:** $O(k^3)$
- **Decryption:** $O(k^3)$

3-CNF satisfiability

Imagine you have a bunch of statements, and you want to figure out if there is a way to make all of them true at the same time by deciding whether certain things are true or false. In this specific problem, each statement is a combination of three smaller parts. These smaller parts are either a variable (which can be true or false) or the opposite of a variable (if the variable is true, this part is false, and vice versa).

Structure of 3-CNF

The statements are connected in a way that is called **3-Conjunctive Normal Form (3-CNF)**. We can define the statement in two different forms, which are as follows:

- **Conjunctive:** All the statements are combined using **AND**, meaning they all need to be true for the whole thing to be true.

- **Normal form:** Each statement is a combination of three parts using **OR**, meaning if at least one part of a statement is true, the whole statement is true.

Let us look at an example formula, shown as follows:

$$(x_1 \vee \neg x_2 \vee x_3) \wedge (\neg x_1 \vee x_2 \vee x_4) \wedge (x_2 \vee \neg x_3 \vee \neg x_4)$$

This means the following:

- Either x_1 is true, or x_2 is false, or x_3 is true (or any combination of these).
- Either x_1 is false, or x_2 is true, or x_4 is true.
- Either x_2 is true, or x_3 is false, or x_4 is false.

Your goal is to find a way to assign true or false values to x_1, x_2, x_3, x_4, so that all these statements are true simultaneously.

The challenge is to see if there is any way to make all the statements true by carefully picking true or false for each variable. If you can do that, the formula is *satisfiable*. If not, it is not satisfiable.

Algorithm 12.8: 3-CNF Satisfiability

The 3-CNF Satisfiability problem is what is known as NP-complete. This term means that we do not have a quick and easy way to solve every possible version of this problem. There is no known method that works efficiently for all cases. However, there are several ways we can try to tackle it as follows:

- **Brute force:** This method involves trying every possible way to assign true or false to the variables and seeing if the formula ends up being true. It is like checking every possible combination until you find one that works. But it takes a lot of time because the number of combinations grows very fast as the number of variables increases.

- **Backtracking:** This is a smarter version of brute force. You start assigning truth values, and if you hit a dead end where the formula cannot be true, you go back and try a different path. It is more efficient than pure brute force because it avoids many unnecessary checks.

- **Heuristic methods:** These are clever shortcuts. Instead of trying all combinations, these methods make educated guesses to find a solution. Techniques like local search, simulated annealing, or genetic algorithms help in finding a satisfying assignment more quickly, although they might not always find the best solution.

- **Satisfiability (SAT) solvers:** These are advanced tools specifically designed to solve SAT problems like 3-CNF. They use complex methods like the **Davis–Putnam–Logemann–Loveland (DPLL)** algorithm (which systematically tries and backtracks on assignments) and **Conflict-Driven Clause Learning (CDCL)**, which learns from conflicts to avoid similar mistakes. These solvers are highly optimized and can handle large and complex problems efficiently.

Complexity analysis

The complexity analysis is calculated based on the approaches, shown as follows:

- **Brute force approach:** The most straightforward way to solve the 3-SAT problem is by trying every possible combination of true or false assignments for the variables as follows:

  - **Number of combinations:** If you have n variables, there are 2^n possible ways to assign true or false values to these variables.

  - **Checking each combination:** For each combination, you need to check if the whole formula becomes true, which can be done relatively quickly (in polynomial time) for each combination.

  - **Time complexity:** Since you have to check 2^n combinations, this method has exponential time complexity, $O(2^n)$. This means the time it takes to solve the problem grows very quickly as the number of variables increases.

- **Backtracking:** Backtracking is a smarter version of brute force. Instead of trying all combinations blindly, you start assigning values and backtrack (go back and try different values) when you find a conflict. The time complexity is as follows:

  - **Efficiency:** While backtracking can still take an exponential amount of time in the worst case, it often works much faster in practice because it avoids many unnecessary checks.

- **Heuristic methods and SAT solvers:** These are advanced techniques designed to solve specific instances more efficiently, and work as follows:

  - **Heuristic methods:** These methods make educated guesses to find a solution faster. They do not guarantee a quick solution for every problem, but often work well in practice.

  - **SAT solvers:** These tools use sophisticated techniques like the DPLL algorithm and CDCL to solve SAT problems much faster than brute force in many cases. However, they can still take exponential time in the worst case.

The clique problem

A clique is a group of people (vertices) where every pair of people is friends (there is an edge between every pair). Imagine you have a network of friends (an undirected graph G) and you want to find out if there is a group of k friends (a clique) where everyone in the group knows each other.

The working of the clique problem is as follows:

1. **Input:** The input consists of the following values:

    • An undirected graph $G = (V, E)$, where V represents the people and E represents the friendships.

    • An integer k, the size of the group you are looking for.

2. **Output:** You need to determine if there is a group of k friends (a clique) in the graph.

For example, consider a network with five people and the following friendships:

$$\{(1,2),(1,3),(1,4),(1,5),(2,3),(2,4),(3,4),(3,5),(4,5)\}$$

This network forms a complete subgraph with all five people, which means there is a clique of size 5. If you want to find a group of four friends, there are several options, such as the group consisting of people {1, 2, 3, 4}.

The clique problem is NP-complete, meaning we do not have a quick method to solve every instance of this problem efficiently. It gets harder to solve as the network grows and as the value of k increases.

Exact algorithms

The following algorithms can be used to solve the clique problem:

• **Brute force approach:** Check all possible groups of k people to see if they form a clique. This method takes a lot of time and is not practical for large networks.

• **Backtracking:** This is a smarter brute-force approach that avoids unnecessary checks by pruning the search space based on certain criteria.

• **Exact algorithms:** Algorithms like Bron–Kerbosch can find cliques more efficiently than brute force.

Approximation algorithms

For large networks, finding an exact solution might be too time-consuming, so we use approximation methods, such as the following:

- **Greedy algorithms:** Build a clique by adding one person at a time based on some criteria.

- **Local search:** Use techniques like simulated annealing to find large cliques in practice, even if they might not be the largest possible.

Complexity analysis

The complexity analysis is as follows:

- **Brute force approach:** The efficiency of the brute force approach is as follows:

  - **Time complexity:** The brute force method involves checking every possible group of k vertices to see if they form a clique. The number of possible groups (combinations) is given by $\binom{n}{k}$, and for each group, we need to check if every pair of vertices is connected, which takes k2 time.

  - **Exponential growth:** This means the total time complexity is $O(\binom{n}{k}, k2)$. Since $\binom{n}{k}$, grows exponentially with n (the number of vertices), this approach becomes impractical for large graphs.

- **Backtracking and exact algorithms:** The complexity analysis of backtracking and exact algorithms reveals the following:

  - **Efficiency in practice:** These methods are designed to be more efficient than brute force by reducing the number of checks needed. They do this by pruning the search space, meaning they skip over parts of the graph that cannot possibly contain a clique of the desired size.

  - **Still exponential:** Despite these improvements, backtracking and exact algorithms still face exponential growth in the worst case as the size of the graph and the desired clique size k increase.

The vertex problem

These problems focus on the vertices (nodes) of a graph and can vary widely.

Vertex cover problem

Imagine you have a network (graph) of cities (vertices) connected by roads (edges). You want to place police stations in a few cities so that every road has at least one police station at either end. The following is a brief explanation of the vertex cover problem:

- **Goal:** Find the smallest number of cities (vertices) where placing police stations ensures all roads are covered.

- **Example:** For a network with cities {1, 2, 3, 4} and roads {(1, 2), (1, 3), (2. 4), (3, 4)}, placing police stations in cities {1, 4} would cover all roads.

- **Complexity:** It is a tough problem (NP-complete), but there are ways to find good enough solutions quickly, like the 2-approximation algorithm, which determines a cover that is at most twice the size of the smallest possible.

Vertex coloring problem

Think of a network where each city needs a unique color, but neighboring cities (connected by a road) cannot share the same color. Refer to the following list for a brief overview of the vertex coloring problem:

- **Goal:** Use the fewest number of colors to color the cities.

- **Example:** For a triangle (three cities each connected to the other twc), you will need three different colors.

- **Complexity:** This problem is generally hard (NP-hard), but for certain networks like bipartite graphs, it is easier and can be done with just two colors.

Dominating set problem

Picture a network where you want to place a few central hubs (vertices), such that every city either has a hub or is directly connected to a city with a hub. A summarized overview of the Dominating Set problem is given as follows:

- **Goal:** Find the smallest number of hubs needed.

- **Example:** In a network where each city is connected to its neighbors, placing a hub in a central city that connects to all others might work.

- **Complexity:** This problem is also very challenging (NP-complete), but there are practical methods to find good solutions.

Maximum independent set problem

Imagine you want to form the largest group of cities (vertices) where no two cities in the group are directly connected by a road. A brief description of the maximum independent set problem is as follows:

- **Goal**: Find the largest such group.

- **Example**: In a network where a group of cities all connect to each other (a clique), the largest group where no two cities are connected is just one city.

- **Complexity**: This is another hard problem (NP-complete). There are strategies for finding approximate solutions or solving specific types of networks efficiently.

Vertex connectivity problem

This problem looks at how connected a network is. Specifically, it asks how many cities (vertices) need to be removed to make the network fall apart (disconnect). A brief overview of the vertex connectivity problem is as follows:

- **Goal:** Determine the minimum number of cities that, when removed, break the network into separate parts.

- **Example:** In a fully connected network (complete graph), you would have to remove almost all cities to disconnect it.

- **Complexity:** Unlike the others, this problem can be solved more easily (in polynomial time) with algorithms like the max-flow min-cut theorem.

Conclusion

This chapter examined fundamental algorithms in sorting, computational geometry, graph theory, number theory, cryptography, and complexity theory. Randomized quicksort demonstrated efficient sorting, while Graham's scan and Jarvis's March tackled convex hull issues. The Fisher-Yates algorithm ensured unbiased permutations, whereas Karger's minimum cut technique elucidated graph partitioning. Euclid's algorithm and the Chinese remainder theorem were essential in number theory, while the traveling salesman approximation method addressed NP-hard optimization challenges. The RSA cryptosystem emphasized computational complexity, 3-CNF satisfiability, the clique problem, and secure encryption; RSA also highlighted security. Collectively, RSA, 3-CNF, and the clique problem provide a robust foundation for understanding algorithmic problem-solving across several domains.

Numerical questions

Let us look at some numerical questions based upon the concepts discussed in this chapter.

Key generation

1. **Given two prime numbers p=61 and q=53, generate the RSA modulus n and the Euler's totient function $\varphi(n)$.**

    Answer:

    - $n = p \times q$
    - $\varphi(n) = (p-1) \times (q-1)$

So,

- n=61×53=3233

- φ(n)=(61−1)×(53−1)=60×52=3120

Public and private keys

2. **For the given n=3233 and φ(n)=3120, choose a public key e such that 1<e<φ(n) and e is coprime with φ(n). Then, find the corresponding private key d such that d×e≡1 (mod φ(n)).**

Answer:

- Let us choose e=17 (a common choice for simplicity).

- To find d, we need to solve 17d≡1 (mod 3120).

Using the extended Euclidean algorithm:

d=2753

Encryption

3. **Given the public key (e, n) = (17, 3233), encrypt the plaintext message m=65.**

Answer:

- Ciphertext c is calculated as c≡ me (mod n).

- So, c≡6517 (mod 3233).

Using modular exponentiation:

- c=2790

Decryption

4. **Using the private key d=2753 and modulus n=3233, decrypt the ciphertext c=2790.**

Answer:

- Plaintext mmm is calculated as m ≡ cd (mod n) m.

- So, m≡27902753 (mod 3233).

Using modular exponentiation:

- m=65

Verification

5. **Verify that the decryption process works correctly by checking that the original plaintext m is recovered.**

   Answer:

   - We previously encrypted m=65 to get c=2790.
   - Then we decrypted c=2790 to get m=65.
   - Since the original plaintext m=65 matches the decrypted plaintext, the encryption and decryption processes are verified to work correctly.

Finding e

6. **For a given φ(n)=3120, find a suitable value for e.**

   Answer:

   - e must be coprime with φ(n) and 1<e<φ(n).
   - Common choices are small prime numbers like 3, 5, 17, or 65537.
   - Let us verify e=65537.

   Using the Euclidean algorithm to check gcd:

   - gcd (65537,3120)=1, so e=65537 is suitable.

Exercise

1. Can randomized quick sort be implemented in a way that it is always in-place?
2. How does Graham's scan algorithm find the convex hull of a set of points?
3. How can the probability of success in Karger's algorithm be increased?
4. Can Euclid's algorithm be extended to find GCD of more than two numbers?
5. Explain the process of reconstructing a number using Chinese Remainder Theorem given its remainders.
6. Why is the clique problem significant in graph theory?

APPENDIX
Most Frequently Asked Questions

Introduction

Understanding the analysis of algorithms is fundamental to computer science and critical for developing efficient, high-performing software. As you delve into this intricate field, you will likely encounter numerous questions that may seem daunting. This chapter aims to address some of the most frequently asked questions to help clarify and reinforce key concepts. Whether you are a student beginning your journey in algorithms, a professional seeking to refresh your knowledge, or someone with a keen interest in computational theory, this chapter provides concise, clear answers to common queries. We will explore topics such as time complexity, space complexity, big O notation, algorithm optimization, and more. By the end of this chapter, you should have a better understanding of the principles that underpin algorithm analysis, enabling you to apply this knowledge to your coding practices and problem-solving techniques. This chapter provides a compilation of the most frequently asked questions related to various algorithms. It aims to reinforce key concepts, clarify doubts, and enhance understanding of algorithms in solving optimization problems. The questions cover fundamental principles, problem-solving approaches, and real-world use cases to help readers grasp the practical significance of branch and bound techniques.

Questions

Question 1: Let $T(n)$ be the recurrence relation defined as follows:

$T(0)=1$,

$T(1)=2$, and

$T(n)=5T(n-1)-6T(n-2)$ for $n \geq 2$

Which one of the following statements is TRUE?

    a. $T(n)=\Theta\,(2^n)$

    b. $T(n)=\Theta\,(n2^n)$

    c. $T(n)=\Theta\,(3^n)$

    d. $T(n)=\Theta\,(n3^n)$ [Gate 2024]

Question 2: Let f and g be functions of natural numbers given by $f(n) = n$ and $g(n) = n^2$. Which of the following statements is or are TRUE?

    a. $f \in O(g)$

    b. $f \in \Omega(g)$

    c. $f \in o(g)$

    d. $f \in \Theta(g)$ [Gate 2023]

Question 3: Let G be a simple, finite, undirected graph with vertex set $\{v_1, \ldots, v_n\}$. Let $\Delta(G)$ denote the maximum degree of G and let $N = \{1, 2, \ldots\}$ denote the set of all possible colors. Color the vertices of G using the following greedy strategy:

for $i = 1, \ldots, n$

$\text{color}(v_i) \leftarrow \min\{j \in N : \text{no neighbor of } v_i \text{ is colored } j\}$

Which of the following statements is or are TRUE?

    a. This procedure results in a proper vertex coloring of G.

    b. The number of colors used is at most $\Delta(G) + 1$.

    c. The number of colors used is at most $\Delta(G)$.

    d. The number of colors used is equal to the chromatic number of G. [Gate 2023]

Question 4: Which statement is not false about comparison-based sorting algorithms?

    a. Comparison-based sorting algorithms take $O(n(\log(n)))$ time for random input arrays.

    b. A comparison-based sorting algorithm can be stable by comparing two elements by location.

c. The counting sort method does not belong to comparison-based sorting.

d. The heap sort method does not belong to comparison-based sorting.

Question 5: What will be the recurrence relation of the code of recursive selection sort?

a. $t(n) = 2t(n/2) + n$

b. $t(n) = 2t(n/2) + c$

c. $t(n) = t(n-1) + n$

d. $t(n) = t(n-1) + c$

Question 6: The recursive program to raise an integer x to the power y uses which of the following algorithms?

a. Dynamic programming

b. Backtracking

c. Divide and conquer

d. Greedy algorithm

Question 7: Which of the following problems should be solved using dynamic programming?

a. Merge sort

b. Binary search

c. Longest common subsequence

d. Quick sort

Question 8: Suppose you have coins of denominations 1, 3, and 4. You use a greedy algorithm, in which you choose the largest denomination coin that is not greater than the remaining sum. For which of the following sums will the algorithm produce an optimal answer?

a. 10

b. 14

c. 100

d. 6

Question 9: Which of the following problems is equivalent to the 0/1 knapsack problem?

a. You are given a bag that can carry a maximum weight of w. You are given n items which have a weight of {w1, w2, w3,...., wn} and a value of {v1, v2, v3,...., vn}. You can break the items into smaller pieces. Choose the items in such a way that you get the maximum value.

b. You are studying for an exam and you have to study n questions. The questions take {t1, t2, t3,...., tn} time (in hours) and carry {m1, m2, m3,...., mn} marks. You can study for a maximum of t hours. You can either study a question or leave it. Choose the questions in such a way that your score is maximized.

c. You are given infinite coins of denominations {v1, v2, v3,....., vn} and a sum s. You have to find the minimum number of coins required to get the sum s.

d. You are given a suitcase that can carry a maximum weight of 15 kg. You are given four items which have a weight of {10, 20, 15,40} and a value of {1, 2, 3,4}. You can break the items into smaller pieces. Choose the items in such a way that you get the maximum value.

Question 10: What is the objective of the knapsack problem?

a. To get the maximum total value in the knapsack.

b. To get the minimum total value in the knapsack.

c. To get the maximum weight in the knapsack.

d. To get the minimum weight in the knapsack.

Question 11: Which of the following statements about 0/1 knapsack and fractional knapsack problem is correct?

a. In the 0/1 knapsack problem, items are divisible, and in the fractional knapsack, items are indivisible.

b. Both are the same.

c. 0/1 knapsack is solved using a greedy algorithm, and fractional knapsack is solved using dynamic programming.

d. In the 0/1 knapsack problem, items are indivisible, and in the fractional knapsack, items are divisible.

Question 12: Given G is a bipartite graph, and the bipartitions of this graph are U and V, respectively. What is the relation between them?

a. Number of vertices in u = number of vertices in v

b. Sum of degrees of vertices in u = sum of degrees of vertices in v

c. Number of vertices in u > number of vertices in v

d. Nothing can be said.

Question 13: Which algorithm is used to solve a maximum flow problem?

a. Prim's algorithm

b. Kruskal's algorithm

c. Dijkstra's algorithm

d. Ford-Fulkerson algorithm

Question 14: Which of the following problems is not NP-complete?

a. Hamiltonian circuit

b. Bin packing

c. Partition problem

d. Halting problem

Question 15: Which of the following problems is similar to that of a Hamiltonian path problem?

a. Knapsack problem

b. Closest pair problem

c. Traveling salesman problem

d. Assignment problem

Question 16: What is the worst-case time complexity of the dynamic programming solution of the set partition problem (sum=sum of set elements)?

a. o(n)

b. o(sum)

c. o(n2)

d. o(sum*n)

Question 17: A networking company uses a compression technique to encode the message before transmitting it over the network. Suppose the message contains the following characters with their frequency:

Characters	Frequency
A	5
B	9
C	12
D	13
E	16
F	45

Each character in the input message takes 1 byte. If the compression technique used is Huffman coding, how many bits will be saved in the message?

a. 224

b. 576

c. 324

d. 328

Question 18: Which of the following is true about Huffman coding?

a. Huffman coding may become lossy in some cases.

b. Huffman codes may not be optimal lossless codes in some cases.

c. In Huffman coding, no code is a prefix of any other code.

d. All of the above

Question 19: A text is made up of the characters a, b, c, d, and e, each occurring with the probability 0.11, 0.40, 0.16, 0.09, and 0.24, respectively. The optimal Huffman coding technique will have an average length of:

a. 2.24

b. 2.16

c. 2.26

d. 2.15

Question 20: F1, F2, F3, F4, F5, and F6 are six files. They have 100, 200, 50, 80, 120, and 150 items, respectively. How should they be stored so that the act works best? Let us say that each file is read the same number of times.

a. F3, F4, F1, F5, F6, F2

b. F3, F4, F1, F5, F6, F2

c. F3, F4, F1, F5, F6, F2

d. All files can be accessed with the same frequencies.

Question 21: Which of the following is true about Kruskal and Prim **minimum spanning tree (MST)** algorithms?

Assume that Prim is implemented for adjacency list representation using binary heap and Kruskal is implemented using union by rank.

a. Worst-case time complexity of both algorithms is the same.

b. Worst-case time complexity of Kruskal is better than Prim.

c. Worst-case time complexity of Prim is better than Kruskal.

d. None of these

Question 22: Consider the string abbccddeee. Each letter in the string must be assigned a binary code satisfying the following properties:

- For any two letters, the code assigned to one letter must not be a prefix of the code assigned to the other letter.

- For any two letters of the same frequency, the letter that occurs earlier in the dictionary order is assigned a code whose length is at most the length of the code assigned to the other letter.

Among the set of all binary code assignments that satisfy the preceding two properties, what is the minimum length of the encoded string (refer to the following figure for the Huffman tree structure)?

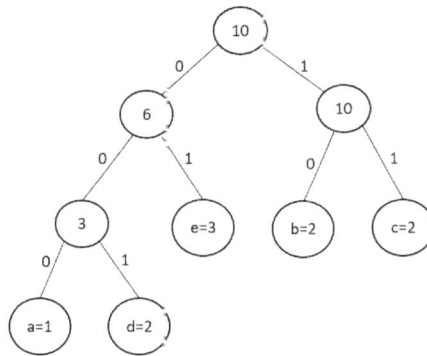

Figure 13.1: Huffman tree structure

a. 29

b. 25

c. 23

d. 21

Question 23: Consider a job scheduling problem with four jobs, J1, J2, J3, and J4, and with corresponding deadlines, (d1, d2, d3, d4) = (4, 2, 4, 2). Which of the following is not a feasible schedule without violating any job schedule?

a. J2, J4, J1, J3

b. J4, J1, J2, J3

c. J4, J2, J1, J3

d. J24 J2, J3, J1

Question 24: Suppose the letters a, b, c, d, e, and f have probabilities 1/2, 1/4, 1/8, 1/16, 1/32, and 1/32, respectively. Which of the following is the Huffman code for the letter a, b, c, d, e, and f?

a. 0, 10, 110, 1110, 11110, 11111

b. 11, 10, 011, 010, 001, 000

    c.   11, 10, 01, 001, 0001, 0000

    d.   110, 100, 010, 000, 001, 111

Question 25: Which of the following standard algorithms is not a greedy algorithm?

    a.   Dijkstra's shortest path algorithm

    b.   Prim's algorithm

    c.   Kruskal algorithm

    d.   Bellman-Ford shortest path algorithm

Question 26: Consider two strings, A = "qpqrr" and B = "pqprqrp". Let x be the length of the longest common subsequence (not necessarily contiguous) between A and B, and let y be the number of such longest common sub-sequences between A and B. Then, $x + 10y$ = ___.

    a.   23

    b.   33

    c.   34

    d.   43

Question 27: In the 0/1 knapsack problem, if an item's weight is greater than the remaining capacity of the knapsack, what action is typically taken?

    a.   Add the fractional part of the item that can fit into the knapsack.

    b.   Remove the least valuable item from the knapsack to make space.

    c.   Remove the most valuable item from the knapsack to make space.

    d.   Ignore the item and move to the next one.

Question 28: The worst-case efficiency of solving a problem in polynomial time is?

    a. $O(p(n))$

    b. $O(p(n \log n))$

    c. $O(p(n^2))$

    d. $O(p(m \log n))$

Question 29: Problems that cannot be solved by any algorithm are called?

    a.   Tractable problems

    b.   Intractable problems

    c.   Undecidable problems

    d.   Decidable problems

Question 30: Which of the following problems is not NP-complete?

    a. Hamiltonian circuit

    b. Bin packing

    c. Partition problem

    d. Halting problem

Question 31: Consider a simple graph G with 18 vertices. What will be the size of the maximum independent set of G if the size of the minimum vertex cover of G is 10?

    a. 18

    b. 08

    c. 10

    d. 28

Question 32: The recursive solution of the Tower of Hanoi problem is an example of which of the following algorithms?

    a. Dynamic programming

    b. Backtracking

    c. Greedy algorithm

    d. Divide and conquer

Question 33: The fractional knapsack problem is solved most efficiently by which of the following algorithms?

    a. Divide and conquer

    b. Dynamic programming

    c. Greedy algorithm

    d. Backtracking

Answers

    1. C

    2. A, C

    3. A, B

    4. D

    5. C

    6. C

    7. C

    8. C

Explanation: Using the greedy algorithm, three coins {4,1,1} will be selected to make a sum of 6. However, the optimal answer is two coins {3,3}. Similarly, four coins {4,4,1,1} will be selected to make a sum of 10, but the optimal answer is three coins {4,3,3}. Also, five coins {4,4,4,1,1} will be selected to make a sum of 14, but the optimal answer is four coins {4,4,3,3}. For a sum of 100, 25 coins {all 4's} will be selected, and the optimal answer is also 25 coins {all 4's}.

9. B

10. A

11. D

Explanation: In the fractional knapsack problem, we can partially include an item into the knapsack, whereas in 0/1 knapsack, we have to either include or exclude the item wholly.

12. B

Explanation: We can prove this by induction. By adding one edge, the degree of vertices in u is equal to 1, as well as in the v vertex. Let us assume that this is true for n-1 edges and add one more edge. Since the given edge adds exactly once to both u and v, we can tell that this statement is true for all n vertices.

13. D

14. D

15. C

16. D

Explanation: The set partition problem has both recursive as well as dynamic programming solutions. The dynamic programming solution has a time complexity of $o(n*sum)$ as it has a nested loop with limits from 1 to n and 1 to sum, respectively.

17. B

Explanation: Total number of characters in the message = 100.

Each character takes 1 byte. So, total number of bits needed = 800.

After Huffman coding, the characters can be represented as follows:

F: 0

C: 100

D: 101

A: 1100

B: 1101

E: 111

Total number of bits needed = 224

Hence, number of bits saved = 800 - 224 = 576

18. C

19. B

Explanation: a = 0.11 b = 0.40 c = 0.16 d = 0.09 e = 0.24

Huffman coding for character:

a = 1111

b = 0

c = 110

d = 1111

e = 10

Length for each character = number of bits * frequency of occurrence:

a = 4 * 0.11 = 0.44

b = 1 * 0.4 = 0.4

c = 3 * 0.16 = 0.48

d = 4 * 0.09 = 0.36

e = 2 * 0.24 = 0.48

Now, add these lengths for average length:

 0.44 + 0.4 + 0.48 + 0.36 + 0.48 = 2.16

20. A

Explanation: This question is based on the optimal storage on tape problem, which uses the greedy approach to find the optimal time to retrieve programs from tape. There are n programs of length L that are to be stored on a computer tape. Associated with each program i is a length Li. So, in order to retrieve these programs most optimally, we need to store them in the non-decreasing order of length Li. So, the correct order is F3, F4, F1, F5, F6, F2.

21. A

22. C

Explanation:

Alphabets	Frequency
a	1
b	2
c	2
d	2
e	3

$1×3 + 2×3 + 3×2 + 2×2 + 2×2 = 23$

23. B

Explanation:

Option A: 2,2,4,4. No problem.

Option B: 2,4,2,4. The third job in this sequence had to be completed under 2-time units. But it took 3-time units. This is not an optimal solution, hence the answer.

Option C: 2,2,4,4. No problem.

Option D: 2,2,4,4. No problem.

24. A

Explanation: The idea is to keep the least probable characters as low as possible by picking them first.

The letters a, b, c, d, e, and f have the probabilities 1/2, 1/4, 1/8, 1/16, 1/32, and 1/32, respectively, as shown in the following Huffman tree after applying the Huffman coding algorithm:

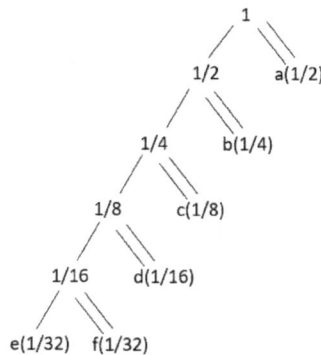

Figure 13.2: Huffman tree structure after applying Huffman coding

25. D

26. C

Explanation: The LCS is of length 4. There are three LCS of length 4: qprr, pqrr, and qpqr. A subsequence is a sequence that can be derived from another sequence by selecting zero or more elements from it without changing the order of the remaining elements. The subsequence need not be contiguous. Since the lengths of the given strings, A = "qpqrr" and B = "pqprqrp", are very small, we do not need to build a 5x7 matrix and solve it using dynamic programming. Rather, we can solve it manually just by brute force. We will first check whether there exists a subsequence of length 5, since min_length (A, B) = 5. Since there is no subsequence, we will now check for length 4. "qprr", "pqrr", and "qpqr" are common in both strings. X = 4 and Y = 3.

X + 10Y = 34

27. D

28. A

29. C

30. D

31. B

Explanation: Removing the vertex cover vertices from the graph results in an isolated graph, and so the remaining vertices would be the independent set in the original graph. Hence, the size of the maximum independent set = 18 – 10 = 8.

32. D

33. C

Conclusion

Reiterating the ideas of branch and bound algorithms is made possible in great part by the section on most often asked questions. It improves the reader's knowledge of optimization methods and their pragmatic uses by addressing typical questions and offering concise answers. This part guarantees a better understanding of problem-solving techniques, helps to strengthen important concepts, and gets readers ready to use branch and bound approaches in practical situations.

Join our Discord space

Join our Discord workspace for latest updates, offers, tech happenings around the world, new releases, and sessions with the authors:

https://discord.bpbonline.com

Index

www.ingramcontent.com/pod-product-compliance
Lightning Source LLC
Chambersburg PA
CBHW061740210326
41599CB00034B/6737